Anti-Slavery

Dialectic

I0094111

Frederick Douglass

CANNAE
PRESS

Anti-Slavery Dialectic

A Frederick Douglass Anthology

Edited, with an Introduction, by

A. Shahid Stover

If ye stay not the hand of the oppressor, if ye fail to safeguard the rights of the downtrodden, what right have ye then to vaunt yourselves among men? What is it of which ye can rightly boast?[1]

-Baha'u'llah (1817-1892)

---

[1] Baha'u'llah, *Writings of Baha'u'llah: A Compilation*, (New Delhi: Bahai Publishing Trust, 2006) p.737.

Dedicated to the African Diaspora as a persistent socio-historical refuge of emancipatory universality and human community, and to Africa herself, the motherland of humanity.

Editorial Note on Texts

Except for writings important enough to prioritize the philosophical emphasis of Douglass' thought with a new appellation drawn from his own discourse, effort has been made to retain as close to the original titles or at least the most familiar designations of Douglass' lectures and essays as possible.

This strategy follows from the example of Philip S. Foner in his *Life and Writings of Frederick Douglass,* who for instance gives some remarks by Douglass on the day of the Emancipation Proclamation a title drawn from the lecture itself, "A Day for Poetry and Song". However, in John W. Blassingame's *The Frederick Douglass Papers* project, which he launched at Yale University, these same remarks are entitled as "The Day of Jubilee Comes", which though certainly an accurate description of the contents, is not a title composed of Douglass' own exact words. As such, both of these naming techniques are utilized for this anthology as discursively appropriate, especially whenever philosophical excerpts are drawn from one of Douglass' lectures or narratives and given new titular designations.

The original source material is referenced as a footnote at the end of each selection. Any slight typographical corrections and/or alterations in spelling or punctuation have been chosen with both clarity and accuracy in mind. For instance, the way Douglass wrote the word "to-day" is now changed to "today" in this anthology.

Although Douglass commonly used the word 'Negro' and 'Black' in his work, he does not consistently capitalize them. However, for the purposes of this anthology, both words are now capitalized throughout for semantic intentionality whenever referring to humanity, community or people. The more vulgar and insulting version of 'Negro' is also now indicated as 'n****r' whenever it appears in this text as well.

Due to the philosophical intentionality of this work, the vast Promethean scope of Douglass' thought is thematically arranged into two distinct sections –

I.   **Revolt Against Human Slavery**
II.   **Intellectual Resistance**

Within each section Douglass' writings and lectures are arranged in chronological order. The only exception to this is the first philosophical passage of the book entitled "Anti-Slavery Dialectic". This selection is excerpted from Douglass' "Lecture on West India Emancipation", and shares this new designation of "Anti-Slavery Dialectic" with the title of this anthology.

In numerous instances where Douglass' lectures were covered and recorded by reporters, all journalistic references indicative of audience response, or attempts to summarize Douglass' thought to the reader, have been edited out. If any additional language not in the original is added to compensate, it is indicated by brackets.

Tremendous gratitude and appreciation should be accorded to the legacy of editors Philip S. Foner for *The Life and Writings of Frederick Douglass*[2] and John W. Blassingame for *The Frederick Douglass*

---

[2] Philip S. Foner, editor, *The Life and Writings of Frederick Douglass, 5 Vols.* (New York: International Publishers, 1950).

Papers[3]. Nor let us forget the invaluable archival efforts of the editorial team and volunteers associated with the Frederick Douglass collection of the Library of Congress.

Indeed, without the distinctive archival work of Foner's and Blassingame's previous pioneering intellectual endeavors of comprehensive historical scholarship combined with the Library of Congress' institutional interest towards sustaining a general level of accessibility with regards to Douglass' massive *oeuvre*, to even attempt to compile and edit a work like this would have been an exercise in futility.

---

[3] John W. Blassingame, editor, *The Frederick Douglass Papers – Series One: Speeches, Debates, and Interviews, 5 Vols*. (New Haven: Yale University Press, 1979-1992).

About the Author

Frederick Douglass (1817? - 1895) is a towering iconic African-American world historical figure who continues to exert a powerful influence upon the popular imagination and historical memory of an ascendant humanity that continues to struggle against all odds for social justice in America.

As a writer, Black radical abolitionist, fugitive slave lecturer and philosopher of human freedom, Douglass was known for his outstanding oratorical prowess, tireless intellectual engagement and existential commitment to the socio-historical struggle against the enslavement of human 'being'.

Douglass himself was born into *chattel* slavery on Maryland's Eastern Shore as the son of an enslaved Black mother and white slavemaster. After learning to read and write, Douglass escaped slavery in 1838 and then became an abolitionist "fugitive slave lecturer" by 1841. Douglass not only lectured throughout the continental United States, but throughout the British Isles on three separate tours from 1845 to 1847, 1859 to 1860 and 1886 to 1887.

Douglass wrote three world renowned autobiographies; first in 1845, entitled *Narrative of the Life of Frederick Douglass, an American Slave: Written by Himself,* followed by *My Bondage and My Freedom* (1855) and culminating with *The Life and Times of Frederick Douglass* (1881, revised 1892).

Frederick Douglass

Anti-Slavery

Dialectic

Edited, with an introduction, by

A. Shahid Stover

CANNAE
PRESS

New York

0 5 2 3 1 8 4 4 3

Published by
Cannae Press
P.O. Box 460
New York, NY 10276
cannaepress.com

Cover Design by Josefina Hernandez

Graphic Arts Consultants – Dario Sanchez-Kennedy, Sultan
Stover and Varsha Mathrani

Library of Congress Control Number: 2025921697
ISBN: 978-1-7335510-5-2 (paperback)

****

Contents

I. Revolt Against Human Slavery

II.   Intellectual Resistance

A Collective Intellectual
History
of
Frederick Douglass

"He belongs in the class of those timeless figures in whom the past and the present are often indistinguishable. Hence even as we view Douglass from this or that perspective, we are willy-nilly showing him to be a hardy perennial, a figure transcending a given hour, ascending beyond a given day. In focusing attention on Douglass, we are simply keeping abreast of the times."[4]

"His own qualities of mind enabled Douglass to move inexorably toward his goals. At the base of these mental qualities was a thirst for knowledge. The first great ambition of the young Douglass was to master the printed page. ... To Douglass freedom from chattel slavery was but half a victory unless followed by a liberation of the mind. ... Always to make a new man of himself – this was his goal."[5]

-Benjamin Quarles

"In February, 1817, a Negro child was born in Maryland who was destined to become one of the nation's most distinguished citizens. Born a slave, he lifted himself up from bondage by his own efforts, taught himself to read and write, developed a great talent as lecturer, editor, and organizer, became a noted figure in American life, and gained worldwide

---

[4] Benjamin Quarles, "Frederick Douglass: Historical and Contemporary Perspectives", *New Directions*, Vol.7, Issue#2, Article 3, January 1st, 1980.
[5] Quarles, "Frederick Douglass: Challenge and Response", Lecture at Morgan State University for Negro History Week, 1967.

recognition as the foremost spokesman for his opp-ressed people and courageous champion of many other progressive causes of his time." ...

"No biography by itself can do the man full justice. For this we still have to read Douglass himself. Fortunately, this is no chore. These writings of a man whom slavery deprived of formal education constitute an important and distinctive contribution to our literature. Here is the clearest articulation of discontent, protest, militant action, and hope of the American Negro. Here one of the most brilliant minds of his time, constantly responsive to the great forces of his day, analyzes every important issue confronting the Negro and the American people generally ..."

"Here are the eloquent words and penetrating thoughts that exerted a decisive influence on the course of national affairs for half a century and moved countless men and women to action in behalf of freedom. Most important of all, here are the militant principles of the outstanding leader of the Negro people whose ideas have remained vital and valid down to the present day."[6]

– Phillip S. Foner

"If we look closely at the words of Frederick Douglass we can detect the theme of resistance once again. His first concrete experience of the possibility of freedom within the limits of slavery comes when he

---

[6] Philip S. Foner, Editor's Preface, Frederick Douglass, *The Life and Writings of Frederick Douglass Vol.1*, (New York: International Publishers, 1950, 1970) pp.11-13.

observes a slave resist a whipping. Now he transforms this resistance into a resistance of the mind, a refusal to accept the will of the master and a determination to find independent means of judging the world."[7]

            –Angela Y. Davis

"To situate Douglass' contribution to existential thought requires an articulation that addresses both slavery and struggle. In Douglass's lifetime, a transition from the combination of *de jure* and *de facto* slavery (the former sanctioned by the U.S. Constitution, the latter wrought via racism and economic exploitation) to only *de facto* slavery (*de jure* slavery having been done away with by the Thirteenth Amendment) was the underlying contradiction. In DuBois, there is the added transition from colonialism to neocolonialism except in the case of prisoners, and Jim Crow discrimination to the contradictions of bourgeois democracy. In Douglass, one is pushed to a concrete challenge to existential thought. Slavery and its legacy must be studied by Africana theorists because of the historical role it has played in the formation of modern Black identity."[8]

            –Lewis R. Gordon

---

[7] Angela Y. Davis, "First Lecture on Liberation", *Narrative of the Life of Frederick Douglass: A New Critical Edition* (San Francisco: City Lights Books, 2010) p.56.

[8] Lewis R. Gordon, *Existentia Africana: Understanding Africana Existential Thought*, (New York: Routledge, 2000) pp.42-43.

"a fugitive slave who had risen from bondage and established himself as one of the foremost orator-editors of the abolition movement. ... By the 1850's he was revered in most antislavery circles in the British Isles, and both loved and resented among American abolitionists. As he spoke with grace and eloquence from countless platforms on two continents, and wrote with increasing skill and force, Douglass presented the greatest living challenge to the American paradox of slavery and freedom."[9]

– David W. Blight

"During this time Douglass identified the racist trajectory of Western philosophy as the principal cause of the entrenchment of racialized slavery and the resultant erection of fixed racial hierarchies in American society. ... Given his growing concern with the Fugitive Slave Laws as evidence of Western racism's intensification, it only stands to reason that he would attack the thought system at slavery's core, which was used to divest enslaved Africans of their humanity, historiographical relevance, and ontological worth. Douglass knew that the battle for African American liberation had to be fought on the philosophical terrain of discourse, which he astutely described as a 'moral battlefield'".[10]

– LaRose T. Parris

---

[9] David W. Blight, *Frederick Douglass' Civil War*, (Baton Rouge: Louisiana State University Press, 1989) p.2.
[10] LaRose T. Parris, *Being Apart: Theoretical and Existential Resistance in Africana Literature*, (Charlottesville: University of Virginia Press, 2014) pp.48-50.

"As events unfolded, however, moral suasion failed both to free the slaves and to reform the slaveholders. Indeed it seemed to have the opposite effect for following the period when it was most vigorously pursued, the slaveholders were emboldened to propose, and managed to push through, the infamous Fugitive Slave Law of 1850. Frustrated by the ineffectiveness of nonviolent moral suasion, Douglass turned to endorsing slave uprisings. But then came to a further and more radical conclusion: it was not only that violent slave resistance was both morally defensible and likely to be more effective in ending slavery than nonviolent moral suasion. Violent slave resistance was also capable of producing the moral benefits that nonviolent moral suasion had promised, but failed to deliver – moral reform of the slaveholders. And it was not only the slavemasters who would benefit morally from slave resistance. The slave was also likely to grow in self-respect if he resisted his master. Of course, Douglass had already claimed in 1845 that he had benefited morally from fighting Covey. After 1850, however, when he became converted to slave resistance, his remarks broadened and hardened. Before 1850 he had not argued that the slave had to resist to gain his self-respect. After 1850, however, he began to make precisely that claim."[11]

– Bernard Boxill

---

[11] Bernard Boxill, "The Fight With Covey", *Existence in Black:An Anthology of Black Existential Philosophy*, edited by Lewis R. Gordon, (New York: Routledge, 1997) p.275.

"Brilliant and to a large degree self-taught, Douglass personified intellectual activism: a sincere concern for the uses and consequences of ideas. Both his people's liberation struggle and his individual experiences, which he envisioned as symbolizing that struggle, provided the basis and structure for his intellectual maturation." ...

"The guiding assumption unifying Douglass's thought was an inveterate belief in a universal and egalitarian brand of humanism. His seemingly innate commitment to the inviolability of freedom and the human spirit best exemplified this overarching assumption."[12]

– Waldo E. Martin Jr

"Douglass, like most Black leaders, held to this view of America seeing a special providence in the presence of the African in America. God would not have suffered such an enormity as the slave trade were it not ultimately to serve some higher end. ... Douglass' faith in the righteousness of this view, in the essential moral capacity of every man, and in the certainty that evil would not go unpunished sustained him in the long, arduous, and frustrating struggle against slavery and racism. A people, no matter how arrogant and self-assured, could not for long work against the laws of God and nature without retribution. The American people had good and evil before them in the starkest terms: the idealism of the Decla-

---

[12] Waldo E. Martin Jr, *The Mind of Frederick Douglass*, (Chapel Hill: University of North Carolina Press, 1984) p.ix.

ration of Independence and the unmitigated evil of slavery. All of human history might well be seen to have led to this dramatic confrontation."[13]

– Nathan Irvin Huggins

"In his crusade against slavery, Douglass ... was an incomparable orator. His booming voice, his sarcasm, his naturalness, his extempore delivery made Douglass a commanding figure. He was poised, fluent, and witty, and had a phenomenal memory. His voice was of unequalled depth, volume, power, and had a great range of intonation. His speeches were always logical, often lyrical and incomparably lucid. Laced with poetic allusions and built on a firm philosophical foundation, they embodied constant appeals to justice, equality, and freedom."[14]

- John W. Blassingame

---

[13] Nathan Irvin Huggins, *Slave and Citizen: The Life of Frederick Douglass*, (Boston: Little, Brown & Company, 1980) pp.74-75.
[14] John W. Blassingame, *The Clarion Voice*, (Washington D.C.: National Park Service, 1976) pp.10-11.

Introducing
an
Insurgent Reading
of
Frederick Douglass

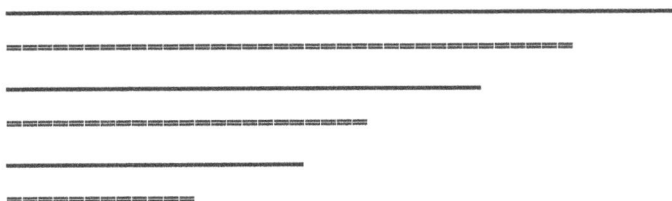

A. Shahid Stover

Anti-Slavery Dialectic: A Frederick Douglass Anthology constitutes an epistemic effort towards restoring the emancipatory thought of Frederick Douglass to insurgent philosophical prominence by collecting his seminal works and peerless contributions to Black liberation discourse in a single comprehensive edition.

In these pages, we see Douglass the Black radical thinker and philosopher "as defender of the principle of human freedom"[15] immersed in a world where the western imperialist imposition of 'objecthood' upon humanity through *chattel* slavery mediates against his choice of resistance to oppression through intellectual engagement. Douglass himself reveals that "The work before us is nothing less than a radical revolution in all the modes of thought which have flourished under the blighting slave system."[16] No doubt, the emancipatory intentionality of radical ontological freedom disclosed by Douglass' insurgent thought commits to a life and death wager of lived universality upon the meaning of human 'being' as implicated by the question of human liberation.

However, for Douglass, there is no possible moral compromise of human consideration, nor any socio-ontological accommodation to an understanding of reality that contributes towards suppressing the universality of human freedom in the confrontation

---

[15] "Shameful Abandonment of Principle", *The North Star*, May 30th 1850.
[16] "The Work of the Future", refer to p.679.

between the meaning of human 'being' as implicated by the question of human liberation in the face of *chattel* slavery. This is crucial, for it epistemically distinguishes the emancipatory gravity and insurgent trajectory of his philosophical discourse from "the three major traditions of mid-nineteenth-century American thought: Protestant Christianity, the Enlightenment, and romanticism"[17] with which he critically engaged in constant and compelling dialogue. And it is from out of such insurgent philosophical dialogue that Douglass' thought discloses an epistemic horizon that introduces the conditions of possibility towards the eventual theoretical formulation of existential liberation critique.

Certainly, the existential liberationist orientation of Douglass' anti-slavery dialectic can thus in no wise be regarded as abstract reasonings on freedom divorced from lived potentialities towards socio-historical insurrection against the violent structural imposition of 'objecthood' upon the human condition by western imperialist power through *chattel* slavery. For as Douglass himself enunciates Revolt, "I am aware that the insurrectionary movements of the slaves were held by many to be prejudicial to their cause. ..." and yet, we were "never nearer emancipation than when General Turner kindled the fires of insurrection at Southampton."[18]

Still, it is worth noting that this work is not meant to represent the full scope of Douglass' thought.

---

[17] Waldo E. Martin, Jr, *The Mind of Frederick Douglass*, (Chapel Hill: University of North Carolina Press, 1984) p.ix.
[18] "Anti-Slavery Dialectic", refer to p.49.

Some aspects of which, especially in the post-Civil War era, lose more and more of their insurgent edge the deeper he wades into the morass of political partisanship intrinsic to the *imperial mainstream-as-civil society* by attempting to build upon "the promise that Blacks would work within the system, rather than agitate from without".[19] This, be it by tragically underestimating the settler colonial imperatives of racialized labor aristocracy that inscribe the American nationalist democratic tradition of 'white' identity politics as class collaboration against the ascendant humanity of Black community, or by pragmatically overlooking the degree to which "the reunited nation would be able to enforce a standard of human rights throughout the land",[20] without being held politically accountable by the threat of direct military intervention during the era of Reconstruction or the emancipatory praxis of organized grassroots socio-historical resistance and spontaneous rebellion in the century that followed.

However, it is only from the vantage point of hindsight, that we dare look puzzled or askance at the historical failure of his realist pragmatic progressive political wager upon an American exceptionalist "assimilation" as an attempt to overcome what Douglass himself describes as "irreconcilable antagonisms" introduced against the normative gaze of modernity by

---

[19] Nathan Irvin Huggins, *Slave and Citizen: The Life of Frederick Douglass*, (Boston: Little, Brown & Company, 1980) p.127.
[20] Ibid.

the assertion of Black subjectivity-as-human 'being'.[21] We have only but to remember that Douglass experienced the American Civil War, in all its contingency, as a dynamic existential unity of spiritual responsibility and geohistorical struggle that introduced conditions of possibility for a fundamental transformation of the social structure. Indeed, "a radical change was needed in our whole system",[22] for as Douglass reveals – "we are not fighting for the Old Union or anything like it."[23] As it turns out, unlike the insurgent slaves and radical abolitionists, that "Old Union", as structurally emblematic of western imperialist power, wasn't fighting for the ascendant humanity of Black community either.

History tells us, in no uncertain terms however, that the emancipatory potentialities of ascendant humanity and social justice introduced by the Civil War were efficiently put to death after the war subsided, making way for new settler colonial reconfigurations of western imperialist power through 'white' identity politics as class collaboration under the nationalist veneer of American exceptionalism.

As such, although Douglass never ceased in the emancipatory responsibility of his philosophical commitment as "an old watchman on the walls of liberty",[24] even to the point of disclosing that "The slave having ceased to be the abject slave of a single master,

---

[21] "We Cannot Remain Half-Slave and Half-Free", lecture on the occasion of the Twenty-First Anniversary of Emancipation in the District of Columbia, April 16, 1883.

[22] "The Mission of the War", refer to p.243.

[23] Ibid, refer to p.252.

[24] "We Cannot Remain Half-Slave and Half-free", April 16, 1883.

his enemies will endeavor to make him the slave of society at large,"[25] the question of the Providential destiny of the African-American community constantly informs Douglass' lived trajectory of intellectual engagement in the face of the disaster of history.

And yet, what is the insurgent philosophical significance of the fact that in the last discursive contribution to his world-renowned trilogy of autobiographical narratives, Douglass made no significant revisions or changes whatsoever with regards to what constitutes his "Third Existential Meditation on Slave Revolt",[26] as phenomenologically disclosed through the lived trajectory of his emancipatory praxis against Edward Covey, the infamous slavebreaking overseer?

Anti-Slavery Dialectic: A Frederick Douglass Anthology is thus singularly concerned with facilitating a discursive dialogue with Douglass' *oeuvre* that aims towards drawing the sword of emancipatory significance and insurgent philosophical contributions of his thought from a scabbard of historical memory that overemphasizes his politically expedient American exceptionalist ideology at the expense of the Black radical imagination. "I have little hope of the freedom of the slave by peaceful means. A long course of peaceful slaveholding has placed the slaveholders beyond the reach of moral and humane considerations. They have neither ears nor hearts for the appeals of justice and humanity. While the slave will tamely submit his neck to the yoke, his back to the lash, and his ankle to the fetter and chain, the

---

[25] "To Be the Slave of Society at Large?", refer to p.685.
[26] Refer to p.268.

Bible will be quoted, and learning invoked to justify slavery. The only penetrable point of a tyrant is the fear of death. The outcry they make, as to the danger of having their throats cut is because they deserve to have them cut. The efforts of John Brown and his brave associates, though apparently unavailing, have done more to upset the logic and shake the security of slavery, than all other efforts in that direction for twenty years."[27]

As such, it is the voice of Douglass the Black radical thinker, philosopher of human freedom, engaged intellectual and uncompromising abolitionist "fugitive slave lecturer",[28] resounding over and above the imperial mainstream familiarity of Douglass as venerable Black spokesman and "representative American",[29] that comes alive through this groundbreaking work of Black liberation discourse. For with regards to the meaning of human 'being' and the question of human liberation, the insurgent orientation of Douglass' thought communicates a tremendous epistemic gravity that, due to the historical continuity of racist dehumanizing oppression in our contemporary world, is as relevant today as ever.

Douglass' lectures speak to the assertion of Black subjectivity-as-human 'being' as an exceptional antagonism that introduces disequilibrium within the normative gaze of modernity as imposed by a western imperialist continuum. "The explanation of the power of

---

[27] "Slaveholders Beyond the Reach of Moral Appeals", refer to p.145.
[28] "Who Will Take Care of the Philosophy?", refer to p.608.
[29] Waldo E. Martin Jr, *The Mind of Frederick Douglass*, p.ix.

anti-slavery is to be found in the inner and spontaneous consciousness, which every man feels of the
comprehensive and stupendous criminality of slavery.
There are many wrongs and abuses in the world that
shock and wound the sensibilities of men. They are
felt to be narrow in their scope, and temporary in
their duration, and to require little effort for their
removal. But not so can men regard slavery. It
compels us to recognize it, as an ever active, ever
increasing, all comprehensive crime against human
nature."[30]

What Douglass discloses about the exceptional
antagonism and singularity of Black liberation struggle
for socio-historical freedom as lived guarantee of the
universality of the human condition, transcends the
academically convenient reduction of his thought to
"basic American values, beliefs, and attitudes"[31] that
he is certainly *in dialogue* with, although never *in
deference* to.

Indeed, to subsume the insurgent philosophical
implications of Douglass' contributions towards existential liberation critique to the imperial mainstream
currents of thought during his era, especially with
regards to any contextualization of his emancipatory
discursive trajectory as somehow being in epistemic
harmony with established structures of meaning that
are themselves predicated upon the absolute negation
of the assertion of Black subjectivity-as-human 'being',
constitutes a calculated distortion of the Black radical

---

[30] "The Power of Anti-Slavery", refer to pp.177-178.
[31] Waldo E. Martin Jr., *The Mind of Frederick Douglass*, p.x.

imagination by *the normative gaze* of established power.

Rather, during the era of his emancipatory discursive contributions as disclosed in this work, Douglass is clearly *a*, if not *the*, insurgent philosophical authority on the existential question of radical ontological freedom situated against the Real of history. For as he phenomenologically enunciates the *anti-slavery dialectic* in the most unambiguous language – "you have seen how a man was made a slave; you shall see how a slave was made a man".[32]

To be sure, the thought of Douglass discloses the irreducibility of human agency and its irreconcilability with the Real of overwhelming socio-historical oppression that severely mediates lived Black experience, though never determines Black subjectivity. "A man is worked upon by what *he* works on. He may carve out his circumstance, but his circumstances will carve him out as well."[33] Thus, the *anti-slavery dialectic* of Douglass reveals the "universal character of the anti-slavery question"[34] as an emancipatory imperative based upon the existential response of human 'being' to the call of the disaster of history through slave Revolt as a socio-ontological phenomenon without geohistorical precedent.

Indeed, the Revolt of human 'being' against *chattel* slavery calls into question established structures of meaning and epistemological presuppositions of mat-

---

[32] "First Existential Meditation on Slave Revolt", refer to p.55.
[33] "The Claims of the Negro Ethnologically Considered", refer to p.560.
[34] "The Power of Anti-Slavery", refer to p.179.

erialistic determinism that reify modern secular humanism within the normative gaze of a western imperialist continuum. For the normative gaze structurally negates the radical ontological freedom of human 'being' through *miseducation of soul* and *objective violence* insofar as "it is necessary to resort to these cruelties, in order to make the slave a slave, and to keep him a slave ... and this can be done only by shutting out the light of education from their minds and brutalizing their persons."[35] The socio-historical insurrection, spiritual upheaval and ontological resistance of human 'being' to *chattel* slavery thus introduces the question of human subjectivity back into history through emancipatory praxis.

As such, what can the Revolt of human 'being' against *chattel* slavery tell us about the human condition? And what then, does human 'being' mean in our contemporary world faced with a globalized system of power that is inscribed with an originary violence of *chattel* slavery and thus disavows ethical responsibility through the structural negation of human consideration when confronted with the assertion of Black subjectivity-as-human 'being'? "Slavery being an utter and entire destruction of all human relations, in opposing it, we are naturally enough bound to consideration of a wide range of topics, involving questions of the greatest importance to all men."[36] For since the onset of modernity as imposed by a western imperialist continuum, emancipatory thought has abdicated to a spiritually impoverished

---

[35] "Slavery is a System", refer to pp.328-329.
[36] "The Power of Anti-Slavery", refer to p.179.

anthropology of Man that legitimizes a violent structural negation of human 'being' by divorcing the cultural diversity of human 'being' from the socio-ontological depth of our lived universality.

Let us not forget the sobering analysis of one of Douglass' notable contemporaries who discloses that "Direct slavery is as much the pivot upon which our present-day industrialism turns as are machinery, credit, etc. Without slavery there would be no cotton, without cotton there would be no modern industry. It is slavery which has given value to the colonies, it is the colonies which have created world trade, and world trade is the necessary condition for large-scale machine industry. Consequently, prior to the slave trade, the colonies sent very few products to the Old World, and did not noticeably change the face of the world. Slavery is therefore an economic category of paramount importance. Without slavery, North America, the most progressive nation, would be transformed into a patriarchal country. Only wipe North America off the map and you will get anarchy, the complete decay of trade and modern civilization. But to do away with slavery would be to wipe America off the map. Being an economic category, slavery has existed in all nations since the beginning of the world. All that modern nations have achieved is to disguise slavery at home and import it openly into the New World."[37] Therefore, how is it possible to pose the question of human 'being' without taking into account

---

[37] Karl Marx, *The Poverty of Philosophy*, (Amherst: Prometheus Books, 1847, 1995) pp.121-2.

emancipatory imperatives towards human liberation against western imperialist power?

And how can we even begin to authentically interrogate the human condition itself without contending with the ontological implications derived from the socio-historical phenomenon of human 'being' in Revolt against *chattel* slavery? Indeed, "The first work of slavery is to mar and deface those characteristics of its victims which distinguish *men* from *things*, and *persons* from *property*. Its first aim is to destroy all sense of high moral and religious responsibility. It reduces man to a mere machine."[38]

As such, Douglass discloses an existential dynamic of "resistance, active and constant resistance, to the forces of physical nature"[39] as fundamental to the constitutive self-determination of human subjectivity and therefore imperative to the anti-slavery dialectic of Revolt, resistance, struggle and progress.

Indeed, the emancipatory thought of Douglass confronts the topographical coherence of a western imperialist continuum as an insurgent movement of *vertical* resistance arising from the *underground of modernity* that ultimately ruptures the normative gaze of established power and introduces the conditions of possibility for slave Revolt emerging out of the radical ontological freedom of human 'being' as the beginnings of the anti-slavery dialectic, rather than an oppositional movement of *lateral* struggle within the *imperial mainstream* aimed at achieving recognition

---

[38] "First Lecture Against Human Slavery", refer to p.456.
[39] "The Struggle to Be as The Question Forced Upon Us", emphasis mine. refer to p.711.

from the normative gaze. For "after resisting" the slavemaster, "I felt as I had never felt before. It was a resurrection from the dark and pestiferous tomb of slavery" as social death, "to the heaven of comparative freedom."[40]

To be certain, the Revolt of human 'being' against *chattel* slavery as a socio-ontological phenomenon without geohistorical precedent cannot be collapsed into the epistemic closure of an Idealist Hegelian framework that prioritizes a 'struggle for recognition' as the means to achieve freedom in history. For the reduction of Black liberation as manifest in history to a Hegelian 'struggle for recognition'[41] between *master* and *slave* ultimately dismembers the anti-slavery dialectic by revalorizing established structures of meaning indebted to the sovereign legitimacy of western imperialist power as the exclusive arbiter as to what constitutes an acceptable horizon of emancipatory praxis.

Nor can the Revolt of human 'being' against *chattel* slavery be psychologically reduced to a mode of Nietzschean *ressentiment*.[42] Inasmuch as slave Revolt against Empire begins as radical ontological freedom becomes socio-historical through the principled creative movement of emancipatory praxis against the imposition of 'objecthood' upon human 'being' by the normative gaze of established power. The Revolt of Black people against human slavery and the culture

---

[40] "Second Existential Meditation on Slave Revolt" refer to p.135.

[41] G.W.F. Hegel, *Phenomenology of Spirit*, (Oxford: Oxford University Press, 1807, 1977) pp.111-119.

[42] Friedrich Nietzsche, *On the Genealogy of Morals*, (New York: Barnes and Noble, 1887, 2006) pp.12-15.

of spiritual resistance that accompanies such an insurgent trajectory of emancipatory praxis against a western imperialist continuum thus introduces new constitutive self-determining potentialities of human subjectivity through a dialectical movement of human liberation as lived response to the call of the disaster of history.

On this point, Douglass leaves no doubt that "The slave is bound to mankind, by the powerful and inextricable network of human brotherhood. His voice is the voice of a man, and his cry is the cry of a man in distress, and man must cease to be man before he can become insensible to that cry. It is the righteousness of the cause – the humanity of the cause – which constitutes its potency."[43] Indeed, is not modern humanism inscribed with a socio-historical insensibility to the *voice of human 'being'* and ontological indifference to the *cry of human subjectivity in distress* towards reifying a secular anthropology of materialist determinism through the rational signification of subhumanity as 'race'?

The Douglassian *anti-slavery dialectic* thus gives birth to the possibility of human subjectivity as the Revolt of human 'being' against the structural-inert violence, miseducation of soul and imposed 'objecthood' of *chattel* slavery, beyond the epistemic scope of a western imperialist continuum, and thus as an unforeseen opening of human 'being' towards the Divine, that inexhaustible horizon of Truth and meaning that is at once socio-historically mediated when manifest into the world through emancipatory praxis.

---

[43] "Comprehending the Vitality of Anti-Slavery", refer to p.569.

"Truth and Error, Liberty and Slavery, in a hand-to-hand conflict. This is what we want. This is what we will have. The utter extinction of Slavery, everywhere...",[44] including all of its contemporary reconfigurations.

-A. Shahid Stover

---

[44] "The Final Struggle", refer to p.141.

Anti-Slavery Dialectic – The general sentiment of mankind is, that a man who will not fight for himself, when he has the means of doing so, is not worth being fought for by others, and this sentiment is just. For a man who does not value freedom for himself will never value it for others, nor put himself to any inconvenience to gain it for others. Such a man the world says, may lay down until he has sense enough to stand up. It is useless and cruel to put a man on his legs, if the next moment his head is to be brought against a curb-stone. ...

In the great struggle now progressing for the freedom and elevation of our people, we should be found at work with all our might, resolved that no man or set of men shall be more abundant in labors, according to the measure of our ability, than ourselves. ...

Let me give you a word of the philosophy of reform. The whole history of the progress of human liberty shows that all concessions yet made to her august claims, have been born of earnest struggle. The conflict has been exciting, agitating, all-absorbing, and for the time being, putting all other tumults to silence. It must do this or it does nothing. If there is no struggle there is no progress. Those who profess to favor freedom and yet deprecate agitation, are men who want crops without plowing up the ground, they want rain without thunder and lightning. They want the ocean without the awful roar of its many waters.

This struggle may be a moral one, or it may be a physical one, and it may be both moral and physical, but it must be a struggle. Power concedes nothing without a demand. It never did and it never will. Find out just what any people will quietly submit to and you have found out the exact measure of injustice and wrong which will be imposed upon them, and these will continue till they are resisted with either words or blows, or with both. The limits of tyrants are prescribed by the endurance of those whom they oppress. In the light of these *ideas,* Negroes will be hunted at the North, and held and flogged at the South so long as they submit to those devilish outrages, and make no resistance, either moral or physical. Men may not get all they pay for in this world, but they must certainly pay for all they get. If we ever get free from the oppressions and wrongs heaped upon us, we must pay for their removal. We must do this by labor, by suffering, by sacrifice, and if needs be, by our lives and the lives of others.

Hence, my friends, every mother who, like Margaret Garner, plunges a knife into the bosom of her infant to save it from the hell of our Christian Slavery, should be held and honored as a benefactress. Every fugitive from slavery who like the noble William Thomas at Wilkesbarre, prefers to perish in a river made red by his own blood, to submission to the hell hounds who were hunting and shooting him, should be esteemed as a glorious martyr, worthy to be held in grateful memory by our people. The fugitive Horace, at Mechanicsburgh, Ohio, the other day, who taught the slave catchers from Kentucky that it was safer to arrest white men than to arrest him, did a most excellent service to our cause. Parker and his noble band of fifteen at Christiana, who defended themselves from the kidnappers with prayers and pistols, are entitled to the honor of making the first successful resistance to the Fugitive Slave Bill. But for that resistance, and the rescue of Jerry, and Shadrack, the man-hunters would have hunted our hills and valleys here with the same freedom with which they now hunt their own dismal swamps.[45]

There was an important lesson in the conduct of that noble Krooman in New York, the other day, who, supposing that the American Christians were about to enslave him, betook himself to the masthead, and with knife in hand, said he would cut his throat before he would be made a slave. Joseph Cinque on the deck of the Amistad, did that which should make his name dear to us. He bore nature's burning protest against slavery. Madison Washington who struck down his oppressor on the deck of the Creole, is more worthy to be remembered than the colored man who shot Pitcairn at Bunker Hill.

My friends, you will observe that I have taken a wide range, and you think it is about time that I should answer the special objection to this celebration. I think so too. This, then, is the truth concerning the inauguration of freedom in the British West Indies. Abolition was the act of the British Government. The motive which led the Government to act, no doubt was mainly a philanthropic one, entitled to our highest admiration and gratitude. The National Religion, the justice, and humanity, cried out in thun-

---

[45] **Editorial Note** - Since at least as early as the 1730's, and on until the end of the Civil War, the Great Dismal Swamp of Southeastern Virginia and Northeastern North Carolina became infamous as an emancipatory refuge for runaway slaves who formed rebel maroon communities and instigated slave resistance throughout the region, as well as eventually becoming an important stop along the Underground Railroad.

derous indignation against the foul abomination, and the government yielded to the storm. Nevertheless a share of the credit of the result falls justly to the slaves themselves. "Though slaves, they were rebellious slaves." They bore themselves well. They did not hug their chains, but according to their opportunities, swelled the general protest against oppression. What Wilberforce was endeavoring to win from the British Senate by his magic eloquence, the Slaves themselves were endeavoring to gain by outbreaks and violence.[46] The combined action of one and the other wrought out the final result. While one showed that slavery was wrong, the other showed that it was dangerous as well as wrong. Mr. Wilberforce, peace man though he was, and a model of piety, availed himself of this element to strengthen his case before the British Parliament, and warned the British government of the danger of continuing slavery in the West Indies. There is no doubt that the fear of the consequences, acting with a sense of the moral evil of slavery, led to its abolition. The spirit of freedom was abroad in the Islands. Insurrection for freedom kept the planters in a constant state of alarm and trepidation. A standing army was necessary to keep the slaves in their chains. This state of facts could not be without weight in deciding the question of freedom in these countries.

I am aware that the rebellious disposition of the slaves was said to arise out of the discussions which

---

[46] **Editorial Note** – Just some significant uprisings against human slavery in the British West Indies alone include – Tacky's Revolt (1760-61) and the Baptist War (1831-32) in Jamaica, Fedon's Rebellion (1795-96) in Grenada, Bussa's Rebellion (1816) in Barbados and the Demerara Rebellion (1823) in Guyana.

the abolitionists were carrying on at home, and it is not necessary to refute this alleged explanation. All that I contend for is this: that the slaves of the West Indies did fight for their freedom, and that the fact of their discontent was known in England, and that it assisted in bringing about that state of public opinion which finally resulted in their emancipation. And if this be true, the objection is answered.

Again, I am aware that the insurrectionary movements of the slaves were held by many to be prejudicial to their cause. This is said now of such movements at the South. The answer is that abolition followed close on the heels of insurrection in the West Indies, and Virginia was never nearer emancipation than when General Turner kindled the fires of insurrection at Southampton.[47]

---

[47] Excerpted from "Lecture on West India Emancipation", delivered at Canandaigua, New York on August 4th, 1857 and published in *Two Speeches, by Frederick Douglass; One on West India Emancipation, Delivered at Canandaigua, Aug. 4th, and the Other on the Dred Scott Decision, Delivered in New York, on the Occasion of the Anniversary of the American Abolition Society, May, 1857*, (Rochester: C.P. Dewey, 1857).

Revolt Against Human Slavery

First Existential Meditation on Slave Revolt – If at any one time of my life more than another, I was made to drink the bitterest dregs of slavery, that time was during the first six months of my stay with Mr. Covey. We were worked in all weathers. It was never too hot or too cold; it could never rain, blow, hail, or snow, too hard for us to work in the field. Work, work, work, was scarcely more the order of the day than of the night. The longest days were too short for him, and the shortest nights too long for him. I was somewhat unmanageable when I first went there, but a few months of this discipline tamed me. Mr. Covey succeeded in breaking me. I was broken in body, soul, and spirit. My natural elasticity was crushed, my intellect languished, the disposition to read departed, the cheerful spark that lingered about my eye died; the dark night of slavery closed in upon me; and behold a man transformed into a brute!

Sunday was my only leisure time. I spent this in a sort of beast-like stupor, between sleep and wake, under some large tree. At times I would rise up, a flash of energetic freedom would dart through my soul, accompanied with a faint beam of hope, that flickered for a moment, and then vanished. I sank down again, mourning over my wretched condition. I was sometimes prompted to take my life, and that of Covey, but was prevented by a combination of hope and fear. My sufferings on this plantation seem now like a dream rather than a stern reality.

Our house stood within a few rods of the Chesapeake Bay, whose broad bosom was ever white with sails from every quarter of the habitable globe. Those beautiful vessels, robed in purest white, so delightful to the eye of freemen, were to me so many shrouded ghosts, to terrify and torment me with thoughts of my wretched condition. I have often, in the deep stillness of a summer's Sabbath, stood all alone upon the lofty banks of that noble bay, and traced, with saddened heart and tearful eye, the countless number of sails moving off to the mighty ocean. The sight of these always affected me powerfully. My thoughts would compel utterance; and there, with no audience but the Almighty, I would pour out my soul's complaint, in my rude way, with an apostrophe to the moving multitude of ships: –

"You are loosed from your moorings, and are free; I am fast in my chains, and am a slave! You move merrily before the gentle gale, and I sadly before the bloody whip! You are freedom's swift-winged angels, that fly round the world; I am confined in bands of iron! O that I were free! O, that I were on one of your gallant decks, and under your protecting wing! Alas! betwixt me and you, the turbid waters roll. Go on, go on. O that I could also go! Could I but swim! If I could fly! O, why was I born a man, of whom to make a brute! The glad ship is gone; she hides in the dim distance. I am left in the hottest hell of unending slavery. O God, save me! God, deliver me! Let me be free! Is there any God? Why am I a slave? I will run away. I will not stand it. Get caught, or get clear, I'll try it. I had as well die with ague as the fever. I have only one life to lose. I had as well be killed running as die standing. Only think of it; one hundred miles straight north, and I am free! Try it? Yes! God helping me, I will. It cannot be that I shall live and die a slave. I will take to the water.

This very bay shall yet bear me into freedom. The steamboats steered in a north-east course from North Point. I will do the same; and when I get to the head of the bay, I will turn my canoe adrift, and walk straight through Delaware Page into Pennsylvania. When I get there, I shall not be required to have a pass; I can travel without being disturbed. Let but the first opportunity offer, and, come what will, I am off. Meanwhile, I will try to bear up under the yoke. I am not the only slave in the world. Why should I fret? I can bear as much as any of them. Besides, I am but a boy, and all boys are bound to someone. It may be that my misery in slavery will only increase my happiness when I get free. There is a better day coming."

Thus I used to think, and thus I used to speak to myself; goaded almost to madness at one moment, and at the next reconciling myself to my wretched lot.

I have already intimated that my condition was much worse, during the first six months of my stay at Mr. Covey's, than in the last six. The circumstances leading to the change in Mr. Covey's course toward me form an epoch in my humble history. You have seen how a man was made a slave; you shall see how a slave was made a man. On one of the hottest days of the month of August, 1833, Bill Smith, William Hughes, a slave named Eli, and myself, were engaged in fanning wheat. Hughes was clearing the fanned wheat from before the fan, Eli was turning, Smith was feeding, and I was carrying wheat to the fan. The work was simple, requiring strength rather than intellect; yet, to one entirely unused to such work, it came very hard. About three o'clock of that day, I broke down; my strength failed me; I was seized with a violent aching of the head, attended with extreme dizziness; I trembled in every limb. Finding what was coming, I nerved myself up, feeling it would never do to stop work. I stood as long as I could stagger to the hopper with grain. When I could stand no longer, I fell, and felt as if held down by an immense weight. The fan of course stopped; everyone had his own work to do; and no one could do the work of the other, and have his own go on at the same time.

Mr. Covey was at the house, about one hundred yards from the treading-yard where we were fanning. On hearing the fan stop, he left immediately, and came to the spot where we were. He hastily inquired what the matter was. Bill answered that I was sick, and there was no one to bring wheat to the fan. I had by this time crawled away under the side of the post and rail-fence by which the yard was enclosed, hoping to find relief by getting out of the sun. He then asked where I was. He was told by one of the hands. He came to the spot, and, after looking at me awhile, asked me what was the matter. I told him as well as I could, for I scarce had strength to speak. He then gave me a savage kick in the side, and told me to get up. I tried to do so, but fell back in the attempt. He gave me another kick, and again told me to rise. I again tried, and succeeded in gaining my feet; but, stooping to get the tub with which I was feeding the fan, I again staggered and fell. While down in this situation, Mr. Covey took up the hickory slat with which Hughes had been striking off the half-bushel measure, and with it gave me a heavy blow upon the head, making a large wound, and the blood ran freely;

and with this again told me to get up. I made no
effort to comply, having now made up my mind to let
him do his worst. In a short time after receiving this
blow, my head grew better. Mr. Covey had now left
me to my fate. At this moment I resolved, for the
first time, to go to my master, enter a complaint, and
ask his protection. In order to do this, I must that
afternoon walk seven miles; and this, under the
circumstances, was truly a severe undertaking. I was
exceedingly feeble; made so as much by the kicks and
blows which I received, as by the severe fit of sickness
to which I had been subjected. I, however, watched
my chance, while Covey was looking in an opposite
direction, and started for St. Michael's. I succeeded
in getting a considerable distance on my way to the
woods, when Covey discovered me, and called after
me to come back, threatening what he would do if I
did not come. I disregarded both his calls and his
threats, and made my way to the woods as fast as my
feeble state would allow; and thinking I might be
overhauled by him if I kept the road, I walked
through the woods, keeping far enough from the road
to avoid detection, and near enough to prevent losing
my way. I had not gone far before my little strength
again failed me. I could go no farther. I fell down,
and lay for a considerable time. The blood was yet
oozing from the wound on my head. For a time I
thought I should bleed to death; and think now that I
should have done so, but that the blood so matted my
hair as to stop the wound. After lying there about
three quarters of an hour, I nerved myself up again,
and started on my way, through bogs and briers,
barefooted and bareheaded, tearing my feet some-

times at nearly every step; and after a journey of about seven miles, occupying some five hours to perform it, I arrived at master's store. I then presented an appearance enough to affect any but a heart of iron. From the crown of my head to my feet, I was covered with blood. My hair was all clotted with dust and blood; my shirt was stiff with blood. My legs and feet were torn in sundry places with briers and thorns, and were also covered with blood. I suppose I looked like a man who had escaped a den of wild beasts, and barely escaped them. In this state I appeared before my master, humbly entreating him to interpose his authority for my protection. I told him all the circumstances as well as I could, and it seemed, as I spoke, at times to affect him. He would then walk the floor, and seek to justify Covey by saying he expected I deserved it. He asked me what I wanted. I told him, to let me get a new home; that as sure as I lived with Mr. Covey again, I should live with but to die with him; that Covey would surely kill me; he was in a fair way for it. Master Thomas ridiculed the idea that there was any danger of Mr. Covey's killing me, and said that he knew Mr. Covey; that he was a good man, and that he could not think of taking me from him; that, should he do so, he would lose the whole year's wages; that I belonged to Mr. Covey for one year, and that I must go back to him, come what might; and that I must not trouble him with any more stories, or that he would himself *get hold of me*. After threatening me thus, he gave me a very large dose of salts, telling me that I might remain in St. Michael's that night, (it being quite late,) but that I must be off back to Mr. Covey's early in the morning; and that if I did not, he would *get hold of me*, which meant that he would whip me. I remained all night, and, according to his orders, I started off to Covey's in the morning, (Saturday morning,) wearied in body and broken in spirit. I got no supper that night, or breakfast that morning. I reached Covey's about nine o'clock; and just as I was getting over the fence that divided Mrs. Kemp's fields from ours, out ran Covey with his cowskin, to give me another whipping. Before he could reach me, I succeeded in getting to the cornfield; and as the corn was very high, it afforded me the means of hiding. He seemed very angry, and searched for me a long time. My behavior was altogether unaccountable. He finally gave up the chase, thinking, I suppose, that I must come home for something to eat; he would give himself no further trouble in looking for me. I spent that day mostly in the woods, having the alternative before me, to go home and be whipped to death, or stay in the woods and be starved to death. That night, I fell in with Sandy Jenkins, a slave with whom I was somewhat acquainted. Sandy had a free wife, who lived about four miles from Mr. Covey's; and it being Saturday, he was on his way to see her. I told him my circumstances, and he very kindly invited me to go home with him. I went home with him, and talked this whole matter over, and got his advice as to what course it was best for me to pursue. I found Sandy an old adviser. He told me, with great solemnity, I must go back to Covey; but that before I went, I must go with him into another part of the woods, where there was a certain *root*, which, if I would take some of it with me, carrying it *always on my right side*, would render it impossible for Mr. Covey, or any other white man, to whip me. He said he had carried it for years; and since he had done so, he had never received a blow, and never expected to while he carried it. I at first rejected the idea, that the simple carrying of a root in my pocket would have any such effect as he had said, and was not disposed to take it; but Sandy impressed the necessity with much earnestness, telling me it could do no harm, if it did no good. To please him, I at length took the root, and, according to his direction, carried it upon my right side. This was Sunday morning. I immediately started for home; and upon entering the yard gate, out came Mr. Covey on his way to meeting. He spoke to me very kindly, bade me drive the pigs from a lot nearby, and passed on towards the church. Now, this singular conduct of Mr. Covey really made me begin to think that there was something in the *root* which Sandy had given me; and had it been on any other day than Sunday, I could have attributed the conduct to no other cause than the influence of that root; and as it was, I was half inclined to think the *root* to be something more than I at first had taken it to be. All went well till Monday morning. On this morning, the virtue of the *root* was fully tested. Long before daylight, I was called to go and rub, curry, and feed, the horses. I obeyed, and was glad to obey. But whilst thus engaged, whilst in the act of throwing down some blades from the loft, Mr. Covey entered the stable with a long rope; and just as I was half out of the loft, he caught hold of my legs, and was about tying me. As soon as I found what he was up to, I gave a sudden spring, and as I did so, he holding to my legs, I was brought sprawling on the stable floor.

Mr. Covey seemed now to think he had me, and could do what he pleased; but at this moment from whence came the spirit I don't know I resolved to fight; and, suiting my action to the resolution, I seized Covey hard by the throat; and as I did so, I rose. He held on to me, and I to him. My resistance was so entirely unexpected, that Covey seemed taken all aback. He trembled like a leaf. This gave me assurance, and I held him uneasy, causing the blood to run where I touched him with the ends of my fingers. Mr. Covey soon called out to Hughes for help. Hughes came, and, while Covey held me, attempted to tie my right hand. While he was in the act of doing so, I watched my chance, and gave him a heavy kick close under the ribs. This kick fairly sickened Hughes, so that he left me in the hands of Mr. Covey. This kick had the effect of not only weakening Hughes, but Covey also. When he saw Hughes bending over with pain, his courage quailed. He asked me if I meant to persist in my resistance. I told him I did, come what might; that he had used me like a brute for six months, and that I was determined to be used so no longer. With that, he strove to drag me to a stick that was lying just out of the stable door. He meant to knock me down. But just as he was leaning over to get the stick, I seized him with both hands by his collar, and brought him by a sudden snatch to the ground. By this time, Bill came. Covey called upon him for assistance. Bill wanted to know what he could do. Covey said, "Take hold of him, take hold of him!" Bill said his master hired him out to work, and not to help to whip me; so he left Covey and myself to fight our own battle out. We were at it for nearly two hours. Covey at length let me go, puffing and blowing at a great rate, saying that if I had not resisted, he would not have whipped me half so much. The truth was, that he had not whipped me at all. I considered him as getting entirely the worst end of the bargain; for he had drawn no blood from me, but I had from him. The whole six months afterwards, that I spent with Mr. Covey, he never laid the weight of his finger upon me in anger. He would occasionally say, he didn't want to get hold of me again. "No," thought I, "you need not; for you will come off worse than you did before."

This battle with Mr. Covey was the turning-point in my career as a slave. It rekindled the few expiring embers of freedom, and revived within me a sense of my own manhood. It recalled the departed self-confidence, and inspired me again with a determination to be free. The gratification afforded by the triumph was a full compensation for whatever else might follow, even death itself. He only can understand the deep satisfaction which I experienced, who has himself repelled by force the bloody arm of slavery. I felt as I never felt before. It was a glorious resurrection, from the tomb of slavery, to the heaven of freedom. My long-crushed spirit rose, cowardice departed, bold defiance took its place; and I now resolved that, however long I might remain a slave in form, the day had passed forever when I could be a slave in fact. I did not hesitate to let it be known of me, that the white man who expected to succeed in whipping, must also succeed in killing me.

From this time I was never again what might be called fairly whipped, though I remained a slave four years after-wards. I had several fights, but was never whipped.

It was for a long time a matter of surprise to me why Mr. Covey did not immediately have me taken by the constable to the whipping-post, and there regularly whipped for the crime of raising my hand against a white man in defence of myself. And the only explanation I can now think of does not entirely satisfy me; but such as it is, I will give it. Mr. Covey enjoyed the most unbounded reputation for being a first-rate overseer and negro-breaker. It was of considerable importance to him. That reputation was at stake; and had he sent me – a boy about sixteen years old – to the public whipping-post, his reputation would have been lost; so, to save his reputation, he suffered me to go unpunished.[48]

---

[48] Excerpted from *Narrative of the Life of Frederick Douglass an American Slave*, (Boston: Anti-Slavery Office, 1845).

Enslave Humanity at Your Own Peril – I am glad to be once more in Faneuil Hall, and to address those whom I regard as among the enslavers of myself and my brethren. What I have to say may not be very pleasant to those who venerate the Constitution, but, nevertheless, I must say to you that, by the support you give to that instrument, you are the enslavers of my southern brethren and sisters. Now you say, through the Constitution, — "If you, slaves, dare to rise and assert your freedom, we of the North will come down upon you like an avalanche, and crush you to pieces." We are frequently taunted with cowardice for being slaves, and for enduring such indignities and sufferings. The taunt comes with an ill grace from you. You stand eighteen million strong, united, educated, armed, ready to put us down; we are weak, ignorant, degraded, unarmed, and three million! Under these circumstances, what can we hope to effect? We call upon you to get out of this relation, — to stand away from the slaveholders' side, and give us fair play. Say to the slaveholders — "If you will imbrue your hands in the blood of your brethren, if you will crush and chain your fellow-men, do it at your own risk and peril!" Would you but do this, oh, men of the North, I know there is a spirit among the slaves which would not much longer brook their degradation and their bondage. There are many Madison Washingtons and Nathaniel Turners in the South, who would assert their right to liberty, if you would take your feet from their necks, and your sympathy and aid from their oppressors.

Nathaniel Turner, a noble, brave and generous soul — patient, disinterested, and fearless of suffering.

How was he treated, for endeavoring to gain his own liberty, and that of his enslaved brethren, by the self-same means which the Revolutionary fathers employed? When taken by his enemies, he was stripped naked, and compelled to walk barefooted, some thirty yards, over burning coals, and, when he reached the end, he fell, pierced by a hundred American bullets! I say to you, get out of this position of bodyguard to slavery! Cease from any longer rendering aid and comfort to the tyrant-master! I know how you will reply to this; you will say that I, and such as I, are not men; you look upon us as beneath you; you look upon us as naturally and necessarily degraded. But, nevertheless, we are *men!* You may pile up statutes against us and our manhood as high as heaven, and still we are not changed thereby. We are *men!* Yes! We are *your* brothers!

[Lest I remind you] of the degradation of the Anglo-Saxon race in England, under their Norman conquerors; yes, of that very race which boasts itself of superiority to all others, and assumes to plunder or enslave all others. You have, too, claimed superiority over France, *infidel* France, as in your pride you have reproachfully called her. But "infidel" France, when she obtains a popular government, emancipates her slaves. And when recently a delegation of colored people in Paris waited upon the Minister Cremieux how were they treated? Rejected? Treated with contempt? Asked to show their free papers? Nothing of the kind. *Infidel* France has not yet learned the lesson from Christian America. Friends, do not think me an infidel to Christianity. I am none. But I *do* go for that infidelity which takes off chains, in preference to that religion which puts them on. [49]

---

[49] Lecture delivered in Boston, Massachusetts at Faneuil Hall on May 30, 1848 and published in *The Liberator*, 9 June 1848.

Blood of the Slave on the Skirts of the Northern People - A victim of your power and oppression, humbly craves your attention to a few words, (in behalf of himself and three millions of his brethren, whom you hold in chains and slavery,) with respect to the election just completed. In doing so, I desire to be regarded as addressing you, individually and collectively. If I should seem severe, remember that the iron of slavery has pierced and rankled in my heart, and that I not only smart under the recollection of a long and cruel enslavement, but am even now passing my life in a country, and among a people, whose prejudices against myself and people subjects me to a thousand poisonous stings. If I speak harshly, my excuse is, that I speak in fetters of your own forging. Remember that oppression hath the power to make even a wise man mad.

In the selection of your national rulers just completed, you have made another broad mark on the page of your nation's history, and have given to the world and the coming generation a certain test by which to determine your present integrity as a people. That actions speak louder than words — that within the character of the representative may be seen that of the constituency — that no people are better than their laws or lawmakers — that a stream cannot rise higher than its source — that a sweet fountain cannot send forth bitter water, and that a tree is to be known by its fruits, are truisms; and in their light let us examine the character and pretensions of your boasted Republic.

As a people, you claim for yourselves a higher civilization — a purer morality — a deeper religious faith — a larger love of liberty, and a broader philanthropy, than any other nation on the globe. In a word, you claim yours to be a model Republic, and promise, by the force and excellence of your institutions, and the purity and brightness of your example, to overthrow the thrones and despotisms of the old world, and substitute your own in their stead. Your missionaries are found in the remotest parts of the globe, while our land swarms with churches and religious institutions. In words of Religion and Liberty, you are abundant and preeminent. You have long desired to get rid of the odium of being regarded as pro-slavery, and have even insisted that the charge of pro-slavery made against you was a slander and that those who made it were animated by wild and fanatical spirit. To make your innocence apparent, you have now had a fair opportunity. The issue for freedom or slavery has been clearly submitted to you, and you have deliberately chosen slavery.

General Taylor and General Cass were the chosen and admitted Southern and slavery candidates for the Presidency. Martin Van Buren, though far from being an abolitionist, yet in some sort represented the Anti-Slavery idea of the North, in a political form — him you have rejected, and elected a slaveholder to rule over you in his stead. When the question was whether New Mexico and California shall be Free or Slave States, you have rejected him who was solemnly pledged to maintain their freedom, and have chosen a man whom you knew to be pledged, by his position, to the maintenance of slavery. By your votes, you have said that slavery is better than freedom — that war is better than peace, and that cruelty is better than humanity. You have given your sanction to slave rule and slavery propagandism, and interposed whatever of moral character and standing you possess, to shield the reputation of slaveholders generally. You have said, that to be a man-stealer is no crime — to traffic in human flesh shall be a passport, rather than a barrier to your suffrages. To slaveholders you have said – *Chain up your men and women, and before the bloody lash drive them to new fields of toil in California and New Mexico.* To the slave in his chains you have said – *Be content in your chains, and if you dare to gain your freedom by force, whether in New Mexico or California, in numbers indicated by our votes, our muskets shall find you out.* In a word, you have again renewed your determination to support the Constitution of the United States, in its parts of freedom to the whites, and slavery to the Blacks. If General Taylor's slaves run away, you have promised again to return them to bondage. While General Taylor is the well-known robber of three hundred human beings of all their hard earnings, and is coining their hard earnings into gold, you have conferred upon him an office worth twenty-five thousand dollars a year, and the highest honor within your power. By this act, you have endorsed his character and history. His murders in Mexico[50] – his "bloodhound" cruelty in the Florida War[51] – his aw-

---

[50] **Editorial Note** – referring to the imperialist annexation war (1846-1848) of the United States against Mexico.

[51] **Editorial Note**–The Florida War refers to the Second Seminole War (1835-1842) of indigenous peoples native to Florida uniting with insurgent runaway slaves as Seminoles(meaning 'runaways', 'renegades', 'outcasts') in Revolt against the imperialist aggress-ions of the occupying United States settler-colonial forces.

ful profanity, together with the crimes attendant upon a slave plantation, such as theft, robbery, murder, and adultery, you have sanctioned as perfectly consistent with your morality, humanity, liberty, religion and civilization. You have said that the most available and suitable person in all this great nation, to preside over this model Republic, is a warrior, slaveholder, swearer, and bloodhound importer. – During the campaign just ended, your leaders have dubbed this man-stealer as an honest man. Yet in the wilderness of a wicked enthusiasm, you have given your countenance and support to this.

Now is it too much to say that you have made his crimes your own, and that the blood of the slave is on your garments? You have covered his theft with honesty, his blasphemy with piety, and, as far as in your power, you have rendered the blows intended to destroy slavery nugatory and innoxious. Before high heaven and the world, you are responsible for the blood of the slave. You may shut your eyes to the fact, sport over it, sleep over it, dance over it, and sing psalms over it, but so sure as there is a God of Justice and an unerring Providence, just so sure will the blood of the bondman be required at your hands – An opportunity was presented to you by which you could have fixed an indelible mark of your utter detestation of slavery, and given a powerful blow to that bitter curse. This you have failed to do. When Christ and Barabbas were presented, you have cried out in your madness, Give us Barabbas the robber, in preference to Christ, the innocent. The perishing slave, with uplifted hands and bleeding hearts, implored you, in the name of God you profess to serve, and the humanity you profess to cherish, not to add this mill-stone to the weight already crushing his heart and hopes. But he has appealed in vain. You have turned a deaf ear to his cries, hardened your hearts to his appeal, turned your back upon his sorrows, and united with the tyrant to perpetuate enslavement. The efforts made in your presence to impress you with the awful sin of slavery, and to awaken you to a sense of your duty to the oppressed, have thus far been unavailing. You continue to fight against God, and declare that *injustice* exalteth a nation, and that sin is an *honor* to any people.

Do you really think to circumvent God? – Do you suppose that you can go on in your present career of injustice and political profligacy undisturbed? Has the law of righteous retribution been repealed from the statutes of the Almighty? Or what mean ye that ye bruise and bind my people? Will justice sleep forever? Oh, that you would lay these things to heart! Oh, that you would consider the enormity of your conduct, and seek forgiveness at the hands of a merciful Creator. Repent of this wickedness, and bring forth fruit meet for repentance, by delivering the despoiled out of the hands of the despoiler.

You may imagine that you have now silenced the annoying cry of abolition – that you have sealed the doom of the slave – that abolition is stabbed and dead; but you will find your mistake. You have stabbed, but the cause is not dead. Though down and bleeding at your feet, she shall rise again, and going before you, shall give you no rest till you break every yoke and let the oppressed go free. The Anti-Slavery Societies of the land will rise up and spring to action again, sending forth from the press and on the voice of the living speaker, words of burning truth, to alarm the guilty, to unmask the hypocrite, expose the frauds of political parties, and rebuke the spirit of a corrupt and sin-sustaining church and clergy. Slavery will be attacked in its stronghold – the compromises of the Constitution, and the cry of disunion shall be more fearlessly proclaimed, till slavery be abolished, the Union dissolved, or the sun of this guilty nation must go down in blood.[52]

[52] *The North Star*, November 17, 1848.

No Tears When Slaveholders Meet with Death – It is a poor rule that won't work both ways. Most people think their Lord is like themselves. A certain very pious man was horribly shocked by hearing an abolitionist say that the Negro was made in the image of God. The Lord is in their image, they seem to think, and the devil in the image of the Black man.

I desire to bear my testimony, after hearing the eulogy pronounced by Mr. Garrison, with regard to our departed brother and co-laborer, John Murray, of Scotland. About three years ago I had the pleasure of bidding that noble man farewell on the shores of Scotland; and I remember well the deep interest he took in the antislavery questions of this country. His last battle in behalf of the slave was with the Free Church of Scotland; and while he lived, that Church, for its alliance with slaveholders — for receiving their money into its treasury, and extending to them its fellowship in return — obtained no repose. He bore a noble testimony against it; he had borne a noble testimony against slavery before. For the last twenty-eight years, John Murray stood up in Scotland, the firm, the untiring, the devoted friend of the slave. There are two or three colored persons, at least, now in this Hall, who have shared his generous hospitality, and received his hearty "God-speed" in their endeavors to break down slavery and prejudice against color in this country, by creating a public sentiment on that side of the Atlantic that should react in favor of human liberty here. I have no more to say respecting this good man; his consistent and irreproachable character is his best eulogy.

Someone has asked me to say a word about General Worth. I only know General Worth by his acts in Mexico and elsewhere, in the service of this slaveholding and slave-trading government. I know why that question is put: it is because one of your city papers, which does not rise to the dignity of being called a paper — a sheet of the basest sort — has said that my tongue ought to be cut out by its roots because, upon hearing of the death of that man, I made use of the remark — (it is not stated in what connection I made it, or where) — that another legalized murderer had gone to his account. I say so yet! I will not undertake to defend what I then said, or to shop up his character or history. You know as well as I do, that Faneuil Hall has resounded with echoing applause of a denunciation of the Mexican war, as a murderous war — as a war against the free states — as a war against freedom, against the Negro, and against the interests of workingmen of this country — and as a means of extending that great evil and damning curse, Negro slavery. Why may not the oppressed say, when an oppressor is dead, either by disease or by the hand of the foeman on the battlefield, that there is one the less of his oppressors left on earth? For my part, I would not care if, tomorrow, I should hear of the death of every man who engaged in that bloody war in Mexico, and that every man had met the fate he went there to perpetrate upon unoffending Mexicans.

A word more. There are three millions of slaves in this land, held by the United States Government, under the sanction of the American Constitution, with all the compromises and guaranties contained in that instrument in favor of the slave system. Among those guaranties and compromises is one by which you, the citizens of Boston, have sworn, before God, that three millions of slaves shall be slaves or die — that your swords and bayonets and arms shall, at any time at the biding of the slaveholder, through the legal magistrate or governor of a slave State, be at his service in putting down the slaves. With eighteen millions of freemen standing upon the quivering hearts of three millions of slaves, my sympathies, of course, must be with the oppressed. I am among them, and you are treading them beneath your feet. The weight of your influence, numbers, political combinations and religious organizations, and the power of your arms, rest heavily upon them, and serve at this moment to keep them in their chains. When I consider their condition — the history of the American people — how they bared their bosoms to the storm of British artillery, in order to resist simply a three-penny tea tax, and to assert their independence of the mother country — I say, in view of these things, I should welcome the intelligence tomorrow, should it come, that the slaves had risen in the South, and that the sable arms which had been engaged in beautifying and adorning the South were engaged in spreading death and devastation there. There is a state of war at the South at this moment. The slaveholder is waging a war of aggression on the oppressed. The slaves are now under his feet. Why, you welcomed the intelligence from France, that Louis Philippe had been barricaded in Paris — you threw up your caps in honor of the victory achieved by Republicanism over Royalty — you shouted aloud — "Long live the republic!" — and joined heartily in the watchword of "Liberty, Equality, Fraternity" — and should you not hail, with equal pleasure, the tidings from the South that the slaves had risen, and achieved for himself, against the iron-hearted slaveholder, what the republicans of France achieved against the royalists of France?[53]

---

[53] Excerpted from a "Lecture on The American Colonization Society" delivered in Boston, Massachusetts at Faneuil Hall on May 31, 1849 and published in *The Liberator*, June 8, 1849.

Nothing Short of the Blood of the Slaveholder – If ever there was a time of trial – of deep solemnity – to those who wish well for the Slave, this is the time. It is a time to test the fidelity of men and women who hitherto have professed to believe in Human Brotherhood.

We have come together to consult as to our duty in reference to the Fugitive Slave Law. This law has had pledged to its support the military and naval power of this Government. It is the only law which, for a long time, it has been deemed necessary, that the Executive should openly pledge for its support the whole power of the army and navy – aye, even to collusion with our citizens, whom he might have to slaughter in its execution.

This is the law. It is one about to be rigorously pressed. Six months ago, this would not have been believed. People would not then believe the bill could be enacted. Mason introduced it, and discussed it; but it was so flagrantly opposed to the Constitution, so scandalous a violation of the plainest principles of justice, that no one of the people at the North believed it could pass.

The people of the North are a hopeful people. The bill passed the Senate – but it could not pass the House. It did pass – but, still hoping, as ever, the good people said Millard Fillmore would not sign it. But Fillmore did sign it.

Then, again, the hopeful people of the North said it would remain a dead letter – that the Northern people did not want these men – and that the North were so repugnant to its operation. But we soon learned that a respectable man in New York was inveighed into a small room, went through a mock trial, and in three hours was on his way to bondage!

The hopeful North again said that this would be the last case. But this proved untrue. We hear of cases now every day. The work under the law had but just begun. The South see a quieting down on the subject – they see prominent clergymen preaching from the pulpit obedience to this law — they see newspapers which once spoke "brave words" for the slave now excluding Abolitionism from their columns.

The question before us is, *Whether we are to make resistance to the execution of this law?* Whether we are to recognize the principle that every man is innocent and free until he is proven to be otherwise, or to admit the Virginia doctrine that every Black man is a slave until proved otherwise? The South have President Fillmore, the Army and the Navy on its side – and they are determined to press this law to the "bitter end."

This Convention must say what ought to be done. I am a peace man. I am opposed to the shedding of blood in all cases where it can be avoided. But this Convention ought to say to Slaveholders that they are in danger of bodily harm if they come here, and attempt to carry men off into bondage. I say to any Fugitive, that nothing short of the blood of the slaveholder who shall attempt to carry him off, ought to satisfy him. The Convention should say so.

Dr. Channing, whose memory [I esteem] so highly, once said that we could frown slaveholders down — the idea being that the indignant flashes of our eyes would frighten them out of countenance. I am for the fullest exercise of moral power — for doing all with moral power that can be done, and for using no other power when that is sufficient for the end. But if anyone should attempt to take me into Slavery, I should strike him down — not with malignity, but as complacently as I would a bloodhound, and think I was doing God service.

The slaveholder has no right to live. We must keep them away. They keep us away from the South. They say they will hang us if we go there — and we keep away. We must make them understand that it is equally important for their safety that they keep away from us on errands of this character.

[I refer] to the case of Hughes, in Boston.[54] He did not deem it safe to remain, and he left. A few cases like that would make the law a dead letter. Make two or three dead men — that will make the law

---

[54] **Editorial Note** – "Our city, for a week past, has been thrown into a state of intense excitement by the appearance of two prowling villains, named Hughes and Knight, from Macon, Georgia, for the purpose of seizing William and Ellen Craft, under the infernal Fugitive Slave Bill, and carrying them back to the hell of Slavery. Since the day of '76, there has not been such a popular demonstration on the side of human freedom in this region. The humane and patriotic contagion has infected all classes. Scarcely any other subject has been talked about in the streets, or in the social circle. On Thursday, of last week, warrants for the arrest of William and Ellen were issued by Judge Levi Woodbury, but no officer has yet been found ready or bold enough to serve them. In the meantime, the Vigilance Committee, appointed at the Faneuil Hall meeting, has not been idle. Their number has been increased to upwards of a hundred "good men and true," including some thirty or forty members of the bar; and they have been in constant session, devising every legal method to baffle the pursuing bloodhounds, and relieve the city of their hateful presence." Excerpted from *The Liberator*, November 1st, 1850.

a dead letter. These men have thrown it in the teeth of the Black men, that they are unfit for freedom — that they have not the spirit to revolt against any degree of oppression. Are we not invited to the work of slaying kidnappers by this theory in regard to ourselves? There will be no more kidnappers from Macon, Georgia.

What we must do is to make it unsafe for a slaveholder or his agent, or a United States officer to undertake to kidnap any man or woman among us. And to show that it is unsafe, we must set some examples. In illustration [I refer] to the recent case in Pennsylvania, where a band of colored men beat off the kidnappers. The slaveholder went home without his prey and declared he would not renew the attempt. The business was accomplished. The rights of the assailed were protected, but only by their own strong arms.

If in Syracuse you allow one to be taken off, another will soon follow. When any human being will so far sink his manhood as to become a wolf, a tiger, a bloodhound, he is not fit to live. I do believe that two or three dead slaveholders will make this law a dead letter. I have said that the South know how to keep Abolitionists away — they say they will hang them on the next tree — and in that way, and in that way only, can we keep these bloodhounds from their errand of robbery at the North.[55]

---

[55] Lecture delivered at City Hall in Syracuse, New York January 7, 1851 for the New York State Anti-Fugitive Slave Bill Mass Convention and published in *New York Daily Tribune* January, 11th, 1851.

Freedom's Battle at Christiana – The fight at Christiana between the slavecatchers and the alleged fugitive slaves, continues to excite general discussion. The sensation produced by the death of the kidnappers is not surpassed by that which occurred throughout the country on hearing of the fate of the Cuban invaders. The failure of these two patriotic expeditions, undertaken so nobly by our *law-abiding* citizens, must long be regarded as among the most memorable events of this eventful year.

Everybody seems astonished, that in this land of gospel light and liberty, after all the sermons of the *Lords, Lathrops, Spencers, Coxes, Springs, Deweys, Sharpes, Tyngs,* and a host of other Doctors of Divinity, there should be found men so firmly attached to liberty and so bitterly averse to slavery, as to be willing to peril even life itself to gain the one and avoid the other. Pro-slavery men especially are in a state of amazement at the strange affair. That the hunted men should fight with the biped bloodhounds that had tracked them, even when the animals had a "*paper*" authorizing them to hunt, is to them inexplicable audacity. 'Tis not that the negroes fought the kidnappers (no, let no one misrepresent) that we are astonished, but that they should fight them and kill them when they knew they had '*papers*'." That they should kill the men-hunters is, perhaps, natural, and may be explained in the light of the generally admitted principles "that self-preservation is the first law of nature;" but, the rascals! they killed their pursuers, when they knew they had "*papers!*" Just here is the point of difficulty. What could have got into these men of sable coating? Didn't they know that slavery, not freedom, is their natural condition? Didn't they know that their legs, arms, eyes, hands and heads, were the rightful property of the white men who claimed them?

Can we in charity suppose these Negroes to have been ignorant of the fact that our *"own dear Fillmore"* (that whom there is none higher – not according to northern Whiggery, not even in the heavens above nor in the earth beneath) did, on the eighteenth day of September, in the year one thousand eight hundred and fifty of the Christian era, and in the seventy-fifth year of the freedom and independence of the American people *from the bondage of a foreign yoke*, approve and send forth a decree, (with all the solemn authority of his great name,) ordaining that thereafter, *Men Should Cease To Be Men*! Oh! ye most naughty and rebellious fellows! Why stand ye up like men, after this mighty decree? Why have not your hands become paws, and your arms, legs? Why are you not down among four-footed beasts with the fox, the wolf and the bear, sharing with them the chances of the chase, but constituting the most choice game – the peculiar game of this free and Christian country? We say again that here is the point of difficulty which demands explanation. For you see, friends and brethren, if the story gets afloat that these Negroes of Christiana did really hear the words of the mighty *Fillmore* commanding them to be brutes instead of men, and they did not change as ordered, why, the dangerous doctrine will also get afloat presently that there is a law higher than the law of *Fillmore*. If his voice cannot change the nature of things, it is certain that there is a power above him, and that that frightful heresy, (which has been so justly condemned by the most learned clergy,) called the "Higher Law," will be received, the evil consequences of which, even the great Daniel cannot portray.

We have said that the pro-slavery people of this country don't know what to make of this demonstration on the part of the alleged fugitive slaves of Christiana. This, however, is possibly a mistake. There is in that translation a lesson which the most obtuse may understand, namely, that all *Negroes Are Not Such Fools and Dastards as to Cling to –* LIFE *– When it is Coupled with Chains and Slavery.*

This lesson, though most dearly bought, is quite worth the price paid. It was needed. The lamb-like submission with which men of color have allowed themselves to be dragged away from liberty, from family and all that is dear to the hearts of man, had well-nigh established the impression that they were conscious of their own fitness for slavery. The frequency of arrests, and the ease with which they were made quickened the rapacity, and invited these aggressions of slavecatchers. The Christiana conflict was therefore needed to check these aggressions and to bring the hunters of men to the sober second thought. But was it right for the colored men to resist their enslavers? We answer, Yes, or the whole structure of the world's theory of right and wrong is a lie. If it be right for any man to resist those who would enslave them, it was right for the men of color at Christiana to resist. If an appeal to arms may ever be innocently made, the appeal in this instance was innocently made; and if it were wrong in them to fight, it can never be right in any case to fight. For never were there, never can there be more sacred rights to defend then were menaced on this occasion. Life and liberty are the most sacred of all man's rights. If these may be invaded with impunity, all others may be, for they comprehend all others. But we take still higher ground. It was right in the light of absolute justice, which says to the aggressor, he that leadeth into captivity shall go into captivity, and he that taketh the sword shall perish by the sword. The man who rushes out of the orbit of his own rights, to strike down the rights of another, does, by that act, divest himself of the right to live; if he be shot down, his punishment is just.

Now what are the facts in the case, for these have been most scandalously misrepresented by the news-papers? The slaveholder's side of the story has been told, but the other side has been dumb, for colored men cannot write. Could they speak for themselves, we dare be sworn that they would testify substantially as follows: Early in the evening of September tenth, a colored man, a fugitive slave, went to the house of Wm. Parker, a sober, well-behaved, and religious man of color, and said to him, William, there is a warrant out for the arrest of some of us, and it is said the kidnappers will be up tonight from Philadelphia. What had we better do? The answer to this, was worthy of the man. Come to my house said Parker. Accordingly, five men of color, all told, spent the night at William's house. They sat up late in apprehension of an attack, but finally went to bed, but sleep they could not. About two hours before day-light, one of the colored men went into the yard, and on raising his eyes, saw, at that unseasonable hour, fifteen men, coming stealthily along the lane. He ran into the house, and told the inmates that the slave-catchers had come, and the truth of his story was soon confirmed, for but a minute elapsed before the whole fifteen men in Parker's yard. The man who went into the yard, did not fasten the door securely, and it was therefore easily forced. The slaveholders rushed into the lower part of the house, and called upon the occupants to give themselves up. Here commenced the conflict. The kidnappers undertook to force their way up stairs, but were met, and compelled to retreat. A parley ensued. Gorsuch was spokesman for himself and his kidnapping comrades, and Parker for himself and guests. Gorsuch said, "you have got my property in your house." "I have not," said Parker; "there is no property here but what belongs to me. I own every trunk, and chair and article of furniture about this house and none but robbers and murderers would make any attack upon me at this hour of the night." "You have got my men in your house" said Gorsuch, "and I will have them, or go to hell in the attempt to get them." Parker said "I have got none of your men, I never owned a man in my life. I believe it to be a sin to own men; I am no slave-owner." Gorsuch here interrupted Parker, saying, "I don't want to hear your abolition lecture." After a long parley, during which Parker repeatedly advised the slave-catchers to go away, stating that he did not wish to hurt them, although they had fired into his house fifteen times, shooting once through his hat crown, the five colored men came down the stairs, and walked in front of the slave-catchers, and both parties were now arrayed face to face. Parker then

took the old man, Gorsuch, by the arm, and said to
him, "old man, we don't want to harm you. You
profess to be a Christian; you are a Methodist class-
leader, and you ought to be ashamed to be in such
business." At this point, the young Gorsuch, said,
"father, do you allow a 'n****r' to talk so to you?
Why don't you shoot him, father?" Parker then
answered: "Young man, I would say to you just what I
have said to your father. You had better go about
your business." Young Gorsuch then fired at Parker,
but missed him, and he Gorsuch, was instantly shot
down. There was now a general shooting, and
striking with clubs, during which the elder Gorsuch
was killed, his son shot through the lungs, and his
nephew dangerously wounded. We must not omit to
state that the first plan to take the advice of the colored preacher (as Parker is called,) was the Marshal
from Philadelphia. He *topped his boom* before the
heat of the battle came on, undoubtedly feeling that
he had barked up the wrong tree, and that it was best
for him to make tracks! The time occupied in
parleying between the two parties, was full two hours.

The colored men who are alleged to have taken
part in the conflict at Christiana, are to be tried, we
are informed, for high treason! This is to cap the
climax of American absurdity, to say nothing of American infamy. Our government has virtually made
every colored man in the land an outlaw, one who
may be hunted by any villain who may think proper
to do so, and if the hunted man, finding himself stript
of all legal protection, shall lift his arms in his own
defense, why, forsooth, he is arrested, arraigned, and

tried for high treason, and found guilty, he must suffer death!

The basis of allegiance is protection. We owe allegiance to the government that protects us, but to the government that destroys us, we owe no allegiance. The only law which the alleged slave has a right to know anything about, is the law of nature. This is his only law. The enactments of this government do not recognize him as a citizen, but as a thing. In the light of the law, a slave can no more commit treason than a horse or an ox can commit treason. A horse kicks out the brains of his master. Do you try the horse for treason? Then why the slave who does the same thing? You answer, because the slave is a man, and he is therefore responsible for his acts. The answer is sound. The slave is a man, and ought not to be treated like a horse, but like a man, and his manhood is his justification for shooting down any creature who shall attempt to reduce him to the condition of a brute.

But there is one consolation after all about this arraignment for treason. It admits our manhood. Sir Walter Scott says, that treason is the crime of a gentleman. We shall watch this trial in Philadelphia, and shall report the result when it transpires. Meanwhile, we think that fugitives may sleep more soundly than formerly.[56]

---

[56] *Frederick Douglass' Paper*, September 25, 1851.

Is Civil Government Right? – This question is raised and summarily disposed of in a letter, which appears in another column, addressed by Mr. Wright to Gerrit Smith, Esq. The writer thinks a just civil government "*an impossibility.*" He does not, in this, object to the abuses of power, but to the power itself, and he classes the assumed right of government with robbery, piracy and slavery. "*To speak of a righteous human ruler is the same as to speak of a righteous thief, a righteous robber, a righteous murderer, a righteous pirate or a righteous slaveholder.*"

To those unacquainted with Mr. Wright's style, this letter will seem an outburst of unusual extravagance on his part; but we must pronounce it *tame* as compared with many of his productions, on this and on kindred subjects. There is in it an absence of startling assertion, and an attempt at reasoning such as Mr. Wright does not always condescend to in dealing with opponents. We, therefore, take pleasure in laying his letter before our readers, that they may have both sides of a subject which is to them, and to us, one of unspeakable interest.

Were we to presume to criticize Mr. Wright's letter, we should object to his limited statement of the assumed right upon which civil government is based. He says, "*the assumption is, that man is invested by God with power to dictate law to man and to punish him if he do not obey.*"

To this statement we object, that the vital principle of government is left out. It contains the skeleton, but the life is not there. The bones and sinews are retained, but the vital spark which should animate them is gone. Were we to make an inquiry into the rightfulness of civil government, we should (perhaps owing to the diffuseness of our intellect) begin by assuming, first, that man is a social as well as an individual being; that he is endowed, by his Creator, with faculties and powers suited to his individuality and to society. Second, that individual isolation is unnatural, unprogressive and against the highest interests of man; and that society is required, by the natural wants and necessities inherent in human existence. Third, that man is endowed with reason and understanding capable of discriminating between good and evil, right and wrong, justice and injustice. Fourth, that while man is constantly liable to do evil, he is still capable of apprehending and pursuing that which is good; and that, upon the whole, his evil tendencies are quite outweighed by the powers within him, impelling him to good. In a word, that crime is the exception, and innocence is the rule of human nature. Fifth, that rewards and punishments are natural agents for restraining evil and for promoting good, man being endowed with faculties keenly alive to both. Finally, that whatever serves to increase the happiness, to preserve the well-being, to give permanence, order and attractiveness to society, and leads to the very highest development of human perfection, is, unless positively prohibited by Divine command, to be esteemed innocent and right. The question then comes, Is human government right? Mark, the question is not: Is arbitrary, despotic, tyrannical, corrupt, unjust, capricious government right? but is society (that is a company of human beings) authorized by their Creator to institute a government for themselves, and to pass and enforce laws which are in accordance with justice, liberty and humanity?   Mr. Wright says that they *have not.* His reasons are, that "*to admit the rightfulness of such government is to admit that human will or discretion is the only tenure by which we hold life, liberty or happiness. That the existence of each one is at the discretion of each and every other. That we must all live or die, be slaves or freemen, be happy or miserable, by act of Congress or Parliament,*" and much more in the same strain.

From a conclusion so revolting and terrible, he, naturally enough, recoils with a shudder.   The fallacy and fatal error which form the basis of this reasoning, are the assumptions that human government is necessarily arbitrary and absolute; and that there is no difference between a righteous and a wicked government.   Human government, from its very nature, is an organization, like every other human institution, limited in its powers, and subject to the very wants of human nature which call it into existence.   A community of men who will organize a government, granting it the power to make them slaves or freemen, to kill them or let them live, to make them happy or miserable at discretion, are in a pitiable condition, and far behind the Liberty Party in right apprehensions of the nature and office of civil government.

"*But,*" says Mr. Wright, "*if a man may rightfully tell his fellow-beings how to act, he may tell them how to speak, how to feel, and how to think.*"   Well, what of it?   Mr. Wright is constantly telling men how to act, how to think, how to feel, and how to speak; and it would be well for the world if it followed some of his telling at least.   But we apprehend that the objection to government does not consist in its telling men how to think, speak, feel or act, but in the punishment which government may see fit to inflict, and that involves the question of the rightfulness of physical force, of which we shall speak anon. Mr. Wright does not object to societies expressing by their votes their dissent or approval of the thoughts, sayings, feelings and actions of men. He, doubtless, deems this proper and praiseworthy; nor does he, as we understand him, object to the principle that majorities ought to rule; at any rate, he certainly cannot think that the minority of the members of the American Anti-Slavery Society ought to adopt measures which are condemned by the majority. Why is this respect to be shown to the majority? Simply because a majority of human hearts and intellects may be presumed, as a general rule, to take a wiser and more comprehensive view of the matters upon which they act than the minority. It is in accordance with the doctrine that good is the rule, and evil the exception in the character and constitution of man. If the fact were otherwise (that is, if men were more disposed to evil than to good), it would, indeed, be dangerous for men to enter into a compact, by which power should be wielded by the mass, for then evil being predominant in man, would predominate in the mass, and innumerable hardships would be inflicted upon the good. The old assertion of the wickedness of the masses, and their consequent unfitness to govern themselves, is the falsehood and corruption out of which have sprung the despotic and tyrannical conspiracies, calling themselves governments, in the old world. They are founded not in the aggregate morality and intelligence of the people, but in a fancied divine authority, resulting from the inherent incompetency of the people to direct their own temporal concerns. Kings and despots flourish in such a soil, poisoning the moral atmosphere with oppression and paralyzing the spirit of progress by choking the utterance of free speech from the platform and the press. It is confounding such government with a righteous democratic government, and charging the crimes of the former upon the latter, that has led such men as Mr. Wright to array them-selves against the Liberty Party.

But how different is the ground assumed by Gerrit Smith and his associates, from that upon which despotic governments are based. The one assumes that the people may be trusted, and the other, that no confidence can be placed in them. The one that the people, the whole people, should have a voice in making the laws under which they live, and the other, that the people should have nothing to do with the laws but to obey them; or (to use a favorite sentiment of Mr. Wright) one regards institutions for men, and the other regards men for institutions. But it is alleged that the power claimed for government by the Liberty Party, is, in essence, the same as that which is claimed by despots, and is, therefore, to be rejected. This allegation is unfounded, since there is all the difference between the cases, that exists between limited and restricted power, and power unlimited and unrestricted. In the one case, the governing power is in the hands of the people, who are supposed to know their rights and to understand their interests; and in the other, the governing power is in the hands of an individual, who, from his very circumstances and environments, can be supposed to have very little sympathy with the people, or very little desire to promote their intelligence as to their best interests.

Mr. Wright will, however, insist that the exercise of governmental power is practically the same, whether it be wielded by King Individual or King Majority; that the will, caprice, or what not, of the majority is as imperious in its tone, and must be as implicitly obeyed as that of the king.

The answer is, that the Liberty Party concedes no governmental authority to pass laws, nor to compel obedience to any laws, against the natural rights and happiness of man. It affirms that the office of government is protection; and when it ceases to protect the rights of man, they repudiate it as a tyrannical usurpation. But our friend asks, "*Who is to decide?*" We answer, the constitution and the common sense of the people, manifested in the choice of their lawmakers. It may still be further asked, will they always decide rightly? They may not, for the individual does not always decide for himself what is for his best interest. What then? Shall we abolish the individual, and deny him the right to govern himself because he may sometimes govern wrongly? The reasoning which would deny the right of society to frame laws for its own protection, preservation and happiness, would, if rigidly adhered to, deny to man the right to govern himself; for is he not a frail mortal, and has he any more right to ruin himself than he has to ruin others? But again, the very fact that a government is instituted by all, and rests upon all for support and direction, is the strongest guarantee that can be given that it will be wielded justly and impartially. With all the drawbacks upon government which fancy can depict, or imagination conjure up, society possessing it, is as paradise to pandemonium, compared with society without it.

Mr. Wright objects to civil government because "there is no crime which man may not and will not perpetrate against man." A strange reason against government truly. – We use the fact in favor of government, not against it. Because there are hardened villains, enemies to themselves and to the well-being of society, who will cheat, steal, rob, burn and murder their fellow-creatures, and because these are the exceptions to the mass of humanity, society has the right to protect itself against their depredations and aggressions upon the common weal. Society without law, is society with a curse, driving men into isolation and depriving them of one of the greatest blessings of which man is susceptible. It is no answer to this to say that if all men would obey the laws of God, lead virtuous lives, do by others as they would be done unto, human government would be unnecessary; for it is enough to know, as Mr. Wright declares, that "there are no crimes which man may not and will not perpetrate against his fellow-man," to justify society in resorting to force, as a means of protecting itself from crime and its consequences.

If it be alleged that to repel aggression by force is to promote aggression; and that to submit to be robbed, plundered and enslaved is the true way to establish justice and liberty among men, the answer is, that the theory is contradicted by the facts of human nature, and by the experience of men in all ages. The present condition of the slave population of this country is a striking illustration of the fallacy that submission is the best remedy for the wrongs and injustice to which they are subjected. Here we have two hundred years of non-resisting submission, and equally two hundred years of cruel injustice; and so far from this submission serving as a remedy for the frightful injustice, it is urged by the oppressors as a reason for persisting in their course. Concessions do but lead to exactions, and submission, to the imposition of still greater hardships, and this is the lesson taught by the facts of human nature, and by the history of the world. Men need to be taught, not only the happy consequences arising from dealing justly, but the dreadful consequences which result from injustice; their fears, therefore, may be as legitimately appealed to as their hopes, and he who repudiates such appeals, throws away an important instrumentality for establishing justice among men, and promoting the peace and happiness of society. All tyrants, all oppressors should be taught, by precept and by example, that, in trampling wantonly and ruthlessly upon the lives and liberties of their unoffending brothermen, they forfeit their own right to liberty, and richly deserve the slavery and death that they inflict upon others. Mr. Wright may say that the slave should appeal to the humanity and to the sense of justice of his master, and thus overcome evil with good; but, once enslaved, the master may forbid such an appeal; for, to use the language of Mr. Wright, the power claimed is such as may enable the slave-holder to tell his slave, not only "how to act," but how to speak, think and feel; and he may deprive his victim of every means of reaching his sense of justice, except through his bodily fears. This, then, is our reasoning: that when every avenue to the understanding and heart of the oppressor is closed, when he is deaf to every moral appeal, and rushes upon his fellow-man to gratify his own selfish propensities at the expense of the rights and liberties of his brother-man, the exercise of physical force, sufficient to repel the aggression, is alike the right and the duty of society.

Truth may withstand falsehood, love may overcome hatred, opinion may be opposed to opinion, the theory of liberty may be opposed to slavery, and common sense alike teaches that physical resistance is the antidote for physical violence.

It is asked, in view of these conclusions, when will wars cease? We answer, when man shall learn to respect the rights of man: "*first pure, then peaceable.*" There can be no peace while there is oppression. The true way to give peace to the world is, to establish justice in the world; and regarding righteous civil government as an important means to this great end, we unhesitatingly and heartily consecrate ourselves, within our humble sphere, to its advocacy.[57]

---

[57] *Frederick Douglass' Paper*, October 23rd, 1851.

The Fugitive Slave Law – Gentlemen, I take it that you are in earnest, and mean all you say by this call, and therefore I will address you. I am taken by surprise, but I never withhold a word on such an occasion as this. The object of this Convention is to organize a party, not merely for the present, but a party identified with eternal principles and therefore permanent. I have come here, not so much of a free soiler as others have come. I am, of course, for circumscribing and damaging slavery in every way I can. But my motto is extermination – not only in New Mexico, but in New Orleans – not only in California but in South Carolina. No where has God ordained that this beautiful land shall be cursed with bondage by enslaving men. Slavery has no rightful existence anywhere. The slaveholders not only forfeit their right to liberty, but to life itself. The earth is God's, and it ought to be covered with righteousness, and not slavery. We expect this great National Convention to lay down some such principle as this. What we want is not a temporary organization, for a temporary want, but a firm, fixed, immovable, liberty party. Had the old liberty party continued true to its principles, we never should have seen such a hell born enactment as the Fugitive Slave Law.

In making your Platform, nothing is to be gained by a timid policy. The more closely we adhere to principle, the more certainly will we command respect. Both National Conventions acted in open contempt of the antislavery sentiment of the North, by incorporating, as the corner stone of their two platforms, the infamous law to which I have alluded – a law which, I think, will never be repealed – it is too bad to be repealed — a law fit only to trampled underfoot, (suiting the action to the word). The only way to make the Fugitive Slave Law a dead letter is to make half a dozen or more dead kidnappers. A half dozen more dead kidnappers carried down South would cool the ardor of Southern gentlemen, and keep their rapacity in check. That is perfectly right as long as the colored man has no protection. The colored men's rights are less than those of a jackass. No man can take away a jackass without submitting the matter to twelve men in any part of this country. A Black man may be carried away without any reference to a jury. It is only necessary to claim him, and that some villain should swear to his identity. There is more protection there for a horse, for a donkey, or anything, rather than a colored man — who is, therefore, justified in the eye of God, in maintaining his right with his arm.

The man who takes the office of a bloodhound ought to be treated as a bloodhound; and I believe that the lines of eternal justice are sometimes so obliterated by a course of long continued oppression that it is necessary to revive them by deepening their traces with the blood of a tyrant. This Fugitive Slave Law had the support of the Lords, and the Coxes, the Tyngs, the Sharps and the flats. It is nevertheless a degradation and a scandalous outrage on religious liberty; and if the American people were not sunk into degradation too deep for one possessing so little eloquence as I do to describe, they would feel it, too. This vile, infernal law does not interfere with singing of psalms, or anything of that kind, but with the weightier matters of the law, judgment, mercy, and faith. It makes it criminal for you, sir, to carry out the principles of Christianity. It forbids you the right to do right — forbids you to show mercy — forbids you to follow the example of the good Samaritan.

Had this law forbidden any of the rites of religion, it would have been a very different thing. Had it been a law to strike at baptism, for instance, it would have been denounced from a 1000 pulpits, and woe to the politician who did not come to the rescue. — But, I am spending my strength for nought; what care we for religious liberty? What are we — an unprincipled set of knaves? You feel it to be so. Not a man of you that looks a fellow Democrat or Whig in the face, but knows it. But it has been said that this law is constitutional — if it were, it would be equally the legitimate sphere of government to repeal it. I am proud to be one of the disciples of Gerrit Smith, and this is his doctrine; and he only utters what all law writers have said who have risen to any eminence. Human government is for the protection of rights; and when human government destroys human rights, it ceases to be a government, and becomes a foul and blasting conspiracy; and is entitled to no respect whatever.

It has been said that our fathers entered into a covenant for this slavecatching. Who were your daddies? I take it they were men, and so are you. You are the sons of your fathers; and if you find your fathers exercising any rights that you don't find among your rights, you may be sure that they have transcended their limits. If they have made a covenant that you should do that which they have no right to do themselves, they transcended their own authority, and surely it is not binding on you. If you look over the list of your rights, you do not find among them any right to make a slave of your brother.

Well, you have just as good a right to do so as your fathers had. It is a fundamental truth that every man is the rightful owner of his own body. If you have no right to the possession of another man's body your fathers had no such right. But suppose that they have written in a constitution that they have a right, you and I have no right to conform to it. Suppose you and I had made a deed to give away two or three acres of blue sky; would the sky fall — and would anybody be able to plough it? You will say that this is an absurdity, and so it is. The binding quality of law, is its reasonableness. I am safe, therefore, in saying, that slavery cannot be legalized at all. I hope, therefore, that you will take the ground that this slavery is a system, not only of wrong, but is of a lawless character, and cannot be Christianized nor legalized.

Can you hear me in that end of the hall now? I trust that this Convention will be the means of laying before the country the principles of the Liberty Party which I have the honor to represent, to some extent, on this floor. Slavery is such a piracy that it is known neither to law nor gospel — it is neither human nor divine — a monstrosity that cannot be legalized. If they took this ground it would be the handwriting on the wall to the Belshazzars of the South. It would strip the crime of its legality, and all the forms of law would shrink back with horror from it. As I have always an object when speaking on such subjects as this, I wish you to supply yourselves with Gerrit Smith's pamphlet on civil government, which I now hold in my hand. I thought you doubted the impossibility of legalizing slavery.

Could a law be made to pass away any of your individual rights? No. And so neither can a law be made to pass away the right of the Black man. This is more important than most of you seem to think. You are about to have a party, but I hope not such a party as will gather up the votes, here and there, to be swallowed up at a meal by the great parties. I think I know what some leading men are now thinking. We hear a great deal of the independent, free democracy — at one time independent and another time dependent — but I want always to be independent, and not hurried to and fro into the ranks of Whigs or Democrats. It has been said that we ought to take the position to gain the greatest number of voters, but that is wrong.

We have had enough of that folly. It was said in 1848 that Martin Van Buren would carry a strong vote in New York; he did so but he almost ruined us. He merely looked at us as into the pigpen to see how the animal grew; but the table was the final prospect in view; he regarded the Free Soil party as a fatling to be devoured. Numbers should not be looked to so much as right. The man who is right is a majority. He who has God and conscience on his side, has a majority against the universe. Though he does not represent the present state, he represents the future state. If he does not represent what we are, he represents what we ought to be. In conclusion, this party ought to extend a hand to the noble, self-sacrificing patriot — glorious Kossuth. But I am a voting delegate, and must now go to the convention. You will excuse me for breaking off so abruptly.[58]

---

[58] Lecture delivered in Pittsburgh, August 11, 1852 at the National Free Soil Convention and published in *Frederick Douglass' Paper*, August, 1852.

A Terror to Kidnappers – Such is the title of a huge and highly finished cane, recently presented to [me] by John Jones and J.D. Bonner, members of the National Council for Illinois. This was a happy thought, this *stick* – present not altogether inappropriate, for it is believed in these parts that a good stick is sometimes as much needed as a good speech and often more effective. Where you have a dog [to] deal with, [a] stick will perform wonders where speech would be powerless! – There are among the children of men, and I have gained the fact through personal observation, to be found representatives of all the animal world, from the most savage and ferocious, to the most gentle and docile. Everything must be dealt with according to its kind. What will do for the Lamb will not do for the Tiger. A man would look foolish if he attempted to bail out a leaking boat with the Bible, or to extinguish a raging fire by throwing in a Prayer Book. Equally foolish would he look if he attempted to soften a slave-catcher's heart without first softening his head. This is a capital stick, and I thank my friends for it. I hope never to meet with a creature requiring its use; but should I meet with such an one, I shall use it with stout arm and humane motive.[59]

---

[59] *Frederick Douglass' Paper*, November 25, 1853.

Is it Right and Wise to Kill a Kidnapper? – A kidnapper has been shot dead while attempting to execute the fugitive slave bill in Boston.[60] The streets of Boston in sight of Bunker Hill Monument have been stained with the warm blood of a man in the act of perpetrating the most atrocious robbery which one man can possibly commit upon another — even the wresting from him his very person and natural powers. The deed of blood, as of course must have been expected, is making a tremendous sensation in all parts of the country, and calling forth all sorts of comments. Many are branding the deed as "murder," and would visit upon the perpetrator the terrible penalty attached to that dreadful crime. The occurrence naturally brings up the question of the reasonableness, and the rightfulness of killing a man who is in the act of forcibly reducing a brother man who is guilty of no crime, to the horrible condition of a slave. The question bids fair to be one of important and solemn interest, since it is evident that the practice of slave-hunting and slave-catching, with all their attendant enormities, will either be pursued indefinitely, or abandoned immediately according to the decision arrived at by the community.

Cherishing a very high respect for the opinions of such of our readers and friends as hold to the invio-

---

[60] **Editorial Note** – James Batchelder was serving as a temporary deputy Federal Marshal at a Boston Courthouse on May 26, 1854 when he was killed during an Abolitionist uprising by the Boston Vigilance Committee that included Thomas Wentworth Higginson who sought to keep Anthony Burns from being re-enslaved. Burns had just recently found his way to Boston after liberating himself from slavery in Richmond, Virginia.

lability of the human life, and differing from them on this vital question, we avail ourselves of the present excitement in the public mind, calmly to state our views and opinions, in reference to the case in hand, asking for them an attentive and candid perusal.

Our moral philosophy on this point is our own — never having read what others may have said in favor of the views which we entertain.

The shedding of human blood at first sight, and without explanation is, and must ever be, regarded with horror; and he who takes pleasure in human slaughter is very properly looked upon as a moral monster. Even the killing of animals produces a shudder in sensitive minds, uncalloused by crime; and men are only reconciled to it by being shown, not only its reasonableness, but its necessity. These tender feelings so susceptible to pain, are most wisely designed by the Creator, for the preservation of life. They are, especially, the affirmation of God, speaking through nature, and asserting man's right to live. Contemplated in the light of warmth of these feelings, it is in all cases, a crime to deprive a human being of life: but God has not left us solely to the guidance of our feelings, having endowed us with reason, as well as with feeling, and it is in the light of reason that this question ought to be decided.

All will agree that human life is valuable or worthless, as to the innocent or criminal use that is made of it. Most evidently, also, the possession of life was permitted and ordained for beneficent ends, and not to defeat those ends, or to render their attainment impossible. Comprehensively stated, the end of man's creation is his own good, and the honor of his

Creator. Life, therefore, is but a means to an end, and must be held in reason to be not superior to the purposes for which it was designed by the All-wise Creator. In this view there is no such thing as an absolute right to live; that is to say, the right to live, like any other human right, may be forfeited, and if forfeited, may be taken away. If the right to *life* stands on the same ground as the right to *liberty*, it is subject to all the exceptions that apply to the right to liberty. All admit that the right to enjoy *liberty* largely depends upon the use made of that liberty; hence Society has erected jails and prisons, with a view to deprive men of their liberty when they are so wicked as to abuse it by invading the liberties of their fellows. We have a right to arrest the locomotion of a man who insists upon walking and trampling on his brother man, instead of upon the highway. This right of society is essential to its preservations; without it a single individual would have it in his power to destroy the peace and the happiness of ten thousand otherwise right-minded people. Precisely on the same ground, we hold that a man may properly, wisely, and even mercifully be deprived of life. Of course life being the most precious is the most sacred of all rights, and cannot be taken away, but under the direst necessity; and not until all reasonable modes had been adopted to prevent this necessity, and to spare the aggressor.

It is no answer to this view to say that society is selfish in sacrificing the life of an individual, or of many individuals, to save the mass of mankind, or society at large. It is in accordance with nature, and the examples of the Almighty, in the execution of his will and beneficent laws. When a man flings himself from the top of some lofty monument, against a granite pavement, in that act he forfeits his right to live. He dies according to law, and however shocking may be the spectacle he presents, it is no argument against the beneficence of the law of gravitation, the suspension of whose operation must work ruin to the well-being of mankind. The observance of this law was necessary to his preservation; and his wickedness or folly, in violating it, could not be excused without imperiling those who are living in obedience to it. The atheist sees no benevolence in the law referred to; but to such minds we address not this article. It is enough for us that the All-Wise has established the law, and determined its character, and the penalty of its violation; and however we may deplore the mangled forms of the foolish and the wicked who transgress it, the beneficence of the law itself is fully vindicated by the security it gives to all who obey it.

We hold, then, in view of this great principle, or rule, in the physical world, we may properly infer that other law or principle of justice in the moral and social world, and vindicate its practical application to the preservation of the rights and liberties of the race, as against such exceptions furnished in the monsters who deliberately violate it by taking pleasure in enslaving, imbruting and murdering their fellow-men. As human life is not superior to the laws for the preservation of the physical universe, so, too, it is not superior to the eternal law of justice, which is essential to the preservation of the rights, and the security, and happiness of the race.

The argument thus far is to the point that society has the right to preserve itself even at the expense of the life of the aggressor; and it may be said that, while what we allege may be right enough, as regards society, it is false as vested in an individual, such as the poor, powerless, and almost friendless wretch, now in the clutches of this proud and powerful republican government. But we take it to be a sound principle, that when government fails to protect the just rights of any individual man, either he or his friends may be held in the sight of God and man, innocent, in exercising any right for his preservation which society may exercise for its preservation. Such an individual is flung, by his untoward circumstances, upon his original right of self-defense. We hold, therefore, that when James Batchelder, the truckman of Boston, abandoned his useful employment, as a common laborer, and took upon himself the revolting business of a kidnapper, and undertook to play the bloodhound on the track of his crimeless brother Burns, he labelled himself the common enemy of mankind, and his slaughter was as innocent, in the sight of God, as would be the slaughter of a ravenous wolf in the act of throttling an infant. We hold that he had forfeited his right to live, and that his death was necessary, as a warning to others liable to pursue a like course.

It may be said, that though the right to kill in defense of one's liberty be admitted, it is still unwise for the fugitive slave or his friends to avail themselves of this right; and that submission, in the circumstances, is far wiser than resistance. To this it is a sufficient answer to show that submission is valuable only so long as it has some chance of being recognized as a virtue. While it has this chance, it is well enough to practice it, as it may then have some moral effect in restraining crime and shaming aggression, but no longer. That submission on the part of the slave has ceased to be a virtue is very evident. While fugitives quietly cross their hands to be tied, adjust their ankles to be chained, and march off unresistingly to the hell of slavery, there will ever be fiends enough to hunt them and carry them back. Nor is this all nor the worst. Such submission, instead of being set to the credit of the poor sable ones, only creates contempt for them in the public mind, and becomes an argument in the mouths of the community, that Negroes are, by nature, only fit for slavery; that slavery is their normal condition. Their patient and unresisting disposition, their unwillingness to peril their own lives, by shooting down their pursuers, is already quoted against them, as marking them as an inferior race. This reproach must be wiped out, and nothing short of resistance on the part of colored men, can wipe it out. Every slavehunter who meets a bloody death in his infernal business, is an argument in favor of the manhood of our race. Resistance is, therefore, wise as well as just.

At this point of our writing, we meet with the following plea, set up for the atrocious wretch, "gone to his own place," by the Rochester *Daily American*, a Silver Grey paper.

"An important inquiry arises, — Who are the murderers of Batchelder? There are several. First, and most guilty, are Wendell Phillips, Theodore Parker, and their Fanueil Hall coadjutors. All just minds will regard their conduct as more atrocious than even that of the ruffians who shot and mangled the unfortunate officer. Cold, remorseless, and bloody as the cruel axe, they deliberately worked up the crowd to a murderous frenzy, and pointed out the path which led to murder. The guilt which rests upon the infuriated assassins is light compared with that which blackens the cowardly orators of Fanueil Hall."

"What had Batchelder done, that Phillips, Parker and their minions should steep their souls in his blood? Why did these men make his wife a widow, — his children fatherless, and send his unwarned spirit to the presence of God?"

This is very pathetic. The *widow* and the *fatherless* of this brutal truckman — a truckman who, it seems, was one of the swell-head bullies of Boston, selected for the office of Marshal or Deputy Marshal, solely because of his brutal nature and ferocious disposition.

We would ask Mr. Mann whether if such a wretch should lay his horney paws upon his own dignified shoulders, with a view to reduce him to bondage, he would hold, as a murderer, any friend of his, who, to save him from such a fate, shot down the brute? — There is not a citizen of Rochester worthy of the name, who would not shoot down any man in defense of his own liberty — or who, if set upon, by a number of robbers, would not thank any friend who interposed, even to the shedding of blood, for his release.— *The widow and orphans* are far better off with such a wretch in the grave, than on the earth. Then again, the law which he undertook to execute, has *no tears* for the *widows and orphans* of poor innocent fugitives, who make their homes at the North. With a hand as relentless as that of death, it snatches the husband from the wife, and the father from his children, and this for no crime. — Oh! that man's ideas of justice and of right depended less upon the circumstance of color, and more upon the indestructible nature of things. For a *white* man to defend his friend unto blood is praiseworthy, but for a *Black* man to do precisely the same thing is crime. It was glorious for Patrick Henry to say, "*Give me liberty or give me death!*" It was glorious for Americans to drench the soil, and crimson the sea with blood, *to escape the payment of three-penny tax upon tea*; but it is crime to shoot down a monster in defense of the liberty of a Black man and to save him from a bondage "one hour of which (in the language of Jefferson) is worse than ages of that which our fathers rose in rebellion to oppose." Until Mr. Mann is willing to be a slave — until he is ready to admit that human legislation can rightfully reduce him to slavery, by a simple vote — until he abandons the right of self-defense — until he ceases to glory in the deeds of Hancock, Adams, and Warren — and ceases to look with pride and patriotic admiration upon the somber pile at Bunker Hill, where the blood of the oppressor was poured out in torrents making thousands of widows and orphans, it does not look graceful in him to brand as murderers those that killed the atrocious Truckman who attempted to play the bloodhound on the track of the poor, defenseless *Burns*. [61]

---

[61] *Frederick Douglass' Paper*, June 2nd, 1854.

Desire for Freedom – I hated slavery, always, and the desire for freedom only needed a favorable breeze, to fan it into a blaze, at any moment. The thought of only being a creature of the present and the past, troubled me, and I longed to have a future – a future with hope in it. To be shut up entirely to the past and present, is abhorrent to the human mind; it is to the soul – whose life and happiness is unceasing progress – what the prison is to the body; a blight and mildew, a hell of horrors.[62]

---

[62] Excerpted from *My Bondage and My Freedom*, (New York and Auburn, New York: Miller, Orton & Mulligan, 1855).

Second Existential Meditation on Slave Revolt – As I have elsewhere intimated that my hardships were much greater during the first six months of my stay at Covey's, than during the remainder of the year, and as the change in my condition was owing to causes which may help the reader to a better understanding of human nature, when subjected to the terrible extremities of slavery, I will narrate the circumstances of this change, although I may seem thereby to applaud my own courage. You have, dear reader, seen me humbled, degraded, broken down, enslaved, and brutalized, and you understand how it was done; now let us see the converse of all this, and how it was brought about; and this will take us through the year 1834. On one of the hottest days of the month of August, of the year just mentioned, had the reader been passing through Covey's farm, he might have seen me at work, in what is there called the "treading yard" – a yard upon which wheat is trodden out from the straw, by the horses' feet. I was there, at work, feeding the "fan," or rather bringing wheat to the fan, while Bill Smith was feeding. Our force consisted of Bill Hughes, Bill Smith, and a slave by the name of Eli; the latter having been hired for this occasion. The work was simple, and required strength and activity, rather than any skill or intelligence, and yet, to one entirely unused to such work, it came very hard. The heat was intense and overpowering, and there was much hurry to get the wheat, trodden out that day, through the fan; since, if that work was done an hour before sundown, the hands would have, according to a promise of Covey, that hour added to their night's rest. I was not behind any of them in the wish to complete the day's work before sundown, and, hence, I struggled with all my might to get the work forward. The promise of one hour's repose on a week day, was sufficient to quicken my pace, and to spur me on to extra endeavor. Besides, we had all planned to go fishing, and I certainly wished to have a hand in that. But I was disappointed, and the day turned out to be one of the bitterest I ever experienced. About three o'clock, while the sun was pouring down his burning rays, and not a breeze was stirring, I broke down; my strength failed me; I was seized with a violent aching of the head, attended with extreme dizziness, and trembling in every limb. Finding what was coming, and feeling it would never do to stop work, I nerved myself up, and staggered on until I fell by the side of the wheat fan, feeling that the earth had fallen upon me. This brought the entire work to a dead stand. There was work for four; each one had his part to perform, and each part depended on the other, so that when one stopped, all were compelled to stop. Covey, who had now become my dread, as well as my tormentor, was at the house, about a hundred yards from where I was fanning, and instantly, upon hearing the fan stop, he came down to the treading yard, to inquire into the cause of our stopping. Bill Smith told him I was sick, and that I was unable longer to bring wheat to the fan.

I had, by this time, crawled away, under the side of a post-and-rail fence, in the shade, and was exceedingly ill. The intense heat of the sun, the heavy dust rising from the fan, the stooping, to take up the wheat from the yard, together with the hurrying, to get through, had caused a rush of blood to my head. In this condition, Covey finding out where I was, came to me; and, after standing over me a while, he asked me what the matter was. I told him as well as I could, for it was with difficulty that I could speak. He then gave me a savage kick in the side, which jarred my whole frame, and commanded me to get up. The man had obtained complete control over me; and if he had commanded me to do any possible thing, I should, in my then state of mind, have endeavored to comply. I made an effort to rise, but fell back in the attempt, before gaining my feet. The brute now gave me another heavy kick, and again told me to rise. I again tried to rise, and succeeded in gaining my feet; but, upon stooping to get the tub with which I was feeding the fan, I again staggered and fell to the ground; and I must have so fallen, had I been sure that a hundred bullets would have pierced me, as the consequence. While down, in this sad condition, and perfectly helpless, the merciless negro breaker took up the hickory slab, with which Hughes had been striking off the wheat to a level with the sides of the half bushel measure, (a very hard weapon,) and with the sharp edge of it, he dealt me a heavy blow on my head which made a large gash, and caused the blood to run freely, saying, at the same time, "*If you have got the headache, I'll cure you.*" This done, he ordered me again to rise, but I made no effort to do so; for I had made up my mind that it was useless, and that the heartless monster might *now* do his worst; he could but kill me, and that might put me out of my misery. Finding me unable to rise, or rather despairing of my doing so, Covey left me, with a view to getting on with the work without me. I was bleeding very freely, and my face was soon covered with my warm blood. Cruel and merciless as was the motive that dealt that blow, dear reader, the wound was fortunate for me. Bleeding was never more efficacious. The pain in my head speedily abated, and I was soon able to rise. Covey had, as I have said, now left me to my fate; and the question was, shall I return to my work, or shall I find my way to St. Michael's, and make Capt. Auld acquainted with the atrocious cruelty of his brother Covey, and beseech him to get me another master? Remembering the object he had in view, in placing me under the management of Covey, and further, his cruel treatment of my poor crippled cousin, Henny, and his meanness in the matter of feeding and clothing his slaves, there was little ground to hope for a favorable reception at the hands of Capt. Thomas Auld. Nevertheless, I resolved to go straight to Capt. Auld, thinking that, if not animated by motives of humanity, he might be induced to interfere on my behalf from selfish considerations. "He cannot," thought I, "allow his property to be thus bruised and battered, marred and defaced; and I will go to him, and tell him the simple truth about the matter." In order to get to St. Michael's, by the most favorable and direct road, I must walk seven miles; and this, in my sad condition, was no easy performance. I had already lost much blood; I was exhausted by over exertion; my sides were sore from the heavy blows planted there by the stout boots of Mr. Covey; and I was, in every way, in an unfavorable plight for the journey. I however watched my chance, while the cruel and cunning Covey was looking in an opposite direction, and started off, across the field, for St. Michael's. This was a daring step; if it failed, it would only exasperate Covey, and increase the rigors of my bondage, during the remainder of my term of service under him; but the step was taken, and I must go forward. I succeeded in getting nearly half way across the broad field, toward the woods, before Mr. Covey observed me. I was still bleeding, and the exertion of running had started the blood afresh. "*Come back! Come back!*" vociferated Covey, with threats of what he would do if I did not return instantly. But, disregarding his calls and his threats, I pressed on toward the woods as fast as my feeble state would allow. Seeing no signs of my stopping, Covey caused his horse to be brought out and saddled, as if he intended to pursue me. The race was now to be an unequal one; and, thinking I might be overhauled by him, if I kept the main road, I walked nearly the whole distance in the woods, keeping far enough from the road to avoid detection and pursuit. But, I had not gone far, before my little strength again failed me, and I laid down. The blood was still oozing from the wound in my head; and, for a time, I suffered more than I can describe. There I was, in the deep woods, sick and emaciated, pursued by a wretch whose character for revolting cruelty beggars all opprobrious speech – bleeding, and almost bloodless. I was not without the fear of bleeding to death. The thought of dying in the woods, all alone, and of being torn to pieces by the buzzards, had not yet been rendered tolerable by my many troubles and hardships, and I was glad when the shade of the trees, and the cool evening breeze, combined with my matted hair to stop the flow of blood. After lying there about three quarters of an hour, brooding over the singular and mournful lot to which I was doomed, my mind passing over the whole scale or circle of belief and unbelief, from faith in the overruling providence of God, to the blackest atheism, I again took up my journey toward St. Michael's, more weary and sad than in the morning when I left Thomas Auld's for the home of Mr. Covey. I was bare-footed and bare-headed, and in my shirt sleeves. The way was through bogs and briers, and I tore my feet often during the journey. I was full five hours in going the seven or eight miles; partly, because of the difficulties of the way, and partly, because of the feebleness induced by my illness, bruises and loss of blood. On gaining my master's store, I presented an appearance of wretchedness and woe, fitted to move any but a heart of stone. From the crown of my head to the sole of my feet, there were marks of blood. My hair was all clotted with dust and blood, and the back of my shirt was literally stiff with the same. Briers and thorns had scarred and torn my feet and legs, leaving blood marks there. Had I escaped from a den of tigers, I could not have looked worse than I did on reaching St. Michael's. In this unhappy plight, I appeared before my professedly *Christian* master, humbly to invoke the interposition of his power and authority, to protect me from further abuse and violence. I had begun to hope, during the latter part of my tedious journey toward St. Michael's, that Capt. Auld would now show himself in a nobler light than I had ever before seen him. I was disappointed. I had jumped from a sinking ship into the sea; I had fled from the tiger to something worse. I told him all the circumstances, as well as I could; how I was endeavoring to please Covey; how hard I was at work in the present instance; how unwillingly I sunk down under the heat, toil and pain; the brutal manner in which Covey had kicked me in the side; the gash cut in my head; my hesitation about troubling him (Capt. Auld) with complaints; but, that now I felt it would not be best longer to conceal from him the outrages committed on me from time to time by Covey. At first, master Thomas seemed somewhat affected by the story of my wrongs, but he soon repressed his feelings and became cold as iron. It was impossible as I stood before him at the first for him to seem indifferent. I distinctly saw his human nature asserting its con-viction against the slave system, which made cases like mine *possible*; but, as I have said, humanity fell before the systematic tyranny of slavery. He first walked the floor, apparently much agitated by my story, and the sad spectacle I presented; but, pres-ently, it was *his* turn to talk. He began moderately, by finding excuses for Covey, and ending with a full justification of him, and a passionate condemnation of me. "He had no doubt I deserved the flogging. He did not believe I was sick; I was only endeavoring to get rid of work. My dizziness was laziness, and Covey did right to flog me, as he had done." After thus fairly annihilating me, and rousing himself by his own eloquence, he fiercely demanded what I wished *him* to do in the case!

With such a complete knock-down to all my hopes, as he had given me, and feeling, as I did, my entire subjection to his power, I had very little heart to reply. I must not affirm my innocence of the allegations which he had piled up against me; for that would be impudence, and would probably call down fresh violence as well as wrath upon me. The guilt of a slave is always, and everywhere, presumed; and the innocence of the slaveholder or the slave employer, is always asserted. The word of the slave, against this presumption, is generally treated as impudence, worthy of punishment. "Do you contradict me, you rascal?" is a final silencer of counter statements from the lips of a slave.

Calming down a little in view of my silence and hesitation, and, perhaps, from a rapid glance at the picture of misery I presented, he inquired again, "what I would have him do?" Thus invited a second time, I told Master Thomas I wished him to allow me to get a new home and to find a new master; that, as sure as I went back to live with Mr. Covey again, I should be killed by him; that he would never forgive my coming to him (Capt. Auld) with a complaint against him (Covey;) that, since I had lived with him, he had almost crushed my spirit, and I believed that he would ruin me for future service; that my life was not safe in his hands. This, Master Thomas (*my brother in the church*) regarded as "nonsense." "There was no danger of Mr. Covey's killing me; he was a good man, industrious and religious, and he would not think of removing me from that home; "besides," said he, and this I found was the most distressing thought of all to him "if you should leave Covey now, that your year has but half expired, I should lose your wages for the entire year. You belong to Mr. Covey for one year, and *you must go back* to him, come what will. You must not trouble me with any more stories about Mr. Covey; and if you do not go immediately home, I will get hold of you myself." This was just what I expected, when I found he had *prejudged* the case against me. "But, Sir," I said, "I am sick and tired, and I cannot get home to-night." At this, he again relented, and finally he allowed me to remain all night at St. Michael's; but said I must be off early in the morning, and concluded his directions by making me swallow a huge dose of – *epsom salts* – about the only medicine ever administered to slaves.

It was quite natural for Master Thomas to presume I was feigning sickness to escape work, for he probably thought that were *he* in the place of a slave with no wages for his work, no praise for well doing, no motive for toil but the lash he would try every possible scheme by which to escape labor. I say I have no doubt of this; the reason is, that there are not, under the whole heavens, a set of men who cultivate such an intense dread of labor as do the slaveholders. The charge of laziness against the slaves is ever on their lips, and is the standing apology for every species of cruelty and brutality. These men literally "bind heavy burdens, grievous to be borne, and lay them on men's shoulders; but they, them-selves, will not move them with one of their fingers." My kind readers shall have, in the next chapter what they were led, perhaps, to expect to find in this namely: an account of my partial disenthrallment from the tyranny of Covey, and the marked change which it brought about.

Sleep itself does not always come to the relief of the weary in body, and the broken in spirit; especially when past troubles only foreshadow coming disasters. The last hope had been extinguished. My master, who I did not venture to hope would protect me as a *man*, had even now refused to protect me as *his property*; and had cast me back, covered with reproaches and bruises, into the hands of a stranger to that mercy which was the soul of the religion he professed. May the reader never spend such a night as that allotted to me, previous to the morning which was to herald my return to the den of horrors from which I had made a temporary escape.

I remained all night – sleep I did not – at St. Michael's; and in the morning (Saturday) I started off, according to the order of Master Thomas, feeling that I had no friend on earth, and doubting if I had one in heaven. I reached Covey's about nine o'clock; and just as I stepped into the field, before I had reached the house, Covey, true to his snakish habits, darted out at me from a fence corner, in which he had secreted himself, for the purpose of securing me. He was amply provided with a cowskin and a rope; and he evidently intended to *tie me up*, and to wreak his vengeance on me to the fullest extent. I should have been an easy prey, had he succeeded in getting his hands upon me, for I had taken no refreshment since noon on Friday; and this, together with the pelting, excitement, and the loss of blood, had reduced my strength. I, however, darted back into the woods, before the ferocious hound could get hold of me, and buried myself in a thicket, where he lost sight of me. The corn-field afforded me cover, in getting to the woods. But for the tall corn, Covey would have overtaken me, and made me his captive. He seemed very much chagrined that he did not catch me, and gave up the chase, very reluctantly; for I could see his angry movements, toward the house from which he had sallied, on his foray.

Well, now I am clear of Covey, and of his wrathful lash, for the present. I am in the wood, buried in its somber gloom, and hushed in its solemn silence; hid from all human eyes; shut in with nature and nature's God, and absent from all human contrivances. Here was a good place to pray; to pray for help for deliverance – a prayer I had often made before. But how could I pray? Covey could pray – Capt. Auld could pray – I would fain pray; but doubts (arising partly from my own neglect of the means of grace, and partly from the sham religion which everywhere prevailed, cast in my mind a doubt upon all religion, and led me to the conviction that prayers were unavailing and delusive) prevented my embracing the opportunity, as a religious one. Life, in itself, had almost become burdensome to me. All my outward relations were against me; I must stay here and starve, (I was already hungry,) or go home to Covey's, and have my flesh torn to pieces, and my spirit humbled under the cruel lash of Covey. This was the painful alternative presented to me. The day was long and irksome. My physical condition was deplorable. I was weak, from the toils of the previous day, and from the want of food and rest; and had been so little concerned about my appearance, that I had not yet washed the blood from my garments. I was an object of horror, even to myself. Life, in Baltimore, when most oppressive, was a paradise to this. What had I done, what had my parents done, that such a life as this should be mine? That day, in the woods, I would have exchanged my manhood for the brutehood of an ox.

Night came. I was still in the woods, unresolved what to do. Hunger had not yet pinched me to the point of going home, and I laid myself down in the leaves to rest; for I had been watching for hunters all day, but not being molested during the day, I expected no disturbance during the night. I had come to the conclusion that Covey relied upon hunger to drive me home; and in this I was quite correct – the facts showed that he had made no effort to catch me, since morning.

During the night, I heard the step of a man in the woods. He was coming toward the place where I lay. A person lying still has the advantage over one walking in the woods, in the day time, and this advantage is much greater at night. I was not able to engage in a physical struggle, and I had recourse to the common resort of the weak. I hid myself in the leaves to prevent discovery. But, as the night rambler in the woods drew nearer, I found him to be a *friend*, not an enemy; it was a slave of Mr. William Groomes, of Easton, a kind hearted fellow, named "Sandy." Sandy lived with Mr. Kemp that year, about four miles from St. Michael's. He, like myself, had been hired out by the year; but, unlike myself, had not been hired out to be broken. Sandy was the husband of a free woman, who lived in the lower part of *"Potpie Neck,"* and he was now on his way through the woods, to see her, and to spend the Sabbath with her.

As soon as I had ascertained that the disturber of my solitude was not an enemy, but the good-hearted

Sandy – a man as famous among the slaves of the neighborhood for his good nature, as for his good sense – I came out from my hiding place, and made myself known to him. I explained the circumstances of the past two days, which had driven me to the woods, and he deeply compassionated my distress. It was a bold thing for him to shelter me, and I could not ask him to do so; for, had I been found in his hut, he would have suffered the penalty of thirty-nine lashes on his bare back, if not something worse. But, Sandy was too generous to permit the fear of punishment to prevent his relieving a brother bondman from hunger and exposure; and, therefore, on his own motion, I accompanied him to his home, or rather to the home of his wife – for the house and lot were hers. His wife was called up – for it was now about midnight – a fire was made, some Indian meal was soon mixed with salt and water, and an ash cake was baked in a hurry to relieve my hunger. Sandy's wife was not behind him in kindness – both seemed to esteem it a privilege to succor me; for, although I was hated by Covey and by my master, I was loved by the colored people, because *they* thought I was hated for my knowledge, and persecuted because I was feared. I was the *only* slave *now* in that region who could read and write. There had been one other man, belonging to Mr. Hugh Hamilton, who could read, (his name was "Jim,") but he, poor fellow, had, shortly after my coming into the neighborhood, been sold off to the far south. I saw Jim ironed, in the cart, to be carried to Easton for sale, – pinioned like a yearling for the slaughter. My knowledge was now the pride of my brother slaves; and, no doubt, Sandy felt something of the general interest in me on that account. The supper was soon ready, and though I have feasted since, with honorables, lord mayors and aldermen, over the sea, my supper on ash cake and cold water, with Sandy, was the meal, of all my life, most sweet to my taste, and now most vivid in my memory.

Supper over, Sandy and I went into a discussion of what was *possible* for me, under the perils and hardships which now overshadowed my path. The question was, must I go back to Covey, or must I now attempt to run away? Upon a careful survey, the latter was found to be impossible; for I was on a narrow neck of land, every avenue from which would bring me in sight of pursuers. There was the Chesapeake Bay to the right, and "Pot-pie" river to the left, and St. Michael's and its neighborhood occupying the only space through which there was any retreat.

I found Sandy an old adviser. He was not only a religious man, but he professed to believe in a system for which I have no name. He was a genuine African, and had inherited some of the so-called magical powers, said to be possessed by African and eastern nations. He told me that he could help me; that, in those very woods, there was an herb, which in the morning might be found, possessing all the powers required for my protection, (I put his thoughts in my own language;) and that, if I would take his advice, he would procure me the root of the herb of which he spoke. He told me further, that if I would take that root and wear it on my right side, it would be impossible for Covey to strike me a blow; that with this root about my person, no white man could whip me.

He said he had carried it for years, and that he had fully tested its virtues. He had never received a blow from a slaveholder since he carried it; and he never expected to receive one, for he always meant to carry that root as a protection. He knew Covey well, for Mrs. Covey was the daughter of Mr. Kemp; and he (Sandy) had heard of the barbarous treatment to which I was subjected, and he wanted to do something for me.

Now all this talk about the root, was, to me, very absurd and ridiculous, if not positively sinful. I at first rejected the idea that the simple carrying a root on my right side, (a root, by the way, over which I walked every time I went into the woods,) could possess any such magic power as he ascribed to it, and I was, therefore, not disposed to cumber my pocket with it. I had a positive aversion to all pretenders to "*divination.*" It was beneath one of my intelligence to countenance such dealings with the devil, as this power implied. But, with all my learning – it was really precious little – Sandy was more than a match for me. "My book learning," he said, "had not kept Covey off me," (a powerful argument just then,) and he entreated me, with flashing eyes, to try this. If it did me no good, it could do me no harm, and it would cost me nothing, anyway. Sandy was so earnest, and so confident of the good qualities of this weed, that, to please him, rather than from any conviction of its excellence, I was induced to take it. He had been to me the good Samaritan, and had, almost providentially, found me, and helped me when I could not help myself; how did I know but that the hand of the Lord was in it? With thoughts of this sort, I took the roots from Sandy, and put them in my right hand pocket.

This was, of course, Sunday morning. Sandy now urged me to go home, with all speed, and to walk up bravely to the house, as though nothing had happened. I saw in Sandy too deep an insight into human nature, with all his superstition, not to have some respect for his advice; and perhaps, too, a slight gleam or shadow of his superstition had fallen upon me. At any rate, I started off toward Covey's, as directed by Sandy. Having, the previous night, poured my griefs into Sandy's ears, and got him enlisted in my behalf, having made his wife a sharer in my sorrows, and having, also, become well refreshed by sleep and food, I moved off, quite courageously, toward the much dreaded Covey's. Singularly enough, just as I entered his yard gate, I met him and his wife, dressed in their Sunday best – looking as smiling as angels – on their way to church. The manner of Covey astonished me. There was something really benignant in his countenance. He spoke to me as never before; told me that the pigs had got into the lot, and he wished me to drive them out; inquired how I was, and seemed an altered man. This extraordinary conduct of Covey, really made me begin to think that Sandy's herb had more virtue in it than I, in my pride, had been willing to allow; and, had the day been other than Sunday, I should have attributed Covey's altered manner solely to the magic power of the root. I suspected, however, that the *Sabbath*, and not the *root*, was the real explanation of Covey's manner. His religion hindered him from breaking the Sabbath, but not from breaking my skin. He had more respect

for the *day* than for the *man,* for whom the day was
mercifully given; for while he would cut and slash my
body during the week, he would not hesitate, on
Sunday, to teach me the value of my soul, or the way
of life and salvation by Jesus Christ.

All went well with me till Monday morning; and
then, whether the root had lost its virtue, or whether
my tormentor had gone deeper into the black art than
myself, (as was sometimes said of him,) or whether he
had obtained a special indulgence, for his faithful
Sabbath day's worship, it is not necessary for me to
know, or to inform the reader; but, this much I may
say, – the pious and benignant smile which graced
Covey's face on *Sunday,* wholly disappeared on
Monday. Long before daylight, I was called up to go
and feed, rub, and curry the horses. I obeyed the
call, and I would have so obeyed it, had it been made
at an earlier hour, for I had brought my mind to a
firm resolve, during that Sunday's reflection, viz: to
obey every order, however unreasonable, if it were
possible, and, if Mr. Covey should then undertake to
beat me, to defend and protect myself to the best of
my ability. My religious views on the subject of
resisting my master, had suffered a serious shock, by
the savage persecution to which I had been subjected,
and my hands were no longer tied by my religion.
Master Thomas's indifference had severed the last
link. I had now to this extent "backslidden" from this
point in the slave's religious creed; and I soon had
occasion to make my fallen state known to my
Sunday-pious brother, Covey.

Whilst I was obeying his order to feed and get the
horses ready for the field, and when in the act of

going up the stable loft for the purpose of throwing down some blades, Covey sneaked into the stable, in his peculiar snake-like way, and seizing me suddenly by the leg, he brought me to the stable floor, giving my newly mended body a fearful jar. I now forgot my *roots*, and remembered my pledge to *stand up in my own defense.* The brute was endeavoring skillfully to get a slip-knot on my legs, before I could draw up my feet. As soon as I found what he was up to, I gave a sudden spring, (my two day's rest had been of much service to me,) and by that means, no doubt, he was able to bring me to the floor so heavily. He was defeated in his plan of tying me. While down, he seemed to think he had me very securely in his power. He little thought he was – as the rowdies say – "in" for a "rough and tumble" fight; but such was the fact. Whence came the daring spirit necessary to grapple with a man who, eight-and-forty hours before, could, with his slightest word have made me tremble like a leaf in a storm, I do not know; at any rate, *I was resolved to fight*, and, what was better still, I was actually hard at it. The fighting madness had come upon me, and I found my strong fingers firmly attached to the throat of my cowardly tormentor; as heedless of consequences, at the moment, as though we stood as equals before the law. The very color of the man was forgotten. I felt as supple as a cat, and was ready for the snakish creature at every turn. Every blow of his was parried, though I dealt no blows in turn. I was strictly on the *defensive*, preventing him from injuring me, rather than trying to injure him. I flung him on the ground several times, when he meant to have hurled me there. I held him so firmly by the throat, that his blood followed my nails. He held me, and I held him.

All was fair, thus far, and the contest was about equal. My resistance was entirely unexpected, and Covey was taken all aback by it, for he trembled in every limb. "*Are you going to resist*, you scoundrel?" said he. To which, I returned a polite "*yes sir*;" steadily gazing my interrogator in the eye, to meet the first approach or dawning of the blow, which I expected my answer would call forth. But, the conflict did not long remain thus equal. Covey soon cried out lustily for help; not that I was obtaining any marked advantage over him, or was injuring him, but because he was gaining none over me, and was not able, single handed, to conquer me. He called for his cousin Hughes, to come to his assistance, and now the scene was changed. I was compelled to give blows, as well as to parry them; and, since I was, in any case, to suffer for resistance, I felt (as the musty proverb goes) that "I might as well be hanged for an old sheep as a lamb." I was still *defensive* toward Covey, but *aggressive* toward Hughes; and, at the first approach of the latter, I dealt a blow, in my desperation, which fairly sickened my youthful assailant. He went off, bending over with pain, and manifesting no disposition to come within my reach again. The poor fellow was in the act of trying to catch and tie my right hand, and while flattering himself with success, I gave him the kick which sent him staggering away in pain, at the same time that I held Covey with a firm hand.

Taken completely by surprise, Covey seemed to have lost his usual strength and coolness. He was frightened, and stood puffing and blowing, seemingly unable to command words or blows. When he saw that poor Hughes was standing half bent with pain – his courage quite gone – the cowardly tyrant asked if I "meant to persist in my resistance." I told him "*I did mean to resist, come what might*," that I had been by him treated like a brute, during the last six months; and that I should stand it *no longer*. With that, he gave me a shake, and attempted to drag me toward a stick of wood, that was lying just outside the stable door. He meant to knock me down with it; but, just as he leaned over to get the stick, I seized him with both hands by the collar, and, with a vigorous and sudden snatch, I brought my assailant harmlessly, his full length, on the *not over* clean ground – for we were now in the cow yard. He had selected the place for the fight, and it was but right that he should have all the advantages of his own selection.

By this time, Bill, the hired man, came home. He had been to Mr. Hemsley's, to spend the Sunday with his nominal wife, and was coming home on Monday morning, to go to work. Covey and I had been skirmishing from before daybreak, till now, that the sun was almost shooting his beams over the eastern woods, and we were still at it. I could not see where the matter was to terminate. He evidently was afraid to let me go, lest I should again make off to the woods; otherwise, he would probably have obtained arms from the house, to frighten me. Holding me, Covey called upon Bill for assistance. The scene here, had something comic about it. "Bill," who knew *precisely* what Covey wished him to do, affected ignorance, and pretended he did not know what to do. "What shall I do, Mr. Covey," said Bill. "Take hold of him – take hold of him!" said Covey. With a toss of his head, peculiar to Bill, he said, "indeed, Mr. Covey, I want to go to work." "*This is* your work," said Covey; "take hold of him." Bill replied, with spirit, "My master hired me here, to work, and not to help you whip Frederick." It was now my turn to speak. "Bill," said I, "don't put your hands on me." To which he replied, "MY GOD! Frederick, I aint goin' to tech ye," and Bill walked off, leaving Covey and myself to settle our matters as best we might.

But, my present advantage was threatened when I saw Caroline (the slave-woman of Covey) coming to the cow yard to milk, for she was a powerful woman, and could have mastered me very easily, exhausted as I now was. As soon as she came into the yard, Covey attempted to rally her to his aid. Strangely – and, I may add, fortunately – Caroline was in no humor to take a hand in any such sport. We were all in open rebellion, that morning. Caroline answered the command of her master to "*take hold of me*," precisely as Bill had answered, but in *her*, it was at greater peril so to answer; she was the slave of Covey, and he could do what he pleased with her. It was not so with Bill, and Bill knew it. Samuel Harris, to whom Bill belonged, did not allow his slaves to be beaten, unless they were guilty of some crime which the law would punish. But, poor Caroline, like myself, was at the mercy of the merciless Covey; nor did she escape the dire effects of her refusal. He gave her several sharp blows.

Covey at length (two hours had elapsed) gave up the contest. Letting me go, he said, – puffing and blowing at a great rate – "now, you scoundrel, go to your work; I would not have whipped you half so much as I have had you not resisted." The fact was, *he had not whipped me at all.* He had not, in all the scuffle, drawn a single drop of blood from me. I had drawn blood from him; and, even without this satisfaction, I should have been victorious, because my aim had not been to injure him, but to prevent his injuring me.

During the whole six months that I lived with Covey, after this transaction, he never laid on me the weight of his finger in anger. He would, occasionally, say he did not want to have to get hold of me again – a declaration which I had no difficulty in believing; and I had a secret feeling, which answered, "you need not wish to get hold of me again, for you will be likely to come off worse in a second fight than you did in the first."

Well, my dear reader, this battle with Mr. Covey, – undignified as it was, and as I fear my narration of it is – was the turning point in my *"life as a slave."* It rekindled in my breast the smouldering embers of liberty; it brought up my Baltimore dreams, and revived a sense of my own manhood. I was a changed being after that fight. I was *nothing* before; I WAS A MAN NOW. It recalled to life my crushed self-respect and my self-confidence, and inspired me with a renewed determination to be A FREEMAN. A man, without force, is without the essential dignity of humanity. Human nature is so constituted, that it cannot *honor* a helpless man, although it can *pity* him; and even this it cannot do long, if the signs of power do not arise.

He only can understand the effect of this combat on my spirit, who has himself incurred something, hazarded something, in repelling the unjust and cruel aggressions of a tyrant. Covey was a tyrant, and a cowardly one, withal. After resisting him, I felt as I had never felt before. It was a resurrection from the dark and pestiferous tomb of slavery, to the heaven of comparative freedom. I was no longer a servile coward, trembling under the frown of a brother worm of the dust, but, my long-cowed spirit was roused to an attitude of manly independence. I had reached the point, at which I was *not afraid to die.* This spirit made me a freeman in *fact*, while I remained a slave in *form*. When a slave cannot be flogged he is more than half free. He has a domain as broad as his own manly heart to defend, and he is really *"a power on earth."* While slaves prefer their lives, with flogging, to instant death, they will always find Christians enough, like unto Covey, to accommodate that preference. From this time, until that of my escape from slavery, I was never fairly whipped. Several attempts were made to whip me, but they were always unsuccessful. Bruises I did get, as I shall hereafter inform the reader; but the case I have been describing, was the end of the brutification to which slavery had subjected me.

The reader will be glad to know why, after I had so grievously offended Mr. Covey, he did not have me taken in hand by the authorities; indeed, why the law of Maryland, which assigns hanging to the slave who resists his master, was not put in force against me; at any rate, why I was not taken up, as is usual in such cases, and publicly whipped, for an example to other slaves, and as a means of deterring me from committing the same offense again. I confess, that the easy manner in which I got off, was, for a long time, a surprise to me, and I cannot, even now, fully explain the cause.

The only explanation I can venture to suggest, is the fact, that Covey was, probably, ashamed to have it known and confessed that he had been mastered by a boy of sixteen. Mr. Covey enjoyed the unbounded and very valuable reputation, of being a first-rate overseer and *negro breaker.* By means of this reputation, he was able to procure his hands for *very trifling* compensation, and with very great ease. His interest and his pride mutually suggested the wisdom of passing the matter by, in silence. The story that he had undertaken to whip a lad, and had been resisted, was, of itself, sufficient to damage him; for his bearing should, in the estimation of slaveholders, be of that imperial order that should make such an occurrence *impossible.* I judge from these circumstances, that Covey deemed it best to give me the go-by. It is, perhaps, not altogether creditable to my natural temper, that, after this conflict with Mr. Covey, I did, at times, purposely aim to provoke him to an attack, by refusing to keep with the other hands in the field, but I could never bully him to another battle. I had made up my mind to do him serious damage, if he ever again attempted to lay violent hands on me. "Hereditary bondmen, know ye not Who would be free, themselves must strike the blow?"[63]

---

[63] Excerpted from *My Bondage and My Freedom*, (New York and Auburn, New York: Miller, Orton & Mulligan, 1855). The last

Slavery Is What Incites Slave Revolt – The slave-holder, kind or cruel, is a slaveholder still – the every hour violator of the just and inalienable rights of man; and he is, therefore, every hour silently whetting the knife of vengeance for his own throat. He never lisps a syllable in commendation of the fathers of this republic, nor denounces any attempted oppression of himself, without inviting the knife to his own throat, and asserting the rights of rebellion for his own slaves.[64]

quote is Douglass citing Lord Byron, *Childe Harold's Pilgrimage*, canto 2, stanza 76.

[64] Excerpted from *My Bondage and My Freedom*, (New York and Auburn, New York: Miller, Orton & Mulligan, 1855).

The Slavemaster Already Recognizes the Humanity of the Enslaved – It is the interest and business of slaveholders to study human nature, with a view to practical results, and many of them attain astonishing proficiency in discerning the thoughts and emotions of slaves. They have to deal not with earth, wood, or stone, but with *men;* and, by every regard they have for their safety and prosperity, they must study to know the material on which they are at work. So much intellect as the slaveholder has around him, requires watching. Their safety depends upon their vigilance. Conscious of the injustice and wrong they are every hour perpetrating, and knowing what they themselves would do if made the victims of such wrongs, they are looking out for the first signs of the dread retribution of justice. They watch, therefore, with skilled and practiced eyes, and have learned to read, with great accuracy, the state of mind and heart of the slaves, through his sable face. These uneasy sinners are quick to inquire into the matter, where the slave is concerned. Unusual sobriety, apparent abstraction, sullenness and indifference – indeed, any mood out of the common way – afford ground for suspicion and inquiry.[65]

---

[65] Excerpted from *My Bondage and My Freedom*, (New York and Auburn, New York: Miller, Orton & Mulligan, 1855).

Bare Suspicion, False Accusations and Torture - Often relying on their superior position and wisdom, they hector and torture the slave into a confession, by affecting to know the truth of their accusations. "You have got the devil in you," say they, "and we will whip him out of you." I have often been put thus to the torture, on bare suspicion. This system has its disadvantages as well as their opposite. The slave is sometimes whipped into the confession of offenses which he never committed. The reader will see that the good old rule — "a man is to be held innocent until proved to be guilty" — does not hold good on the slave plantation. Suspicion and torture are the approved methods of getting at the truth, here. It was necessary for me, therefore, to keep a watch over my deportment, lest the enemy should get the better of me.[66]

---

[66] Excerpted from *My Bondage and My Freedom*, (New York and Auburn, New York: Miller, Orton & Mulligan, 1855).

The Final Struggle – Among the varied and multitudinous array of opposition to the anti-slavery movement, no Abolitionist should abate his zeal, or relax his energy, but rather redouble his diligence, and resolve, if need be, to die upon the battlefield, struggling for the victory. There is some consolation in the reflection, that the conflict will not, cannot, last forever. The hour which shall witness *the final struggle*, is on the wing. Already we hear the *booming* of the bell which shall yet toll the death knell of human slavery.

Liberty and Slavery cannot dwell together forever in the same country. There is not one iota of affinity existing between them. They hate each other, with a hatred which is unto Death. They ever have been, and they ever must remain, in a state of irreconcilable hostility. Before a union can be effected between them, the laws which govern the moral universe must be repealed. It is absurd in any one to expect to witness the spirit of Liberty being led, by the demon of Slavery, to the hymeneal altar. – As well expect the pains and sorrows of hell, to mingle, in happy unison, with the pleasures and the joys of heaven; the spirits of just men made perfect, with the spirits of the lost.

It is useless, then, to attempt to effect a union between them. No compromise can effect it. No legislation can change the inflexible law of adaptation, the eternal fitness of things. No compact can make that Right, which is wrong from its first principles to its crowning assumptions.

It is, then, perfectly apparent to every reflecting mind, that a crisis more critical than any which has preceded it, is pending. This crisis cannot much

longer be delayed. It must come to pass as the legitimate result of the past and the present struggle for
the mastery in which we behold these deadly enemies
engaged. We may attempt to bind up the wounds of
the respective hostile parties, with mollifying oint-
ment, but this will not avert the impending hour. It
must come, as sure as the laws of God cannot be
trampled upon with impunity.

Then, as a nation, if we are wise, we will prepare
for the last conflict, for that final struggle in which the
enemy of Freedom must capitulate. Instead of indul-
ging in delusive dreams of safety, the Slave Power
should prepare for the era of its disastrous doom; it
will be wise and consider its latter end.

The motto to be inscribed upon the banner of
Freedom, in the last conflict is not, "No *more* Slave
States," nor "No Slavery outside of the Slave States";
but no Slavery where it does exist; no Slavery in the
Republic. We shall not be burdened or annoyed by
unhallowed compromises, we shall make no contracts
with the perfidious enemy. Not one word of concession or compromise, shall escape our lips, not one
syllable of apology. Truth and Error, Liberty and
Slavery, in a hand-to-hand conflict. This is what we
want; this is what we will have. The utter extinction of
Slavery, everywhere in our national domain; the
subversion of the black Power, wherever, in all our
widespread territory, it dare lift its defiant head toward Heaven.

Again; in the final struggle, in order to be successful, there must exist a thorough organization of
freemen, with the single issue presented, Liberty
everywhere, Slavery nowhere; there must be unity of

effort; every man who loves freedom, must array himself in her defence, whatever may have been his past political predilections. The magnet of Human Freedom, must be held high above the din of party tumult, and every man who is willing to peril his life, his fortune, and his sacred honor, in its defence, will ultimately be attracted to the magnet, whether Whig, or Democrat, or Freesoiler, or Abolitionist. This will form the great Abolition Party of the land. In fact, there must be, and there will be, but two Parties in the country; these will be known not as Whigs, nor as Democrats, nor as Republicans, so far as party names are concerned, but simply as the Anti-Slavery, and Pro-Slavery parties of the country. All who are desirous of maintaining a sort of assumed neutrality on the question, as well as the most inveterate haters of the Abolition movement, will constitute the Pro-Slavery Party. Neither of these parties, in the last conflict, will be *wheedled* from the arena, by the presentation of incidental issues. Each party, forming a unit, and rallying under its own banner, will fight for the triumph of its respective Principles.

We do not fear the result of such a struggle. The sooner the last battle shall be fought, the sooner victory will perch upon the standard of the free. The Principles which form the basis of the Abolition movement, are as unchanging and as undying as their Eternal Author. They must triumph, *for Heaven has nowhere promised to delegate his power to another.* Let us then prepare for the battle, and for victory. Already are the masses moving. The disintegration of the once powerful political Parties, is a cheering and significant sign of the times. The throne of the despot is trembling to its deep foundations. There is a good time coming. We yet shall make the welkin ring with the mighty hallelujahs of the free.[67]

---

[67] *Frederick Douglass' Paper*, November 16, 1855.

Peaceful Annihilation of Slavery is Hopeless – While we feel bound to use all our powers of persuasion and argument; to welcome every instrumentality that promises to peacefully destroy that perpetual contemner of God's laws, and disturber of a nation's peace – Slavery; we yet feel that its peaceful annihilation is almost hopeless, and hence stand by the doctrines enunciated in those resolutions, and contend that the slave's right to revolt is perfect, and only wants the occurrence of favourable circumstances to become a duty . . . We cannot but shudder as we call to mind the horrors that have ever marked servile insurrections – we would avert them if we could; but shall the millions forever submit to robbery, to murder, to ignorance, and every unnamed evil which an irresponsible tyranny can devise, because the overthrow of that tyranny would be productive of horrors? We say not. The recoil, when it comes, will be in exact proportion to the wrongs inflicted; terrible as it will be, we accept and hope for it. The slaveholder has been tried and sentenced, his execution only waits the finish to the training of his executioners. He is training his own executioners.[68]

---

[68] *Frederick Douglass' Paper*, November 28, 1856 and quoted by William Chambers, *American Slavery and Colour*, (London: W.&R. Chambers, Paternoster Row and New York: Dix and Edwards, 1857) p.174.

Slaveholders Beyond the Reach of Moral Appeals – I have little hope of the freedom of the slave by peaceful means. A long course of peaceful slaveholding has placed the slaveholders beyond the reach of moral and humane considerations. They have neither ears nor hearts for the appeals to justice and humanity. While the slave will tamely submit his neck to the yoke, his back to the lash, and his ankle to the fetter and chain, the Bible will be quoted, and learning invoked to justify slavery. The only penetrable point of a tyrant is the fear of death. The outcry that they make, as to the danger of having their throats cut is because they deserve to have them cut. The efforts of John Brown and his brave associates, though apparently unavailing, have done more to upset the logic and shake the security of slavery, than all other efforts in that direction for twenty years.

The sleeping dust, over which yourself and friends proposed to meet on the 4th cannot be revived; but the noble principles and disinterested devotion which led John Brown to step serenely to the gallows and lay down his life will never die. They are all the more potent for his death.

Not anxiously are the eyes and the hearts of the American slaves and their friends turned to the lofty peaks of the Alleghanies. The innumerable glens, caves, ravines and rocks of the mountains, will yet be the hiding-places of hunted liberty. The eight-and-forty hours of John Brown's school in Virginia taught the slaves more than they could have otherwise learned in a half-century. Even the mistake of remaining in the arsenal after the first blow was struck, may prove the key to future successes. The tender regard which the dear old man evinced for the life of the tyrants – and which should have secured him his life – will not be imitated by future insurgents. Slaveholders are as insensible to magnanimity as to justice, and the measure they meter must be meted out to them again.[69]

---

[69] Excerpted from a Letter to James Redpath on June 29, 1860 and published in *The Liberator*, July 27, 1860.

Slaveholders Must Feel Death in the Air – This is a meeting to discuss the best method of abolishing slavery, and each speaker is expected to present what he regards as the best way of prosecuting the anti-slavery movement. From my heart of hearts I endorse the sentiment expressed by Mr. Phillips, of approval of all methods of proceeding against slavery, politics, religion, peace, war, Bible, Constitution, disunion, Union – every possible way known in opposition to slavery is my way. But the moral and social means of opposing slavery have had a greater prominence, during the last twenty-five years, than the way indicated by the celebration of this day – I mean the John Brown way. This is a recent way of opposing slavery; and I think, since it is in consequence of this peculiar mode of advocating the overthrow of slavery that we have had a mob in Boston today, it may be well for me to occupy the few moments I have in advocating John Brown's way of accomplishing our object.

Sir, we have seen the number of slaves increase from half a million to four millions. We have seen, for the last sixty years, more or less of resistance to slavery in the United States. As early as the beginning of the U. S. Government, there were abolition societies in the land. There were abolition societies in Virginia, abolition societies in Maryland, abolition societies in South Carolina, abolition societies in

Pennsylvania. These societies appealed to the sense of justice, appealed to humanity, in behalf of the slave. They appealed to the magnanimity of the slaveholders and the nation; they appealed to the Christianity of the South and of the nation, in behalf of the slave. Pictures of slavery were presented. The ten thousand enormities daily occurring in the Southern States were held up – men sold on the auction block – women scourged with a heavy lash – men tied to the stake and deliberately burned, the blood gushing from their nose and eyes, asking rather to be shot than to be murdered by such slow torture. The facts of these charges have been flung before the public by ten thousand eloquent lips, and by more than ten thousand eloquent pens. The humanity, the common human nature of the country has been again and again appealed to. Four millions have bowed before this nation, and with uplifted hands to Heaven and to you, have asked, in the name of God, and in the name of humanity, to break our chains! To this hour, however, the nation is dumb and indifferent to these cries for deliverance, coming up from the South; and instead of the slaveholders becoming softened, becoming more disposed to listen to the claims of justice and humanity – instead of being more and more disposed to listen to the suggestions of reason, they have become madder and madder, and with every attempt to rescue the bondman from the clutch of his enslaver, his grip has become tighter and tighter, his conscience more and more callous. He has become harder and harder, with every appeal made to his sense of justice, with every appeal made to his humanity, until at length he has come even to confront the world with the pretension that to rob a man of his liberty, to pocket his wages, or to pocket the fruits of his labor without giving him compensation for his work, is not only right according to the law of nature and the laws of the land, but that it is right and just in the sight of the living God. Doctors of Divinity – the Stuarts and the Lords, the Springs, the Blagdens, the Adamses and ten thousand others all over the country – have come out in open defense of the slave system. Not only is this the case, but the very submission of the slave to his chains is held as evidence of his fitness to be a slave; it is regarded as one of the strongest proofs of the divinity of slavery, that the negro tamely submits to his fetters. His very non-resistance – what would be here regarded a Christian virtue – is quoted in proof of his cowardice, and his unwillingness to suffer and to sacrifice for his liberty.

Now what remains? What remains? Sir, it is possible for men to trample on justice and liberty so long as to become entirely oblivious of the principles of justice and liberty. It is possible for men so far to transgress the laws of justice as to cease to have any sense of justice. What is to be done in that case? You meet a man on the sidewalk, in the morning, and you give him the way. He thanks you for it. You meet him again, and you give him the way, and he may thank you for it, but with a little less emphasis than at first. Meet him again and give him the way, and he almost forgets to thank you for it. Meet him again, and give the way, and he comes to think that you are conscious either of your inferiority or of his superiority; and he begins to claim the inside of the walk as his right. This is human nature; this is the nature of the slaveholders. Now, something must be done to make these slaveholders feel the injustice of their course. We must, as John Brown, Jr. – thank God that he lives and is with us tonight! – we must, as John Brown Jr., has taught us this evening, reach the slaveholder's conscience through his fear of personal danger. We must make him feel that there is death in the air about him, that there is death in the pot before him, that there is death all around him. We must do this in some way. It can be done. When you have a good horse, a kind and gentle horse, a horse that your wife can drive, you are disposed to keep him – you wouldn't take any money for that horse. But when you have one that at the first pull of the reins takes the bit in his teeth, kicks up behind, and knocks off the dasher-board, you generally want to get rid of that horse. The Negroes of the South must do this; they must make these slaveholders feel that there is something uncomfortable about slavery – must make them feel that it is not so pleasant, after all, to go to bed with bowie-knives, and revolvers, and pistols, as they must. This can be done, and will be done – yes, I say will be done. Let not, however, these suggestions of mine be construed into the slightest disparagement of the various other efforts, political and moral.

I believe in agitation; and it was largely this belief which brought me five hundred miles from my home to attend this meeting. I am sorry – not for the part I humbly took in the meeting this morning – but I am sorry that Mr. Phillips was not there to look that Fay in the face. I believe that he, and a few Abolitionists like him in the city of Boston, well-known, honorable men, esteemed among their fellow-citizens – had they been there to help us take the initiatory steps in the organization of that meeting, we might, perhaps, have been broken up, but it would have been a greater struggle, certainly, than that which it cost to break up the meeting this morning.

I say, sir, that I want the slaveholders to be made uncomfortable. Every slave that escapes helps to add to their discomfort. I rejoice in every uprising at the South. Although the men may be shot down, they may be butchered upon the spot, the blow tells, notwithstanding, and cannot but tell. Slaveholders sleep more uneasily than they used to. They are more careful to know that the doors are locked than they formerly were. They are more careful to know that their bowie-knives are sharp; they are more careful to know that their pistols are loaded. This element will play its part in the abolition of slavery. I know that all hope of a general insurrection is vain. We do not need a general insurrection to bring about this result. We only need the fact to be known in the Southern States generally, that there is liberty in yonder mountains, planted by John Brown. The slaveholders have but to know, and they do now know, but will be made to know it even more certainly before long – that from the Alleghanies, from the State of Pennsylvania, there is a vast broken country extending clear down into the heart of Alabama – mountains where there are rocks, and ravines, and fastnesses, dens and caves, ten thousand Sebastopols piled up by the hand of the living God, where one man for defense will be as good as a hundred for attack.[70] There let them learn that there are men hid in those fastnesses, who will sally out upon them and conduct their slaves from the chains and fetters in which they are now bound, to breathe the free air of liberty upon those mountains. Let, I say, only a thousand men be scattered in those

---

[70] **Editorial Note** – Douglass endorsed Brown's initial plans of establishing maroon communities of fugitive slaves in the mountains from which to launch guerilla campaigns against slaveholders, but broke with Brown when the plans changed into a frontal assault to seize the Federal arsenal at Harper's Ferry, Virginia.

hills, and slavery is dead. It cannot live in the presence of such a danger. Such a state of things would put an end to planting cotton; it would put an end not only to planting cotton, but to planting anything in that region.

Something is said about the dissolution of the Union under Mr. Lincoln or under Mr. Buchanan. I am for dissolution of the Union – decidedly for dissolution of the Union! Under an abolition President, who would wield the army and the navy of the Government for the abolition of slavery, I should be for the union of these States. If this Union is dissolved, I see many ways in which slavery may be attacked by force, but very few in which it could be attacked by moral means. I see that the moment you dissolve the union between the South and the North, the slave part going by itself, and doing so peaceably – as the cry is from the Tribune and the Albany Evening Journal, and other such papers, that it shall do – establishing an independent government – that very moment the feeling of responsibility for slavery in the North is at an end. But men will tell us to mind our own business. We shall care no more for slavery in the Carolinas or in Georgia than we care for kingcraft or priestcraft in Canada, or slavery in the Brazils or in Cuba. My opinion is that if we only had an abolition President to hold these men in the Union and execute the declared provisions of the Constitution, execute that part of the Constitution which is in favor of liberty, as well as put upon those passages which have been construed in favor of slavery, a construction different from that and more in harmony with the principles of eternal justice that lie at the foundation of the government – if we could have such a government, a government that would force the South to behave herself, under those circumstances I should be for the continuance of the Union. If, on the contrary – no if about it – we have what we have, I shall be glad of the news, come when it will, that the slave States are an independent government, and that you are no longer called upon to deliver fugitive slaves to their masters, and that you are no longer called upon to shoulder your arms and guard with your swords those States – no longer called to go into them to put down John Brown, or anybody else who may strike for liberty there. In case of such a dissolution, I believe that men could be found at least as brave as Walker, and more skillful than any other fillibuster, who would venture into those States and raise the standard of liberty there, and have ten thousand and more hearts at the North beating in sympathy with them. I believe a Garibaldi would arise who would march into those States with a thousand men, and summon to his standard sixty thousand, if necessary, to accomplish the freedom of the slave.

We need not only to appeal to the moral sense of these slaveholders; we have need, and a right, to appeal to their fears. Sir, moral means are good, but we need something else. Moral means were very little to poor John Thomas on the banks of the Wilkesbarre river, in Pennsylvania, when the slavecatchers called upon him to provide them with a breakfast at the hotel, that while in the act of serving them with their beef steak they might fall upon him and return him to slavery. They did fall upon him; they struck him down; but, recovering himself, he ran and plunged into the Wilkesbarre. There he stood, up to his shoulders, and the slavecatchers gathered on the banks – and the moral suasion people of that vicinity gathered also on the banks – they looked indignantly on the slavecatchers. But the slavecatchers did not heed the cries of indignation and shame; they fired their revolvers until the river about that man was red with his blood, and no hand was lifted to strike down those assassins. They went off, indeed, without their victim, but they supposed he was dead. Sir, what was wanted at that time was just what John Brown, Jr., has told us tonight – a few resolute men, determined to be free, and to free others, resolved, when men were being shot, to shoot again. Had a few balls there whistled, as at Christiana, about the heads of the slavecatchers, it would have been the end of this slavecatching business there. There is no necessity of permitting it. The only way to make the Fugitive Slave Law a dead letter, is to make a few dead slave-catchers. There is no need to kill them either – shoot them in the legs, and send them to the South living epistles of the free gospel preached here at the North.

But, Sir, I am occupying too much time. I see a friend on my right, whose voice tonight I have not heard for many years. These troublous times in which we live, and have been living for a few years past, make that voice doubly dear to me on this occasion; and I seize this occasion, as the first that has happened to me in at least six to eight years, to say that I rejoice, most heartily rejoice, in the privilege – for a privilege I esteem it – not only of hearing Mr. Phillips's voice, but of standing on a platform with him in vindication of free speech. But I hope to speak in Boston on Friday. I, therefore, will not prolong my remarks further. I thank you for this hearing.[71]

---

[71] Originally published as "Speech on John Brown", *Douglass' Monthly*, January 1861. Douglass first planned on delivering this lecture at Tremont Temple in Boston on December 3rd, 1860 – the one-year anniversary of John Brown's state execution for his role in the attempt to capture the federal arsenal at Harper's Ferry, Virginia by force of arms. And yet, the venue for the lecture was subsequently moved to Joy Street Baptist Church, Boston that same day after Douglass and his fellow abolitionists vociferously fought off an anti-abolitionist mob. Aside from Douglass' Lecture, the following first-hand coverage of the event was also published in *Douglass' Monthly* and merits being read in full.

AN ANTI-SLAVERY MEETING BROKEN UP BY A MOB IN BOSTON. Special Dispatch to the N.Y. Tribune. BOSTON, Monday, Dec. 3 - 5 P. M.

The Convention called today at the Tremont Temple, to commemorate the anniversary of John Brown's execution, by a discussion of the question, 'How can American slavery be abolished?' was broken up in the morning by a diversified mob, composed chiefly of North street aristocrats and Beacon street roughs. A determination to prevent this proposed public expression of anti-Southern feeling in Boston had been very noisily avowed by the merchants and bankers of this city; but, as various experiences had shown that riotous demonstrations here seldom go beyond words, no disturbance was anticipated. In the present case, however, the prospects of financial distress roused the commercial interest to an unusual excitement, and the resolution to save the Union by destroying the Tremont Temple Convention, was really carried out.

At the hour of opening, the majority of persons present was evidently opposed to the peaceful fulfillment of the object of the meeting. On the platform were Fred. Douglass, Messrs. Redpath, Sanborn, J. Sella Martin, the colored clergyman, and others of less distinction in the Garrisonian party. Mr. Garrison came later. On the floor were a few score of ladies, as many policemen, and a multitude of representatives of the enlightenment which hovers around the State-House, and the muscular force of the North End.

The first attempt to organize was frustrated by the howlings and screamings of the confederated majority, who presently took the management of affairs into their own hands, and elected for Chairman, Richard S. Fay, Constitutional broker and ex-candidate for Congress. Mr. Fay was escorted to the platform by a number of his friends, and proceeded to make a speech, which finished with a set of resolutions exactly opposite to the sentiments of those who called the Convention. The resolutions were adopted viva voce, amid a great deal of boisterous confusion. No person was allowed to speak excepting in their favor. They are as follows:

Whereas, it is fitting upon the occasion of the anniversary of the execution of John Brown, for his piratical and bloody attempts to create an insurrection among the slaves of the State of Virginia, for the people of this Commonwealth to assemble and express their horror of the man, and of the principles which led to the foray; therefore, it is

Resolved, That no virtuous and law-abiding citizen of the Commonwealth ought to countenance, sympathize or hold communion with any man who believes that John Brown and his aiders and abettors in that nefarious enterprise were right, in any sense of the word.

Resolved, That the present perilous juncture in our political affairs, in which our existence as a nation is imperiled, requires of every citizen who loves his country to come forward, and to express his sense of the value of the Union, alike important to the free labor of the North, the slave labor of the South, and to the interests of the commerce, manufactures and agriculture of the world.

Resolved, That we tender to our brethren in Virginia our warmest thanks for the conservative spirit they have manifested, notwithstanding the unprovoked and lawless attack made upon them by John Brown and his associates, acting, if not with the connivance, at least with the sympathy of a few fanatics from the Northern States and that we hope they will continue to aid in opposing the fanaticism which is even now attempting to subvert the Constitution and the Union.

Resolved, That the people of this city have submitted too long in allowing irresponsible persons and political demagogues of every description to hold public meetings to disturb the public peace and misrepresent us abroad; they have become a nuisance, which, in self-defence, we are determined shall henceforth be summarily abated.

Resolved, That a copy of these resolutions be sent to each of the persons named in the call for this meeting.

After their passage, however, F. Douglass replied to Mr. Fay, and, without touching much upon the subject of the day, showered ridicule so plentifully and so effectively among his opponents, that the joint forces of Beacon and North streets rose in wrath and drowned his voice.

Up to this time the disturbances had been confined to violent declamation on both sides, with occasional feeble attempts at pacification by the Chief of Police. But when it was found that Mr. Douglass could not be silenced, a party rushed upon the platform and endeavored to sweep it clear of the negroes. The police here interfered for the first time against the majority, and a wild fight of two or three minutes ensued, from which a part of the flower of Beacon street emerged, much battered and far less ornamented than usual. No person, however, was severely injured in the fray.

The tumult rather increased after the platform squabble was checked, and threatened to result very seriously. The miserable inefficiency of the Chief of Police, who at one moment declared his intention of clearing the hall, and the next fell back bewildered upon his subordinates for counsel--who, by turns, avowed to sustain the Douglass part of the company, and promised to stand by the Beacon and North street brotherhood, added greatly to the confusion.

As a temporary expedient, every negro was removed from the platform, and immediately after, every one was suffered to return.--The Chief of Police announced an incubation of purpose, and for a quarter of an hour there was tolerable quiet, but the promised purpose was not hatched, and the clamor revived. On one side cheers for Gov. Wise and the Fugitive Slave Bill were launched.--On the other, cheers for freedom and liberty of speech. Mr. Douglass again essayed to speak, but the combined voice of Beacon st. overpowered his voice.

At about noon, Mr. Fay rejoined the audience, Mr. James A. Howe, a State street banker, was elected chairman in a corner, and was straightway led to the platform. Mr. Sanborn, who claimed the chair on the other side, received him certainly with courtesy, and was forthwith insulted in reply. During a brief debate between the two, a person attempted to take Mr. Sanborn's chair and place it behind Mr. Howe, upon which Mr. Douglass stepped up to interpose. Then Beacon street, led by Thomas H. Perkins, dashed in boldly, and a second fight ensued. -- Weapons were drawn, and, probably, handled with caution, for they did not go off. Nevertheless, the affray was serious enough. -- Men were thrown boldly from the platform down among the audience.

The women were greatly frightened, and helped the turbulence by loud cries. Mr. Douglass fought like a trained pugilist; and, although a score opposed him, he cleared his way through the crowd to the rostrum, which he clutched with an air that indicated his determination to hold to his place. His friends, however, were less combative, and so he was left, unaided, in the hands of a strong number of police, who dragged him away and threw him down the staircase to the floor of the hall. Mr. Sanborn was dragged out by the neck.

Finally the platform was cleared of all those who had joined in the call for the Convention and engaged in the hall, and left in possession of the opposition. Having gained their object, the majority remained tranquil for half an hour, without purposing any movement whatever.

At one time Mr. Douglass re-appeared on the platform, seeking for his portfolio, and then the clamor set in again. But this soon subsided, and at half-past one o'clock, when everything was quiet, and no trouble appeared likely to arise, the Chief of Police came to a prompt and energetic decision that the hall should be cleared, and this was done.

It was announced by the Douglass party that no other meeting would be held in the Tremont Temple, but that, in the evening, the friends of John Brown would re-assemble in J. Sella Martin's Church.

The multitude then dispersed, and the high-minded majority betook itself to mobbing the negroes as they came forth. This sport was, on Tremont street, continued for a long time. At last, it was given over to make arrangements for the breaking up of the evening meeting. Placards were prepared, calling upon Union-lovers to assemble and look for its suppression, in view of the impending troubles. The Cadets and the Second Battalion of Infantry are now under arms at their armories, by order of the Mayor.

Ten o'clock P. M. -- An hour before the time fixed for the evening meeting, Mr. Martin's Church was filled. The police, this time under the abler direction of the Deputy Chief, prevented it from being overcrowded, and the throngs of opponents who came later were accordingly unable to enter.

At 8 o'clock the Church was surrounded by a vast mob, which extended through several adjoining streets. Some outside speeches were made, but the Deputy Chief, in order to prevent the meeting from being disturbed, had the court, in which the Church is situated, entirely cleared, an operation of considerable difficulty.

There was very little tumult within the building -- the disturbers being in the minority and less confident of their strength than in the morning. Only one man attempted interruptions, and he was laughed down and left unmolested. The speakers were John Brown Jr., Wendell Phillips, F. Sanborn, F. Douglass, H. Ford Douglass, and others.

Mr. Phillips's remarks were more than usually bitter, and excited the only angry demonstrations of disfavor that were shown during the evening.

A set of resolutions was passed, fixing the blame of the morning interruption upon Mayor Lincoln, who, it was shown, had failed to exercise the right he might have employed to preserve order. The resolutions are as follows:

Resolved, That the riotous interruption of a meeting this day assembled in Tremont Temple, to discuss the question of the abolition of slavery, by a mob of merchants and other evil-disposed persons, headed by R. S. Fay, Esq., who organized their raid outside, and stole into the hall while the meeting was being organized, trampled on the rights of those who had hired the hall, and called it, was a mean and unconstitutional, as well as an unmanly act, unworthy of Massachusetts and even of Boston.

Resolved, That this cowardly act betrays the undoubted fact that these 'gentlemen of property and standing' have no arguments satisfactory even to themselves to urge against those who called the meeting, and who are the practical friends of free speech.

Resolved, That the efforts of the mob to break up the meeting, in our opinion, would have been unsuccessful but for the Mayor's command to remove the friends of order and the originators of the meeting from the platform -- by which act he became the real ringleader of the mob, and stands responsible for the destruction of the meeting.

At 9 o'clock Mr. Phillips excused himself, saying that the sickness of his wife called him home. He retired, accompanied by about a dozen of his friends, and was conveyed away by a narrow private passage -- so narrow that the party was obliged to creep in single file to Belknap street, where the mob was less dense than in the nearer vicinity of the church. -- But even here he was recognized, and a rush was at once made for him. He had two ladies beside him, and around the three his friends gathered closely, forming a circle with locked hands. There were loud cries of 'Stone him! 'Hit him with a brick!' 'Hang him!' 'Kill Phillips, but save the ladies!' and the like. Mr. Phillips appeared wholly unmoved, and went on his way laughing; but the ladies with him were greatly distressed. -- His companions marched very determinedly, and gave such manifestations of their temper as induced the mob, some hundreds in number, to confine themselves to verbal insult.-- The procession crossed the Common leisurely, the mob still hooting Phillips and invoking vengeance upon him without ever attempting to wreak it. As Essex street was approached,
the number diminished, and it was evident there would be no real trouble, although Mr. Phillips's peril had just before seemed imm-

inent. The mob as he entered his house sent volleys of groans and hisses after him, which were responded to by cheers of exultation from his friends. Mr. Phillips stood for some seconds upon his steps uncovered, and in full view, a prominent mark for any messenger of mischief; but the humor of the crowd evaporated in expletives, and no violence was attempted.

Eleven o'clock P. M. - After the adjournment of the meeting, the street mob took to hunting negroes as they came forth. Some were knocked down and trampled upon, and a few more seriously injured. Occasionally a beaten negro would take refuge in his house, upon which the windows thereof would be straightway smashed. One colored man, disliking the rattling of the glass about his ears, sallied forth with a hatchet, and chopped somebody in the leg, for which he was duly arrested - a distinction of which he was the solitary example. Pistols were here and there discharged, but it did not appear that anybody was injured thereby. A great many buildings, and one chapel, belonging to colored people, were attacked after a fashion, and their windows broken. Beyond this the ire of the mob did not reach. At this hour all seems again quiet.

The following is a copy of the poster which was issued and conspicuously displayed in the streets after the day meeting had been broken up by the rioters:

'CITIZENS OF BOSTON! - The sympathizers of JOHN BROWN say they will hold a meeting at Martin's Church, in Joy Street, this Monday evening, Dec 3d. UNION MEN, SHALL IT BE ALLOWED? LET BOSTON SPEAK!'

THE MEETING IN JOY STREET CHURCH.

The church was filled to repletion, and would have been if it had been ten-fold its capacity.

The meeting was called to order by Rev. J. Sella Martin.

Frank B. Sanborn was introduced as Chairman. On taking the chair, he said it gave him pleasure to be present at this, what might be termed an adjourned meeting of the one broken up by Mr. Fay, as he believed it was.

The organization of the meeting was perfected by the choice of J. H. Fowler and John Oliver as Secretaries.

A motion was made by Mr. Martin, that a Committee on Resolutions be appointed.

After a brief discussion as to the policy of offering any resolutions, the motion was carried, and Mr. Elizur Wright, Rev. J. B. Smith, and Dr. Knox were appointed.

Mr. McClure here arose and said that he wished to contradict reports in the public prints and elsewhere that he drew a revolver at the Tremont Temple, and for the reason that he had none. All that he had were his own good arms.

John Brown, Jr, of Ohio, was then introduced. He had, he said, come prepared to repel mob violence by force, if necessary. If that meeting were permitted to be broken up, the fighting powers of the Abolitionists were greatly demoralized. (Applause.) Liberty of speech must be preserved, at all events. - He hoped his life would never be saved by dodging his responsibilities. He had a speech prepared, and if they wished, he would deliver it. He then proceeded to read a speech on the question, 'How shall African Slavery be Abolished?' He should address himself to those who believed slavery must and should be abolished. Mr. Brown then proceeded to allude to the aggressions of slavery, and the outrages it had committed. They had fought against this Slave Power, and had got to do it again. He recounted the hardships endured by freemen in Kansas.

[A lady in the gallery here said that there were some persons in the gallery to break up the meeting. This created some little excitement. 'Put them out!' was shouted in every part of the church. Mr. Sanborn begged the audience to be quiet. They had taken measures to preserve order.]

Mr. Brown resumed his remarks, saying that they should be quiet, for there was true courage in this. Their rule should be acts, not words. Mr. Brown next proceeded to discuss the methods of abolishing slavery, among which was one that should make slave property as uncertain as possible. In relation to the free colored people, he said they should be thoroughly organized and armed. (Applause.) Of slave-catchers, he would take them - alive, if possible, but secure them, anyway - and give them seventy-eight lashes; - after which, he would have them washed down in salt and water. (Laughter.) Alluding to Gov. Wise, he said, 'My father forgives - so do I.' He continued by urging a firm and courageous course against slavery. Their watchword should not be, 'Give me liberty or give me death,' but 'Give me liberty, or I will give you death.' (Applause.) In conclusion, he trusted that slavery would ere long be abolished.

Elizur Wright, Esq., from the Committee on Resolutions, here reported the following:

[The resolutions will be found in another column.]

Mr. Martin moved that the resolutions be adopted.

Stephen S. Foster thought that part relating to the Mayor was too weak. The responsibility of the outrage today lay upon his shoulders. He had talked with many of the police, and they were heartily disgusted at the course he pursued.

A Mr. Marble here eulogized Mayor Lincoln.

Dr. Knox said that he knew certain things of Mayor Lincoln which he should like to state. He said that the Mayor had been represented as acting by advice of the Trustees of the Tremont Temple.

Mr. Martin said that the Chief of Police had told him that he could not protect the meeting, and that he acted in part by suggestion of the Mayor.

This, Deacon Converse denied. The speaker thought the Mayor did not desire to take any action in the matter.

Mr. Hayes, Superintendent of Tremont Temple, said that if it had not been for the imbecility of the Chief of Police, the meetings would have been held forenoon, afternoon and evening, at the Tremont Temple. - Six policemen could at any time have stopped the disturbance. The police themselves were heartily ashamed of the affair.

Wendell Phillips was the next speaker. - On rising he was received with prolonged applause and cheers. At its conclusion, he proceeded to speak. The meeting itself, he said, was a speech to which little could be added. This is Boston, which vindicates itself for two hundred years. They were profoundly grateful that when driven out of other places, they found a colored church. Just a year since, the speaker carried the remains of John Brown to their resting place. He was happy to say to North Elba that Boston welcomes his son. (Cheers.) Mr. Phillips next took up the subject of the Boston Mayoralty. We Abolitionists, he said, are accustomed to live without a government. He did not remember a decent Mayor of Boston for twenty years. - [Some one in the audience here hissed.] Mr. Phillips said that the right to hiss was as clear as to speak. With two exceptions, there was not a city north of Baltimore, in which Abolitionist meetings had not been broken up. In alluding to the meeting at Tremont Temple, he said the rioters only were allowed to go free. He praised the prompt action of Mayor Henry of Philadelphia, when the mob attempted to disturb George W. Curtis. When asked what he would do with these disturbers, Mayor Henry replied, 'Send them to the watch-house' - a decision and a pluck he thought they would look for in vain in Boston. The speaker next proceeded to criticise with much severity the course of Mr. Lincoln during the day. Mr. Phillips was thankful that the meeting tonight was not governed by State Street. They had kicked South Carolina out of the Union, and set her cringing sycophants shaking. He thanked God Richard S. Fay was not a Boston man, nor was he a gentleman. Should it be said, he continued, that we are to surrender at home that which we ask our Representatives in Congress to carry out? If they could not have met in any hall in the city, they should have held a meeting on the Common. John Brown, Jr., had advised colored men to arm themselves with revolvers. This meeting was a revolver. In relation to the abolition of slavery, Mr. Phillips said he was in favor of all methods, but principally of free discussion. State Street can't bear free speech, and that is what we want to give it. The smell of disunion is the jubilee of the slave. Again referring to the meeting of Tremont Temple, he said that men on State Street, whose notes command thousands, had been guilty of meanly stealing the hall. Mr. Phillips concluded, urging the friends of freedom to continue in the good work, which was sure to triumph.

The resolutions were then adopted.

Brief addresses were subsequently made by Messrs. Parker Pillsbury and H. Ford Douglass, and Rev. J. Sella Martin. At a quarter to 10 o'clock, the meeting adjourned with cheers.

The Liberator mentions among the colored men who were seriously injured by the mob, after the adjournment of the evening meeting, the names of G. W. Crawford, Daniel Butcher, George Rhoades, Thomas Prout, George Roberts, and several others. Attacks were also made upon several dwelling-houses, which were more or less injured. The windows of the Howard Boarding House, and also those of Gregory's Saloon on Cambridge St., were smashed in. The Cambridge cars were, in several instances, beset in quest of colored victims, on which to wreak their murderous hate.

Speaking of the different reports of the meeting, the Tribune's correspondent says:

The Tribune's report of the riot is the best I have seen, and is indeed the only report of the attempted attack upon Mr. Phillips after the meeting in Joy Street. The Traveller had a very good report of the evening meeting, but most of the accounts were more or less colored with friendship for the rioters. - The Post's report professes to be verbatim, and is in general fair, but Mr. Douglass's report upon Fay is omitted purposely. Fay had remarked that a negro slave-driver is the most cruel in the world. 'Yes, Sir,' said Douglass, 'and for the precise reason that a Northern Doughface is inconceivably meaner than a Southern slaveholder.' I don't think Mr. Fay is a rapid reasoner, but he seemed to understand this allusion. Some say he hung his head and blushed, but I do not credit this.

Another correspondent says:

Setting aside all view as to the original intentions of the meeting, and leaving out the question of the propriety of holding it at all, I am bound to say that the conduct and temper of the negroes and their companions were throughout incomparably better and more manly than those of their opponents. They resisted nothing, except when personally attacked, and in the two affrays which occurred, they were not the aggressors. And when Douglass did fight, he fought rather better, on the whole, than any of his well-educated opponents, and cleared his way through the crowd that assailed him in a way that Tom Sayers would have taken off his hat in honor to. The Tremont Temple meeting, however, had to be broken up. That was determined upon. The Mayor was appealed to, and, after sundry vacillations, directed that the hall should be cleared by the police. Up to this time, the efforts of the police had been vigorously applied to the suppression and extinction of the party which had called, and wished to hold, the meeting. The only persons harshly treated were the negroes and their associates - the very ones who had engaged the hall, and were accountable for the payment for its use.

How to End the War – To our mind, there is but one easy, short and effectual way to suppress and put down the desolating war which the slaveholders and their rebel minions are now waging against the American Government and its loyal citizens. Fire must be met with water, darkness with light, and war for the destruction of liberty must be met with war for the destruction of slavery. *The simple way, then, to put an end to the savage and desolating war now waged by the slaveholders, is to strike down slavery itself,* the primal cause of that war.

Freedom to the slave should now be proclaimed from the Capitol, and should be seen above the smoke and fire of every battle field, waving from every loyal flag! The time for mild measures is past. They are pearls cast before swine, and only increase and aggravate the crime which they would conciliate and repress. The weak point must be found, and when found should be struck with the utmost vigor. Any war is a calamity; but a peace that can only breed war is a far greater calamity. A long and tame war, waged without aim or spirit, paralyzes business, arrests the wheels of civilization, benumbs the national feeling, corrodes the national heart, and diffuses its baleful influence universally. Sharp, quick, wise, strong and sudden, are the elements for the occasion. The sooner this rebellion is put out of its misery, the better for all concerned. A lenient war is a lengthy war, and therefore the worst kind of war. Let us stop it, and stop it effectually— stop it before its evils are diffused throughout the Northern States — stop it on the soil upon which it originated, and among the traitors and rebels who originated the war. This can be done at once, by "*carrying the war into Africa.*" *Let the slaves and free colored people be called into service, and formed into a liberating army*, to march into the South and raise the banner of Emancipation among the slaves. The South having brought revolution and war upon the country, and having elected and consented to play at that fearful game, she has no right to complain if some good as well as calamity shall result from her own act and deed.

The slaveholders have not hesitated to employ the sable arms of the Negroes at the South in erecting the fortifications which silenced the guns of Fort Sumter, and brought the star-spangled banner to the dust. They often boast, and not without cause, that their negroes will fight for them against the North. They have no scruples against employing the Negroes to exterminate freedom, and in overturning the Government. They work with spade and barrow with them, and they will stand with them on the field of battle, shoulder to shoulder, with guns in their hands, to shoot down the troops of the U. S. Government — They have neither pride, prejudice nor *pity* to restrain them from employing negroes *against white men, where slavery is to be protected and made secure.* Oh! that this Government would only now be as true to liberty as the rebels, who are attempting to batter it down, are true to slavery. We have no hesitation in saying that ten thousand Black soldiers might be raised in the next thirty days to march upon the South. One Black regiment alone would be, in such a war, the full equal of two white ones. The very fact of color in this case would be more terrible than powder and balls. The slaves would learn more as to the nature of the conflict from the presence of one such regiment, than from a thousand preachers. Every consideration of justice, humanity and sound policy confirms the wisdom of calling upon Black men just now to take up arms in behalf of their country.

We are often asked by persons in the street as well as by letter, what our people will do in the present solemn crisis in the affairs of the country. Our answer is, would to God you would let us do something! We lack nothing but your consent. We are ready and would go, counting ourselves happy in being permitted to serve and suffer for the cause of freedom and free institutions. But you won't let us go. Read the heart-rending account we publish elsewhere of the treatment received by the brave fellows, who broke away from their chains and went through marvelous suffering to defend Fort Pickens against the rebels. — They were instantly seized and put in irons and returned to their guilty masters to be whipped to death! Witness Gen. Butler's offer to put down the slave insurrection in the State of Maryland. The colored citizens of Boston have offered their services to the Government, and were refused. There is, even now, while the slaveholders are marshaling armed Negroes against the Government, covering the ocean with pirates, destroying innocent lives, to sweep down the commerce of the country, tearing up railways, burning bridges to prevent the march of Government troops to the defence of its capital, exciting mobs to stone the Yankee soldiers; there is still, we say, weak and contemptible tenderness towards the blood-thirsty, slaveholding traitors, by the Government and people of the country. Until the nation shall repent of this weakness and folly, until they shall make the cause of their country the cause of freedom, until they shall strike down slavery, the source and center of this gigantic rebellion, they don't deserve the support of a single sable arm, nor will it succeed in crushing the cause of our present troubles.[72]

---

[72] *Douglass' Monthly*, May 1861.

The Power of Anti-Slavery – I am not surprised, my respected hearers, though I am most deeply gratified by the continued interest which you have manifested in these now somewhat protracted anti-slavery lectures. The subject of slavery is a most fruitful one, and it seems impossible to exhaust it. I seldom retire from this place without thinking of something left unsaid, which might have been said to profit.

More than thirty years of earnest discussion has augmented rather than diminished the interest which surrounds the subject. Tongues the most eloquent, and pens the most persuasive, the highest talent and genius of the country have been arduously employed in the attempt to unfold the matchless and measureless abominations comprehended in that one little word — slavery. Yet those who have succeeded best, own that they have fallen far short of the terrible reality. You, yourselves, have read much, thought much, and have felt much respecting the slave system, and yet you come up here and crowd this church every Sunday to hear the subject further discussed.

Vain as I may be, I have not the vanity to suppose that you come here because of any eloquence of mine, or any curiosity to hear a colored man speak — for I have been speaking among you more or less frequently nearly a score of years; and I recognize among my hearers today some of those kind friends who greeted me the first time I attempted to plead the cause of the slave in this city. No — the explanation of this continued, and I may say increasing interest, is not to be found in your humble speaker; nor can it be ascribed altogether to the temper of the times, and the mighty events now transpiring in the country. We shall find it in the deep significance, the solemn importance and unfathomable fullness of the subject itself. It sweeps the whole horizon of human rights, powers, duties and responsibilities. The grand primal principles which form the basis of human society are here.

Those who love peace more than justice; those who prefer grim and hoary oppression to agitation and liberty, condemn the discussion of slavery because it is an exciting subject. They cry, away with it; we have had enough of it; it excites the people, excites the Church, excites Congress, excites the North, excites the South, and excites everybody. It is, in a word, an exciting subject. I admit it all. The subject is, indeed, an exciting one. Herein is one proof of its importance. Small pots boil quick; empty barrels make the most noise when rolled; but that which has the power to stir a nation's heart, and shake the foundations of Church and State, is something more than empty clamor. Individual men of excitable temperament may be moved by trifles; they may give to an inch the importance of a mile — elevate a mote to the grandeur of a mountain — but the masses of men are not of this description. Only mighty forces, resting deep down among the foundations of nature and life, can lash the deep and tranquil sea of humanity into a storm, like that which the world is now witnessing.

The human mind is so constructed as that, when left free from the blinding and hardening power of selfishness, it bows reverently to the mandates of truth and justice. It becomes loyal and devoted to an idea. Good men, once fully possessed of this loyalty, this devotion, have bravely sacrificed fortune, reputation, and life itself. All the progress towards perfection ever made by mankind, and all the blessings which are now enjoyed, are ascribable to some brave and good man, who, catching the illumination of a heaven-born truth, has counted it a joy, precious and unspeakable, to toil, suffer, and often to die for the glorious real-ization of that heaven-born truth. Hence the excite-ment. Cold water added to cold water, makes no disturbance. Error added to error causes no jar. Selfishness and selfishness walk together in peace, because they are agreed; but when fire is brought in direct contact with water, when flaming truth grapples with some loathsome error, when the clear and sweet current of benevolence sets against the foul and bitter stream of selfishness, when mercy and humanity confront iron-hearted cruelty, and ignorant brutality, there cannot fail to be agitation and excitement.

Men have their choice in this world. They can be angels, or they may be demons. In the apocalyptic vision, John describes a war in heaven. You have only to strip that vision of its gorgeous Oriental drapery, divest it of its shining and celestial ornaments, clothe it in the simple and familiar language of common sense, and you will have before you the eternal conflict between right and wrong, good and evil, liberty and slavery, truth and falsehood, the glorious light of love, and the appalling darkness of human selfishness and sin. The human heart is a seat of constant war. Michael and his angels are still contending against the infernal host of bad passions, and excitement will last while the fight continues, and the fight will continue till one or the other is subdued. Just what takes place in individual human hearts, often takes place between nations, and between individuals of the same nation. Such is the struggle now going on in the United States. The slaveholders had rather reign in hell than serve in heaven.

What a whirlwind, what a tempest of malignant passion greets us from that quarter! Behold how they storm with rage, and yet grow pale with terror! Their demonstrations of offended pride are only equaled by their consummate impudence and desperate lying. Let me read you a paragraph from a recent speech of Mr. Henry A. Wise, as a specimen of the lies with which the leaders of this slaveholding rebellion inflame the base passions of their ignorant followers. He lyingly says of the Northern people:

"Your political powers and rights, which were enthroned in the Capitol when you were united with them under the old constitutional bond of the Confederacy, have been annihilated. They have undertaken to annul laws within their own limits that would render your property unsafe within those limits. They have abolitionized your border, as the disgraced North-West will show. They have invaded your moral strongholds, and the rights of your religion, and have undertaken to teach you what should be the moral duties of men. They have invaded the sanctity of your homes and firesides, and endeavored to play master, father and husband for you in your households."

Such lies answer themselves at the North, but do their work at the South. The strong and enduring power which anti-slavery truth naturally exercises upon the minds of men, when earnestly presented, is explained, as I have already intimated, not by the cunning arts of rhetoric, for often the simplest and most broken utterances of the uneducated fugitive slave, will be far more touching and powerful than the finest flights of oratory. The explanation of the power of anti-slavery is to be found in the inner and spontaneous consciousness, which every man feels of the comprehensive and stupendous criminality of slavery. There are many wrongs and abuses in the world that shock and wound the sensibilities of men. They are felt to be narrow in their scope, and temporary in their duration, and to require little effort for their removal. But not so can men regard slavery. It compels us to recognize it, as an ever active, ever increasing, all comprehensive crime against human nature. It is not an earthquake swallowing up a town or city, and then leaving the solid earth undisturbed for centuries. It is not a Vesuvius which, belching forth its fire and lava at intervals, causes ruin in a limited territory; but slavery is felt to be a moral volcano, a burning lake, a hell on the earth, the smoke and stench of whose torments ascend upward forever. Every breeze that sweeps over it comes to us tainted with its foul miasma, and weighed down with the sighs and groans of its victims. It is a compendium of all the wrongs which one man can inflict upon a helpless brother. It does not cut off a right hand, nor pluck out a right eye, but strikes down at a single blow the God-like form of man. It does not merely restrict the rights, or lay heavy burdens upon its victims, grievous to be borne; but makes deliberate and constant war upon human nature itself, robs the slave of personality, cuts him off from the human family, and sinks him below even the brute. It leaves nothing standing to tell the world that here was a man and a brother.

In the eye of the law of slavery, the slave is only property. He cannot be a father, a husband, a brother, or a citizen, in any just sense of these words. To be a father, a husband, a brother, and a citizen, implies the personal possession of rights, powers, duties and responsibilities, all of which are denied the slave. Slavery being the utter and entire destruction of all human relations, in opposing it, we are naturally enough bound to the consideration of a wide range of topics, involving questions of the greatest importance to all men. But for the universal character of the anti-slavery question, it would have been impossible to have held the public mind suspended upon this discussion during the space of thirty years. The best informed men have candidly confessed that anti-slavery meetings have been the very best schools of the nation during the last quarter of a century. The nation has been taught here, as nowhere else, law, morals and Christianity. Untrammelled by prescription, unrestrained by popular usage, unfettered by mouldy creeds, despising all the scorn of vulgar prejudice, our anti-slavery speakers and writers have dared to call in question every doctrine and device of man, which could strengthen the hands of tyrants, and bind down the bodies and souls of men. The manhood of the slave has been the test of all our laws, customs, morals, civilization, governments, and our religions. With a single eye here, the whole anti-slavery body has been full of light. With the golden rule, they have measured American Christianity, and found it hollow — its votaries doing precisely unto others that which they would shoot, stab, burn and devour others for doing unto themselves. To all who press the Bible into the service of slavery, we have said, if you would not be the slave, you cannot be the master.

The fact is, slavery is at the bottom of all mischief amongst us, and will be until we shall put an end to it. We have seen three attempts within less than thirty years to break up the American Government in this the first century of its existence, and slavery has been the moving cause in each instance. The attempt was made in 1832, again in 1850, and again in 1860. Some of us were surprised and astonished that the slaveholders should rebel against the American Government, simply because they could not rule the Government to the full extent of their wishes. Little cause had we for such surprise and astonishment. We ought to have known slaveholders better.

What is a slaveholder but a rebel and a traitor? That is, and must be in the nature of his vocation, his true character. Treason and rebellion are the warp and woof of the relation of master and slave. A man cannot be a slaveholder without being a traitor to humanity and a rebel against the law and government of the ever-living God. He is a usurper, a spoiler. His patriotism means plunder, and his principles are those of the highway robber. Out of such miserable stuff you can make nothing but conspirators and rebels.

So far as the American Government is entitled to the loyal support and obedience of American citizens, so far that Government is, in the main, in harmony with the highest good and the just convictions of the people. Justice, goodness, conscience are divine. Conformity to these, on the part of human governments, make them binding and authoritative. These attributes, wherever exhibited, whether in the government of States, in the government of families, or wherever else exhibited, command the reverence and loyal regard of honest men and women. But slaveholders, by the very act of slaveholding, have thrown off all the trammels of conscience and right. They are open, brazen, self-declared rebels and traitors to all that makes loyalty a virtue, and fidelity a duty. The greater includes the lesser crime. In the one high handed act of rebellion against truth, justice and humanity, comprehended in making one man the slave of another, we have the ascertained sum of treason and rebellion which now rages and desolates the whole slaveholding territory in the United States.

This is no new idea in these lectures. I have presented it before, and shall probably repeat it again. I wish at any rate to underscore it now, for I deem it important that we should thoroughly understand the foe with which we have to deal. Let it, then, be written down in every man's mind, as no longer a matter of dispute, that a thief and a robber cannot be safely trusted; that a slaveholder cannot be a good citizen of a free republic; and that the relation of master and slave is, in the nature of it, treason and rebellion. It has long been obvious to common sense — it is now known to common experience — that a slaveholder who is a slaveholder at heart is a natural born traitor and rebel. He is a rebel against manhood, woman-hood and brotherhood. The essence of his crime is nothing less than the complete destruction of all that dignifies and ennobles human character.

I don't know how it seems to you, in reading the authoritative utterances of our Government, and the officers of our army, respecting slavery; but it really seems to me that they are woefully mistaken if they think this country can ever have peace while slavery is allowed to live. Every little while you learn that slaves have been sent back to their loyal masters. We hear that while other property is freely confiscated, this peculiar property is only held to the end of the war, and the inference seems to be that these slaves, by and by, are to enter into the basis of negotiations between the Government and the slaveholding rebels. I am anxious to look charitably upon everything looking to the suppression of rebellion and treason. I want to see the monster destroyed; but I think that while our Government uses its soldiers to catch and hold slaves, and offers to put down slave insurrect-ions, and subject them to the control and authority of

their rebel masters, it will make precious little head-
way in putting down the rebels, or in establishing the
peace of the country hereafter.

There is still an effort to conciliate the Border
States. Our Government does not know slavery. Our
rulers do not yet know slaveholders. We are likely to
find them out after a while. We are just now in a
pretty good school. The revolution through which we
are passing is an excellent instructor. We are likely to
find out what is meant by Southern chivalry and
Southern honor. When you have watched a while
longer the course of Southern men, whether in the
cotton States or in the slave-breeding States, you will
have become convinced that they are all of the same
species, and that the Border States are as bad as any.
John Bell, the Union man, is as much a traitor as
Frank Pickens of South Carolina. We shall learn by
and by that such men as Letcher of Virginia, Jackson
of Missouri, Magoffin of Kentucky, were traitors and
rebels in the egg, only waiting to be hatched by the
heat of surrounding treason. The ties that bind
slaveholders together are stronger than all other ties,
and in every State where they hold the reins of
government, they will take sides openly or secretly
with the slaveholding rebels. Conciliation is out of the
question. They know no law, and will respect no law
but the law of force. The safety of the Government

can be attained only in one way, and that is, by rendering the slaveholders powerless.

Slavery, like all other gross and powerful forms of wrong which appeal directly to human pride and selfishness, when once admitted into the framework of society, has the ability and tendency to beget a character in the whole network of society surrounding it, favorable to its continuance. The very law of its existence is growth and dominion. Natural and harmonious relations easily repose in their own rectitude, while all such as are false and unnatural are conscious of their own weakness, and must seek strength from without. Hence the explanation of the uneasy, restless, eager anxiety of slaveholders. Our history shows that from the formation of this Government, until the attempt now making to break it up, this class of men have been constantly pushing schemes for the safety and supremacy of the slave system. They have had marvelous success. They have completely destroyed freedom in the slave States, and were doing their best to accomplish the same in the free States. He is a very imperfect reasoner who attributes the steady rise and ascendency of slavery to anything else than the nature of slavery itself. Truth may be careless and forgetful, but a lie cannot afford to be either. Truth may repose upon its inherent strength, but a falsehood rests for support upon external props. Slavery is the most stupendous of all lies, and depends for existence upon a favorable adjustment of all its surroundings. Freedom of speech, of the press, of education, of labor, of locomotion, and indeed all kinds of freedom, are felt to be a standing menace to slavery. Hence, the friends of slavery are bound by the necessity of their system to do just what the history of the country shows they have done — that is, to seek to subvert all liberty, and to pervert all the safeguards of human rights. They could not do otherwise. It was the controlling law of their situation.

Now, if these views be sound, and are borne out by the whole history of American slavery, then for the statesman of this hour to permit any settlement of the present war between slavery and freedom, which will leave untouched and undestroyed the relation of master and slave, would not only be a great crime, but a great mistake, the bitter fruits of which would poison the life blood of unborn generations. No grander opportunity was ever given to any nation to signalize, either its justice and humanity, or its intelligence and statesmanship, than is now given to the loyal American people. We are brought to a point in our National career where two roads meet and diverge. It is the critical moment for us. The destiny of the mightiest Republic in the modern world hangs upon the decision of that hour. If our Government shall have the wisdom to see, and the nerve to act, we are safe. If it fails, we perish, and go to our own place with those nations of antiquity long blotted from the maps of the world. I have only one voice, and that is neither loud nor strong. I speak to but few, and have little influence; but whatever I am or may be, I may, at such a time as this, in the name of justice, liberty and humanity, and in that of the permanent security and welfare of the whole nation, urge all men, and especially the Government, to the abolition of slavery. Not a slave should be left a slave in the returning footprints of the American army gone to put down this slaveholding rebellion. Sound policy, not less than humanity, demands the instant liberation of every slave in the rebel States.[73]

---

[73] Delivered at Zion Church on June 16th, 1861 in Rochester, New York and published as "Substance of a Lecture" in *Douglass' Monthly*, July 1861.

Fighting Rebels with Only One Hand – What upon earth is the matter with the American Government and people? Do they really covet the world's ridicule as well as their own social and political ruin? What are they thinking about, or don't they condescend to think at all? So, indeed, it would seem from their blindness in dealing with the tremendous issue now upon them. Was there ever anything like it before? They are sorely pressed on every hand by a vast army of slaveholding rebels, flushed with success, and infuriated by the darkest inspirations of a deadly hate, bound to rule or ruin. Washington, the seat of Government, after ten thousand assurances to the contrary, is now positively in danger of falling before the rebel army. Maryland, a little while ago considered safe for the Union, is now admitted to be studded with the materials for insurrection, and which may flame forth at any moment. – Every resource of the nation, whether of men or money, whether of wisdom or strength, could be well employed to avert the impending ruin. Yet most evidently the demands of the hour are not comprehended by the Cabinet or the crowd. Our Presidents, Governors, Generals and Secretaries are calling, with almost frantic vehemence, for men. – "Men! men! send us men!" they scream, or the cause of the Union is gone, the life of a great nation is ruthlessly sacrificed, and the hopes of a great nation go out in darkness; and yet these very officers, representing the people and Government, steadily and persistently refuse to receive the very class of men which have a deeper interest in the defeat and humiliation of the rebels, than all others. — Men are wanted in Missouri — wanted in Western Virginia, to hold and defend what has been already gained; they are wanted in Texas, and all along the sea coast, and though the Government has at its command a class in the country deeply interested in suppressing the insurrection, it sternly refuses to summon from among the vast multitude a single man, and degrades and insults the whole class by refusing to allow any of their number to defend with their strong arms and brave hearts the national cause. What a spectacle of blind, unreasoning prejudice and pusillanimity is this! The national edifice is on fire. Every man who can carry a bucket of water, or remove a brick, is wanted; but those who have the care of the building, having a profound respect for the feeling of the national burglars who set the building on fire, are determined that the flames shall only be extinguished by Indo-Caucasian hands, and to have the building burnt rather than save it by means of any other. Such is the pride, the stupid prejudice and folly that rules the hour.

Why does the Government reject the Negro? Is he not a man? Can he not wield a sword, fire a gun, march and countermarch, and obey orders like any other? Is there the least reason to believe that a regiment of well-drilled Negroes would deport themselves less soldier-like on the battle field than the raw troops gathered up generally from the towns and cities of the State of New York? We do believe that such soldiers, if allowed now to take up arms in defense of the Government, and made to feel that they are hereafter to be recognized as persons having rights, would set the highest example of order and general good behavior to their fellow soldiers, and in every way add to the national power.

If persons so humble as we can be allowed to speak to the President of the United States, we should ask him if this dark and terrible hour of the nation's extremity is a time for consulting a mere vulgar and unnatural prejudice? We should ask him if national preservation and necessity were not better guides in this emergency than either the tastes of the rebels, or the pride and prejudices of the vulgar? We would tell him that General Jackson in a slave State fought side by side with Negroes at New Orleans, and like a true man, despising meanness, he bore testimony to their bravery at the close of the war. We would tell him that colored men in Rhode Island and Connecticut performed their full share in the war of the Revolution, and that men of the same color, such as the noble Shields Green, Nathaniel Turner and Denmark Vesey stand ready to peril everything at the command of the Government. We would tell him that this is no time to fight with one hand, when both are needed; that this is no time to fight only with your white hand, and allow your black hand to remain tied.

Whatever may be the folly and absurdity of the North, the South at least is true and wise. The Southern papers no longer indulge in the vulgar expression, "free n****rs." That class of bipeds are now called "colored residents." The Charleston papers say: "The colored residents of this city can challenge comparison with their class, in any city or town, in loyalty or devotion to the cause of the South. Many of them individually, and without ostentation, have been contributing liberally, and on Wednesday evening, the 7th inst., a very large meeting was held by them, and a Committee appointed to provide for more efficient aid. The proceedings of the meeting will appear in results hereafter to be reported."

It is now pretty well established, that there are at the present moment many colored men in the Confederate army doing duty not only as cooks, servants and laborers, but as real soldiers, having muskets on their shoulders, and bullets in their pockets, ready to shoot down loyal troops, and do all that soldiers may to destroy the Federal Government and build up that of the traitors and rebels. There were such soldiers at Manassas, and they are probably there still. There is a Negro in the army as well as in the fence, and our

Government is likely to find it out before the war comes to an end. That the Negroes are numerous in the rebel army, and do for that army its heaviest work, is beyond question. They have been the chief laborers upon those temporary defenses in which the rebels have been able to mow down our men. Negroes helped to build the batteries at Charleston. They relieve their gentlemanly and military masters from the stiffening drudgery of the camp, and devote them to the nimble and dexterous use of arms. Rising above vulgar prejudice, the slaveholding rebel accepts the aid of the Black man as readily as that of any other. If a bad cause can do this, why should a good cause be less wisely conducted? We insist upon it, that one Black regiment in such a war as this is, without being any more brave and orderly, would be worth to the Government more than two of any other; and that, while the Government continues to refuse the aid of colored men, thus alienating them from the national cause, and giving the rebels the advantage of them, it will not deserve better fortunes than it has thus far experienced. — Men in earnest don't fight with one hand, when they might fight with two, and a man drowning would not refuse to be saved even by a colored hand.[74]

---

[74] *Douglass' Monthly*, September 1861.

The Proclamation and the Negro Army – I congratulate you, upon what may be called the greatest event of our nation's history, if not the greatest event of the century. In the eye of the Constitution, the supreme law of the land, there is not now, and there has not been, since the first day of January, a single slave lawfully deprived of Liberty in any of the States now recognized as in Rebellion against the National Government. In all those States Slavery is now in law, as in fact, a system of lawless violence, against which the slave may lawfully defend himself. In the hurry and excitement of the moment, it is difficult to grasp the full and complete significance of President Lincoln's proclamation. The change in the attitude of the Government is vast and startling. For more than sixty years the Federal Government has been little better than a stupendous engine of Slavery and oppression, through which Slavery has ruled us, as with a rod of iron. The boast that Cotton is King was no empty boast. Assuming that our Government and people will sustain the President and his Proclamation, we can scarcely conceive of a more complete revolution in the position of a nation. England, no longer ruled by a king, the Pope turned Protestant, Austria — a Republic, would not present a greater revolution. I hail it as the doom of Slavery in all the States. I hail it as the end of all that miserable statesmanship, which has for sixty years juggled and deceived the people, by professing to reconcile what is irreconcileable. No politician need now hope to rise to power, by crooking the pregnant hinges of the knee to Slavery. We part company forever with that amphibious animal called a Northern man with Southern principles. Color is no longer a crime or a badge of bondage. At last the outspread wings of the American Eagle afford shelter and protection to men of all colors, all countries, and all climes, and the long oppressed Black man may honorably fall or gloriously flourish under the star-spangled banner. I stand here tonight not only as a colored man and an American, but, by the express decision of the Attorney General of the United States, as a colored citizen, having, in common with all other citizens, a stake in the safety, prosperity, honor, and glory of a common country. We are all liberated by this proclamation. Everybody is liberated. The white man is liberated, the Black man is liberated, the brave men now fighting the battles of their country against rebels and traitors are now liberated, and may strike with all their might, even if they do by thus manfully striking hurt the Rebels, at their most sensitive point. I congratulate you upon this amazing change — this amazing approximation toward the sacred truth of human liberty. All the space between man's mind and God's mind, says Parker, is crowded with truths that wait to be discovered and organized into law for the better government of society. Mr.

Lincoln has not exactly discovered a new truth, but he has dared, in this dark hour of national peril, to apply an old truth, long ago acknowledged in theory by the nation — a truth which carried the American people safely through the war for independence, and one which will carry us, as I believe, safely through the present terrible and sanguinary conflict for national life, if we shall but faithfully live up to that great truth. Born and reared as a slave, as I was, and wearing on my back the marks of the slavedriver's lash, as I do, it is natural that I should value the Emancipation Proclamation for what it is destined to do for the slaves. I do value it for that. It is a mighty event for the bondman, but it is a still mightier event for the nation at large, and mighty as it is for both, the slave and the nation, it is still mightier when viewed in its relation to the cause of truth and justice throughout the world. It is in this last character that I prefer to consider it. There are certain great national acts, which by their relation to universal principles, properly belong to the whole human family, and Abraham Lincoln's Proclamation of the 1st of January, 1863, is one of these acts. Henceforth that day shall take rank with the Fourth of July. Henceforth it becomes the date of a new and glorious era in the history of American liberty. Henceforth it shall stand associated in the minds of men, with all those stately steps of mankind, from the regions of error and oppression, which have lifted

them from the trial by poison and fire to the trial by
Jury — from the arbitrary will of a despot to the sacred
writ of habeas corpus — from abject serfdom to
absolute citizenship. It will stand in the history of
civilization with Catholic Emancipation, with the
British Reform Bill, with the repeal of Corn Laws and
with that noble act of Russian liberty, by which twenty
millions of serfs, against the clamors of haughty
tyrants, have been released from servitude. Aye! It
will stand with every distinguished event which marks
any advance made by mankind from the thraldom
and darkness of error to the glorious liberty of truth.
I believe in the millenium — the final perfection of the
race, and hail this Proclamation, though wrung out
under the goading lash of a stern military necessity, as
one reason of the hope that is in me. Men may see in
it only a military necessity. To me it has a higher
significance. It is a grand moral necessity. "Thrice is
he armed who hath his quarrel just, And he but
naked, though wrapped up in steel, Whose conscience with injustice is corrupted."

The conscience of the North has been troubled
during all this war. It has seen the inconsistency of
fighting for Slavery. It has seen the absurdity of killing
the Rebel, while asserting the Rebel's right to his
slave. It has seen the folly of fighting the Rebels with
our soft white hands, and keeping back our iron
Black hands.

This whole subject of the war and the President's proclamation naturally brings us to the consideration of first principles, the nature of truth and error, and their respective powers and prospects, in the Government of mankind. I attempt no scientific definition either of truth or of error. The occasion does not require it. Truth is that view or theory of things which describes them as they really are. It describes a man as a man, a horse as a horse, and never confounds the distinction between men and horses. Error is any and every contradiction of truth, in much or in little. The one is in its nature a unit. The other is in its nature multitudinous. The devil gave his name correctly when he called himself legion — for there are a thousand wrong ways to but one right way.

Nevertheless, truth as one, shall be more than a match for error as a thousand — and all nations shall yet be brought into harmony with its absolute requirements. Either in the truth, or man himself, there is a compensating force, which renders him, in a high sense superior to the numerical advantages of error. By some means or other, whatever may be said of innate depravity, men do and will in the end prefer truth to error, and the right way to the wrong one.

When we meet with facts in our experience of the world, which seem to contradict this, the explanation can always be found in considerations entirely apart from the qualities of truth on the one hand, and of error on the other. Men never prefer the crooked to the straight road, because the one is crooked and the other is straight. It is always done because of some fancied advantage gained, or some disadvantage avoided — and done in the name of expediency, as choosing the least between two evils.

But little hope would there be for this world covered with error as with a cloud of thick darkness, and studded with all abounding injustice, wrong, oppression, intemperance, and monopolies, bigotry, superstition, King-craft, priest-craft, pride of race, prejudice of color, chattel-slavery — the grand sum of all human woes, and villanies if there were not in man, deep down, and it may be very deep down, in his soul or in the truth itself, an elective power, or an attractive force, call it by what name you will, which makes truth in her simple beauty and excellence, ever preferred to the grim and ghastly powers of error.

Hence, though this life voyage of ours offers a thousand opportunities to drown, to only one of being saved; hence, though the sea is broad, and the ship is narrow; hence, though the billows are mighty, and the bark frail, there is a power on board, a captain at the helm whose presence forbids despair even in the darkest hours.

The hope of the world — the progress of nations — the triumph of the truth and the reign of reason and righteousness among men are conditioned on free discussion. Good old John Brown was a madman at Harper's Ferry. Two years pass away, and the nation is as mad as he. Every General and every soldier that now goes in good faith to Old Virginia, goes there for the very purpose that sent honest John Brown to Harper's Ferry.

One of the peculiarities of our times compels notice here. Parties have to some extent changed sides on the subject of free speech. The men who would a few years ago mob and hang Abolitionists for exercising the sacred right of free thought and speech, have all at once become the most urgent for the largest liberty of speech. And I must say, detestable as are the motives that have brought them to the defense of free speech, I think they have the right in the controversy. I do not know where I would limit the right of simple utterance of opinion. If anyone is base enough to spit upon the grave of his mother, or to shout for Jefferson Davis, let him, and do not lock him up for it.

After that almost inspired announcement of equal rights contained in the Declaration of Independence, Jefferson has left us nothing more worthy of his profound mind than his saying that error may be safely tolerated where truth is left free to combat it. Equally true, though not always equally manifest, is it that error can never be safely tolerated when truth is not left free to combat it. Whence came the terrible conflict which now rocks our land with the thundering tramp of hostile armies? Why does the cold and greedy earth now drink up the warm red blood of our patriot sons, brothers, husbands, and fathers — carrying sorrow and agony into every household? Many answers have been returned to these questions. This, however, is the true one. A stupendous error, long tolerated, and protected even from discussion, held too sacred to be called in question, has at last become belligerent and snatched the sword of treason for permanent dominion. Nothing strange has happened unto us; the result has been reached naturally. Our trouble is a logical part of the conflict of ages, past, present, and future. It will go on. It cannot be stopped. Here, as elsewhere, the fire will go out only when the fuel is exhausted. The moral chemistry of the universe makes peace between Liberty and Slavery impossible. Moral necessity is upon the slaveholders to stand up for Slavery. The dream and delusion of the hour is the thought of restoring the country to the condition it occupied previous to the war. What good would come of such restoration? What is the tremendous war but the ripened fruit of that past condition? Our present, horrible as it is, is the legitimate child of our previous; and to go back to what we were is simply to ask us to come back again to what we are. The conflict has changed its form from words to blows, and it may change again from blows to words; but the conflict itself, in one form or the other, will go on till truth is slain or error is driven from the field.

Much as I hate Slavery, and glad as I should be to see it instantly abolished, I would consent gladly to any peace if but the right of speech, and the liberty of peaceably assembling could be secured in every part of the Union.

When error consents to reason, truth may also consent to reason. But when error takes the sword, truth must also take the sword. Not to do this, and to cry out "peace at any price," is to desert the truth, and give up the world to the powers of darkness. The man who now preaches peace, preaches treason to his country and to the paramount claims of truth and justice. The slaveholders are fighting for Slavery. The boldness with which they avow this object would astonish the world, but that the world knows that cunning, not courage, is the cause of their making it. They know that all attempt at concealment would be absurd and fruitless. They are fighting for Slavery — and the slave system being against nature — they are fighting against the eternal laws of nature, and though they should for a time succeed — dissolve the Union, capture a part of our territory, compel the North to sue for peace, and obtain peace upon the usual terms of compromise by which the South gets all and the North nothing, nature with the aid of free discussion would set herself right in the end. Great is truth, great is humanity, and they must prevail.

A great man once said it was useless to re-enact the laws of God, meaning thereby the laws of Nature. But a greater man than he will yet teach the world that it is useless to re-enact any other laws with any hope of their permanence. There are said to be some towns in this country which are finished, nothing more will or can be done for them, and that they might be fenced in without detriment. There are individuals of the same description whose greatest alarm seems to be that things may change after they are dead.

As the nerves of one of your dwellers in a finished town would be shocked by the sound of a hammer, those of our respectable Hunkers are shocked by the sound of a newly discovered truth. They recognize it as a disturber of the world's peace. But the world, like the fish preached to in the stream, moves on in obedience to the laws of its being, bearing away all excrescences and imperfections in its progress. It has its periods of illumination as well as of darkness, and often bounds forward a greater distance in a single year than in an age before. The rosy morning light of a great truth breaks upon the vision of some early riser — and straightway he wakes up the drowsy world with the announcement of the day and the work. Sleepy people don't like to be disturbed. They hate the troubler, call him names, draw their curtains, close their blinds, turn their backs to the light — but the sun rises nevertheless, and the most conservative Hunker of them all is compelled in time to acknowledge it.

Less than one hundred years ago it is said that the people of the West Coast of Ireland thought that the proper way to attach a horse to a plow was by the tail. It seemed to them that that was what the tail was made for. Only two hundred years ago, we are told by the pious Godwin, that the Christian people of the British West Indies thought it a sin to baptize persons of color who were slaves. The argument against such baptism was quite logical. They said that Negroes are property, and it is not right to baptize property; and a learned divine thought it necessary to write a book to prove that it was not a sin to baptize a Negro.

At a time less remote than that, even in New England, now so remarkable for its enlightenment and its liberality, if any aged woman were in any wise distinguished for talent, and a little eccentric withal, as most gifted women are supposed to be, she stood a smart chance of being hanged as a witch. New England has outgrown this folly, and is condemned by some who reproach her, for refusing now to fall in with the barbarism of Slavery. At one time to hate and despise a Jew, simply for being a Jew, was almost a Christian virtue. The Jews were treated with every species of indignity, and not allowed to learn trades, nor to live in the same part of the city with other people. Now kings cannot go to war without the consent of a Jew. The Jew has come up, and the Negro will come up by and by. The world is not much older than it was when to torture and burn men for a difference of speculative religious belief was deemed simple fidelity to the Christian faith. All the wisdom of Boston could devise no better way a hundred years ago to cure a woman of Quakerism than by the cart-whip. Roger Williams found more toleration among the Indians of Rhode Island than among the Puritans of Massachusetts. It is only thirty years ago when gentlemen of property and standing in the very Athens of America felt it a patriotic duty to mob Wm. L. Garrison and break up a woman's Anti-Slavery prayer-meeting. Only two years ago there remained enough of this brutality and barbarism in Boston to block the streets of that city with a mob of 10,000 men clamoring for the blood of an eminent Boston citizen, for simply daring to speak against Slavery.

These facts are notorious and oft repeated. I mention them here not to cast reproach but as a part of the struggle between truth and error, and as a proof of progress. Fortunately for mankind, error is a bad reasoner. It can fight better than it can reason. It can make mouths, call names, and fling brickbats, but cannot reason except to damage itself. All the powers of the universe fight steadily against it. Brooks could knock down the Senator, but the whole South in arms could not knock down the Senator's argument. Such is my confidence in the potency of truth, in the power of reason, I hold that had the right of free discussion been preserved during the last thirty years, had the Northern parties and politicians been half so diligent in protecting this high constitutional right, from the first ruthlessly struck down all over the South, as they have been in framing laws for the recapture of poor, toil-worn and foot-sore slaves, we should now have no Slavery to breed Rebellion, nor war, black with dismal terror, to drench our land with blood, and fill our dwellings with sorrow and mourning. Slavery would have fallen as it fell in the West Indies, as it has fallen in the Free States, as it has fallen in Russia, and elsewhere, and as it will fall everywhere, when men can assail it with the weapons of reason and the facts of experience.

No men better understand the moral weakness of Slavery than the slaveholders themselves. The simple ones among them may think the system strong in reason; but the leading minds at the South know and confess the contrary. The Columbia (S.C.) Telegraph only echoed the sentiment of the whole South when it said thirty years ago: "Let us declare through the public journals of the country that the question of

Slavery is not and shall not be open to discussion, that the moment any private individual shall attempt to lecture upon its evils and immorality, and the necessity of putting means in operation to secure us from them, in that same moment, his tongue shall be cut out and cast upon a dung hill."

The Augusta (Ga.) Chronicle, of the same period, speaking of one who had attempted thus to lecture, says: "He should have been hanged up as high as Haman, to rot till the wind whistled through his bones. The cry of the whole South should be death to the Abolitionists, wherever found."

The Lords of the Lash have often boasted of late that discussion has convinced them that Slavery is right. That in this respect they are wiser than Washington, who desired to see Slavery abolished, and would gladly give his vote for such abolition; wiser than Jefferson, who said he trembled for his country when he reflected that God was just, and that his justice would not sleep forever; wiser than Franklin, who was President of the first Abolition Society in America; wiser than Madison, who did not wish to have it seen in the Constitution that there could be any such thing as property in man; wiser than the Congress of 1807, which abolished the Slave Trade, and wiser than the men of 1787, who abolished Slavery in all the Territory then belonging to the United States.

They tell us that discussion has made them thus wise. Discussion indeed! Discussion which only permits one side to be heard, and compels the other to remain silent, would be likely to produce just such a result. The slaveholder has spoken but the slave has remained dumb. On the side of the oppressor is power, on the side of the slave weakness. The whole array of Southern lawyers, priests, and politicians — the whole power of the Southern press, pulpit, and platform have for 30 years stifled the very groans of the millions in bondage. Valuing itself at twenty hundred millions of dollars — a mountain of gold — it has bribed and bought up all the subtle machinery of religion, science, and law, in favor of Slavery. While denouncing rails, tar and feathers, faggots and fire against any who should dare call in question the accursed system of Slavery, and this they call discussion.

Thus the moral eyes of Southern society were put out. They banished from among them every moral antidote for the dreadful evil of Slavery and have chosen to walk blindfold into the very jaws of death. I confess that when I consider the common people of the South, especially helpless women and children, who are often startled at midnight, and made to leave their beds and homes, half clad, to find their way to the woods through darkness, rain, mud, and snow, I feel something like pity for these people, while I feel a burning indignation, for those who have blinded and deceived them. Under the whole heavens there never was a people more completely given over to believe a lie that they might be destroyed. They are suffering all the horrors of war at this moment because [they were] deluded by their moral teachers, both at the North and at the South.

Look at it! If they went to the church where men profess to speak by the authority of God, what did they hear on the subject of Slavery? Why, this: That Jesus Christ and his Apostles, though they walked in the presence of Roman Slavery — which was far more severe than ours — nowhere condemned the system; that the New Testament prescribed and enjoined obedience from slaves to their masters; that even to catch and return runaway slaves was in accordance with apostolic example, and that the main feature of the Fugitive Slave bill was in harmony with Paul's Epistle to Philemon. They learned from their moral teachers that they might whip, hold, buy, and sell men and women, innocently, for Slavery was of Divine appointment, established by the law of Christ. Slave-holders are the modern Abrahams, Isaacs and Jacobs in the Church of God. Such was the teaching at the South.

Was the case much better at the North? You know and I know that even here, the black mantle of Slavery was everywhere flaunted in our faces from Northern pulpits. If at any time during the last thirty years preceding the firing upon Fort Sumter any slaveholder had consulted the leading divines of the North as to the sinfulness of Slavery, he would have found that the teachings of the Northern pulpit differed very little from that of the South. A few heterodox, and still fewer orthodox ministers, filling humble pulpits and living upon small salaries, have espoused the cause of the slave; but the ministers of high standing — the $5,000 divines — were almost to a man on the side of Slavery, and did their best to defend the system from the assaults of the Abolitionists. They steadily denied the inherent sinfulness of Slavery and so far from being rebuked as an offender, the slaveholder was received and welcomed as a saint.

Every influential pulpit of Rochester, where I live, was open to slaveholders so lately as two or three years ago. The old school General Assembly met there — the city survived it — at that time. The late Dr. Thornwall, a champion, alike of Secession and of Slavery, was there. He was courted and welcomed by every prominent pulpit of the city, while that faithful champion of the rights of human nature, Dr. George B. Cheever, was coldly repulsed from all such pulpits. What was true of Rochester three years ago, and true of the whole North, would become true again if this war were settled on the basis of compromise. Nay, I should expect that the Press would be fettered at the North nearly as heavily as it is at the South. Slavery would be welcomed and honored in Northern pulpits, with a servility more disgusting and shocking than ever before.

Why do I make these remarks? I will tell you. Much as I value the present apparent hostility to Slavery at the North, I plainly see that it is less the outgrowth of high and intelligent moral conviction against Slavery, as such, than because of the trouble its friends have brought upon the country. I would have Slavery hated for that and more. A man that hates Slavery only for what it does to the white man, stands ready to embrace it the moment its injuries are confined to the Black man, and he ceases to feel those injuries in his own person.

I confess, if I could possibly doubt the salvation of this nation, it would not be because the traitors and Rebels are strong, but because we are weak at this vital point. There is yet among us a cowardly shrinking from a full and frank acknowledgment of the manhood of the Negro, and a whole-souled recognition of his power to help in the great struggle through which we are passing.

But to proceed: The saying that the children of this world are in their day and generation wiser than the children of light, is verified in the history of the conflict between Slavery and Freedom. History will accord to the Abolitionists a large measure of wisdom, and heroic courage and fortitude in assailing

Slavery in its strongholds of Church and State; but it cannot award to them that prophetic vision that sees the end from the beginning. It is fortunate, I think, that they did not see it — fortunate that they walked by faith and not by sight. Could they have foreseen their country torn and rent by the giant footsteps of this terrible rebellion — could they have seen a million of men, confronting each other, discussing the question of Slavery with cannon — could they have seen the rivers red with blood, and the fields whitened with human bones, they might have shrunk back from the moral contest, and thus only have postponed this physical contest to a future day, and upon a more dreadful scale than the one now going on.

From the very first the enemies of Abolitionism comprehended one feature in the nature of the contest between Freedom and Slavery. They saw at least the evils attendant on that conflict. Merchants saw their trade with the South embarrassed and ruined. Churches saw their denominations divided. The old political parties saw their organizations broken up. Statesmen saw the Union dissolved and terrible border wars inaugurated. Worshiping at mammon's altar themselves they knew the mighty hold which mammon held upon its Southern worshipers. They said that the slaveholders would strike down the Government before they would give up Slavery. They predicted that the South would secede if we did not stop talking and voting against Slavery. By their very predictions, they helped on the fulfillment. The South was flattered and encouraged by what was thus expected of her by leading men at the North. She doubtless expected that those who said she would dissolve her connection with the Union without once denouncing her doing so as a crime, recognized her right to do so, and would rather think her wanting in spirit if she did not do so.

Foreseeing the evils thus predicted, these men cried with one accord: "Give us the Union; give us Slavery and prosperity; give us Slavery and peace; give us error, if Slavery be an error; and as for what you call truth and human liberty, crucify them." The world has seen no greater example of patience and perseverance than that exhibited by the Abolitionists in meeting the objections of their opponents. Weapons of war they had cast from the battle. No Abolitionist ever drew sword against Slavery until Slavery drew its exterminating sword against Liberty on the soil of Kansas. It was only after he saw his brave sons hunted like felons and shot down like wolves, that noble old John Brown went to Harper's Ferry.

Until this, Anti-Slavery men, of all shades of opinion were eminently peaceful. The grand mistake of the Abolitionists was in supposing the American people better than they were. They did not see that an evil so gigantic as Slavery, so interwoven with the social arrangements, manners, and morals of the country, could not be removed without something like the social earthquake now upon us. They ought to have known that the huge Leviathan would cause the deep to boil — aye, to howl, and hiss, and foam in sevenfold agony.

Great however, as was our mistake, incomparably greater and vastly more harmful was the mistake of those who flattered themselves and the nation that all was peace and prosperity, and that the nation had nothing to fear from anything but Abolitionists. They thought that this nation could go on year after year and century after century, outraging and trampling upon the sacred rights of human nature, and that it could still enjoy peace, and prosperity. To them the world was without a moral Government and might was right. The war now on our hands is sometimes described as a school for the moral education of the nation. I like the designation. It certainly is a school, and a very severe and costly one. But who will say that it will not be worth all it costs if it shall correct our errors concerning Slavery and free us from that barbarism.

Slavery from the first has not only been our great national crime, but our great national scandal and mistake. The first grand error of which this war is likely to cure us is: That a nation can outlaw one part of its people without endangering the rights and liberties of all the people. They will learn that they cannot put a chain on the ankle of the bondmen without finding the other end of it about their own necks. Hitherto the white laborer has been deluded into the belief that to degrade the Black laborer is to elevate the white. We shall learn by-and-by that labor will always be degraded where idleness is the badge of respectability. Whence came the degrading phrases, fast growing popular before the war, "hireling labor," "greasy mechanics," "mudsills of society." The laborer should be "owned by the capitalists." — Poor "white trash" — and a dozen others of the same class: They come from Slavery. I think I never saw anywhere such contempt for poor white people as in the South.

Gen. Butler has only made a discovery which any man having two eyes could not fail to make in the South, that the war of the Rebels — is a war of the rich against the poor. Let Slavery go down with the war, and let labor cease to be fettered, chained, flogged, and branded. Let it be paid honest wages for honest work, and then we shall see as never before, the laborers in all sections of this country rising to respectability and power.

That this war is to abolish Slavery I have no manner of doubt. The process may be long and tedious, but the event will come at last. It is among the undoubted certainties of the future.

It is objected to the Proclamation of Freedom, that it only abolishes Slavery in the Rebel States. To me it seems a blunder that Slavery was not declared abolished everywhere in the Republic. Slavery anywhere endangers the National cause, and should perish everywhere.

But even in this omission of the Proclamation the evil is more seeming than real. When Virginia is a free State, Maryland cannot be a slave State. When Missouri is a free State, Kentucky cannot be a slave State. Slavery must stand or fall together. Strike it at either extreme — either on the head or at the heel, and it dies. A brick knocked down at either end of the row brings every brick in it to the ground.

You have heard the story of the Irishman who paid the price of two spurs — but refused to carry away but one; on the ground, as he said, that if he could make one side of his horse go, he would risk the other.

So I say, if we can strike down Slavery in the Rebel States, I will risk the downfall of Slavery in the Border States. It is again objected to this Proclamation that it is only an ink and paper proclamation. I admit it. The objector might go a step further, and assert that there was a time when this Proclamation was only a thought, a sentiment, an idea — a hope of some radical Abolitionist — for such it truly was. But what of it? The world has never advanced a single inch in the right direction, when the movement could not be traced to some such small beginning. The bill abolishing Slavery, and giving freedom to eight hundred thousand people in the West Indies, was a paper bill. The Reform bill, that broke up the rotten borough system in England, was a paper bill. The act of Catholic Emancipation was a paper act; and so was the bill repealing the Corn Laws. Greater than all, our own Declaration of Independence was at one time but ink and paper.

The freedom of the American colonies dates from no particular battle during the war. No man can tell upon what particular day we won our national independence. But the birth of our freedom is fixed on the day of the going forth of the Declaration of Independence. In like manner aftercoming generations will celebrate the first of January as the day which brought liberty and manhood to the American slaves.

How shall this be done? I answer: That the paper Proclamation must now be made iron, lead and fire, by the prompt employment of the Negro's arm in this contest.

I hold that the Proclamation, good as it is, will be worthless — a miserable mockery — unless the nation shall so far conquer its prejudice as to welcome into the army full-grown Black men to help fight the battles of the Republic.

I know it is said that the Negroes won't fight. But I distrust the accuser. In one breath the Copperheads tell you that the slaves won't fight, and in the next they tell you that the only effect of the Proclamation is to make the slaves cut their masters' throats and stir up insurrections all over the South. The same men tell you that the Negroes are lazy and good for nothing, and in the next breath they tell you that they will all come North and take the labor away from the laboring white men here. In one breath they tell you that the Negro can never learn the military art, and in the next they tell you that there is danger that white men may be outranked by colored men. I may be pardoned if I leave these objections to their own contradictions and absurdities. They are like the Kilkenny cats, and there is a fair probability of their reaching the same result.

But we are asked why have the Negroes remained silent spectators of the dreadful struggle now going on? I am not annoyed by this question. The course pursued by them is creditable to their wisdom. The Negro has proved that he is much like the white man. He will fight, but he must have a reasonable prospect of whipping somebody. Up to the first day of last month there was no earthly chance of success in a rising among the slaves. Both the Union and the Confederate armies were in the field against the Negro. Madness itself could not counsel the slaves to rise in such circumstances. Their not doing so should be charged not to their cowardice, but to their good sense.

But who are those who are now opposing the measure of putting arms in the hands of colored men? Who are those who are opposed to raising colored troops? They are the men who would gladly disarm every white soldier now fighting for their country, and hand the country over, bound hand and foot, into the hands of Jefferson Davis. You know the men, and ought to know how much weight should be given to the counsels of such men. Would these men rather drown than be saved by a Black man? Would they prefer to see their dwellings burnt to ashes than to have the flames extinguished by colored men? If they would not, then are they traitors in disguise and very thin disguise at that, when they refuse to the country, now in its peril, what they would gladly claim for themselves. They exhibit their unmitigated hollowness by opposing the enrollment of colored troops.

Do you ask me whether Black men will freely enlist in the service of the country? I tell you that that depends upon the white men of the country. The Government must assure them of protection as soldiers, and give them a fair chance of winning distinction and glory in common with other soldiers. They must not be made the mere hewers of wood and drawers of water for the army.

When a man leaves home, family, and security, to risk his limbs and life in the field of battle, for God's sake let him have all the honor which he may achieve, let his color be what it may. If, by the fortunes of war he is flung into the hands of the Rebels, let him be assured that the loyal Government will not desert him, but will hold the Confederate Government strictly responsible, as much for a Black as for a white soldier. Give us fair play, and open here your recruiting offices, and their doors shall be crowded with Black recruits to fight the battles of the country. Do your part, my white fellow-countrymen, and we will do ours.

> "*Oh! where's the slave so lowly,*
> *Condemned to chains unholy,*
> *Who, could he burst his chains at fight,*
> *Would pine beneath them slowly?*"

The colored man only waits for honorable admission into the service of the country. They know that who would be free, themselves must strike the blow, and they long for the opportunity to strike that blow. Thus far, however, the colored men of the Free States, and for the most part, of the Slave States, have had their military ardor chilled by the contempt with which their offer to serve their country has been refused. We asked the Governor of New York if he would accept colored troops, and he said it would be impossible for him to receive them. We asked Gov. Curtin of Pennsylvania, and he would not receive colored soldiers at any rate. So that our ardor was chilled. But I know, colored men now in the army passing for white not much whiter than I, but by shaving their heads very closely they manage to get in. I know one from my own town who has been promoted recently. If I could speak loud enough to be heard by the Government at Washington I should say, have a care, lest you let slip the last moment when your call for help can be answered. You have wronged us long and wronged us greatly, but it is not yet too late to retrieve the past. We still stand ready to serve you, and will do it with a will, at the first sound of your war-trumpet. I know the colored men of the North; I know the colored men of the South. They are ready to rally under the stars and stripes at the first tap of the drum. Give them a chance; stop calling them "n****rs," and call them soldiers.

Give them a chance to seek the bauble reputation at the cannon's mouth. Stop telling them they can't fight, and tell them they can fight and shall fight, and they will fight, and fight with vengeance. Give them a chance. The most delicate lady in the city of New York can ride by the side of a Black man, if he is there as a servant. Even the most fastidious of our Generals can be waited on by colored men. Why should they object to our fighting? We were with you on the banks of the Mobile, good enough to fight with you under Gen. Jackson. Why not let us fight by your side under Gen. Hooker?

We shall have a chance yet, and I tell you to whom I am looking for this. I have great faith, as I told you more than a year ago, in the virtue of the people of the North; I have more in the persistent villainy of the South. I tell you that under their tent we shall yet be able to accept the aid of the colored man. Away with prejudice, away with folly, and in this death struggle for liberty, country, and permanent security, let the Black, iron hand of the colored man fall heavily on the head of the slaveholding traitors and rebels and lay them low. Give them a chance! Give them a chance. I don't say they are great fighters. I don't say they will fight better than other men. All I say is, give them a chance. I feel that we are living in a glorious time. I felt so on the first of January, and have been feeling so ever since. I felt whiter, and I have combed my hair with less difficulty. You had a grand time here, and we had a grand time at Boston, on the first of January.

We had two machines running — at Music Hall and Tremont Temple — more than three thousand at each. You want to know what the colored people think. I will tell you how joyfully they received the Proclamation of Abraham Lincoln. We were not all colored either; but we all seemed to be about of one color that day. We met in good spirits at 10 o'clock expecting before the adjournment to have the Proclamation. We had waited on each speaker keeping our eye on the door. No Proclamation. The President said we would meet again at two when he had no doubt we should have the Proclamation. We met again but no Proclamation. We did not know whether to shout or hold our peace but we adjourned again with the understanding that it was on the wires and we should certainly see it in the evening. But no Proclamation came. We went on until 11 o'clock and I said, we won't go home till morning. By and by Judge Russell went to one of the newspaper offices and obtained a slip containing the Proclamation. I never saw enthusiasm before. I never saw joy before.

Men, women, young and old, were up; hats and bonnets were in the air, and we gave three cheers for Abraham Lincoln and three cheers for almost everybody else. Some prayed and some sang, and finally we adjourned from that place to meet in the Rev. Mr. Grimes' Church; that good old soul and we continued greeting them till three o'clock. There was shouting and singing, "Glory, Hallelujah," "Old John Brown," "Marching On," and "Blow Ye, the Trumpet Blow!" — till we got up such a state of enthusiasm that almost anything seemed to be witty — and entirely appropriate to the glorious occasion.

There was one Black man who stood in a corner, and I thought I never saw a blacker man and I think I never saw whiter teeth. Occasionally he would bound up like a fish out of water, and as he was standing in a dark place, you could see nothing going up but a little white streak. About the last he said he must speak, and I will make you his speech. It was all in place. We were up to the point when everything was in order. "Brethren," said he, "I was born in North Carolina, where my brother Douglass was born, thank God!" I didn't happen to be born there, but I could not for the life of me interrupt him. Said he, "I was born there, and was born and held a slave there, thank God! I grew up from childhood to manhood there, thank God!" And the audience shouted. And said he: "When I got to be grown up to man's estate I wanted to marry a wife, thank God!" And said he: "I courted no less than sixteen women, thank God!" And said he: "The woman I married is here tonight, thank God!" We all rose up to see this little woman, and she was told to get up, and we looked at her, and she was nothing extraordinary; but still it was all in place. The feeling of the whole of this Black Congregation — for it was mainly Black — was that they were ready to offer their services at any moment this Government should call for them. And I want to assure you, and the Government, and everybody, that we are ready, and we only ask to be called into this service.

What a glorious day when Slavery shall be no more in this country, when we have blotted out this system of wrong, and made this United States in fact and in truth what it is in theory — The land of the Free and the Home of the Brave.[75]

---

[75] Lecture delivered at The Cooper Union in New York City on February 6th, 1863 and published in *Douglass' Monthly*, March 1863.

Men of Color, To Arms! – When first the rebel cannon shattered the walls of Sumter and drove away its starving garrison, I predicted that the war then and there inaugurated would not be fought out entirely by white men. Every month's experience during these dreary years has confirmed that opinion. A war undertaken and brazenly carried on for the perpetual enslavement of colored men, calls logically and loudly for colored men to help suppress it. Only a moderate share of sagacity was needed to see that the arm of the slave was the best defense against the arm of the slaveholder. Hence with every reverse to the national arms, with every exulting shout of victory raised by the slaveholding rebels, I have implored the imperiled nation to unchain against her foes, her powerful Black hand. Slowly and reluctantly that appeal is beginning to be heeded. Stop not now to complain that it was not heeded sooner. It may or it may not have been best that it should not. This is not the time to discuss that question. Leave it to the future. When the war is over, the country is saved, peace is established, and the Black man's rights are secured, as they will be, history with an impartial hand will dispose of that and sundry other questions. Action! Action! not criticism, is the plain duty of this hour. Words are now useful only as they stimulate to blows. The office of speech now is only to point out when, where, and how to strike to the best advantage. There is no time to delay.

The tide is at its flood that leads on to fortune. From East to West, from North to South, the sky is written all over, "Now or never." Liberty won by white men would lose half its luster. "Who would be free themselves must strike the blow." "Better even die free, than to live slaves." This is the sentiment of every brave colored man amongst us. There are weak and cowardly men in all nations. We have them amongst us. They tell you this is the "white man's war"; that you will be "no better off after than before the war"; that the getting of you into the army is to "sacrifice you on the first opportunity." Believe them not; cowards themselves, they do not wish to have their cowardice shamed by your brave example. Leave them to their timidity, or to whatever motive may hold them back.

I have not thought lightly of the words I am now addressing you. The counsel I give comes of close observation of the great struggle now in progress, and of the deep conviction that this is your hour and mine.

In good earnest then, and after the best deliberation, I now for the first time during this war feel at liberty to call and counsel you to arms. By every consideration which binds you to your enslaved fellow-countrymen, and the peace and welfare of your country; by every aspiration which you cherish for the freedom and equality of yourselves and your children;

by all the ties of blood and identity which make us one with the brave Black men now fighting our battles in Louisiana and in South Carolina, I urge you to fly to arms, and smite with death the power that would bury the government and your liberty in the same hopeless grave. I wish I could tell you that the State of New York calls you to this high honor. For the moment her constituted authorities are silent on the subject. They will speak by and by, and doubtless on the right side; but we are not compelled to wait for her. We can get at the throat of treason and slavery through the State of Massachusetts.

She was first in the War of Independence; first to break the chains of her slaves; first to make the Black man equal before the law; first to admit colored children to her common schools, and she was first to answer with her blood the alarm cry of the nation, when its capital was menaced by rebels. You know her patriotic governor, and you know Charles Sumner. I need not add more.

Massachusetts now welcomes you to arms as soldiers. She has but a small colored population from which to recruit. She has full leave of the general government to send one regiment to the war, and she has undertaken to do it. Go quickly and help fill up the first colored regiment from the North. I am authorized to assure you that you will receive the same wages, the same rations, the same equipments, the same protection, the same treatment, and the same bounty, secured to the white soldiers. You will be led by able and skillful officers, men who will take especial pride in your efficiency and success. They will be quick to accord to you all the honor you shall merit by your valor, and see that your rights and feelings are respected by other soldiers. I have assured myself on these points, and can speak with authority. More than twenty years of unswerving devotion to our common cause may give me some humble claim to be trusted at this momentous crisis.

I will not argue. To do so implies hesitation and doubt, and you do not hesitate. You do not doubt. The day dawns; the morning star is bright upon the horizon! The iron gate of our prison stands half open. One gallant rush from the North will fling it wide open, while four millions of our brothers and sisters shall march out into liberty. The chance is now given you to end in a day the bondage of centuries, and to rise in one bound from social degradation to the plane of common equality with all other varieties of men. Remember Denmark Vesey of Charleston; remember Nathaniel Turner of South-ampton; remember Shields Green and Copeland, who followed noble John Brown, and fell as glorious martyrs for the cause of the slave. Remember that in a contest with oppression, the Almighty has no attribute which can take sides with oppressors. The case is before you. This is our golden opportunity. Let us accept it, and forever wipe out the dark reproaches unsparingly hurled against us by our enemies. Let us win for ourselves the gratitude of our country, and the best blessings of our posterity through all time. The nucleus of this first regiment is now in camp at Readville, a short distance from Boston. I will undertake to forward to Boston all persons adjudged fit to be mustered into the regiment, who shall apply to me at any time within the next two weeks.[76]

---

[76] Printed as a *Broadside*, Rochester, March 21st,1863, yet based upon a Lecture delivered in Rochester on March 2, 1863.

Why Should a Colored Man Enlist? – This question has been repeatedly put to us while raising men for the 54th Massachusetts regiment during the past five weeks, and perhaps we cannot at present do a better service to the cause of our people or to the cause of the country than by giving a few of the many reasons why a colored man should enlist.

First – You are a man, although a colored man. If you were only a horse or an ox, incapable of deciding whether the rebels are right or wrong, you would have no responsibility, and might like the horse or the ox go on eating your corn or grass, in total indifference, as to which side is victorious or vanquished in this conflict. You are however no horse, and no ox, but a man, and whatever concerns man should interest you. He who looks upon a conflict between right and wrong, and does not help the right against the wrong, despises and insults his own nature, and invites the contempt of mankind. As between the North and South, the North is clearly in the right and the South is flagrantly in the wrong. You should therefore, simply as a matter of right and wrong, give your utmost aid to the North. In presence of such a contest there is no neutrality for any man. You are either for the Government or against the Government. Manhood requires you to take sides, and you are mean or noble according to how you choose between action and inaction. – If you are sound in body and mind, there is nothing in your color to excuse you from enlisting in the service of the republic against its enemies. If color should not be a criterion of rights, neither should it be a standard of duty. The whole duty of a man, belongs alike to white and Black. "A man's a man for a' that."

Second – You are however, not only a man, but an American citizen, so declared by the highest legal adviser of the Government, and you have hitherto expressed in various ways, not only your willingness but your earnest desire to fulfil any and every obligation which the relation of citizenship imposes. Indeed, you have hitherto felt wronged and slighted, because while white men of all other nations have been freely enrolled to serve the country, you a native born citizen have been coldly denied the honor of aiding in defense of the land of your birth. The injustice thus done you is now repented of by the Government and you are welcomed to a place in the army of the nation. Should you refuse to enlist *now*, you will justify the past contempt of the Government towards you and lead it to regret having honored you with a call to take up arms in its defense. You cannot but see that here is a good reason why you should promptly enlist.

Third – A third reason why a colored man should enlist is found in the fact that every Negro-hater and slavery-lover in the land regards the arming of

Negroes as a calamity and is doing his best to prevent it. Even now all the weapons of malice, in the shape of slander and ridicule are used to defeat the filling up of the 54th Massachusetts (colored) regiment. In nine cases out of ten, you will find it safe to do just what your enemy would gladly have you leave undone. What helps you hurts him. Find out what he does not want and give him a plenty of it.

Fourth – You should enlist to learn the use of arms, to become familiar with the means of securing, protecting and defending your own liberty. A day may come when men shall learn war no more, when justice shall be so clearly apprehended, so universally practiced, and humanity shall be so profoundly loved and respected, that war and bloodshed, shall be confined only to beasts of prey. Manifestly however, that time has not yet come, and while all men should labor to hasten its coming, by the cultivation of all the elements conducive to peace, it is plain that for the present no race of men can depend wholly upon moral means for the maintenance of their rights. Men must either be governed by love or by fear. They must love to do right or fear to do wrong. The only way open to any race to make their rights respected is to learn how to defend them. When it is seen that Black men no more than white men can be enslaved with impunity, men will be less enclined to enslave and oppress them. Enlist therefore, that you may learn the art and assert the ability to defend yourself and your race.

Fifth – You are a member of a long enslaved and despised race. Men have set down your submission to Slavery and insult, to a lack of manly courage. They point to this fact as demonstrating your fitness only to be a servile class. You should enlist and disprove the slander, and wipe out the reproach. When you shall be seen nobly defending the liberties of your own country against rebels and traitors — brass itself will blush to use such arguments imputing cowardice against you.

Sixth – Whether you are or are not, entitled to all the rights of citizenship in this country has long been a matter of dispute to your prejudice. By enlisting in the service of your country at this trial hour, and upholding the National Flag, you will stop the mouths of traducers and win applause even from the iron lips of ingratitude. Enlist and you make this your country in common with all other men born in the country or out of it.

Seventh – Enlist for your own sake. Decried and derided as you have been and still are, you need an act of this kind by which to recover your own self-respect. You have to some extent rated your value by the estimate of your enemies and hence have counted yourself less than you are. You owe it to yourself and your race to rise from your social debasement and take your place among the soldiers of your country, a man among men. Depend upon it, the subjective effect of this one act of enlisting will be immense and highly beneficial. You will stand more erect, walk more assured, feel more at ease, and be less liable to insult than you ever were before. He who fights the battles of America may claim America as his country — and have that claim respected. Thus in defending your country now against rebels and traitors you are defending your own Liberty, honor, manhood and self-respect.

Eighth – You should enlist because your doing so will be one of the most certain means of preventing the country from drifting back into the whirlpool of Pro-Slavery Compromise at the end of the war, which is now our greatest danger. He who shall witness another Compromise with Slavery in this country will see the free colored man of the North more than ever a victim of the pride, lust, scorn and violence of all classes of white men. The whole North will be but another Detroit, where every white fiend may with impunity revel in unrestrained beastliness towards people of color; they may burn their houses, insult their wives and daughters, and kill indiscriminately. If you mean to live in this country now is the time for you to do your full share in making it a country where you and your children after you can live in comp-arative safety. Prevent a compromise with the traitors, compel them to come back to the Union whipped and humbled into obedience and all will be well. But let them come back as masters and all their hate and hellish ingenuity will be exerted to stir up the ignorant masses of the North to hate, hinder and persecute the free colored people of the North. That most inhuman of all modern enactments, with its bribed judges, and summary process, the Fugitive Slave Law, with all its infernal train of canting divines, preaching the gospel of kidnapping, as twelve years ago, will be revived against the free colored people of the North. One or two Black brigades will do much to prevent all this.

Ninth – You should enlist because the war for the Union, whether men so call it or not, is a war for Emancipation. The salvation of the country, by the inexorable relation of cause and effect, can be secured only by the complete abolition of Slavery. The President has already proclaimed emancipation to the Slaves in the rebel States which is tantamount to declaring Emancipation in all the States, for Slavery must exist everywhere in the South in order to exist anywhere in the South. Can you ask for a more inviting, ennobling and soul enlarging work, than that of making one of the glorious Band who shall carry Liberty to your enslaved people? Remember that identified with the Slave in color, you will have a power that white soldiers have not, to attract them to your lines and induce them to take up arms in a common cause. One Black Brigade will, for this work, be worth more than two white ones. Enlist, therefore, enlist without delay, enlist now, and forever put an end to the human barter and butchery which have stained the whole South with the warm blood of your people, and loaded its air with their groans. Enlist, and deserve not only well of your country, and win for yourselves, a name and a place among men, but secure to yourself what is infinitely more precious, the fast dropping tears of gratitude of your kith and kin marked out for destruction, and who are but now ready to perish.

When time's ample curtain shall fall upon our national tragedy, and our hillsides and valleys shall neither redden with the blood nor whiten with the bones of kinsmen and country-men who have fallen in the sanguinary and wicked strife; when grim visaged war has smoothed his wrinkled front and our country shall have regained its normal condition as a leader of nations in the occupation and blessings of peace — and history shall record the names of heroes and martyrs — who bravely answered the call of patriotism and Liberty — against traitors thieves and assassins — let it not be said that in the long list of glory, composed of men of all nations — there appears the name of no colored man.[77]

---

[77] *Douglass' Monthly*, April 1863.

The Mission of the War – By the mission of the war I mean nothing occult, arbitrary or difficult to be understood, but simply those great moral changes in the fundamental condition of the people, demanded by the situation of the country, plainly involved in the nature of the war, and which if the war is conducted in accordance with its true character, it is naturally and logically fitted to accomplish.

Speaking in the name of Providence, some men tell us that Slavery is already dead, that it expired with the first shot at Sumter. This may be so, but I do not share the confidence with which it is asserted. In a grand Crisis like this, we should all prefer to look facts sternly in the face, and to accept their verdict whether it bless or blast us. I look for no miraculous destruction of Slavery. The war looms before me simply as a great national opportunity, which may be improved to national salvation, or neglected to national ruin. I hope much from the bravery of our soldiers, but in vain is the might of armies if our rulers fail to profit by experience, and refuse to listen to the suggestions of wisdom and justice. The most hopeful fact of the hour is that we are now in a salutary school — the school of affliction. If sharp and signal retribution, long protracted, widesweeping and over-whelming, can teach a great nation respect for the long-despised claims of justice, surely we shall be taught now and for all time to come. But if, on the other hand, this potent teacher, whose lessons are written in characters of blood, and thundered to us from a hundred battlefields shall fail, we shall go down, as we shall deserve to go down, as a warning to all other nations which shall come after us. It is not pleasant to contemplate the hour as one of doubt and danger. We naturally prefer the bright side, but when there is a dark side it is folly to shut our eyes to it or deny its existence.

I know that the acorn involves the oak, but I know also that the commonest accident may destroy its potential character and defeat its natural destiny. One wave brings its treasure from the briny deep, but another often sweeps it back to its primal depths. The saying that revolutions never go backward must be taken with limitations. The revolution of 1848 was one of the grandest that ever dazzled a gazing world. It overturned the French throne, sent Louis Philippe into exile, shook every throne in Europe, and inaugurated a glorious Republic. Looking on from a distance, the friends of democratic liberty saw in the convulsion the death of kingcraft in Europe and throughout the world. Great was their disappointment. Almost in the twinkling of an eye, the latent forces of despotism rallied. The Republic disappeared. Her noblest defenders were sent into exile, and the hopes of democratic liberty were blasted in the moment of their bloom. Politics and perfidy proved too strong for the principles of liberty and justice in that contest. I wish I could say that no such liabilities darken the horizon around us. But the same elements are plainly involved here as there. Though the portents are that we shall flourish, it is too much to say that we cannot fail and fall. Our destiny is not to be taken out of our own hands. It is cowardly to shuffle our responsibilities upon the shoulders of Providence. I do not intend to argue but to state facts.

We are now wading deep into the third year of conflict with a fierce and sanguinary rebellion, one which, at the beginning of it, we were hopefully assured by one of our most sagacious and trusted political prophets, would be ended in less than ninety days: a rebellion which, in its worst features, stands alone among rebellions a solitary and ghastly horror, without a parallel in the history of any nation, ancient or modern: a rebellion inspired by no love of liberty and by no hatred of oppression, as most other rebellions have been, and therefore utterly indefensible upon any moral or social grounds: a rebellion which openly and shamelessly sets at defiance the world's judgment of right and wrong, appeals from light to darkness, from intelligence to ignorance, from the ever-increasing prospects and blessings of a high and glorious civilization to the cold and withering blasts of a naked barbarism: a rebellion which even at this unfinished stage of it, counts the number of its slain not by thousands nor tens of thousands, but by hundreds of thousands. A rebellion which in the destruction of human life and property has rivalled the earthquake, the whirlwind and the pestilence that walketh in darkness, and wasteth at noonday. It has planted agony at a million hearthstones, thronged our streets with the weeds of mourning, filled our land with mere stumps of men, ridged our soil with 200,000 rudely-formed graves, and mantled it all over with the shadow of death. A rebellion which, while it has arrested the wheels of peaceful industry and checked the flow of commerce, has piled up a debt, heavier than a mountain of gold to weigh down the necks of our children's children. There is no end to the mischiefs wrought. It has brought ruin at home, contempt abroad, cooled our friends, heated our enemies, and endangered our existence as a nation.

Now, for what is all this desolation, ruin, shame, suffering, and sorrow? Can anybody want the answer? Can anybody be ignorant of the answer? It has been given a thousand times from this and other platforms. We all know it is Slavery. Less than a half a million of Southern slaveholders — holding in bondage four million slaves — finding themselves outvoted in the effort to get possession of the United States Government, in order to serve the interests of Slavery, have madly resorted to the sword — have undertaken to accomplish by bullets what they failed to accomplish by ballots. That is the answer.

It is worthy of remark that Secession was an afterthought with the Rebels. Their aim was higher; Secession was only their second choice. Wise was going to fight for Slavery in the Union. It was not separation, but subversion. It was not Richmond, but Washington. It was not the Confederate rag, but the glorious Star-Spangled Banner.

Whence came the guilty ambition equal to this atrocious crime? A peculiar education was necessary to this bold wickedness. Here all is plain again. Slavery —the peculiar institution— is aptly fitted to produce just such patriots, who first plunder and then seek to destroy their country. A system which rewards labor with stripes and chains!— which robs the slave of his manhood, and the master of all just consideration for the rights of his fellow-man — has prepared the characters — male and female — that figure in this Rebellion — and for all its coldblooded and hellish atrocities. In all the most horrid details of torture, starvation and murder, in the treatment of our prisoners, I beheld the features of the monster in whose presence I was born, and that is Slavery. From no source less foul and wicked could such a Rebellion come. I need not dwell here. The country knows the story by heart. But I am one of those who think this Rebellion —inaugurated and carried on for a cause so unspeakably guilty and distinguished by barbarities which would extort a cry of shame from the painted savage— is quite enough for the whole lifetime of any one nation —though that lifetime should cover the space of a thousand years. We ought not to want a repetition of it —nor can we wisely risk a possible repetition of it. Looking at the matter from no higher ground than patriotism — setting aside the high considerations of justice, liberty, progress, and civilization — the American people should resolve that this shall be the last slaveholding Rebellion that shall ever curse this continent. Let the War cost much or cost little — let it be long or short — the work now begun should suffer no pause, no abatement, until it is done and done forever.

I know that many are appalled and disappointed by the apparently interminable character of this war. I am neither appalled nor disappointed. Without pretending to any higher wisdom than other men, I know well enough and often said it — Once let the North and South confront each other on the battlefield, and Slavery and Freedom be the inspiring motives of the respective sections, the contest will be fierce, long and sanguinary. Gov. Seymour charges us with prolonging the war, and I say the longer the better if it must be so — in order to put an end to the hell black cause out of which the Rebellion has risen.

Say not that I am indifferent to the horrors and hardships of the war. I am not indifferent. In common with the American people generally, I feel the prolongation of the war a heavy calamity — private as well [as] public. There are vacant spaces at my hearthstone which I shall rejoice to see filled again by the boys who once occupied them — but which cannot be thus filled while the war lasts — for they have enlisted — "during the war."

But even from the length of this struggle, we who mourn over it may well enough draw some consolation when we reflect upon the vastness and grandeur of its mission. The world has witnessed many wars — and history records and perpetuates their memory, but the world has not seen a nobler and grander war than that which the loyal people of this country are now waging against the slaveholding Rebels. The blow we strike is not merely to free a country or continent — but the whole world from Slavery — for when Slavery falls here — it will fall everywhere. We have no business to mourn over our mission. We are writing the statutes of eternal justice and liberty in the blood of the worst of tyrants as a warning to all aftercomers. We should rejoice that there was moral life and health enough in us to stand in our appointed place, and do this great service for mankind.

It is true that the war seems long. But this very slow progress is an essential element of its effectiveness. Like the slow convalescence of some patients the fault is less chargeable to the medicine than to the deep-seated character of the disease. We were in a very low condition before the remedy was applied. The whole head was sick and the whole heart faint. Dr. Buchanan and his Democratic friends had given us up, and were preparing to celebrate the nation's funeral. We had been drugged nearly to death by Pro-Slavery compromises. A radical change was needed in our whole system. Nothing is better calculated to effect the desired change than the slow, steady and certain progress of the war.

I know that this view of the case is not very consoling to the peace Democracy. I was not sent and am not come to console this branch of our political church. They regard this grand moral revolution in the mind and heart of the nation as the most distressing attribute of the war, and howl over it like certain characters of whom we read — who thought themselves tormented before their time.

Upon the whole, I like their mode of characterizing the war. They charge that it is no longer conducted upon constitutional principles. The same was said by Breckinridge and Vallandigham. They charge that it is not waged to establish the Union as it was. The same idea has occurred to Jefferson Davis. They charge that this is a war for the subjugation of the South. In a word, that it is an Abolition war.

For one, I am not careful to deny this charge. But it is instructive to observe how this charge is brought and how it is met. Both warn us of danger. Why is this war fiercely denounced as an Abolition war? I answer, because the nation has long and bitterly hated Abolition, and the enemies of the war confidently rely upon this hatred to serve the ends of treason. Why do the loyal people deny the charge? I answer, because they know that Abolition, though now a vast power, is still odious. Both the charge and the denial tell how the people hate and despise the only measure that can save the country.

An Abolition war! Well, let us thank the Democracy for teaching us this word. The charge in a comprehensive sense is most true, and it is not a pity that it is true, but it would be a vast pity if it were not true. Would that it were more true than it is. When our Government and people shall bravely avow this to be an Abolition war, then the country will be safe. Then our work will be fairly mapped out. Then the uplifted arm of the nation will swing unfettered to its work, and the spirit and power of the Rebellion will be broken. Had Slavery been abolished in the Border States at the very beginning of this war, as it ought to have been — had it been abolished in Missouri, as it would have been but for Presidential interference — there would now be no Rebellion in the Southern States — for instead of having to watch these Border

States, as they have done, our armies would have marched in overpowering numbers directly upon the Rebels and overwhelmed them. I now hold that a sacred regard for truth, as well as sound policy, makes it our duty to own and avow before Heaven and earth that this war is, and of right ought to be, an Abolition war.

The Abolition of Slavery is the comprehensive and logical object of the war, for it includes everything else which the struggle involves. It is a war for the union, a war for the Constitution, I admit; but it is logically such a war only in the sense that the greater includes the lesser. Slavery has proved itself the strong man of our national house. In every Rebel State it proved itself stronger than the Union, stronger than the Constitution, and stronger than Republican Institutions. It overrode majorities, made no account of the ballot-box, and had everything its own way. It is plain that this strong man must be bound and cast out of our house before Union, Constitution and Republican institutions can become possible. An Abolition war, therefore, includes Union, Constitution, Republican Institutions, and all else that goes to make up the greatness and glory of our common country. On the other hand, exclude Abolition, and you exclude all else for which you are fighting.

The position of the Democratic party in relation to the war ought to surprise nobody. It is consistent with the history of the party for thirty years past. Slavery, and only Slavery, has been its recognized master during all that time. It early won for itself the title of being the natural ally of the South and of Slavery. It has always been for peace or against peace, for war and against war, precisely as dictated by Slavery. Ask why it was for the Florida War, and it answers, Slavery. Ask why it was for the Mexican War, and it answers, Slavery. Ask why it was for the annexation of Texas, and it answers, Slavery. Ask why it was opposed to the *habeas corpus* when a negro was the applicant, and it answers, Slavery. Ask why it is now in favor of the *habeas corpus*, when Rebels and traitors are the applicants for its benefits, and it answers, Slavery. Ask why it was for mobbing down freedom of speech a few years ago, when that freedom was claimed by the Abolitionists, and it answers, Slavery. Ask why it now asserts freedom of speech, when sympathizers with traitors claim that freedom, and again Slavery is the answer. Ask why it denied the right of a State to protect itself against possible abuses of the Fugitive-Slave bill, and you have the same old answer. Ask why it now asserts the sovereignty of the States separately, as against the States united, and again Slavery is the answer. Ask why it was opposed to giving persons claimed as fugitive slaves a jury trial before returning them to slavery; ask why it is now in favor of giving jury trial to traitors before sending them to the forts for safe keeping; ask why it was for war at the beginning of the Rebellion; ask why it has attempted to embarrass and hinder the loyal Government at every step of its progress, and you have but one answer, Slavery.

The fact is, the party in question, I say nothing of individual men who were once members of it, has had but one vital and animating principle for thirty years, and that has been the same old horrible and hell-born principle of Negro Slavery.

It has now assumed a saintly character. Its members would receive the benediction due to peacemakers. At one time they would stop bloodshed at the South by inaugurating bloody revolution at the North. The livery of peace is a beautiful livery, but in this case it is a stolen livery and sits badly on the wearer. These new apostles of peace call themselves Peace Democrats, and boast that they belong to the only party which can restore the country to peace. I neither dispute their title nor the pretensions founded upon it. The best that can be said of the peacemaking ability of this class of men is their bitterest condemnation. It consists in their known treachery to the loyal Government. They have but to cross the Rebel lines to be hailed by the traitors as countrymen, clansmen, kinsmen, and brothers beloved in a common conspiracy. But, fellow-citizens, I have far less solicitude about the position and the influence of this party than I have about that of the great loyal party of the country. We have much less to fear from the bold and shameless wickedness of the one than from the timid and shortsighted policy of the other.

I know we have recently gained a great political victory; but it remains to be seen whether we shall wisely avail ourselves of its manifest advantages. There is danger that, like some of our Generals in the field, who, after soundly whipping the foe, generously allow him time to retreat in order, reorganize his forces, and intrench himself in a new and stronger position, where it will require more power and skill to dislodge him than was required to vanquish him in the first instance. The game is now in our hands. We can put an end to this disloyal party by putting an end to Slavery. While the Democratic party is in existence as an organization, we are in danger of a slaveholding peace, and of Rebel rule. There is but one way to avert this calamity, and that is, destroy Slavery and enfranchise the Black man while we have the power. While there is a vestige of Slavery remaining, it will unite the South with itself, and carry with it the Democracy of the North. The South united and the North divided, we shall be hereafter as heretofore, firmly held under the heels of Slavery.

Here is a part of the platform of principles upon which it seems to me every loyal man should take his stand at this hour:

First: That this war, which we are compelled to wage against slaveholding Rebels and traitors, at untold cost of blood and treasure, shall be, and of right ought to be, an Abolition War.

Secondly: That we, the loyal people of the North and of the whole country, while determined to make this a short and final war, will offer no peace, accept no peace, consent to no peace, which shall not be to all intents and purposes an Abolition peace.

Thirdly: That we regard the whole colored population of the country, in the loyal as well as in the disloyal States, as our countrymen — valuable in peace as laborers, valuable in war as soldiers — entitled to all the rights, protection, and opportunities for achieving distinction enjoyed by any other class of our countrymen.

Fourthly: Believing that the white race has nothing to fear from fair competition with the Black race, and that the freedom and elevation of one race are not to be purchased or in any manner rightfully subserved by the disfranchisement of another, we shall favor immediate and unconditional emancipation in all the States, invest the Black man everywhere with the right to vote and to be voted for, and remove all discriminations against his rights on account of his color, whether as a citizen or as a soldier.

Ladies and gentlemen, there was a time when I hoped that events unaided by discussions would couple this Rebellion and Slavery in a common grave. But as I have before intimated, the facts do still fall short of our hopes. The question as to what shall be done with Slavery — and more especially what shall be done with the Negro — threaten to remain open questions for some time yet.

It is true we have the Proclamation of January, 1863. It was a vast and glorious step in the right direction. But unhappily, excellent as that paper is — and much as it has accomplished temporarily — it settles nothing. It is still open to decision by courts, canons and Congresses. I have applauded that paper and do now applaud it, as a wise measure — while I detest the motive and principle upon which it is based. By it the holding and flogging of Negroes is the exclusive luxury of loyal men.

Our chief danger lies in the absence of all moral feeling in the utterances of our rulers. In his letter to Mr. Greeley the President told the country virtually that the abolition or non-abolition of Slavery was a matter of indifference to him. He would save the Union with Slavery or without Slavery. In his last Message he shows the same moral indifference, by saying as he does say that he had hoped that the Rebellion could be put down without the abolition of Slavery.

When the late Stephen A. Douglas uttered the sentiment that he did not care whether Slavery were voted up or voted down in the Territories, we thought him lost to all genuine feeling on the subject, and no man more than Mr. Lincoln denounced that sentiment as unworthy of the lips of any American statesman. But today, after nearly three years of a Slaveholding Rebellion, we find Mr. Lincoln uttering substantially the same heartless sentiments. Douglas wanted Popular Sovereignty; Mr. Lincoln wants the Union. Now did a warm heart and a high moral feeling control the utterances of the President, he would welcome, with joy unspeakable and full of glory, the opportunity afforded by the Rebellion to free the country from the matchless crime and infamy. But policy, policy, everlasting policy, has robbed our statesmanship of all soul-moving utterances.

The great misfortune is and has been during all the progress of this war, that the Government and loyal people have not understood and accepted its true mission. Hence we have been floundering in the depths of dead issues. Endeavoring to impose old and worn-out conditions upon new relations — putting new wine into old bottles, new cloth into old garments, and thus making the rent worse than before.

Had we been wise, we should have recognized the war at the outset as at once the signal and the necessity for a new order of social and political relations among the whole people. We could, like the ancients, discern the face of the sky, but not the signs of the times. Hence we have been talking of the importance of carrying on the war within the limits of a Constitution broken down by the very people in whose behalf the Constitution is pleaded! Hence we have from the first been deluding ourselves with the miserable dream, that the old Union can be revived in the States where it has been abolished.

Now, we of the North have seen many strange things, and may see many more; but that old Union, whose canonized bones we saw hearsed in death and inurned under the frowning battlements of Sumter, we shall never see again while the world standeth. The issue before us is a living issue. We are not fighting for the dead past, but for the living present and the glorious future. We are not fighting for the old Union, nor for anything like it, but for that which is ten thousand times more important; and that thing, crisply rendered, is National unity. Both sections have tried Union. It has failed.

The lesson for the statesman at this hour is to discover and apply some principle of Government which shall produce unity of sentiment, unity of idea, unity of object. Union without unity is, as we have seen, body without soul, marriage without love, a barrel without hoops, which falls at the first touch.

The statesmen of the South understood this matter earlier and better than the statesmen of the North. The dissolution of the Union on the old bases of compromise, was plainly foreseen and predicted 30 years ago. Mr. Calhoun and not Mr. Seward, is the original author of the doctrine of the irrepressible conflict. The South is logical and consistent. Under the teachings of their great leader they admit into their form of Government no disturbing force. They have based their Confederacy squarely on their corner-stone. Their two great, and all commanding ideas are first, that Slavery is right, and second, that the slaveholders are a superior order or class. Around these two ideas their manners, morals, politics, religion, and laws revolve. Slavery being right, all that is inconsistent with its entire security is necessarily wrong, and of course ought to be put down. There is no flaw in their logic.

They first endeavored to make the Federal Government stand upon their accursed corner-stone; and we but barely escaped, as you well know, that calamity. Fugitive Slave laws, Slavery Extension laws, and Dred Scott decisions were among the steps to get the nation squarely upon the corner-stone now chosen by the Confederate States. The loyal North is less logical, less consistent, and less definite in regard to the necessity of principles of National Unity. Yet, unconsciously to ourselves, and against our own prot-estations, we are in reality, like the South, fighting for national unity — a unity of which the great principles of liberty and equality, and not Slavery and class superiority, are the cornerstone.

Long before this rude and terrible war came to tell us of a broken Constitution and a dead Union, the better portion of the loyal people had outlived and outgrown what they had been taught to believe were the requirements of the old Union. We had come to detest the principle by which Slavery had a strong representation in Congress. We had come to abhor the idea of being called upon to suppress slave insurrections. We had come to be ashamed of slave-hunting, and being made the watchdogs of slave-holders, who were too proud to scent out and hunt down their slaves for themselves. We had so far outlived the old Union four years ago that we thought the little finger of the hero of Harper's Ferry of more value to the world struggling for liberty than all the first families of old Virginia put together.

What business, then, have we to be pouring out our treasure and shedding our best blood like water for that old worn-out, dead and buried Union, which had already become a calamity and a curse? The fact is, we are not fighting for any such thing, and we ought to come out under our own true colors, and let the South and the whole world know that we don't want and will not have anything analogous to the old Union.

What we now want is a country — a free country — a country nowhere saddened by the footprints of a single slave — and nowhere cursed by the presence of a slaveholder. We want a country, and we are fighting for a country, which shall not brand the Declaration of Independence as a lie. We want a country whose fundamental institutions we can proudly defend before the highest intelligence and civilization of the age. Hitherto we have opposed European scorn of our Slavery with a blush of shame as our best defense. We now want a country in which the obligations of patriotism shall not conflict with fidelity to justice and Liberty. We want a country, and are fighting for a country, which shall be free from sectional political parties — free from sectional religious denominations — free from sectional benevolent associations — free from every kind and description of sect, party, and combination of a sectional character. We want a country where men may assemble from any part of it, without prejudice to their interests or peril to their persons. We are in fact, and from absolute necessity, transplanting the whole South with the higher civilization of the North. The New England schoolhouse is bound to take the place of the Southern whipping-post. Not because we love the Negro, but the nation; not because we prefer to do this, because we must or give up the contest, and give up the country. We want a country, and are fighting for a country, where social intercourse and commercial relations shall neither be embarrassed nor embittered by the imperious exactions of an insolent slaveholding Oligarchy, which required Northern merchants to sell their souls as a condition precedent to selling their goods. We want a country, and are fighting for a country, through the length and breadth of which the literature and learning of any section of it may float to its extremities unimpaired, and thus become the common property of all the people — a country in which no man shall be fined for reading a book, or imprisoned for selling a book — a country where no man can be imprisoned or flogged or sold for learning to read, or teaching a fellow mortal how to read. We want a country, and are fighting for a country, in any part of which to be called an American citizen, shall mean as much as it did to be called a Roman citizen in the palmiest days of the Roman Empire.

We have heard much in other days of manifest destiny. I don't go all the lengths to which such theories are pressed, but I do believe that it is the manifest destiny of this war to unify and reorganize the institutions of this country — and that herein is the secret of the strength, the fortitude, the persistent energy, in a word the sacred significance of this war. Strike out the high ends and aims thus indicated, and the war would appear to the impartial eye of an onlooking world little better than a gigantic enterprise for shedding human blood.

A most interesting and gratifying confirmation of this theory of its mission is furnished in the varying fortunes of the struggle itself. Just in proportion to the progress made in taking upon itself the character I have ascribed to it, has the war prospered and the Rebellion lost ground.

Justice and humanity are often overpowered — but they are persistent and eternal forces — and fearful to contend against. Let but our rulers place the Government fully within these trade winds of Omnipotence, and the hand of death is upon the Confederate Rebels. A war waged as ours seemed to be at first, merely for power and empire, repels sympathy though supported by legitimacy. If Ireland should strike for independence tomorrow, the sympathy of this country would be with her, and I doubt if American statesmen would be more discreet in the expression of their opinions of the merits of the contest, than British statesmen have been concerning the merits of ours. When we were merely fighting for the old Union the world looked coldly upon our Government. But now the world begins to see something more than legitimacy — something more than national pride. It sees national wisdom aiming at national unity; and national justice breaking the chains of a long enslaved people. It is this new complexion of our cause which warms our hearts and strengthens our hands at home, disarms our enemies and increases our friends abroad. It is this more than all else which has carried consternation into the blood-stained halls of the South. It has sealed the fiery and scornful lips of the Roebucks and Lindsays of England, and caused even the eloquent Mr. Gladstone to restrain the expression of his admiration for Jeff. Davis and his Rebel nation. It has placed the broad arrow of British suspicion on the prows of the Rebel rams in the Mersey, and performed a like service for those in France. It has driven Mason, the shameless man-hunter, from London, where he never should have been allowed to stay for an hour, except as a bloodhound is tolerated in Regent Park for exhibition.

We have had from the first warm friends in England. We owe a debt of respect and gratitude to William Edward Forster, John Bright, Richard Cobden, and other British statesmen, in that they outran us in comprehending the high character of our struggle. They saw that this must be a war for human nature, and walked by faith to its defense while all was darkness about us — while we were yet conducting it in profound reverence for Slavery.

I know we are not to be praised for this changed character of the war. We did our very best to prevent it. We had but one object at the beginning, and that was, as I have said, the restoration of the old Union; and for the first two years the war was kept to that object strictly, and you know full well and bitterly with what results. I will not stop here to blame and denounce the past; but I will say that most of the blunders and disasters of the earlier part of the war might have been avoided had our armies and Generals not repelled the only true friends the Union cause had in the Rebel States. The Army of the Potomac took up an anti-Negro position from the first, and has not entirely renounced it yet. The colored people told me a few days ago in Washington that they were the victims of the most brutal treatment by these Northern soldiers when they first came there. But let that pass. Few men, however great their wisdom, are permitted to see the end from the beginning. Events are mightier than our rulers, and these Divine forces, with overpowering logic, have fixed upon this war, against the wishes of our Government, the comprehensive character and mission I have ascribed to it. The collecting of revenue in the Rebel ports, the repossession of a few forts and arsenals and other public property stolen by the Rebels, have almost disappeared from the recollection of the people. The war has been a growing war in every sense of the word. It began weak, and has risen strong. It began low, and has risen high. It began narrow, and has become broad.

It began with few, and now, behold, the country is full of armed men, ready, with courage and fortitude, to make the wisest and best idea of American statesmanship the law of the land.

Let, then, the war proceed in its strong, high, and broad course till the Rebellion is put down and our country is saved beyond the necessity of being saved again!

I have already hinted at our danger. Let me be a little more direct and pronounced.

The Democratic party, though defeated in the elections last Fall, is still a power. It is the ready organized nucleus of a powerful Pro-Slavery and Pro-Rebel reaction. Though it has lost in numbers, it retains all the elements of its former power and malevolence.

That party has five very strong points in its favor, and its public men and journals know well how to take advantage of them.

First: There is the absence of any deep moral feeling among the loyal people against Slavery itself — their feeling against it being on account of its rebellion against the Government, and not because it is a stupendous crime against human nature.

Secondly: The vast expense of the war and the heavy taxes in money as well as men which the war requires for its prosecution. Loyalty has a strong back, but taxation has often broken it.

Thirdly: The earnest desire for peace which is shared by all classes except Government contractors who are making money out of the war; a feeling which may be kindled to a flame by any serious reverses to our arms. It is silent in victory but vehement and dangerous in defeat.

Fourthly: And superior to all others, is the national prejudice and hatred toward the colored people of the country, a feeling which has done more to encourage the hopes of the Rebels than all other powers beside.

Fifthly: An Abolitionist is an object of popular dislike. The guilty Rebel who with broad blades and bloody hands seeks the life of the nation, is at this hour more acceptable to the northern Democracy than an Abolitionist guilty of no crime. Whatever may be a man's abilities, virtue, or service, the fact that he is an Abolitionist makes him an object of popular hate.

Upon these five strings the Democracy still have hopes of playing themselves into power, and not without reason. While our Government has the meanness to ask Northern colored men to give up the comfort of home, good wages, and personal security, to join the army, endure untold hardships, peril health, limbs and life itself, in its defense, and then degrades them in the eyes of other soldiers, by offering them the paltry sum of $7 per month, and refuses to reward their valor with even the hope of promotion — the Democratic party may well enough presume upon the strength of popular prejudice for support.

While our Republican Government at Washington makes color and not character the criterion of promotion in the army, and degrades colored commissioned officers at New Orleans below the rank to which even the Rebel Government had elevated them, I think we are in danger of a compromise with Slavery.

Our hopeful Republican friends tell me this is impossible — that the day of compromise with Slavery is past. This may do for some men, but it will not do for me.

The Northern people have always been remarkably confident of their own virtue. They are hopeful to the last. Twenty years ago we hoped that Texas could not be annexed; but if that could not be prevented we hoped that she would come in as a Free State. Thirteen years ago we were quite sure that no such abomination as the Fugitive Slave Bill could get itself on our National statute book; but when it got there we were equally sure that it never could be enforced. Four years ago we were sure that the Slave States would not rebel, but if they did we were sure it would be a very short rebellion. I know that times have changed very rapidly, and that we have changed with them. Nevertheless, I know also that we are the same old American people, and that what we have done once we may possibly do again. The leaven of compromise is among us — I repeat, while we have a Democratic party at the North trimming its sails to catch the Southern breeze in the next Presidential election, we are in danger of compromise. Tell me not of amnesties and oaths of allegiance. They are valueless in the presence of twenty hundred millions invested in human flesh. Let but the little finger of Slavery get back into this Union, and in one year you shall see its whole body again upon our backs.

While a respectable colored man or woman can be kicked out of the commonest street car in New York — where any white ruffian may ride unquestioned — we are in danger of a compromise with Slavery. While the North is full of such papers as The New York *World*, *Express*, and *Herald*, firing the nation's heart with hatred to Negroes and Abolitionists, we are in danger of a slaveholding peace. While the major part of all Anti-Slavery profession is based upon devotion to the Union rather than hostility to Slavery, there is danger of a slaveholding peace. Until we shall see the election of November next, and know that it has resulted in the election of a sound Anti-Slavery man as President, we shall be in danger of a slaveholding compromise. Indeed, so long as Slavery has any life left in it, anywhere in the country, we are in danger of such a compromise.

Then there is the danger arising from the impatience of the people on account of the prolongation of the war. I know the American people. They are an impulsive people, impatient of delay, clamorous for change — and often look for results out of all proportion to the means employed in attaining them.

You and I know that the mission of this war is National regeneration. We know and consider that a nation is not born in a day. We know that large bodies move slowly — and often seem to move thus — when, could we perceive their actual velocity, we should be astonished at its greatness. A great battle lost or won is easily described, understood and appreciated, but the moral growth of a great nation requires reflection, as well as observation, to appreciate it. There are vast numbers of voters, who make no account of the moral growth of the nation, and who only look at the war as a calamity to be endured only so long as they have no power to arrest it. Now, this is just the sort of people whose vote may turn the scale against us in the last event.

Thoughts of this kind tell me that there never was a time when Anti-Slavery work was more needed than now. The day that shall see the Rebels at our feet, their weapons flung away, will be the day of trial. We have need to prepare for that trial. We have long been saved a Pro-Slavery peace by the stubborn, unbending persistence of the Rebels. Let them bend as they will bend — there will come the test of our sternest virtues.

I have now given, very briefly, some of the grounds of danger. A word as to the grounds of hope. The best that can be offered is, that we have made progress — vast and striking progress — within the last two years.

President Lincoln introduced his administration to the country as one which would faithfully catch, hold, and return runaway slaves to their masters. He avowed his determination to protect and defend the slaveholder's right to plunder the Black laborer of his hard earnings. Europe was assured by Mr. Seward that no slave should gain his freedom by this war. Both the President and the Secretary of State have made progress since then.

Our Generals, at the beginning of the war, were horribly Pro-Slavery. They took to slave-catching and slave-killing like ducks to water. They are now very generally and very earnestly in favor of putting an end to Slavery. Some of them, like Hunter and Butler, because they hate Slavery on its own account, and others, because Slavery is in arms against the Government.

The Rebellion has been a rapid educator. Congress was the first to respond to the instinctive judgment of the people, and fixed the broad brand of its reprobation upon slave-hunting in shoulder-straps. Then came very temperate talk about confiscation, which soon came to be pretty radical talk. Then came propositions for Border-State, gradual, compensated, colonized Emancipation. Then came the threat of a proclamation, and then came the proclamation. Meanwhile the negro had passed along from a loyal spade and pickax to a Springfield rifle.

Haiti and Liberia are recognized. Slavery is humbled in Maryland, threatened in Tennessee, stunned nearly to death in Western Virginia, doomed in Missouri, trembling in Kentucky, and gradually melting away before our arms in the rebellious States.

The hour is one of hope as well as danger. But whatever may come to pass, one thing is clear: The principles involved in the contest, the necessities of both sections of the country, the obvious requirements of the age, and every suggestion of enlightened policy demand the utter extirpation of Slavery from every foot of American soil, and the enfranchisement of the entire colored population of the country. Elsewhere we may find peace, but it will be a hollow and deceitful peace. Elsewhere we may find prosperity, but it will be a transient prosperity. Elsewhere we may find greatness and renown, but if these are based upon anything less substantial than justice they will vanish, for righteousness alone can permanently exalt a nation.

I end where I began — no war but an Abolition war; no peace but an Abolition peace; liberty for all, chains for none; the Black man a soldier in war, a laborer in peace; a voter at the South as well as at the North; America his permanent home, and all Americans his fellow-countrymen. Such, fellow-citizens, is my idea of the mission of the war. If accomplished, our glory as a nation will be complete, our peace will flow like a river, and our foundations will be the everlasting rocks.[78]

---

[78] Lecture delivered at The Cooper Union in New York and several other venues during the winter of 1863–64 and published in *New York Daily Tribune*, January 14th, 1864.

Third Existential Meditation on Slave Revolt – As I have intimated that my hardships were much greater during the first six months of my stay at Covey's than during the remainder of the year, and as the change in my condition was owing to causes which may help the reader to a better understanding of human nature, when subjected to the terrible extremities of slavery, I will narrate the circumstances of this change, although I may seem thereby to applaud my own courage.

You have, dear reader, seen me humbled, degraded, broken down, enslaved, and brutalized; and you understand how it was done; now let us see the converse of all this, and how it was brought about; and this will take us through the year 1834.

On one of the hottest days of the month of August of the year just mentioned, had the reader been passing through Covey's farm, he might have seen me at work in what was called the "treading-yard" a yard upon which wheat was trodden out from the straw by the horses' feet. I was there at work feeding the "fan," or rather bringing wheat to the fan, while Bill Smith was feeding. Our force consisted of Bill Hughes, Bill Smith, and a slave by the name of Eli, the latter having been hired for the occasion. The work was simple, and required strength and activity, rather than any skill or intelligence; and yet to one entirely unused to such work, it came very hard. The heat was intense and overpowering, and there was much hurry to get the wheat trodden out that day, through the fan; since if that work was done an hour before sundown, the hands would have, according to a promise of Covey, that hour added to their night's rest. I was not behind any of them in the wish to complete the day's work before sundown, and hence I struggled with all my might to get it forward. The promise of one hour's repose on a week day was sufficient to quicken my pace, and to spur me on to extra endeavor. Besides, we had all planned to go fishing, and I certainly wished to have a hand in that. But I was disappointed, and the day turned out to be one of the bitterest I ever experienced.

About three o'clock, while the sun was pouring down his burning rays, and not a breeze was stirring, I broke down; my strength failed me; I was seized with a violent aching of the head, attended with extreme dizziness, and trembling in every limb. Finding what was coming, and feeling that it would never do to stop work, I nerved myself up and staggered on, until I fell by the side of the wheat fan, with a feeling that the earth had fallen in upon me. This brought the entire work to a dead stand. There was work for four: each one had his part to perform, and each part depended on the other, so that when one stopped, all were compelled to stop. Covey, who had become my dread, was at the house, about a hundred yards from where I was fanning, and instantly, upon hearing the fan stop, he came down to the treading-yard to inquire into the cause of the interruption. Bill Smith told him that I was sick and unable longer to bring wheat to the fan.

I had by this time crawled away in the shade, under the side of a post-and-rail fence, and was exceedingly ill. The intense heat of the sun, the heavy dust rising from the fan, and the stooping to take up the wheat from the yard, together with the hurrying to get through, had caused a rush of blood to my head. In this condition Covey, finding out where I was, came to me, and after standing over me a while asked what the matter was. I told him as well as I could, for it was with difficulty that I could speak. He gave me a savage kick in the side which jarred my whole frame, and commanded me to get up. The monster had obtained complete control over me, and if he had commanded me to do any possible thing I should, in my then state of mind, have endeavored to comply. I made an effort to rise, but fell back in the attempt before gaining my feet. He gave me another heavy kick, and again told me to rise. I again tried, and succeeded in standing up; but upon stooping to get the tub with which I was feeding the fan I again staggered and fell to the ground. I must have so fallen had I been sure that a hundred bullets would have pierced me through as the consequence. While down in this sad condition, and perfectly helpless, the merciless negro-breaker took up the hickory slab with which Hughes had been striking off the wheat to a level with the sides of the half-bushel measure, (a very hard weapon), and, with the edge of it, he dealt me a heavy blow on my head which made a large gash, and caused the blood to run freely, saying at the same time, "If you have got the headache I'll cure you." This done, he ordered me again to rise, but I made no effort to do so, for I had now made up my mind that it was useless and that the heartless villain might do his worst. He could but kill me and that might put me out of my misery. Finding me unable to rise, or rather despairing of my doing so, Covey left me, with a view to getting on with the work without me. I was bleeding very freely, and my face was soon covered with my warm blood. Cruel and merciless as was the motive that dealt that blow, the wound was a fortunate one for me. Bleeding was never more efficacious. The pain in my head speedily abated, and I was soon able to rise. Covey had, as I have said, left me to my fate, and the question was, shall I return to my work, or shall I find my way to St. Michaels and make Capt. Auld acquainted with the atrocious cruelty of his brother Covey, and beseech him to get me another master? Remembering the object he had in view in placing me under the management of Covey, and further, his cruel treatment of my poor crippled cousin Henny, and his meanness in the matter of feeding and clothing his slaves, there was little ground to hope for a favorable reception at the hands of Capt. Thomas Auld. Nevertheless, I resolved to go straight to him, thinking that, if not animated by motives of humanity, he might be induced to interfere on my behalf from selfish considerations. "He cannot," I thought, "allow his property to be thus bruised and battered, marred and defaced, and I will go to him about the matter."

In order to get to St. Michaels by the most favorable and direct road I must walk seven miles, and this, in my sad condition, was no easy performance. I had already lost much blood, I was exhausted by over-exertion, my sides were sore from the heavy blows planted there by the stout boots of Mr. Covey, and I was in every way in an unfavorable plight for the journey. I however watched my chance while the cruel and cunning Covey was looking in an opposite direction, and started off across the field for St. Michaels. This was a daring step. If it failed it would only exasperate Covey and increase during the remainder of my term of service under him, the rigors of my bondage. But the step was taken and I must go forward. I succeeded in getting nearly half way across the broad field toward the woods, when Covey observed me. I was still bleeding and the exertion of running had started the blood afresh. "Come back! Come back!" he vociferated, with threats of what he would do if I did not instantly return. But, disregard-

ding his calls and threats, I pressed on toward the
woods as fast as my feeble state would allow. Seeing
no signs of my stopping, he caused his horse to be
brought out and saddled, as if he intended to pursue
me. The race was now to be an unequal one, and
thinking I might be overhauled by him if I kept the
main road, I walked nearly the whole distance in the
woods, keeping far enough from the road to avoid
detection and pursuit. But I had not gone far before
my little strength again failed me, and I was obliged to
lie down. The blood was still oozing from the wound
in my head, and for a time I suffered more than I can
describe. There I was in the deep woods, sick and
emaciated, bleeding and almost bloodless, and pursued by a wretch whose character for revolting cruelty
beggars all opprobrious speech. I was not without the
fear of bleeding to death. The thought of dying all
alone in the woods, and of being torn in pieces by the
buzzards, had not yet been rendered tolerable by my
many troubles and hardships, and I was glad when the
shade of the trees and the cool evening breeze combined with my matted hair to stop the flow of blood.
After lying there about three-quarters of an hour,
brooding over the singular and mournful lot to which
I was doomed, my mind passing over the whole scale
or circle of belief and unbelief, from faith in the overruling Providence of God, to the blackest atheism, I
again took up my journey toward St. Michaels, more

weary and sad than on the morning when I left Thomas Auld's for the home of Covey. I was barefooted, bare-headed, and in my shirt-sleeves. The way was through briers and bogs, and I tore my feet often during the journey. I was full five hours in going the seven or eight miles; partly because of the difficulties of the way, and partly because of the difficulties of the way, and partly because of the feebleness induced by my illness, bruises, and loss of blood.

On gaining my master's store, I presented an appearance of wretchedness and woe calculated to move any but a heart of stone. From the crown of my head to the sole of my feet, there were marks of blood. My hair was all clotted with dust and blood, and the back of my shirt was literally stiff with the same. Briers and thorns had scarred and torn my feet and legs. Had I escaped from a den of tigers, I could not have looked worse. In this plight I appeared before my professedly *Christian* master, humbly to invoke the interposition of his power and authority, to protect me from further abuse and violence. During the latter part of my tedious journey I had begun to hope that my master would now show himself in a nobler light than I had before seen him. But I was disappointed. I had jumped from a sinking ship into the sea. I had fled from a tiger to something worse. I told him as well as I could, all the circumstances; how I was endeavoring to please Covey; how hard I was at work in the present instance; how unwillingly I sank down under the heat, toil, and pain; the brutal manner in which Covey had kicked me in the side, the gash cut in my head; my hesitation about troubling him (Capt. Auld) with complaints; but that now I felt it would not be best longer to conceal from him the outrages committed from time to time upon me. At first Master Thomas seemed somewhat affected by the story of my wrongs, but he soon repressed whatever feeling he may have had, and became as cold and hard as iron. It was impossible, at first, as I stood before him, to seem indifferent. I distinctly saw his human nature asserting its conviction against the slave system, which made cases like mine possible; but, as I have said, humanity fell before the systematic tyranny of slavery. He first walked the floor, apparently much agitated by my story, and the spectacle I presented; but soon it was his turn to talk. He began moderately by finding excuses for Covey, and ended with a full justification of him, and a passionate condemnation of me. He had no doubt I deserved the flogging. He did not believe I was sick; I was only endeavoring to get rid of work. My dizziness was laziness, and Covey did right to flog me as he had done. After thus fairly annihilating me, and arousing himself by his eloquence, he fiercely demanded what I wished him to do in the case! With such a knock-down to all my hopes, and feeling as I did my entire subjection to his power,

I had very little heart to reply. I must not assert my innocence of the allegations he had piled up against me, for that would be impudence. The guilt of a slave was always and everywhere presumed, and the innocence of the slaveholder, or employer, was always asserted. The word of the slave against this presumption was generally treated as impudence, worthy of punishment. "Do you dare to contradict me, you rascal?" was a final silencer of counter-statements from the lips of a slave. Calming down a little, in view of my silence and hesitation, and perhaps a little touched at my forlorn and miserable appearance, he inquired again, what I wanted him to do? Thus invited a second time, I told him I wished him to allow me to get a new home, and to find a new master; that as sure as I went back to live again with Mr. Covey, I should be killed by him; that he would never forgive my coming home with complaints; that since I had lived with him he had almost crushed my spirit, and I believed he would ruin me for future service and that my life was not safe in his hands. This Master Thomas (*my brother in the church*) regarded as "nonsense." There was no danger that Mr. Covey would kill me; he was a good man, industrious and religious, and he would not think of removing me from that home; "besides," said he – and this I found was the most distressing thought of all to him – "if you should leave Covey now that your year is but half expired, I should lose your wages for the entire year. You belong to Mr. Covey for one year, and you *must go back* to him, come what will; and you must not trouble me with any more stories; and if you don't go immediately home, I'll get hold of you myself." This was just what I expected when I found he had prejudged the case against me. "But, sir," I said, "I am sick and tired, and I cannot get home tonight." At this he somewhat relented, and finally allowed me to stay the night, but said I must be off early in the morning, and concluded his directions by making me swallow a huge dose of Epsom salts, which was about the only medicine ever administered to slaves.

It was quite natural for Master Thomas to presume I was feigning sickness to escape work, for he probably thought that were he in the place of a slave, with no wages for his work, no praise for welldoing, no motive for toil but the lash, he would try every possible scheme by which to escape labor. I say I have no doubt of this; the reason is, that there were not, under the whole heavens, a set of men who cultivated such a dread of labor as did the slaveholders. The charge of laziness against the slaves was ever on their lips and was the standing apology for every species of cruelty and brutality. These men did indeed literally "bind heavy burdens, grievous to be borne, and laid them upon men's shoulders, but they themselves would not move them with one of their fingers."

Sleep does not always come to the relief of the weary in body, and broken in spirit; especially is it so when past troubles only foreshadow coming disasters. My last hope had been extinguished. My master, who I did not venture to hope would protect me *as a MAN*, had now refused to protect me *as his property*, and had cast back, covered with reproaches and bruises, into the hands of one who was a stranger to that mercy which is the soul of the religion he professed. May the reader never know what it is to spend such a night as to me was that which heralded my return to the den of horrors from which I had made a temporary escape.

I remained – sleep I did not – all night at St. Michaels, and in the morning (Saturday) I started off, obedient to the order of Master Thomas, feeling that I had no friend on earth, and doubting if I had one in heaven. I reached Covey's about nine o'clock; and just as I stepped into the field, before I had reached the house, true to his snakish habits, Covey darted out at me from a fence corner, in which he had secreted himself for the purpose of securing me. He was provided with a cowskin and a rope, and he evidently intended to tie me up, and wreak his vengeance on me to the fullest extent. I should have been an easy prey had he succeeded in getting his hands upon me, for I had taken no refreshment since noon on Friday; and this, with the other trying circumstances, had greatly reduced my strength. I, however, darted back into the woods before the ferocious hound could reach me, and buried myself in a thicket, where he lost sight of me. The cornfield afforded me shelter in getting to the woods. But for the tall corn, Covey would have overtaken me, and made me his captive. He was much chagrined that he did not, and gave up the chase very reluctantly, as I could see by his angry movements, as he returned to the house.

For a little time I was clear of Covey and his lash. I was in the wood, buried in its somber gloom and hushed in its solemn silence; hidden from all human eyes; shut in with nature and with nature's God, and absent from all human contrivances. Here was a good place to pray; to pray for help, for deliverance – a prayer I had often before made. But how could I pray? Covey could pray – Capt. Auld could pray. I would fain pray; but doubts arising, partly from my neglect of the means of grace and partly from the sham religion which everywhere prevailed, there was awakened in my mind a distrust of all religion and the conviction that prayers were unavailing and delusive.

Life in itself had almost become burdensome to me. All my outward relations were against me. I must stay here and starve, or go home to Covey's and have my flesh torn to pieces and my spirit humbled under his cruel lash. These were the alternatives before me. The day was long and irksome. I was weak from the toils of the previous day and from want of food and sleep, and I had been so little concerned about my appearance that I had not yet washed the blood from my garments. I was an object of horror, even to myself. Life in Baltimore, when most oppressive, was a paradise to this. What had I done, what had my parents done, that such a life as this should be mine? That day, in the woods, I would have exchanged my manhood for the brutehood of an ox.

Night came. I was still in the woods, and still unresolved what to do. Hunger had not yet pinched me to the point of going home, and I laid myself down in the leaves to rest; for I had been watching for hunters all day, but not being molested by them during the day, I expected no disturbance from them during the night. I had come to the conclusion that Covey relied upon hunger to drive me home, and in this I was quite correct, for he made no effort to catch me after the morning.

During the night I heard the step of a man in the woods. He was coming toward the place where I lay. A person lying still in the woods in the day-time has the advantage over one walking, and this advantage is much greater at night. I was not able to engage in a physical struggle, and I had recourse to the common resort of the weak. I hid myself in the leaves to prevent discovery. But as the night rambler in the woods drew nearer I found him to be a friend, not an enemy; a slave of Mr. William Groomes of Easton, a kindhearted fellow named "Sandy." Sandy lived that year with Mr. Kemp, about four miles from St. Michaels. He, like myself, had been hired out, but unlike myself had not been hired out to be broken. He was the husband of a free woman who lived in the lower part of "Poppie Neck," and he was now on his way through the woods to see her and to spend the Sabbath with her.

As soon as I had ascertained that the disturber of my solitude was not an enemy, but the good-hearted Sandy, – a man as famous among the slaves of the neighborhood for his good nature as for his good sense – I came out from my hiding-place and made myself known to him. I explained the circumstances of the past two days which had driven me to the woods, and he deeply compassionated my distress. It was a bold thing for him to shelter me, and I could not ask him to do so, for had I been found in his hut he would have suffered the penalty of thirty-nine lashes on his bare back, if not something worse. But Sandy was too generous to permit the fear of punishment to prevent his relieving a brother bondman from hunger and exposure, and therefore, on his own motion, I accompanied him home to his wife – for the house and lot were hers, as she was a free woman. It was about midnight, but his wife was called up, a fire was made, some Indian meal was soon mixed with salt and water, and an ash-cake was baked in a hurry, to relieve my hunger. Sandy's wife was not behind him in kindness; both seemed to esteem it a privilege to succor me, for although I was hated by Covey and by my master I was loved by the colored people, because they thought I was hated for my knowledge, and persecuted because I was feared. I was the only slave in that region who could read or write. There had been one other man, belonging to Mr. Hugh Hamilton, who could read, but he, poor fellow, had, shortly after coming into the neighborhood, been sold off to the far south. I saw him in the cart, to be carried to Easton for sale, ironed and pinioned like a yearling for the slaughter. My knowledge was now the pride of my brother slaves, and no doubt Sandy felt on that account something of the general interest in me. The supper was soon ready, and though over the sea I have since feasted with honorables, lord mayors and aldermen, my supper on ash-cake and cold water, with Sandy, was the meal of all my life most sweet to my taste and now most vivid to my memory.

Supper over, Sandy and I went into a discussion of what was possible for me, under the perils and hardships which overshadowed my path. The question was, must I go back to Covey, or must I attempt to run away? Upon a careful survey the latter was found to be impossible; for I was on a narrow neck of land, every avenue from which would bring me in sight of pursuers. There was Chesapeake Bay to the right, and "Pot-pie" river to the left, and St. Michaels and its neighborhood occupied the only space through which there was any retreat.

I found Sandy an old adviser. He was not only a religious man, but he professed to believe in a system for which I have no name. He was a genuine African, and had inherited some of the so-called magical powers said to be possessed by the eastern nations. He told me that he could help me; that in those very woods there was an herb which in the morning might be found, possessing all the powers required for my protection (I put his words in my own language), and that if I would take his advice he would procure me the root of the herb of which he spoke. He told me, further, that if I would take that root and wear it on my right side it would be impossible for Covey to strike me a blow, and that, with this root about my person, no white man could whip me. He said he had carried it for years, and that he had fully tested its virtues. He had never received a blow from a slave-holder since he carried it, and he never expected to receive one, for he meant always to carry that root for protection. He knew Covey well, for Mrs. Covey was the daughter of Mrs. Kemp; and he (Sandy) had heard of the barbarous treatment to which I had been subjected, and he wanted to do something for me.

Now all this talk about the root was to me very absurd and ridiculous, if not positively sinful. I at first rejected the idea that the simple carrying a root on my right side (a root, by the way, over which I walked every time I went into the woods) could possess any such magic power as he ascribed to it, and I was, therefore, not disposed to cumber my pocket with it. I had a positive aversion to all pretenders to "divination." It was beneath one of my intelligence to countenance such dealings with the devil as this power implied. But with all my learning – it was really precious little – Sandy was more than a match for me. "My book-learning," he said, "had not kept Covey off me" (a powerful argument just then), and he entreated me, with flashing eyes, to try this. If it did me no good it could do me no harm, and it would cost me nothing any way. Sandy was so earnest and so confident of the good qualities of this weed that, to please him, I was induced to take it. He had been to me the good Samaritan, and had, almost providentially, found me and helped me when I could not help myself; how did I know but that the hand of the Lord was in it? With thoughts of this sort I took the roots from Sandy and put them in my right-hand pocket.

This was of course Sunday morning. Sandy now urged me to go home with all speed, and to walk up bravely to the house, as though nothing had happened. I saw in Sandy, with all his superstition, too deep an insight into human nature not to have some respect for his advice; and perhaps, too, a slight gleam or shadow of his superstition had fallen on me. At any rate, I started off toward Covey's, as directed. Having, the previous night, poured my griefs into Sandy's ears and enlisted him in my behalf, having made his wife a sharer in my sorrows, and having also become well refreshed by sleep and food, I moved off quite courageously toward the dreaded Covey's. Singularly enough, just as I entered the yardgate I met him and his wife on their way to church, dressed in their Sunday best, and looking as smiling as angels. His manner perfectly astonished me. There was some-thing really benignant in his countenance. He spoke to me as never before, told me that the pigs had got into the lot and he wished me to go to drive them out; inquired how I was, and seemed an altered man. This extraordinary conduct really made me begin to think that Sandy's herb had more virtue in it than I, in my pride, had been willing to allow, and, had the day been other than Sunday, I should have attributed Covey's altered manner solely to the power of the root. I suspected, however, that the Sabbath, not the root, was the real explanation of the change. His religion hindered him from breaking the Sabbath, but not from breaking my skin on any other day than Sunday. He had more respect for the day than for the man for whom the day was mercifully given; for while he would cut and slash my body during the week, he would on Sunday teach me the value of my soul, and the way of life and salvation by Jesus Christ.

All went well with me till Monday morning; and then, whether the root had lost its virtue, or whether my tormentor had gone deeper into the black art than I had, (as was sometimes said of him), or whether he had obtained a special indulgence for his faithful Sunday's worship, it is not necessary for me to know or to inform the reader; but this much I may say, the pious and benignant smile which graced the face of Covey on *Sunday* wholly disappeared on *Monday.*

Long before daylight I was called up to go feed, rub, and curry the horses. I obeyed the call, as I should have done had it been made at an earlier hour, for I had brought my mind to a firm resolve during that Sunday's reflection to obey every order, however unreasonable, if it were possible, and if Mr. Covey should then undertake to beat me to defend and protect myself to the best of my ability. My religious views on the subject of resisting my master had suffered a serious shock by the savage persecution to which I had been subjected, and my hands were no longer tied by my religion. Master Thomas's indifference had severed the last link. I had backslidden from this point in the slaves' religious creed, and I soon had occasion to make my fallen state known to my Sunday-pious brother, Covey.

While I was obeying his order to feed and get the
horses ready for the field, and when I was in the act of
going up the stable-loft, for the purpose of throwing
down some blades, Covey sneaked into the stable, in
his peculiar way, and seizing me suddenly by the leg,
he brought me to the stable-floor, giving my newly-
mended body a terrible jar. I now forgot all about my
roots, and remembered my pledge to stand up in my
own defense. The brute was skillfully endeavoring to
get a slip-knot on my legs, before I could draw up my
feet. As soon as I found what he was up to, I gave a
sudden spring (my two days' rest had been of much
service to me) and by that means, no doubt, he was
able to bring me to the floor so heavily. He was defeated in his plan of tying me. While down, he seemed
to think that he had me very securely in his power.
He little thought he was – as the rowdies say – "in" for
a "rough and tumble" fight; but such was the fact.
Whence came the daring spirit necessary to grapple
with a man who, eight-and-forty hours before, could,
with his slightest word, have made me tremble like a
leaf in a storm, I do not know; at any rate, I was
resolved to fight, and what was better still, I actually
was hard at it. The fighting madness had come upon
me, and I found my strong fingers firmly attached to
the throat of the tyrant, as heedless of consequences,
at the moment, as if we stood as equals before the
law. The very color of the man was forgotten. I felt

supple as a cat, and was ready for him at every turn. Every blow of his was parried, though I dealt no blows in return. I was strictly on the *defensive*, preventing him from injuring me, rather than trying to injure him. I flung him on the ground several times when he meant to have hurled me there. I held him so firmly by the throat that his blood followed my nails. He held me, and I held him.

All was fair thus far, and the contest was about equal. My resistance was entirely unexpected and Covey was taken all aback by it. He trembled in every limb. "*Are you going to resist*, you scoundrel?" said he. To which I returned a polite " *Yes, sir*," steadily gazing my interrogator in the eye, to meet the first approach or dawning of the blow which I expected my answer would call forth. But the conflict did not long remain equal. Covey soon cried lustily for help; not that I was obtaining any marked advantage over him, or was injuring him, but because he was gaining none over me, and was not able, single-handed, to conquer me. He called for his cousin Hughes to come to his assistance, and now the scene was changed. I was compelled to give blows, as well as to parry them, and since I was in any case to suffer for resistance, I felt (as the musty proverb goes) that I "might as well be hanged for an old sheep as a lamb." I was still defensive toward Covey, but aggressive toward Hughes, on whom, at his first approach, I dealt a blow which fairly sickened him. He went off, bending over with pain, and manifesting no disposition to come again within my reach. The poor fellow was in the act of trying to catch and tie my right hand, and while flattering himself with success, I gave him the kick which sent him staggering away in pain, at the same time that I held Covey with a firm hand.

Taken completely by surprise, Covey seemed to have lost his usual strength and coolness. He was frightened, and stood puffing and blowing, seemingly unable to command words or blows. When he saw that Hughes was standing half bent with pain, his courage quite gone, the cowardly tyrant asked if I "meant to persist in my resistance." I told him I "*did mean to resist*, come what might; that I had been treated like a brute during the last six months, and that I should stand it no longer." With that he gave me a shake, and attempted to drag me toward a stick of wood that was lying just outside the stable-door. He meant to knock me down with it; but, just as he leaned over to get the stick, I seized him with both hands, by the collar, and with a vigorous and sudden snatch brought my assailant harmlessly, his full length, on the not over-clean ground, for we were now in the cow-yard. He had selected the place for the fight, and it was but right that he should have all the advantages of his own selection.

By this time Bill, the hired man, came home. He had been to Mr. Helmsley's to spend Sunday with his nominal wife. Covey and I had been skirmishing from before daybreak till now. The sun was shooting his beams almost over the eastern woods, and we were still at it. I could not see where the matter was to terminate. He evidently was afraid to let me go, lest I should again make off to the woods, otherwise he would probably have obtained arms from the house to frighten me. Holding me, he called upon Bill to assist him. The scene here had something comic about it. Bill, who knew precisely what Covey wished him to do, affected ignorance, and pretended he did not know what to do. "What shall I do, Master Covey?" said Bill. "Take hold of him! take hold of him!" cried Covey. With a toss of his head, peculiar to Bill, he said: "Indeed, Master Covey, I want to go to work." "This is your work," said Covey; "take hold of him." Bill replied, with spirit: "My master hired me here to work, and not to help you whip Frederick." It was my turn to speak. "Bill," said I, "don't put your hands on me." To which he replied: "My God, Frederick, I ain't goin' to tech ye"; and Bill walked off, leaving Covey and myself to settle our differences as best we might.

But my present advantage was threatened when I saw Caroline (the slave woman of Covey) coming to the cow-yard to milk, for she was a powerful woman, and could have mastered me easily, exhausted as I was.

As soon as she came near, Covey attempted to rally her to his aid. Strangely and fortunately, Caroline was in no humor to take a hand in any such sport. We were all in open rebellion that morning. Caroline answered the command of her master to "take hold of me," precisely as Bill had done, but in her it was at far greater peril, for she was the slave of Covey, and he could do what he pleased with her. It was not so with Bill, and Bill knew it. Samuel Harris, to whom Bill belonged, did not allow his slaves to be beaten unless they were guilty of some crime which the law would punish. But poor Caroline, like myself, was at the mercy of the merciless Covey, nor did she escape the dire effects of her refusal: he gave her several sharp blows.

At length (two hours had elapsed) the contest was given over. Letting go of me, puffing and blowing at a great rate, Covey said: "Now, you scoundrel, go to your work; I would not have whipped you half so hard if you had not resisted." The fact was, he had not whipped me at all. He had not, in all the scuffle, drawn a single drop of blood from me. I had drawn blood from him, and should even without this satisfaction have been victorious, because my aim had not been to injure him, but to prevent his injuring me.

During the whole six months that I lived with Covey after this transaction, he never again laid the weight of his finger on me in anger. He would occasionally say he did not want to have to get hold of me again – a declaration which I had no difficulty in believing; and I had a secret feeling which answered, "You had better not wish to get hold of me again, for you will be likely to come off worse in a second fight than you did in the first."

This battle with Mr. Covey, undignified as it was and as I fear my narration of it is, was the turning-point in my "life as a slave." It rekindled in my breast the smouldering embers of liberty. It brought up my Baltimore dreams and revived a sense of my own manhood. I was a changed being after that fight. I was *nothing* before; *I was a man* now. It recalled to life my crushed self-respect, and my self-confidence, and inspired me with a renewed determination to be a *free man.* A man without force is without the essential dignity of humanity. Human nature is so constituted, that it cannot *honor* a helpless man, though it can *pity* him, and even this it cannot do long if signs of power do not arise.

He only can understand the effect of this combat on my spirit, who has himself incurred something, or hazarded something, in repelling the unjust and cruel aggressions of a tyrant. Covey was a tyrant and a cowardly one withal. After resisting him, I felt as I had never felt before. It was a resurrection from the dark and pestiferous tomb of slavery, to the heaven of comparative freedom. I was no longer a servile coward, trembling under the frown of a brother worm of the dust, but my long-cowed spirit was roused to an attitude of independence. I had reached the point at which I was *not afraid to die.* This spirit made me a freeman in *fact,* though I still remained a slave in *form.* When a slave cannot be flogged, he is more than half free. He has a domain as broad as his own manly heart to defend, and he is really "a power on earth." From this time until my escape from slavery, I was never fairly whipped. Several attempts were made, but they were always unsuccessful. Bruised I did get, but the instance I have described was the end of the brutification to which slavery had subjected me.

The reader may like to know why, after I had so grievously offended Mr. Covey, he did not have me taken in hand by the authorities; indeed, why the law of Maryland, which assigned hanging to the slave who resisted his master, was not put in force against me, at any rate why I was not taken up, as was usual in such cases, and publicly whipped as an example to other slaves, and as a means of deterring me from again committing the same offence. I confess that the easy manner in which I got off was always a surprise to me, and even now I cannot fully explain the cause, though the probability is that Covey was ashamed to have it known that he had been mastered by a boy of sixteen. He enjoyed the unbounded and very valuable reputation of being a first-rate overseer and negro-breaker, and by means of this reputation he was able to procure his hands at very trifling compensation and with very great ease. His interest and his pride would mutually suggest the wisdom of passing the matter by in silence. The story that he had undertaken to whip a lad and had been resisted, would of itself be damaging to him in the estimation of slaveholders.

It is perhaps not altogether creditable to my natural temper that after this conflict with Mr. Covey I did, at times, purposely aim to provoke him to an attack, by refusing to keep with the other hands in the field; but I could never bully him to another battle. I was determined on doing him serious damage if he ever again attempted to lay violent hands on me. "Hereditary bondmen, know ye not Who would be free, themselves must strike the blow?"[79]

---

[79] Excerpted from *Life and Times of Frederick Douglass* (Hartford, CT: Park Publishing Co., 1881).

Intellectual Resistance

First Existential Meditation on Intellectual Resistance – My new mistress proved to be all she appeared when I first met her at the door, a woman of the kindest heart and finest feelings. She had never had a slave under her control previously to myself, and prior to her marriage she had been dependent upon her own industry for a living. She was by trade a weaver; and by constant application to her business, she had been in a good degree preserved from the blighting and dehumanizing effects of slavery. I was utterly astonished at her goodness. I scarcely knew how to behave towards her. She was entirely unlike any other white woman I had ever seen. I could not approach her as I was accustomed to approach other white ladies. My early instruction was all out of place. The crouching servility, usually so acceptable a quality in a slave, did not answer when manifested toward her. Her favor was not gained by it; she seemed to be disturbed by it. She did not deem it impudent or unmannerly for a slave to look her in the face. The meanest slave was put fully at ease in her presence, and none left without feeling better for having seen her. Her face was made of heavenly smiles, and her voice of tranquil music.

But, alas! this kind heart had but a short time to remain such. The fatal poison of irresponsible power was already in her hands, and soon commenced its infernal work. That cheerful eye, under the influence of slavery, soon became red with rage; that voice, made all of sweet accord, changed to one of harsh and horrid discord; and that angelic face gave place to that of a demon. Thus is slavery the enemy of both the slave and the slaveholder.

Very soon after I went to live with Mr. and Mrs. Auld, she very kindly commenced to teach me the A, B, C. After I had learned this, she assisted me in learning to spell words of three or four letters. Just at this point of my progress, Mr. Auld found out what was going on, and at once forbade Mrs. Auld to instruct me further, telling her, among other things, that it was unlawful, as well as unsafe, to teach a slave to read. To use his own words, further, he said, "If you give a n****r an inch, he will take an ell. A n****r should know nothing but to obey his master to do as he is told to do. Learning would *spoil* the best n****r in the world. Now," said he, "if you teach that n****r (speaking of myself) how to read, there would be no keeping him. It would forever unfit him to be slave. He would at once become unmanageable, and of no value to his master. As to himself, it could do him no good, but a great deal of harm. It would make him discontented and un-happy." These words sank deep into my heart, stirred up sentiments within that lay slumbering, and called into existence an entirely new train of thought. It was a new and special revelation, explaining dark

and mysterious things, with which my youthful understanding had struggled, but struggled in vain. I now
understood what had been to me a most perplexing
difficulty to wit, the white man's power to enslave the
Black man. It was a grand achievement, and I prized
it highly. From that moment, I understood the
pathway from slavery to freedom. It was just what I
wanted, and I got it at a time when I the least expected it. Whilst I was saddened by the thought of losing
the aid of my kind mistress, I was gladdened by the
invaluable instruction which, by the merest accident, I
had gained from my master. Though conscious of
the difficulty of learning without a teacher, I set out
with high hope, and a fixed purpose, at whatever cost
of trouble, to learn how to read. The very decided
manner with which he spoke, and strove to impress
his wife with the evil consequences of giving me
instruction, served to convince me that he was deeply
sensible of the truths he was uttering. It gave me the
best assurance that I might rely with the utmost
confidence on the results which, he said, would flow
from teaching me to read. What he most dreaded,
that I most desired. What he most loved, that I most
hated. That which to him was a great evil, to be
carefully shunned, was to me a great good, to be
diligently sought; and the argument which he so
warmly urged, against my learning to read, only
served to inspire me with a desire and determination

to learn. In learning to read, I owe almost as much to the bitter opposition of my master, as to the kindly aid of my mistress. I acknowledge the benefit of both. . . .

I lived in Master Hugh's family about seven years. During this time, I succeeded in learning to read and write. In accomplishing this, I was compelled to resort to various stratagems. I had no regular teacher. My mistress, who had kindly commenced to instruct me, had, in compliance with the advice and direction of her husband, not only ceased to instruct, but had set her face against my being instructed by anyone else. It is due, however, to my mistress to say of her, that she did not adopt this course of treatment immediately. She at first lacked the depravity indispensable to shutting me up in mental darkness. It was at least necessary for her to have some training in the exercise of irresponsible power, to make her equal to the task of treating me as though I were a brute.

My mistress was, as I have said, a kind and tender-hearted woman, and in the simplicity of her soul she commenced, when I first went to live with her, to treat me as she supposed one human being ought to treat another. In entering upon the duties of a slaveholder, she did not seem to perceive that I sustained to her the relation of a mere chattel, and that for her to treat me as a human being was not only wrong, but dangerously so. Slavery proved as injurious to her as it did to me. When I went there, she was a pious, warm, and tender-hearted woman. There was no sorrow or suffering for which she had not a tear. She had bread for the hungry, clothes for the naked, and comfort for every mourner that came within her reach. Slavery soon proved its ability to divest her of these heavenly qualities. Under its influence, the tender heart became stone, and the lamblike disposition gave way to one of tiger-like fierceness. The first step in her downward course was in her ceasing to instruct me. She now commenced to practice her husband's precepts. She finally became even more violent in her opposition than her husband himself. She was not satisfied with simply doing as well as he had commanded; she seemed anxious to do better. Nothing seemed to make her more angry than to see me with a newspaper. She seemed to think that here lay the danger. I have had her rush at me with a face made all up of fury, and snatch from me a newspaper, in a manner that fully revealed her apprehension. She was an apt woman; and a little experience soon demonstrated, to her satisfaction, that education and slavery were incompatible with each other.

From this time I was most narrowly watched. If I was in a separate room any considerable length of time, I was sure to be suspected of having a book, and was at once called to give an account of myself. All this, however, was too late. The first step had been taken. Mistress, in teaching me the alphabet, had given me the *inch*, and no precaution could prevent me from taking the *ell*.

The plan which I adopted, and the one by which I was most successful, was that of making friends of all the little white boys whom I met in the street. As many of these as I could, I converted into teachers. With their kindly aid, obtained at different times and in different places, I finally succeeded in learning to read. When I was sent of errands, I always took my book with me, and by going one part of my errand quickly, I found time to get a lesson before my return. I used also to carry bread with me, enough of which was always in the house, and to which I was always welcome; for I was much better off in this regard than many of the poor white children in our neighborhood. This bread I used to bestow upon the hungry little urchins, who, in return, would give me that more valuable bread of knowledge. I am strongly tempted to give the names of two or three of those little boys, as a testimonial of the gratitude and affection I bear them; but prudence forbids; not that it would injure me, but it might embarrass them; for it is almost an unpardonable offence to teach slaves to read in this Christian country. It is enough to say of the dear little fellows, that they lived on Philpot Street, very near Durgin and Bailey's shipyard. I used to talk this matter of slavery over with them. I would sometimes say to them, I wished I could be as free as they would be when they got to be men. "You will be free as soon as you are twenty-one, *but I am a slave for life*! Have not I as good a right to be free as you have?" These words used to trouble them; they would express for me the liveliest sympathy, and console me with the hope that something would occur by which I might be free.

I was now about twelve years old, and the thought of being *a slave for life* began to bear heavily upon my heart. Just about this time, I got hold of a book entitled *The Columbian Orator*. Every opportunity I got, I used to read this book. Among much of other interesting matter, I found in it a dialogue between a master and his slave. The slave was represented as having run away from his master three times. The dialogue represented the conversation which took place between them, when the slave was retaken the third time. In this dialogue, the whole argument in behalf of slavery was brought forward by the master, all of which was disposed of by the slave. The slave was made to say some very smart as well as impressive things in reply to his master – things which had the desired though unexpected effect; for the conversation resulted in the voluntary emancipation of the slave on the part of the master.

In the same book, I met with one of Sheridan's mighty speeches on and in behalf of Catholic emancipation. These were choice documents to me. I read them over and over again with unabated interest. They gave tongue to interesting thoughts of my own soul, which had frequently flashed through my mind, and died away for want of utterance. The moral which I gained from the dialogue was the power of truth over the conscience of even a slaveholder. What I got from Sheridan was a bold denunciation of slavery, and a powerful vindication of human rights. The reading of these documents enabled me to utter my thoughts, and to meet the arguments brought forward to sustain slavery; but while they relieved me of one difficulty, they brought on another even more painful than the one of which I was relieved. The more I read, the more I was led to abhor and detest my enslavers. I could regard them in no other light than a band of successful robbers, who had left their homes, and gone to Africa, and stolen us from our homes, and in a strange land reduced us to slavery. I loathed them as being the meanest as well as the most wicked of men. As I read and contemplated the subject, behold! that very discontentment which Master Hugh had predicted would follow my learning to read had already come, to torment and sting my soul to unutterable anguish. As I writhed under it, I would at times feel that learning to read had been a curse rather than a blessing. It had given me a view of my wretched condition, without the remedy. It opened my eyes to the horrible pit, but to no ladder upon which to get out. In moments of agony, I envied my fellow-slaves for their stupidity. I have often wished myself a beast. I preferred the condition of the meanest reptile to my own. Anything, no matter what, to get rid of thinking! It was this everlasting thinking of my condition that tormented me. There was no getting rid of it. It was pressed upon me by every object within sight or hearing, animate or inanimate. The silver trump of freedom had roused my soul to eternal wakefulness. Freedom now appeared, to disappear no more forever. It was heard in every sound, and seen in everything. It was ever present to torment me with a sense of my wretched condition. I saw nothing without seeing it, I heard nothing without hearing it, and felt nothing without feeling it. It looked from every star, it smiled in every calm, breathed in every wind, and moved in every storm.

I often found myself regretting my own existence, and wishing myself dead; and but for the hope of being free, I have no doubt but that I should have killed myself, or done something for which I should have been killed. While in this state of mind, I was eager to hear any one speak of slavery. I was a ready listener. Every little while, I could hear something about the abolitionists. It was some time before I found what the word meant. It was always used in such connections as to make it an interesting word to me. If a slave ran away and succeeded in getting clear, or if a slave killed his master, set fire to a barn, or did anything very wrong in the mind of a slaveholder, it was spoken of as the fruit of abolition. Hearing the word in this connection very often, I set about learning what it meant. The dictionary afforded me little or no help. I found it was "the act of abolishing;" but then I did not know what was to be abolished. Here I was perplexed. I did not dare to ask anyone about its meaning, for I was satisfied that it was something they wanted me to know very little about. After a patient waiting, I got one of our city papers, containing an account of the number of petitions from the north, praying for the abolition of slavery in the District of Columbia, and of the slave trade between the States. From this time I understood the words abolition and abolitionist, and always drew near when that word was spoken, expecting to hear something of importance to myself and fellow-slaves. The light broke in upon me by degrees. I went one day down on the wharf of Mr. Waters; and seeing two Irishmen unloading a scow of stone, I went unasked, and helped them. When we had finished, one of them came to me and asked me if I were a slave. I told him I was. He asked, "Are ye a slave for life?" I told him that I was. The good Irishman seemed to be deeply affected by the statement. He said to the other that it was a pity so fine a little fellow as myself should be a slave for life.

He said it was a shame to hold me. They both advised me to run away to the north; that I should find friends there, and that I should be free. I pretended not to be interested in what they said, and treated them as if I did not understand them; for I feared they might be treacherous. White men have been known to encourage slaves to escape, and then, to get the reward, catch them and return them to their masters. I was afraid that these seemingly good men might use me so; but I nevertheless remembered their advice, and from that time I resolved to run away. I looked forward to a time at which it would be safe for me to escape. I was too young to think of doing so immediately; besides, I wished to learn how to write, as I might have occasion to write my own pass. I consoled myself with the hope that I should one day find a good chance. Meanwhile, I would learn to write. The idea as to how I might learn to write was suggested to me by being in Durgin and Bailey's shipyard, and frequently seeing the ship carpenters, after hewing, and getting a piece of timber ready for use, write on the timber the name of that part of the ship for which it was intended. When a piece of timber was intended for the larboard side, it would be marked thus "L." When a piece was for the starboard side, it would be marked thus "S." A piece for the larboard side forward, would be marked thus "L. F." When a piece was for starboard side forward, it would be marked thus "S. F." For larboard aft, it would be marked thus "L. A." For starboard aft, it would be marked thus "S. A." I soon learned the names of these letters, and for what they were intended when placed upon a piece of timber in the shipyard. I immediately commenced copying them, and in a short time was able to make the four letters named. After that, when I met with any boy who I knew could write, I would tell him I could write as well as he. The next word would be, "I don't believe you. Let me see you try it." I would then make the letters which I had been so fortunate as to learn, and ask him to beat that. In this way I got a good many lessons in writing, which it is quite possible I should never have gotten in any other way. During this time, my copy-book was the board fence, brick wall, and pavement; my pen and ink was a lump of chalk. With these, I learned mainly how to write. I then commenced and continued copying the Italics in Webster's Spelling Book, until I could make them all without looking on the book. By this time, my little Master Thomas had gone to school, and learned how to write, and had written over a number of copy-books. These had been brought home, and shown to some of our near neighbors, and then laid aside. My mistress used to go to class meeting at the Wilk Street meeting-house every Monday afternoon, and leave me to take care of the house. When left thus, I used to spend the time in writing in the spaces left in Master Thomas's copy-book, copying what he had written. I continued to do this until I could write a hand very similar to that of Master Thomas. Thus, after a long, tedious effort for years, I finally succeeded in learning how to write.[80]

---

[80] Excerpted from *Narrative of the Life of Frederick Douglass an American Slave*, (Boston: Anti-Slavery Office, 1845).

Every Tone as Testimony Against Slavery – The slaves selected to go to the Great House Farm, for the monthly allowance for themselves and their fellow-slaves, were peculiarly enthusiastic. While on their way, they would make the dense old woods, for miles around, reverberate with their wild songs, revealing at once the highest joy and the deepest sadness. They would compose and sing as they went along, consulting neither time nor tune. The thought that came up, came out — if not in the word, in the sound; — and as frequently in the one as in the other. They would sometimes sing the most pathetic sentiment in the most rapturous tone, and the most rapturous sentiment in the most pathetic tone. Into all of their songs they would manage to weave something of the Great House Farm. Especially would they do this, when leaving home. They would then sing most exultingly the following words: — *"I am going away to the Great House Farm! O, yea! O, yea! O!"* This they would sing, as a chorus, to words which to many would seem unmeaning jargon, but which, nevertheless, were full of meaning to themselves. I have sometimes thought that the mere hearing of those songs would do more to impress some minds with the horrible character of slavery, than the reading of whole volumes of philosophy on the subject could do.

I did not, when a slave, understand the deep meaning of those rude and apparently incoherent songs. I was myself within the circle; so that I neither saw nor heard as those without might see and hear. They told a tale of woe which was then altogether beyond my feeble comprehension; they were tones loud, long, and deep; they breathed the prayer and complaint of souls boiling over with the bitterest anguish. Every tone was a testimony against slavery, and a prayer to God for deliverance from chains. The hearing of those wild notes always depressed my spirit, and filled me with ineffable sadness. I have frequently found myself in tears while hearing them. The mere recurrence to those songs, even now, afflicts me; and while I am writing these lines, an expression of feeling has already found its way down my cheek. To those songs I trace my first glimmering conception of the dehumanizing character of slavery. I can never get rid of that conception. Those songs still follow me, to deepen my hatred of slavery, and quicken my sympathies for my brethren in bonds. If any one wishes to be impressed with the soul-killing effects of slavery, let him go to Colonel Lloyd's plantation, and, on allowance-day, place himself in the deep pine woods, and there let him, in silence, analyze the sounds that shall pass through the chambers of his soul, — and if he is not thus impressed, it will only be because "there is no flesh in his obdurate heart."

I have often been utterly astonished, since I came to the north, to find persons who could speak of the

singing, among slaves, as evidence of their contentment and happiness. It is impossible to conceive of a
greater mistake. Slaves sing most when they are most
unhappy. The songs of the slave represent the
sorrows of his heart; and he is relieved by them, only
as an aching heart is relieved by its tears. At least,
such is my experience. I have often sung to drown
my sorrow, but seldom to express my happiness.
Crying for joy, and singing for joy, were alike
uncommon to me while in the jaws of slavery. The
singing of a man cast away upon a desolate island
might be as appropriately considered as evidence of
contentment and happiness, as the singing of a slave;
the songs of the one and of the other are prompted
by the same emotion.[81]

---

[81] Excerpted from *Narrative of the Life of Frederick Douglass an American Slave*, (Boston: Anti-Slavery Office, 1845).

A Still Tongue Makes a Wise Head – Slaves, when inquired of as to their condition and the character of their masters, almost universally say they are contented, and that their masters are kind. The slaveholders have been known to send in spies among their slaves, to ascertain their views and feelings in regard to their condition. The frequency of this has had the effect to establish among the slaves the maxim, that a still tongue makes a wise head. They suppress the truth rather than take the consequences of telling it, and in so doing prove themselves a part of the human family. If they have anything to say of their masters, it is generally in their masters' favor, especially when speaking to an untried man. I have been frequently asked, when a slave, if I had a kind master, and do not remember ever to have given a negative answer; nor did I, in pursuing this course, consider myself as uttering what was absolutely false; for I always measured the kindness of my master by the standard of kindness set up among slaveholders around us. Moreover, slaves are like other people, and imbibe prejudices quite common to others. They think their own better than that of others. Many, under the influence of this prejudice, think their own masters are better than the masters of other slaves; and this, too, in some cases, when the very reverse is true. Indeed, it is not uncommon for slaves even to fall out and quarrel among themselves about the relative goodness of their masters, each contending for the superior goodness of his own over that of the others. At the very same time, they mutually execrate their masters when viewed separately. It was so on our plantation. When Colonel Lloyd's slaves met the slaves of Jacob Jepson, they seldom parted without a quarrel about their masters; Colonel Lloyd's slaves contending that he was the richest, and Mr. Jepson's slaves that he was the smartest, and most of a man. Colonel Lloyd's slaves would boast his ability to buy and sell Jacob Jepson. Mr. Jepson's slaves would boast his ability to whip Colonel Lloyd. These quarrels would almost always end in a fight between the parties, and those that whipped were supposed to have gained the point at issue. They seemed to think that the greatness of their masters was transferable to themselves. It was considered as being bad enough to be a slave; but to be a poor man's slave was deemed a disgrace indeed![82]

---

[82] Excerpted from *Narrative of the Life of Frederick Douglass an American Slave*, (Boston: Anti-Slavery Office, 1845).

Keeping Down the Spirit of Insurrection pt. I – The days between Christmas and New Year's day are allowed as holidays; and, accordingly, we were not required to perform any labor, more than to feed and take care of the stock. This time we regarded as our own, by the grace of our masters; and we therefore used or abused it nearly as we pleased. Those of us who had families at a distance, were generally allowed to spend the whole six days in their society. This time, however, was spent in various ways. The staid, sober, thinking and industrious ones of our number would employ themselves in making corn-brooms, mats, horse-collars, and baskets; and another class of us would spend the time in hunting opossums, hares, and coons. But by far the larger part engaged in such sports and merriments as playing ball, wrestling, running foot-races, fiddling, dancing, and drinking whisky; and this latter mode of spending the time was by far the most agreeable to the feelings of our masters. A slave who would work during the holidays was considered by our masters as scarcely deserving them. He was regarded as one who rejected the favor of his master. It was deemed a disgrace not to get drunk at Christmas; and he was regarded as lazy indeed, who had not provided himself with the necessary means, during the year, to get whisky enough to last him through Christmas.

From what I know of the effect of these holidays upon the slave, I believe them to be among the most effective means in the hands of the slaveholder in keeping down the spirit of insurrection. Were the slaveholders at once to abandon this practice, I have not the slightest doubt it would lead to an immediate insurrection among the slaves. These holidays serve as conductors, or safety-valves, to carry off the rebellious spirit of enslaved humanity. But for these, the slave would be forced up to the wildest desperation; and woe betide the slaveholder, the day he ventures to remove or hinder the operation of those conductors! I warn him that, in such an event, a spirit will go forth in their midst, more to be dreaded than the most appalling earthquake.

The holidays are part and parcel of the gross fraud, wrong, and inhumanity of slavery. They are professedly a custom established by the benevolence of the slaveholders; but I undertake to say, it is the result of selfishness, and one of the grossest frauds committed upon the down-trodden slave. They do not give the slaves this time because they would not like to have their work during its continuance, but because they know it would be unsafe to deprive them of it. This will be seen by the fact, that the slaveholders like to have their slaves spend those days just in such a manner as to make them as glad of their ending as of their beginning. Their object seems to be, to disgust their slaves with freedom, by plunging them into the lowest depths of dissipation. For instance, the slaveholders not only like to see the slave drink of his own accord, but will adopt various plans to make him drunk. One plan is, to make bets on their slaves, as to who can drink the most whisky without getting drunk; and in this way they succeed in getting whole multitudes to drink to excess. Thus, when the slave asks for virtuous freedom, the cunning slaveholder, knowing his ignorance, cheats him with a dose of vicious dissipation, artfully labelled with the name of liberty. The most of us used to drink it down, and the result was just what might be supposed: many of us were led to think that there was little to choose between liberty and slavery. We felt, and very properly too, that we had almost as well be slaves to man as to rum. So, when the holidays ended, we staggered up from the filth of our wallowing, took a long breath, and marched to the field, feeling, upon the whole, rather glad to go, from what our master had deceived us into a belief was freedom, back to the arms of slavery.

I have said that this mode of treatment is a part of the whole system of fraud and inhumanity of slavery. It is so. The mode here adopted to disgust the slave with freedom, by allowing him to see only the abuse of it, is carried out in other things.[83]

---

[83] Excerpted from *Narrative of the Life of Frederick Douglass an American Slave*, (Boston: Anti-Slavery Office, 1845).

Sober Mind a Threat to Slavery pt. I - The coloured man in the United States has great difficulties in the way of his moral, social, and religious advancement. Almost every step he takes towards mental, moral, or social improvement is repulsed by the cold indifference or the active mob of the white. He is compelled to live an outcast from society; he is, as it were, a border or salvage on the great cloth of humanity, and the very fact of his degradation is given as a reason why he should be continued in the condition of a slave.

The Blacks are to a considerable extent intemperate, and if intemperate, of course vicious in other respects, and this is counted against them as a reason why their emancipation should not take place. As I desire, therefore, their freedom from physical chains, so I desire their emancipation from intemperance, because I believe it would be the means — a great and glorious means — towards helping to break their physical chains and letting them go free.

To give you some idea of the strength of this prejudice and passion against the coloured people, I may state that they formed themselves into a temperance procession in Philadelphia, on the day on which the legislature in this country had by a benevolent act awarded freed-om to the Negroes in the West Indian islands. They formed themselves into a procession with appropriate banners, but they had not proceeded up two streets before they were attacked by a reckless mob, their procession broken up, their banners destroyed, their houses and churches burned, and all because they had dared to have a temperance procession on the 1st of August. They had saved enough to build a hall, besides their churches. These were not saved, they were burned down, and the mob was backed up by the most respectable people in Philadelphia. These are the difficulties which beset their path.

And yet the Americans, those demons in human shape, they speak to us, and say that we are morally and religiously incapacitated for enjoying liberty with themselves. I am afraid I am making this an anti-slavery meeting. ... I have had some experiences of intemperance as well as of slavery. In the Southern States, masters induce their slaves to drink whiskey, in order to keep them from devising ways and means by which to attain their freedom.

In order to make a man a slave, it is necessary to silence or drown his mind. It is not the flesh that objects to being bound — it is the spirit. It is not the mere animal part — it is the immortal mind which distinguishes man from the brute creation.

To blind his affections, it is necessary to bedim and bedizzy his understanding. In no other way can this be so well accomplished as by using ardent spirits! On Saturday evening, it is the custom of the slaveholder to give his slaves drink, and why? Because if they had time to think, if left to reflection on the Sabbath day, they might devise means by which to obtain their liberty.[84]

---

[84] Extracted from "Lecture on Temperance and Anti-Slavery", delivered in Paisley, Scotland on March 30th, 1846 and published in *Glasgow Saturday Post,* April 4th, 1846 and *Renfrewshire Advertiser,* April 11th, 1846.

Slavery is a System – I feel exceedingly glad of the opportunity now afforded me of presenting the claims of my brethren in bonds in the United States, to so many in London and from various parts of Britain, who have assembled here on the present occasion. I have nothing to commend me to your consideration in the way of learning, nothing in the way of education, to entitle me to your attention; and you are aware that slavery is a very bad school for rearing teachers of morality and religion. Twenty-one years of my life have been spent in slavery – personal slavery – surrounded by degrading influences, such as can exist nowhere beyond the pale of slavery; and it will not be strange, if under such circumstances, I should betray, in what I have to say to you, a deficiency of that refinement which is seldom or ever found, except among persons that have experienced superior advantages to those which I have enjoyed. But I will take it for granted that you know something about the degrading influences of slavery, and that you will not expect great things from me this evening, but simply such facts as I may be able to advance immediately in connection with my own experience of slavery.

Now, what is this system of slavery? This is the subject of my lecture this evening – what is the character of this institution? I am about to answer the inquiry, what is American slavery? I do this the more readily, since I have found persons in this country who have identified the term slavery with that which I think it is not, and in some instances, I have feared, in so doing, have rather (unwittingly, I know) detracted much from the horror with which the term slavery is contemplated. It is common in this country to distinguish every bad thing by the name of slavery. Intemperance is slavery; to be deprived of the right to vote is slavery, says one; to have to work hard is slavery, says another; and I do not know but that if we should let them go on, they would say that to eat when we are hungry, to walk when we desire to have exercise, or to minister to our necessities, or have necessities at all, is slavery. I do not wish for a moment to detract from the horror with which the evil of intemperance is contemplated — not at all; nor do I wish to throw the slightest obstruction in the way of any political freedom that any class of persons in this country may desire to obtain. But I am here to say that I think the term slavery is sometimes abused by identifying it with that which it is not. Slavery in the United States is the granting of that power by which one man exercises and enforces a right of property in the body and soul of another. The condition of a slave is simply that of the brute beast. He is a piece of property — a marketable commodity, in the language of the law, to be bought or sold at the will and caprice of the master who claims him to be his property; he is spoken of, thought of, and treated as property. His own good, his conscience, his intellect, his affections, are all set aside by the master. The will and the wishes of the master are the law of the slave. He is as much a piece of property as a horse. If he is fed, he is fed because he is property. If he is clothed, it is with a view to the increase of his value as property. Whatever of comfort is necessary to him for his body or soul that is inconsistent with his being property, is carefully wrested from him, not only by public opinion, but by the law of the country. He is carefully deprived of everything that tends in the slightest degree to detract from his value as property. He is deprived of education. God has given him an intellect; the slaveholder declares it shall not be cultivated. If his moral perception leads him in a course contrary to his value as property, the slaveholder declares he shall not exercise it. The marriage institution cannot exist among slaves, and one-sixth of the population of democratic America is denied its privileges by the law of the land. What is to be thought of a nation boasting of its liberty, boasting of its humanity, boasting of its Christianity, boasting of its love of justice and purity, and yet having within its own borders three millions of persons denied by law the right of marriage? — what must be the condition of that people? I need not lift up the veil by giving you any experience of my own. Every one that can put two ideas together, must see the most fearful results from such a state of things as I have just mentioned. If any of these three millions find for themselves companions, and prove themselves honest, upright, virtuous persons to each other, yet in these cases — few as I am bound to confess they are — the virtuous live in constant apprehension of being torn asunder by the merciless men-stealers that claim them as their property. This is American slavery; no marriage — no education — the light of the gospel shut out from the dark mind of the bondman — and he forbidden by law to learn to read. If a mother shall teach her children to read, the law in Louisiana proclaims that she may be hanged by the neck. If the father attempt to give his son a knowledge of letters, he may be punished by the whip in one instance, and in another be killed, at the discretion of the court. Three millions of people shut out from the light of knowledge! It is easy for you to conceive the evil that must result from such a state of things.

I now come to the physical evils of slavery. I do not wish to dwell at length upon these, but it seems right to speak of them, not so much to influence your minds on this question, as to let the slaveholders of America know that the curtain which conceals their crimes is being lifted abroad; that we are opening the dark cell, and leading the people into the horrible recesses of what they are pleased to call their domestic institution. We want them to know that a knowledge of their whippings, their scourgings, their brandings, their chainings, is not confined to their plantations, but that some Negro of theirs has broken loose from his chains — has burst through the dark incrustation of slavery, and is now exposing their deeds of deep damnation to the gaze of the Christian people of England.

The slaveholders resort to all kinds of cruelty. If I were disposed, I have matter enough to interest you on this question for five or six evenings, but I will not dwell at length upon these cruelties. Suffice it to say, that all of the peculiar modes of torture that were resorted to in the West India islands, are resorted to, I believe, even more frequently, in the United States of America. Starvation, the bloody whip, the chain, the gag, the thumb-screw, cat-hauling, the cat-o'-nine-tails, the dungeon, the bloodhound, are all in requisition to keep the slave in his condition as a slave in the United States. If anyone has a doubt upon this point, I would ask him to read the chapter on slavery in Dickens's *Notes on America*. If any man has a doubt upon it, I have here the "testimony of a thousand witnesses," which I can give at any length, all going to prove the truth of my statement. The blood-hound is regularly trained in the United States, and advertisements are to be found in the southern papers of the Union, from persons advertising themselves as bloodhound trainers, and offering to hunt down slaves at fifteen dollars a piece, recommending their hounds as the fleetest in the neighborhood, never known to fail. Advertisements are from time to time inserted, stating that slaves have escaped with iron collars about their necks, with bands of iron about their feet, marked with the lash, branded with red-hot irons, the initials of their master's name burned into their flesh; and the masters advertise the fact of their being thus branded with their own signature, thereby proving to the world, that, however damning it may appear to non-slavers, such practices are not regarded discreditable among the slaveholders themselves. Why, I believe if a man should brand his horse in this country — burn the initials of his name into any of his cattle, and publish the ferocious deed here — that the united execrations of Christians in Britain would descend upon him. Yet in the United States, human beings are thus branded. As Whittier says —

...Our countrymen in chains,
The whip on woman's shrinking flesh,
Our soil yet reddening with the stains
Caught from her scourgings warm and fresh.

The slave-dealer boldly publishes his infamous acts to the world. Of all things that have been said of slavery to which exception has been taken by slaveholders, this, the charge of cruelty, stands foremost, and yet there is no charge capable of clearer demonstration, than that of the most barbarous inhumanity on the part of the slaveholders toward their slaves. And all this is necessary; it is necessary to resort to these cruelties, in order to make the slave a slave, and to keep him a slave. Why, my experience all goes to prove the truth of what you will call a marvelous proposition, that the better you treat a slave, the more you destroy his value as a slave, and enhance the probability of his eluding the grasp of the slaveholder; the more kindly you treat him, the more wretched you make him, while you keep him in the condition of a slave. My experience, I say, confirms the truth of this proposition. When I was treated exceedingly ill; when my back was being scourged daily; when I was whipped within an inch of my life — life was all I cared for. "Spare my life," was my continual prayer. When I was looking for the blow about to be inflicted upon my head, I was not thinking of my liberty; it was my life. But, as soon as the blow was not to be feared, then came the longing for liberty. If a slave has a bad master, his ambition is to get a better; when he gets a better, he aspires to have the best; and when he gets the best, he aspires to be his own master. But the slave must be brutalized to keep him as a slave. The slaveholder feels this necessity. I admit this necessity. If it be right to hold slaves at all, it is right to hold them in the only way in which they can be held; and this can be done only by shutting out the light of education from their minds, and brutalizing their persons. The whip, the chain, the gag, the thumb-screw, the bloodhound, the stocks, and all the other bloody paraphernalia of the slave system, are indispensably necessary to the relation of master and slave. The slave must be subjected to these, or he ceases to be a slave. Let him know that the whip is burned; that the fetters have been turned to some useful and profitable employment; that the chain is no longer for his limbs; that the bloodhound is no longer to be put upon his track; that his master's authority over him is no longer to be enforced by taking his life — and immediately he walks out from the house of bondage and asserts his freedom as a man. The slaveholder finds it necessary to have these implements to keep the slave in bondage; finds it necessary to be able to say, "Unless you do so and so; unless you do as I bid you — I will take away your life!"

Some of the most awful scenes of cruelty are constantly taking place in the middle states of the Union. We have in those states what are called the slave-breeding states. Allow me to speak plainly. Although it is harrowing to your feelings, it is necessary that the facts of the case should be stated. We have in the United States slave-breeding states. The very state from which the minister from our court to yours comes, is one of these states — Maryland, where men, women, and children are reared for the market, just as horses, sheep, and swine are raised for the market. Slave-rearing is there looked upon as a legitimate trade; the law sanctions it, public opinion upholds it, the church does not condemn it. It goes on in all its bloody horrors, sustained by the auctioneer's block. If you would see the cruelties of this system, hear the following narrative. Not long since the following scene occurred. A slave-woman and a slaveman had united themselves as man and wife in the absence of any law to protect them as man and wife. They had lived together by the permission, not by right, of their master, and they had reared a family. The master found it expedient, and for his interest, to sell them. He did not ask them their wishes in regard to the matter at all; they were not consulted. The man and woman were brought to the auctioneer's block, under the sound of the hammer. The cry was raised, "Here goes; who bids cash?" Think of it — a man and wife to be sold! The woman was placed on the auctioneer's block; her limbs, as is customary, were brutally exposed to the purchasers, who examined her with all the freedom with which they would examine a horse. There stood the husband, powerless; no right to his wife; the master's right preeminent. She was sold. He was next brought to the auctioneer's block. His eyes followed his wife in the distance; and he looked beseechingly, imploringly, to the man that had bought his wife, to buy him also. But he was at length bid off to another person. He was about to be separated forever from her he loved. No word of his, no work of his, could save him from this separation. He asked permission of his new master to go and take the hand of his wife at parting. It was denied him. In the agony of his soul he rushed from the man who had just bought him, that he might take a farewell of his wife; but his way was obstructed, he was struck over the head with a loaded whip, and was held for a moment; but his agony was too great. When he was let go, he fell a corpse at the feet of his master. His heart was broken. Such scenes are the everyday fruits of American slavery. Some two years since, the Hon. Seth. M. Gates, an anti-slavery gentleman of the state of New York, a representative in the congress of the United States, told me he saw with his own eyes the following circumstances. In the national District of Columbia, over which the star-spangled emblem is constantly waving, where orators are ever holding forth on the subject of American liberty, American democracy, American republicanism, there are two slave prisons. When going across a bridge, leading to one of these prisons, he saw a young woman run out, bare-footed and bare-headed, and with very little clothing on. She was running with all speed to the bridge he was approaching. His eye was fixed upon her, and he stopped to see what was the matter. He had not paused long before he saw three men run out after her. He now knew what the nature of the case was; a slave escaping from her chains — a young woman, a sister — escaping from the bondage in which she had been held. She made her way to the bridge, but had not reached, ere from the Virginia side there came two slaveholders. As soon as they saw them, her pursuers called out, "Stop her!" True to their Virginian instincts, they came to the rescue of their brother kidnappers, across the bridge. The poor girl now saw that there was no chance for her. It was a trying time. She knew if she went back, she must be a slave forever — she must be dragged down to the scenes of pollution which the slaveholders continually provide for most of the poor, sinking, wretched young women, whom they call their property. She formed her resolution; and just as those who were about to take her, were going to put hands upon her, to drag her back, she leaped over the balustrades of the bridge, and down she went to rise no more. She chose death, rather than to go back into the hands of those Christian slaveholders from whom she had escaped.

Can it be possible that such things as these exist in the United States? Are not these the exceptions? Are any such scenes as this general? Are not such deeds condemned by the law and denounced by public opinion? Let me read to you a few of the laws of the slaveholding states of America. I think no better exposure of slavery can be made than is made by the laws of the states in which slavery exists. I prefer reading the laws to making any statement in confirmation of what I have said myself; for the slaveholders cannot object to this testimony, since it is the calm, the cool, the deliberate enactment of their wisest heads, of their most clear-sighted, their own constituted representatives. "If more than seven slaves together are found in any road without a white person, twenty lashes a piece; for visiting a plantation without a written pass, ten lashes; for letting loose a boat from where it is made fast, thirty-nine lashes for the first offense; and for the second, shall have cut off from his head one ear; for keeping or carrying a club, thirty-nine lashes; for having any article for sale, without a ticket from his master, ten lashes; for traveling in any other than the most usual and accustomed road, when going alone to any place, forty lashes; for traveling in the night without a pass, forty lashes." I am afraid you do not understand the awful character of these lashes. You must bring it before your mind. A human being in a perfect state of nudity, tied hand and foot to a stake, and a strong man standing behind with a heavy whip, knotted at the end, each blow cutting into the flesh, and leaving the warm blood dripping to the feet; and for these trifles. "For being found in another person's Negro-quarters, forty lashes; for hunting with dogs in the woods, thirty lashes;

for being on horseback without the written permission of his master, twenty-five lashes; for riding or going abroad in the night, or riding horses in the day time, without leave, a slave may be whipped, cropped, or branded in the cheek with the letter R. or otherwise punished, such punishment not extending to life, or so as to render him unfit for labor." The laws referred to, may be found by consulting Brevard's Digest; Haywood's Manual; Virginia Revised Code; Prince's Digest; Missouri Laws; Mississippi Revised Code. A man, for going to visit his brethren, without the permission of his master — and in many instances he may not have that permission; his master, from caprice or other reasons, may not be willing to allow it — may be caught on his way, dragged to a post, the branding-iron heated, and the name of his master or the letter R branded into his cheek or on his forehead. They treat slaves thus, on the principle that they must punish for light offenses, in order to prevent the commission of larger ones. I wish you to mark that in the single state of Virginia there are seventy-one crimes for which a colored man may be executed; while there are only three of these crimes, which, when committed by a white man, will subject him to that punishment. There are many of these crimes which if the white man did not commit, he would be regarded as a scoundrel and a coward. In the state of Maryland, there is a law to this effect: that if a slave shall strike his master, he may be hanged, his head severed from his body, his body quartered, and his head and quarters set up in the most prominent places in the neighborhood. If a colored woman, in the defense of her own virtue, in defense of her own person, should shield herself from the brutal attacks of her tyrannical master, or make the slightest resistance, she may be killed on the spot. No law whatever will bring the guilty man to justice for the crime.

But you will ask me, can these things be possible in a land professing Christianity? Yes, they are so; and this is not the worst. No; a darker feature is yet to be presented than the mere existence of these facts. I have to inform you that the religion of the southern states, at this time, is the great supporter, the great sanctioner of the bloody atrocities to which I have referred. While America is printing tracts and bibles; sending missionaries abroad to convert the heathen; expending her money in various ways for the promotion of the gospel in foreign lands — the slave not only lies forgotten, uncared for, but is trampled under foot by the very churches of the land. What have we in America? Why, we have slavery made part of the religion of the land. Yes, the pulpit there stands up as the great defender of this cursed institution, as it is called. Ministers of religion come forward and torture the hallowed pages of inspired wisdom to sanction the bloody deed. They stand forth as the foremost, the strongest defenders of this "institution." As a proof of this, I need not do more than state the general fact, that slavery has existed under the droppings of the sanctuary of the south for the last two hundred years, and there has not been any war between the religion and the slavery of the south. Whips, chains, gags, and thumb-screws have all lain under the droppings of the sanctuary, and instead of rusting from off the limbs of the bondman, those droppings have served to preserve them in all their strength. Instead of preaching the gospel against this tyranny, rebuke, and wrong, ministers of religion have sought, by all and every means, to throw in the background whatever in the bible could be construed into opposition to slavery, and to bring forward that which they could torture into its support. This I conceive to be the darkest feature of slavery, and the most difficult to attack, because it is identified with religion, and exposes those who denounce it to the charge of infidelity. Yes, those with whom I have been laboring, namely, the old organization anti-slavery society of America, have been again and again stigmatized as infidels, and for what reason? Why, solely in consequence of the faithfulness of their attacks upon the slaveholding religion of the southern states, and the northern religion that sympathizes with it. I have found it difficult to speak on this matter without persons coming forward and saying, "Douglass, are you not afraid of injuring the cause of Christ? You do not desire to do so, we know; but are you not undermining religion?" This has been said to me again and again, even since I came to this country, but I cannot be induced to leave off these exposures. I love the religion of our blessed Savior. I love that religion that comes from above, in the "wisdom of God," which is first pure, then peaceable, gentle, and easy to be entreated, full of mercy and good fruits, without partiality and without hypocrisy. I love that religion that sends its votaries to bind up the wounds of him that has fallen among thieves. I love that religion that makes it the duty of its disciples to visit the father less and the widow in their affliction. I love that religion that is based upon the glorious principle, of love to God and love to man; which makes its followers do unto others as they themselves would be done by. If you demand liberty to yourself, it says, grant it to your neighbors. If you claim a right to think for yourself, it says, allow your neighbors the same right. If you claim to act for yourself, it says, allow your neighbors the same right. It is because I love this religion that I hate the slave-holding, the woman-whipping, the mind-darkening, the soul-destroying religion that exists in the southern states of America. It is because I regard the one as good, and pure, and holy, that I cannot but regard the other as bad, corrupt, and wicked. Loving the one I must hate the other; holding to the one I must reject the other.

I may be asked, why I am so anxious to bring this subject before the British public — why I do not confine my efforts to the United States? My answer is, first, that slavery is the common enemy of mankind, and all mankind should be made acquainted with its abominable character. My next answer is, that the slave is a man, and, as such, is entitled to your sympathy as a brother. All the feelings, all the susceptibilities, all the capacities, which you have, he has. He is a part of the human family. He has been the prey — the common prey — of Christendom for the last three hundred years, and it is but right, it is but just, it is but proper, that his wrongs should be known throughout the world. I have another reason for bringing this matter before the British public, and it is this: slavery is a system of wrong, so blinding to all around, so hardening to the heart, so corrupting to the morals, so deleterious to religion, so sapping to all the principles of justice in its immediate vicinity, that the community surrounding it lack the moral stamina necessary to its removal. It is a system of such gigantic evil, so strong, so overwhelming in its power, that no one nation is equal to its removal. It requires the humanity of Christianity, the morality of the world to remove it. Hence, I call upon the people of Britain to look at this matter, and to exert the influence I am about to show they possess, for the removal of slavery from America. I can appeal to them, as strongly by their regard for the slaveholder as for the slave, to labor in this cause. I am here, because you have an influence on America that no other nation can have. You have been drawn together by the power of steam to a marvelous extent; the distance between London and Boston is now reduced to some twelve or fourteen days, so that the denunciations against slavery, uttered in London this week, may be heard in a fortnight in the streets of Boston, and reverberating amidst the hills of Massachusetts. There is nothing said here against slavery that will not be recorded in the United States. I am here, also, because the slaveholders do not want me to be here; they would rather that I were not here. I have adopted a maxim laid down by Napoleon, never to occupy ground which the enemy would like me to occupy. The slaveholders would much rather have me, if I will denounce slavery, denounce it in the northern states, where their friends and supporters are, who will stand by and mob me for denouncing it. They feel something as the man felt, when he uttered his prayer, in which he made out a most horrible case for himself, and one of his neighbors touched him and said, "My friend, I always had the opinion of you that you have now expressed for yourself — that you are a very great sinner." Coming from himself, it was all very well, but coming from a stranger it was rather cutting. The slaveholders felt that when slavery was denounced among themselves, it was not so bad; but let one of the slaves get loose, let him summon the people of Britain, and make known to them the conduct of the slaveholders toward their slaves, and it cuts them to the quick, and produces a sensation such as would be produced by nothing else. The power I exert now is something like the power that is exerted by the man at the end of the lever; my influence now is just in proportion to the distance that I am from the United States. My exposure of slavery abroad will tell more upon the hearts and consciences of slave-holders, than if I was attacking them in America; for almost every paper that I now receive from the United States, comes teeming with statements about this fugitive Negro, calling him a "glib-tongued scoun-drel," and saying that he is running out against the institutions and people of America. I deny the charge that I am saying a word against the institutions of America, or the people, as such. What I have to say is against slavery and slaveholders. I feel at liberty to speak on this subject. I have on my back the marks of the lash; I have four sisters and one brother now under the galling chain. I feel it my duty to cry aloud and spare not. I am not averse to having the good opinion of my fellow creatures. I am not averse to being kindly regarded by all men; but I am bound, even at the hazard of making a large class of religionists in this country hate me, oppose me, and malign me as they have done — I am bound by the prayers, and tears, and entreaties of three millions of kneeling bondsmen, to have no compromise with men who are in any shape or form connected with the slaveholders of America. I expose slavery in this country, because to expose it is to kill it. Slavery is one of those monsters of darkness to whom the light of truth is death. Expose slavery, and it dies. Light is to slavery what the heat of the sun is to the root of a tree; it must die under it. All the slaveholder asks of me is silence. He does not ask me to go abroad and preach in favor of slavery; he does not ask anyone to do that. He would not say that slavery is a good thing, but the best under the circumstances. The slaveholders want total darkness on the subject. They want the hatchway shut down, that the monster may crawl in his den of darkness, crushing human hopes and happiness, destroying the bondman at will, and having no one to reprove or rebuke him. Slavery shrinks from the light; it hateth the light, neither cometh to the light, lest its deeds should be reproved. To tear off the mask from this abominable system, to expose it to the light of heaven, aye, to the heat of the sun, that it may burn and wither it out of existence, is my object in coming to this country. I want the slaveholder surrounded, as by a wall of anti-slavery fire, so that he may see the condemnation of himself and his system glaring down in letters of light. I want him to feel that he has no sympathy in England, Scotland, or Ireland; that he has none in Canada, none in Mexico, none among the poor wild Indians; that the voice of the civilized, aye, and savage world is against him. I would have condemnation blaze down upon him in every direction, till, stunned and over-whelmed with shame and confusion, he is compelled to let go the grasp he holds upon the persons of his victims, and restore them to their long-lost rights.[85]

---

[85] Reception Lecture at Finsbury Chapel, Moorfields, England, May 12, 1846 and published as *Report of a public meeting held at Finsbury Chapel, Moorfields, to receive Frederick Douglass, the American slave on Friday, May 12th, 1846*, London, 1846.

Overthrowing the Accursed System of Bondage – Mr. Chairman, Ladies and Gentlemen, — I never appear before an audience like that which I now behold, without feeling my incompetency to do justice to the cause which I am here to advocate, or to meet the expectations which are generally created for me, by the friends who usually precede me in speaking. Certainly, if the eulogiums bestowed upon me this evening were correct, I should be able to chain the attention of this audience for hours by my eloquence. But, sir, I claim none of these qualities. While I feel grateful for the generosity of my friends in bestowing them upon me, I am conscious of possessing very little just right to them; for I am but a plain, blunt man — a poor slave, or, rather, one who has been a slave. Never had I a day's schooling in my life; all that I have of education I have stolen.

I am desirous, therefore, at once to relieve you from any anticipation of a great speech, which, from what you have heard from our esteemed friend, the chairman, and the gentlemen who preceded me, you might have been led to expect. That I am deeply, earnestly, and devotedly engaged in advocating the cause of my oppressed brethren, is most true; and in that character, as their representative, I hail your kind expression of feeling towards me this evening, and receive it with the profoundest gratitude. I will make use of these demonstrations of your warm approbation hereafter; I will take them home in my memory; they shall be written upon my heart; and I will employ them in that land of boasted liberty and light, but, at the same time, of abject slavery, to which I am going, for the purpose of overthrowing that accursed system of bondage, and restoring the Negroes, throughout its wide domain, to their lost liberty and rights.

Sir, the time for argument upon this question is over, so far as the right of the slave to himself is concerned; and hence I feel less freedom in speaking here this evening, than I should have done under other circumstances. Place me in the midst of a pro-slavery mob in the United States, where my rights as a man are cloven down — let me be in an assembly of ministers or politicians who call in question my claim to freedom — and then, indeed, I can stand up and open my mouth; then assert boldly and strongly the rights of my manhood. But where all is admitted — where almost every man is waiting for the end of a sentence that he may respond to it with a cheer — listening for the last words of the most radical resolution that he may hold up his hand in favour of it — why, then, under such circumstances, I certainly have very little to do. You have done all for me. Still, sir, I may manage, out of the scraps of the cloth which you have left, to make a coat of many colours, not such an one as Joseph was clothed in, yet still bearing some resemblance to it. I do not, however, promise to make you a very connected speech.

I have listened to the patriotic, or rather respectful, language applied to America and Americans this evening. I confess, that although I am going back to that country, though I have many dear friends there, though I expect to end my days upon its soil, I am, nevertheless, not here to make any profession whatever of respect for that country, of attachment to its politicians, or love for its churches or national institutions. The fact is, the whole system, the entire network of American society, is one great falsehood, from beginning to end.

I might say, that the present generation of Americans have become dishonest men from the circumstances by which they are surrounded. Seventy years ago, they went to the battlefield in defence of liberty. Sixty years ago, they framed a constitution, over the very gateway of which they inscribed, "To secure the blessings of liberty to ourselves and posterity." In their celebrated Declaration of Independence, they made the loudest and clearest assertions of the rights of man; and yet at that very time the identical men who drew up that Declaration of Independence, and framed the American democratic constitution, were trafficking in the blood and souls of their fellow men. From the period of the first adoption of the constitution of the United States downward, everything good and great in the heart of the American people everything patriotic within their breasts — has been summoned to defend this great lie before the world. They have been driven from their very patriotism to defend this great falsehood.

How have they done it? Why, by wrapping it up in honeyed words. By disguising it, and calling it "our peculiar institution;" "our social system;" our patriarchal institution;" "our domestic institution;" and so forth. They have spoken of it in every possible way, except the right way. In no less than three clauses of their constitution may be found a spirit of the most deadly hostility to the liberty of the Black man in that country, and yet clothed in such language as no Englishman, to whom its meaning was unknown, could take offence at.

For instance, the President of the United States is required, at all times and under any circumstances, to call out the army and navy to suppress "domestic insurrection." Of course, all Englishmen, upon a superficial reading of that clause of the constitution, would very readily assent to the justice of the proposition involved in it; they would agree at once in its perfect propriety. "The army and navy! what are they good for if not to suppress insurrections, and preserve the peace, tranquillity, and harmony of the state?" But what does this language really mean, sir? What is its signification, as shadowed forth practically, in that constitution? What is the idea it conveys to the mind of the American? Why, that every man who casts a ball into the American ballot-box — every man who pledges himself to raise his hand in support of the American constitution every individual who swears to support this instrument — at the same time swears that the slaves of that country shall either remain slaves or die. This clause of the constitution, in fact, converts every white American into an enemy to the Black man in that land of professed liberty. Every bayonet, sword, musket, and cannon has its deadly aim at the bosom of the Negro: 3,000,000 of the coloured race are lying there under the heels of 17,000,000 of their white fellow creatures. There they stand, with all their education, with all their religion, with all their moral influence, with all their means of co-operation — there they stand, sworn before God and the universe, that the slave shall continue a slave or die.

Then, take another clause of the American constitution. "No person held in service or labour, in any state within the limits thereof, escaping into another, shall in consequence of any law or regulation therein, be released from such service or labour, but shall be delivered up to be claimed by the party to whom such service or labour may be due." Upon the face of this clause there is nothing of injustice or inhumanity in it. It appears perfectly in accordance with justice, and in every respect humane. It is, indeed, just what it should be, according to your English notion of things and the general use of words.

But what does it mean in the United States? I will tell you what it signifies there — that if any slave, in the darkness of midnight, looks down upon himself, feeling his limbs and thinking himself a man, and entitled to the rights of a man, shall steal away from his hovel or quarter, snap the chain that bound his leg, break the fetter that linked him to slavery, and seek refuge from the free institutions of a democracy, within the boundary of a monarchy, that that slave, in all his windings by night and by day, in his way from the land of slavery to the abode of freedom, shall be liable to be hunted down like a felon, and dragged back to the hopeless bondage from which he was endeavouring to escape.

So that this clause of the constitution is one of the most effective safeguards of that slave system of which we have met here this evening to express our detestation. This clause of the American constitution makes the whole land one vast hunting-ground for men: it gives to the slaveholder the right at any moment to set his well-trained bloodhounds upon the track of the poor fugitive; hunt him down like a wild beast, and hurl him back to the jaws of slavery, from which he had, for a brief space of time, escaped. This clause of the constitution consecrates every rood of earth in that land over which the star-spangled banner waves as slave-hunting-ground. Sir, there is no valley so deep, no mountain so high, no plain so expansive, no spot so sacred, throughout the length and breadth of America, as to enable a man, not having a skin coloured like your own, to enjoy the free and unrestrained right to his own hands. If he attempt to assert such a right he may be hunted down in a moment.

Sir, in the Mosaic economy, to which reference has been made this evening by a preceding speaker, we have a command given, as it were, amid the thunders and lightenings from Sinai, "Thou shalt not deliver unto his master the servant that is escaped unto thee: he shall dwell with thee in the place that liketh him best: thou shalt not oppress him!" America, religious America, has run into the very face of Jehovah, and said, "Thou shalt deliver him unto his master." "Thou shalt deliver unto the tyrant, who usurps authority over his fellow man, the trembling bondman that escapes into your midst."

Sir, this clause of the American constitution is one of the most deadly enactments against the natural rights of man; above and beyond all its other provisions, it serves to keep up that system of fraud, wrong, and inhumanity which is now crushing 3,000,000 of human beings identified with me in their complexion, and formerly in their chains. How is it? Why, the slaveholders of the South would be wholly unable to hold their slaves were it not for the existence of the protection afforded by this constitution; but for this the slaves would run away. No, no; they do not love their masters so well as the tyrants sometimes flatter themselves; they do frequently run away. You have an instance of their disposition to run away before you.

Why, sir, the Northern States claim to be exempt from all responsibility in the matter of the slave-holding of America, because they do not actually hold slaves themselves upon their own soil. But this is a mere subterfuge. What is the actual position of those Northern States? If they are not actual slaveholders, they stand around the slave system and support it. They say to the slaveholder, "We have a sentiment against — we have a feeling opposed to — we have an abhorrence of — slavery. We would not hold slaves ourselves, and we are most sincerely opposed to slavery; but, still, if your Negroes run away from you to us, we will return them to you. And, while you can make the slaves believe that we will so return them, why, of course, they will not run away into our states; and, then, if they should attempt to gain their freedom by force, why, we will bring down upon them the whole civil, military, and naval power of the nation and crush them again into subjection. While we make them believe that we will do this, we give them the most complete evidence that we will, by our votes in congress and in the senate, by our religious assemblies, our synods, presbyteries and conferences, by our individual votes, by our deadly hate and deep prejudice against the coloured man, even when he is free, we will, by all these evidences, give you the means of convincing the slave, that, if he does attempt to gain his freedom, we will kill him. But still, notwithstanding all this, let it be clearly understood that we hate slavery."

This is the guilty position even of those who do not themselves hold slaves in America. And, under such circumstances, I really cannot be very patriotic when speaking of their national institutions and boasted constitution, and, therefore, I hope you will not expect any very eloquent outbursts of eulogy or praise of America from me upon the present occasion.

No, my friends; I am going back, determined to be honest with America. I am going to the United States in a few days, but I go there to do, as I have done here, to unmask her pretensions to republicanism, and expose her hypocritical professions of Christianity; to denounce her high claims to civilization, and proclaim in her ears the wrongs of those who cry day and night to Heaven, "How long! how long! O Lord God of Sabaoth!"

I go to that land, not to foster her national pride, or utter fulsome words about her greatness. She is great in territory; great in numerical strength; great in intellectual sagacity; great in her enterprise and industry.

She may boast of her broad lakes and mighty rivers; but, sir, while I remember, that with her broadest lakes and finest rivers, the tears and blood of my brethren are mingled and forgotten, I cannot speak well of her; I cannot be loud in her praise, or pour forth warm eulogiums upon her name or institutions. No; she is unworthy of the name of great or free. She stands upon the quivering heart-strings of 3,000,000 of people.

She punishes the Black man for crimes, for which she allows the white man to escape. She declares in her statute-book, that the Black man shall be seventy times more liable to the punishment of death than the white man. In the state of Virginia, there are seventy-one crimes for which a Black man may be punished with death, only one of which crimes will bring upon the white man a like punishment. She will not allow her Black population to meet together and worship God according to the dictates of their own consciences. If they assemble together more than seven in number for the purpose of worshipping God, or improving their minds in any way, shape, or form, each one of them may legally be taken and whipped with thirty-nine lashes upon his bare back. If any one of them shall be found riding a horse, by day or by night, he may be taken and whipped forty lashes on his naked back, have his ears cropped, and his cheek branded with a red-hot iron.

In all the slave states south, they make it a crime punishable with severe fines, and imprisonment in many cases, to teach or instruct a slave to read the pages of Inspired Wisdom. In the state of Mississippi, a man is liable to a heavy fine for teaching a slave to read. In the state of Alabama, for the third offence, it is death to teach a slave to read. In the state of Louisiana, for the second offence, it is death to teach a slave to read. In the state of South Carolina, for the third offence of teaching a slave to read, it is death by the law. To aid a slave in escaping from a brutal owner, no matter how inhuman the treatment he may have received at the hands of his tyrannical master, it is death by the law. For a woman, in defence of her own person and dignity, against the brutal and infernal designs of a determined master, to raise her hand in protection of her chastity, may legally subject her to be put to death upon the spot.

Sir, I cannot speak of such a nation as this with any degree of complacency, and more especially when that very nation is loud and long in its boasts of holy liberty and light; when, upon the wings of the press, she is hurling her denunciations at the despotisms of Europe, when she is embracing every opportunity to scorn and scoff at the English government, and taunt and denounce her people as a community of slaves, bowing under a haughty monarchy; when she has stamped upon her coin, from the cent to the dollar, from the dollar to the eagle, the sacred name of liberty; when upon every hill may be seen erected, a pole, bearing the cap of liberty, under which waves the star-spangled banner; when upon every 4th of July we hear declarations like this: "O God! we thank Thee that we live in a land of religious and civil liberty!"; when from every platform, upon that day, we hear orators rise and say: — "Ours is a glorious land; Her broad arms stretch from shore to shore, The broad Pacific chafes her strand, She hears the dark Atlantic roar; Enamelled on her ample breast, A many a goodly prospect stands."

"Ours is the land of the free and the home of the brave."

I say, when professions like these are put forth vauntingly before the world, and I remember the scenes I have witnessed in, and the facts I know, respecting that country, why, then, let others do as they will, I have no word of patriotic applause for America or her institutions. America presents to the world an anomaly, such as no other nation ever did or can present before mankind. The people of the United States are the boldest in their pretensions to freedom, and the loudest in their profession of love of liberty; yet no nation upon the face of the globe can exhibit a statute-book so full of all that is cruel, malicious, and infernal, as the American code of laws. Every page is red with the blood of the American slave. O'Connell once said, speaking of Ireland — no matter for my illustration, how truly or falsely — that "her history may be traced, like the track of a wounded man through a crowd." If this description can be given of Ireland, how much more true is it when applied to the sons and daughters of Africa, in the United States? Their history is nothing but blood! blood! blood! — blood in the morning, blood at noon, blood at night! They have had blood to drink; they have had their own blood shed. At this moment we may exclaim "What, ho! our countrymen in chains! The whip on woman's shrinking flesh! Our soil still redd'ning with the stains Caught from her scourging, warm and fresh! What! mothers from their children riven! What! God's own image bought and sold! Americans to market driven, And barter'd, as the brutes, for gold!"

And this, too, sir, in the midst of a people professing, not merely republicanism, not merely democratical institutions, but civilization; nay, more — Christianity, in its highest, purest, and broadest sense; claiming to be the heaven-appointed nation, in connexion with the British, to civilise, Christianise, and evangelise the world. For this purpose, sir, we have our Tract, Bible, and Missionary Societies; our Sabbath-school and Education Societies; we have in array all these manifestations of religious life, and yet, in the midst of them all — amid the eloquence of the orators who swagger at all these meetings — may be heard the clanking of the fetter, the rattling of the chain, and the crack of the slave-driver's whip.

The very man who ascends the platform, and is greeted with rounds of applause when he comes forward to speak on the subject of extending the victories of the cross of Christ, "from the rivers to the ends of the earth," has actually come to that missionary meeting with money red with the blood of the slave; with gold dripping with gore from the plantations. The very man who stands up there — Dr. Plummer, for instance, Dr. Marsh, Dr. Anderson, Dr. Cooper, or some other such doctor — comes to the missionary meeting for the purpose of promoting Christianity, Evangelical Christianity, with the price of blood in his possession. He stands up and preaches with it in his pocket, and gives it to aid the holy cause of sending missionaries to heathen lands. This is the spectacle we witness annually at New York and Philadelphia; and sometimes they have the temerity to come as far as Boston with their blood-stained money.

We are a nation of inconsistencies; completely made up of inconsistencies. Mr. John C. Calhoun, the great Southern statesman of the United States, is regarded in that country as a real democrat, "dyed in the wool," "a right out-and-out democrat," "a back-bone democrat." By these and similar phrases they speak of him; and yet, sir, that very man stands upon the floor of the senate, and actually boasts that he is a robber! that he is an owner of slaves in the Southern states. He positively makes his boast of this disgraceful fact, and assigns it as a reason why he should be listened to as a man of consequence — a person of great importance. All his pretensions are founded upon the fact of his being a slaveowner.

The audacity of these men is actually astounding; I scarcely know what to say in America, when I hear men deliberately get up and assert a right to property in my limbs — my very body and soul; that they have a right to me! that I am in their hands, "a chattel personal to all intents, purposes, and constructions whatsoever;" "a thing" to be bought and sold! — to be sure, having moral perceptions; certainly possessing intellect, and a sense of my own rights, and endowed with resolution to assert them whenever an opportunity occurred; and yet, notwithstanding, a slave! a marketable commodity! I do not know what to think of these men; I hardly know how to answer them when they speak in this manner. And, yet, this self-same John C. Calhoun, while he vehemently declaims for liberty, and asserts that any attempt to abridge the rights of the people should be met with the sternest resistance on all hands, deliberately stands forth at the head of the democracy of that country and talks of his right to property in me; and not only in my body, but in the bodies and souls of hundreds and thousands of others in the United States.

As with this honourable gentleman, so is it with the doctors of divinity in America; for, after all, slavery finds no defenders there so formidable as them. They are more skilful, adroit, and persevering, and will descend even to greater meannesses, than any other class of opponents with whom the abolitionists have to contend in that country. The church in America is, beyond all question, the chief refuge of slavery. When we attack it in the state, it runs into the street, to the mob; when we attack it in the mob, it flies to the church; and, sir, it is a melancholy fact, that it finds a better, safer, and more secure protection from the shafts of abolitionism within the sacred enclosure of the Christian temple than from any other quarter whatever. Slavery finds no champions so bold, brave, and uncompromising as the ministers of religion. These men come forth, clad in all the sanctity of the pastoral office, and enforce slavery with the Bible in their hands, and under the awful name of the Everlasting God. We there find them preaching sermon after sermon in support of the system of slavery as an institution consistent with the Gospel of Jesus Christ. We have commentary after commentary attempting to wrest the sacred pages of the Bible into a justification of the iniquitous system.

And, sir, this may explain to you what might otherwise appear unaccountable in regard to the conduct and proceedings of American abolitionists. I am very desirous of saying a word or two on this point, upon which there has been much misrepresentation. I say, the fact that slavery takes refuge in the churches of the United States will explain to you another fact, which is, that the opponents of slavery in America are almost universally branded there — and, I am sorry to say, to some extent in this country also — as infidels. Why is this? Simply because slavery is sheltered by the church.

The warfare in favor of emancipation in America is a very different thing from the warfare which you had to wage on behalf of freedom in the West India Islands. On that occasion, thank God! religion was in its right position, and slavery in its proper place — in fierce antagonism to each other. Religion and slavery were then the enemies of each other. Slavery hated Religion with the utmost intensity; it pursued the missionary with the greatest malignity, burning down his chapel, mobbing his house, jeopardising his life, and rendering his property utterly insecure. There was an antipathy deep and lasting between slavery and the exponents of Christianity in the West India Islands. All honour to the names of Knibb and Burchell! Those men were indeed found faithful to Him who commanded them to, "Preach deliverance to the captive and the opening of the prison to them that were bound." But, sir, the natural consequence of such faithfulness was, that these men were hated with the most deadly hate by the slaveowners, who with their abettors, used every effort to crush that living voice of truth coming from the bosom of the Christian church, which was endeavoring to dash down the bloody altars of slavery, and scatter its guilty profits to the winds.

Slavery was opposed by the church in the West Indies: not so in America; there, religion and slavery are linked and interlinked with each other — woven and interwoven together. In the United States we have slaveholders as class-leaders, ministers of the Gospel, elders, deacons, doctors of divinity, professors of theology, and even bishops. We have the slaveholder in all parts of the church. Wherever he is, he is an active, energetic, vigilant man.

Slavery never sleeps or slumbers. The slaveholder who goes to his bed for the purpose of taking rest does not pass his night in tranquillity and peace; but, knowing his danger, he takes his pistol, bowie-knife, and dirk with him. He is uneasy; he is aware that he lies upon bleeding heartstrings, that he sleeps upon the wretchedness of men, that he rests himself upon the quivering flesh of his fellow creatures around him; he is conscious that there is intellect burning — a spark of divinity enkindled — within the bosoms of the men he oppresses, who are watching for, and will seize upon, the first opportunity to burst their bonds asunder, and mete out justice to the wretch who has doomed them to slavery. The slaveowner, therefore, is compelled to be watchful; he cannot sleep; there is a morbid sensitiveness in his breast upon this subject: everything that looks like opposition to slavery is promptly met by him and put down.

Whatever, either in the church or the state, may appear to have a tendency to undermine, sap, or destroy the foundation of slavery is instantly grappled with; and, by their religion, their energy, their perseverance, their unity of feeling, and identity of interest, the slaveholder and the church have ever had the power to command a majority to put down any efforts for the emancipation of the coloured race, and to sustain slavery in all its horrors. Thus has slavery been protected and sheltered by the church. Slavery has not only framed our civil and criminal code, it has not only nominated our presidents, judges, and diplomatic agents, but it has also given to us the most popular commentators on the Bible in America. It has given to us our religion, shaped our morality, and fashioned it favourable to its own existence.

Thus is it that slavery is ensconced at this moment; and, when the abolitionist sees slavery thus woven and interwoven with the very texture — with the whole network — of our social and religious organisations, why he resolves, at whatever hazard of reputation, ease, comfort, luxury, or even of life itself, to pursue, and, if possible, destroy it. Sir, to illustrate our principle of action, I might say that we adopt the motto of Pat, upon entering a Tipperary row. Said he, "Wherever you see a head, hit it!" So, the abolitionists have resolved, that wherever slavery manifests itself in the United States, they will hit it. They will deal out their heaviest blows upon it. Hence, having followed it from the state to the street, from the mob to the church, from the church to the pulpit, they are now hunting it down there.

But slavery in the present day affects to be very pious; it is uncommonly devotional, all at once. It feels disposed to pray the very moment you touch it. The hideous fiend kneels down and pretends to engage in devotional exercises; and when we come to attack it, it howls piously — "Off! you are an infidel;" and straightway the press in America, and some portion of the press in this land also, take up the false cry. Forthwith a clamour is got up here, not against the slaveholder, but against the man who is virtuously labouring for the overthrow of that which his assailants profess to hate — slavery. A fierce outcry is raised, not in favour of the slave, but against him and against his best and only friends.

Sir, when the history of the emancipation movement shall have been fairly written, it will be found that the abolitionists of the nineteenth century were the only men who dared to defend the Bible from the blasphemous charge of sanctioning and sanctifying negro slavery. It will be found that they were the only men who dared to stand up and demand, that the churches calling themselves by the name of Christ, should entirely, and forever, purify themselves from all contact, connection, and fellowship with men who gain their fortunes by the blood of souls. It will be found that they were the men who "cried aloud and spared not;" who "lifted their voices like trumpets," against the giant iniquity by which they were surrounded. It will then be seen that they were the men who planted themselves on the immutable, eternal, and all-comprehensive principle of the sacred New Testament — "All things whatsoever ye would that men should do unto you, do ye even so unto them" — that, acting on this principle, and feeling that if the fetters were on their own limbs, the chain upon their own persons, the lash falling quick and hard upon their own quivering bodies, they would desire their fellow men about them to be faithful to their cause; and, therefore, carrying out this principle, they have dared to risk their lives, fortunes, nay, their all, for the purpose of rescuing from the tyrannous grasp of the slaveholder these 3,000,000 of trampled-down children of men.

Sir, the foremost, strongest, and mightiest among those who have completely identified themselves with the negroes in the United States, I will now name here; and I do so because his name has been most unjustly coupled with odium in this country. I will name, if only as an expression of gratitude on my part, my beloved, esteemed, and almost venerated friend, William Lloyd Garrison.

Sir, I have now been in this country for nineteen months; I have gone through its length and breadth; I have had sympathy here and sympathy there; co-operation here, and co-operation there; in fact, I have scarcely met a man who has withheld fellowship from me as an abolitionist, standing unconnected with William Lloyd Garrison. Had I stood disconnected from that great and good man, then numerous and influential parties would have held out to me the right hand of fellowship, sanctioned my proceedings in England, backed me up with money and praise, and have given me a great reputation, so far as they were capable; and they were men of influence.

And why, sir, is William Lloyd Garrison hated and despised by certain parties in this country? What has he done to deserve such treatment at their hands? He has done that which all great reformers and pioneers in the cause of freedom or religion have ever been called upon to do — made himself unpopular for life in the maintenance of great principles. He has thrown himself, as it were, over the ditch as a bridge; his own body, his personal reputation, his individual property, his wide and giant-hearted intellect, all were sacrificed to form a bridge that others might pass over and enjoy a rich reward from the labours that he had bestowed, and the seed which he had sown. He has made himself disreputable. How? By his uncompromising hostility to slavery, by his bold, scathing denunciation of tyranny; his unwavering, inflexible adherence to principle; and by his frank, open, determined spirit of opposition to everything like cant and hypocrisy. Such is the position in which he stands among the American people. And the same feeling exists in this country to a great extent. Because William Lloyd Garrison has upon both sides of the Atlantic fearlessly unmasked hypocrisy, and branded impiety in language in which impiety deserves to be characterized, he has thereby brought down upon himself the fierce execrations of a religious party in this land.

But, sir, I do not like, upon the present occasion, even to allude to this subject; for the party who have acted in this matter is small and insignificant; so impotent for good, so well known for its recklessness of statement, so proverbial for harshness of spirit, that I will not dwell any longer on their conduct. I feel that I ought not to trespass upon your patience any further.

Well, then, as you are so indulgent to me, I will refer to another matter. It would not be right and proper, from any consideration of regard and esteem which I feel for those who have honoured me by assembling here this evening to bid me farewell — especially to some who have honoured me and the cause I am identified with, honoured themselves and our common humanity, by being present tonight upon this platform — I say it would not be proper in me, out of deference to any such persons, on this occasion, to fail to advert to what I deem one of the greatest sins of omission ever committed by British Christians in this country. I allude to the recent meeting of the Ecumenical Evangelical Alliance. Sir, I must be permitted to say a word or two upon this matter.

From my very love of British Christians — out of esteem for the very motives of those excellent men who composed the British part of that great convention — from all these considerations, I am bound to state here my firm belief, that they suffered themselves to be sadly hoodwinked upon this point. They were misled and cajoled into a position on this question, which no subsequent action can completely obliterate or entirely atone for. They had it in their power to have given slavery a blow which would have sent it reeling to its grave, as if smitten by a voice or an arm from Heaven. They had moral power; they had more — they had religious power. They were in a position which no other body ever occupied, and in which no other association will ever stand, while slavery exists in the United States. They were raised up on a pinnacle of great eminence: they were "a city set on a hill." They were a body to whom the whole evangelical world was looking, during that memorable month of August.

Pressed down deep among evangelical Christians, under the feet of some there, were 3,000,000 of slaves looking to the Evangelical Alliance, with uplifted hands, with imploring tones — or, rather, I should say in the absence of tones, for the slave is dead; he has no voice in such assemblies; he can send no delegates to Bible and Missionary Societies, Temperance Conventions, or Evangelical Alliances; he is not permitted to send representatives there to tell his wrongs. He has his pressing evils and deeply aggravated wrongs, to which he is constantly subject; but he is not allowed to depute any voice to plead his cause. Still, in the silence of annihilation — of mental and moral annihilation — in the very eloquence of extinction, he cried to the Evangelical Alliance to utter a word on behalf of his freedom. They "passed him by on the other side."

Sir, I am sorry for this, deeply sorry; sorry on their own account, for I know they are not satisfied with their position. I am sorry that they should, from a timidity on their part — a fear of offending those who were called "The American brethren" — have given themselves the pain and trouble to repent on this question. But still, I hope they will repent; and I believe that many of them have already repented; I believe that those who were hoodwinked on that occasion, when they shall be brought to see that they were miserably deceived — misled by the jack o' lanterns from America — that they will add another element to their former opposition to slavery, and that is, the pain and sense of injustice done to themselves on the part of the American delegates. From the very feeling of having been betrayed into a wrong position, they will feel bound to deal a sharp, powerful, and pungent rebuke to those guilty men who dared to lead them astray.

Sir, after all, I do not wonder at the manner in which the British delegates were deluded; when I reflect upon the subtlety of the Americans, their apparently open, free, frank, candid, and unsophisticated disposition — how they stood up and declared to the British brethren that they were honest, and looked so honestly, and smiled so blandly at the same time. No; I do not wonder at their success, when I think how old and skilful they are in the practice of misrepresentation — in the art of lying. Coarse as the expression I have here applied to them may be, Mr. Chairman, it is, nevertheless, true; the thing exists. If

I am branded for coarseness on the present occasion, I must excuse myself by telling you I have a coarse thing and a foul business to lay before you.

As with the president, so with those deputations from America; there is not a single inaugural speech, not an annual message, but teems with lies like this — that "in this land every man enjoys the protection of the law, the protection of his property, the protection of his person, the protection of his liberty." They iterate and reiterate these statements over and over again. Thus, these Americans, as I said before, are skilled in the art of falsehood. I do not wonder at their success, when I recollect that they brought religion to and them in their fraud; for they not only told their falsehood with the blandness, oratory, and smiling looks of the politicians in their own country, but they combined with those seductive qualities a loud profession of piety; and in this way they have succeeded well in misleading the judgements of some of the most intrepid, bright, and illustrious of slavery's foes in the ranks of the ministers of religion of England.

Among the arguments used at the meeting of the Evangelical Alliance, the following stood pre-eminent: "You, British ministers, should not interfere with slavery, or pass resolutions to exclude slaveholders from your fellowship, because," it was coolly said, "the slaveholders are placed in difficult circumstances." It was stated that the slaveholders could not get rid of their slaves if they wished; that they were anxiously desirous of emancipating their slaves, but that the laws of the states in which they lived were such as to compel them to hold them whether they would or not. It was alleged that their peculiar circumstances make it a matter of Christian duty in them to hold their slaves.

Sir, I know the stubborn and dogged manner in which these statements were made; and I am conscious how well calculated they were to excite sympathy for the slaveholders: but I am here to tell you, that there was not one word of truth in any of those plausible assertions. There was, indeed, a slight shadow of light; a glimmering might be detected by an argue eye, but not certainly by the eye of man. There was a faint semblance of truth in it, a slight shadow; but, after all, it was only a semblance.

What are the facts of the case? Just these: that in three or four of the Southern states, when a man emancipates his slaves, he is obliged to give a bond that such slaves shall not become chargeable to the state as paupers. That is all the "impediment;" that is the whole of the "difficulty" as regards the law. But the fact is, that the free Negroes never become paupers. I do not know that I ever saw a Black pauper. The free Negroes in Philadelphia, 25,000 in number, not only support their own poor, by their own benevolent societies, but actually pay 500 dollars per annum for the support of the white paupers in the state. No, sir, the statement is false; we do not have Black paupers in America; we leave pauperism to be fostered and taken care of by white people; not that I intend any disrespect to my audience in making this statement. I can assure you I am in nowise prejudiced against colour. But the idea of a Black pauper in the United States is most absurd.

But, after all, what does the objection amount to? What if really they have to give a bond to the State that the slaves whom they emancipate should not become chargeable to the state? Why, sir, one would think this would be a very little matter of consideration to a just and Christian man; considering that all the wealth that this conscientious slave-holder possesses, he has wrung from the unrequited toil of the slave. It is not much, when it is recollected that he kept the poor Negro in ignorance, and worked him twenty-eight or thirty years of his life, and that he has had the fruit of his labour during the best part of his days. But yet, it is gravely stated, that the slaveowner looks on it as a great hardship, that if he emancipates his slave he is bound not to suffer him to become chargeable to the state. Why, the money which the slave should have earned in his youthful days, to support him in the season of age, has been wrung from him by his Christian master. But the slaveholder of America had no occasion ever to have had such a difficulty as this to contend with before he gets rid of his slave.

I may mention a fact, which is not generally known here, that this law was adopted in the slave states — for what purpose? I will tell you why: because it was previously the custom of a large class of slaveholders to hold their slaves in bondage from infancy to old age, so long as they could toil and struggle and were worth a penny a day to their masters. While they could do this, they were kept; but, as soon as they became old and decrepit — the moment they were unable to toil — their masters, from very benevolence and humanity of course, gave them their freedom. The inhabitants of the states, to prevent this burden upon their community, made the masters liable for their support under such circumstances. Dr. Cox did not tell you that in his famous speech in the Evangelical Alliance. I mean Dr. Cox of America. I do rejoice that there is another Dr. Cox in the world, of a very different character from the one in America, to redeem the name of Cox from the infamy that must necessarily settle down upon the head of that Cox, who, with wiles and subtlety, led the Evangelical Alliance astray upon this question. I am glad — I am delighted — I am grateful — profoundly grateful, in review of all the facts, that my friend — the slave's friend — Dr. Cox of Hackney, has been pleased to give us his presence tonight.

But now, really if the slaveholder is watching for an opportunity to get rid of his slaves, what has he to do? Why, just nothing at all — he has only to cease to do. He has to undo what he has already done; nothing more. He has only to tell the slave, "I have no longer any claim upon you as a slave." That is all that is necessary; and then the work is done. The Negro, simple in his understanding as he was represented this evening — somewhat unjustly, by the [remarks made by Mr. Henry Russell] — would take care of the rest of the matter. He would have no difficulty in finding some way to gain his freedom, if his master only gave him permission so to do.

The truth is, that the whole of America is cursed with slavery. There is upon our Northern and Western borders a land uncurled by slavery — a territory ruled over by the British power. There — "The lion at a virgin's feet Crouches, and lays his mighty paw Upon her lap — an emblem meet Of England's queen and England's law."

From the slave plantations of America the slave could run, under the guidance of the North Star, to that same land, and in the mane of the British lion he might find himself secure from the talons and beak of the American eagle. The American slaveholder has only to say to his slave, "Tomorrow, I shall no longer hold you in bondage," and the slave forthwith goes, and is permitted — not merely "permitted" — oh! no, he is welcomed and received with open arms, by the British authorities; he is welcomed, not as a slave, but as a man; not as a bondman, but as a freeman; not as a captive, but as a brother. He is received with kindness, and regarded and treated with respect as a man. The Americans have only to say to their slaves, "Go and be free;" and they go and are free. No power within the states, or out of the states, attempts to disturb the master in the exercise of his right of transferring his negro from one country to the other.

"Oh! but then," Dr. Cox would say, "brethren, although all this which Douglass states may be very true, yet you must know that there are some very poor masters, who are so situated in regard to pecuniary matters" — for the doctor is a very indirect speaker— "so situated, in regard to pecuniary concerns, that they would not be able to remove their slaves. I know a brother in the South — a dear brother to whom I spoke on this subject; and I told him what a great sin I thought it was for him to hold slaves, but he said to me, 'Brother, I feel it as much as you do', 'but what can I do? Here are my slaves; take them; you may have them; you may take them out of the state if you please.'" Said he [Cox], "I could not; and I left them." "Now what would you do?" said the doctor to the brethren at Manchester and Liverpool —

"what would you do, if placed in such difficult circumstances?"

The fact is, there is no truth in the existence of these difficulties at all. Sir, let me tell you what has stood as a standing article in our anti-slavery journals for the last ten years. When this plea was first put forth in America, and those intrepid champions of the slave, Gerrit Smith, Arthur Tappan, and other noble-minded abolitionists heard of it, what did they do? They inserted their cards in all the most respectable papers in America, and stated that there were 10,000 dollars ready at the service of any poor slaveholders who might not have the means of removing the Negroes they were desirous of emancipating. Now, sir, the slaveholder must have seen this advertisement, for whatever difficulties they have to encounter, they find none in seeing money. But, sir, was there ever a demand for a single red copper of the whole of those 10,000 dollars? Never; never.

Now what does this fact prove? Why, that there were no slaveholders who stood in need of such assistance; not one who wanted it for the purpose for which it might have been easily obtained, to meet the "difficult circumstances" stated by Dr. Cox. How Dr. Cox could, knowing that fact, as he must have done — for he is not so blind that he cannot see a dollar — I say how he could set up this false and contemptible plea before the world, and attempt to mislead the public mind of England upon the subject — I will not use a harsh expression, but I will say — that I cannot see how he could reconcile its concealment with honesty at any rate. That is the strongest word I will use in regard to this portion of his conduct. He certainly knew better; at least, I think he must have known better; he ought to have done so; for it is astonishing how quickly he sees things generally.

Another brother, the Reverend Doctor Marsh, also went into this subject, and told the brethren of the difficult circumstances in which the slaveholders were placed, especially the "Christian slaveholders;" for, mark this, they never apologise for infidel slave-holders! You never heard one of the whole deputation apologise for that brutal man — the uneducated slave-driver. No; it is the refined, polite, highly civilised, general, Christian part of the slaveholders, for whom they stand up and plead. Yes; they apologise for what they call "Christian slaveholders" — white blackbirds! Dr. Marsh stated, that if any persons in the United States were to emancipate their slaves, they would instantly be put into the penitentiary. I have sometimes been astonished at the credulity of their English auditory; but I do not wonder at it, for John Bull is pretty honest himself, and he thinks other people are so also. But, yet, I must say that I am surprised when I find sagacious, intelligent men really carried away by such assertions as these.

Why, sir, if this statement were true, another tinge, deeper and darker than any previously exhibited, would have appeared in the character of the American people. What! men are not only permitted to enslave, not only allowed by the government to rob and plunder, but actually compelled by the first government upon earth to live by plunder! Why, these men, by such statements, stamp their country with an infamy deeper than I can cast upon it by anything I could say; that is, admitting their statements were true.

But, sir, America, deeply fallen and lost as she is to moral principle, has not embodied in the form of law any such compulsion of slavery as that which these reverend gentlemen attempt to make out. No, sir; the slaveholder can free his slaves. Why, he has the same right to emancipate as he has to whip his Negro. He whips him; he has a right to do what he pleases with his own; he may give his slave away.

I was given away; I was given away by my father, or the man who was called my father, to his own brother. My master was a Methodist class-leader. When he found that I had made my escape, and was a good distance out of his reach, he felt a little spark of benevolence kindled up in his heart; and he cast his eyes upon a poor brother of his — a poor, wretched, out-at-elbows, hat-crown-knocked-in brother, reckless brother, who had not been so fortunate as to possess such a number of slaves as he had done. Well, looking over the pages of some British newspaper, he saw his son Frederick a fugitive slave in a foreign country, in a state of exile; and he determined now, for once in his life, that he would be a little generous to this brother out at the elbows, and he therefore said to him, "Brother, I have got a Negro; that is, I have not got him, but the English have. When a slave, his name was Frederick — Fred. Bailey. We called him Fred" — (for the Negroes never have but one name) — "but he fancied that he was something better than a slave, and so he gave himself two names. Well, that same Fred. is now actually changed into Frederick Douglass, and is going through the length and breadth of Great Britain, telling the wrongs of the slaves. Now, as you are very poor, and certainly will not be made poorer by the gift I am about to bestow upon you, I transfer to you all legal right to property in the body and soul of the said Frederick Douglass." Thus was I transferred by my father to my uncle.

Well, really, after all, I feel a little sympathy for my uncle, Hugh Auld. I did not wish to be altogether a losing game for Hugh, although, certainly, I had no desire myself to pay him any money; but if anyone else felt disposed to pay him money, of course they might do so. But at any rate I confess I had less reluctance at seeing £150 paid to poor Hugh Auld than I should have had to see the same amount of money paid to his brother, Thomas Auld, for I really think poor Hugh needed it, while Thomas did not. Hugh is a poor scamp. I hope he may read or hear of what I am now saying. I have no doubt he will, for I intend to send him a paper containing a report of this meeting.

By the by, though, I want to tell the audience one thing which I forgot, and that is, that I have as much right to sell Hugh Auld as Hugh Auld had to sell me. If any of you are disposed to make a purchase of him, just say the word. However, whatever Hugh and Thomas Auld may have done, I will not traffic in human flesh at all; so let Hugh Auld pass, for I will not sell him.

As to the kind friends who have made the purchase of my freedom, I am deeply grateful to them. I would never have solicited them to have done so, or have asked them for money for such a purpose. I never could have suggested to them the propriety of such an act. It was done from the prompting or suggestion of their own hearts, entirely independent of myself. While I entertain the deepest gratitude to them for what they have done, I do not feel like shouldering the responsibility of the act. I do, however, believe that there has been no right or noble principle sacrificed in the transaction. Had I thought otherwise, I would have been willingly "a stranger and a foreigner, as all my fathers were," through my life, in a strange land, supported by those dear friends whom I love in this country. I would have contented myself to have lived here rather than have had my freedom purchased at the violation or expense of principle. But, as I said before, I do not believe that any good principle has been violated. If there is anything to which exception may be taken, it is in the expediency, and not the principle, involved in the transaction.

I wish to say one word more respecting another body who have been alluded to this evening. You see that I keep harping on the church and its ministers, and I do so for the best of all reasons, that however low the ministry in a country may be (they may take this admission and make what they can of it: I know they will interpret it in their own favour, as it may be so interpreted) — that however corrupt the stream of politics and religion, nevertheless the fountain of the purity, as well as of the corruption, of the community may be found in the pulpit.

It is in the pulpit and the press — in the publications especially of the religious press — that we are to look for our right moral sentiment. I assert this as my deliberate opinion, I know, against the views of many of those with whom I co-operate. I do believe, however dark and corrupt they may be in any country, the ministers of religion are always higher —

of necessity higher — than the community about
them. I mean, of course, as a whole. There are
exceptions. They cannot be enunciating those great
abstract principles of right without their exerting, to
some extent, a healthy influence upon their own
conduct, although their own conduct is often in
violation of those great principles. I go, therefore, to
the churches, and I ask the churches of England for
their sympathy and support in this contest.

Sir, the growing contact and communication between this country and the United States, renders it a
matter of the utmost importance that the subject of
slavery in America should be kept before the British
public. The reciprocity of religious deputations — the
interchange of national addresses — the friendly
addresses on peace and upon the subject of temperance — the ecclesiastical connections of the two
countries — their vastly increasing commercial
intercourse resulting from the recent relaxation of the
restrictive laws upon the commerce of this country —
the influx of British literature into the United States as
well as of American literature into this country — the
constant tourists — the frequent visits to America by
literary and philanthropic men — the improvement in
the facility for the transportation of letters through the
post-office, in steam navigation, as well as other
means of locomotion — the extraordinary power and
rapidity with which intelligence is transmitted from

one country to another — all conspire to make it a matter of the utmost importance that Great Britain should maintain a healthy moral sentiment on the subject of slavery.

Why, sir, does slavery exist in the United States? Because it is reputable: that is the reason. Why is it thus reputable in America? Because it is not so disreputable out of America as it ought to be. Why, then, is it not so disreputable out of the United States as it should be? Because its real character has not been so fully known as it ought to have been. Hence, sir, the necessity of an Anti-Slavery Leagues — of men leaguing themselves together for the purpose of enlightening, raising, and fixing the public attention upon this foulest of all blots upon our common humanity. Let us, then, agitate this question.

But, sir, I am met by the objection, that to do so in this country, is to excite, irritate, and disturb the slaveholder. Sir, this is just what I want. I wish the slaveholder to be irritated. I want him jealous. I desire to see him alarmed and disturbed. Sir, by thus alarming him, you have the means of blistering his conscience, and it can have no life in it unless it is blistered. Sir, I want every Englishman to point to the star-spangled banner and say — "United States! your banner wears Two emblems, one of fame: Alas! the other that it bears Reminds us of your shame. The white man's liberty in types Stands blazoned on your stars;

But what's the meaning of your stripes? They mean your Negroes' scars."

"Oh!" it is said, "but by so doing you would stir up war between the two countries." Said a learned gentleman to me, "You will only excite angry feelings, and bring on war, which is a far greater evil than slavery." Sir, you need not be afraid of war with America while they have slavery in the United States. We have 3,000,000 of peace-makers there. Yes, 3,000,000, sir — 3,000,000 who have never signed the pledge of the noble Burrit, but who are, nevertheless, as strong and as invincible peace-men as even our friend Elihu Burrit himself.

Sir, the American slaveholders can appreciate these peace-makers; 3,000,000 of them stand there on the shores of America, and when our statesmen get warm, why these 3,000,000 keep cool. When our legislators' tempers are excited, these peace-makers say, "Keep your tempers down, brethren!" The Congress talks about going to war, but these peace-makers suggest, "But what will you do at home?" When these slaveholders declaim about shouldering their muskets, buckling on their knapsacks, girding on their swords, and going to beat back and scourge the foreign invaders, they are told by these friendly monitors, "Remember, your wives and children are at home! Reflect that we are at home! We are on the plantations. You had better stay at home and look after us. True, we eat the bread of freemen; we take up the room of freemen; we consume the same commodities as freemen: but still we have no interest in the state, no attachment for the country: we are slaves! You cannot fight a battle in your own land, but, at the first tap of a foreign drum — the very moment the British standard shall be erected upon your soil, at the first trumpet-call to freedom — millions of slaves are ready to rise and to strike for their own liberty." The slaveholders know this; they understand it well enough.

No, no; you need not fear about war between Great Britain and America. When Mr. Polk tells you that he will have the whole of Oregon, he only means to brag a little. When this boasting president tells you that he will have all that territory or go to war, he intends to retract his words the first favourable opportunity. When Mr. Webster says, fiercely, If you do not give back Madison Washington — the noble Madison Washington, who broke his fetters on the deck of the Creole, achieved liberty for himself and one hundred and thirty-five others, and took refuge within your dominions — when this proud statesman tells you, that if you do not send this noble negro back to chains and slavery, he will go to war with you, do not be alarmed; he does not mean any such thing. Leave him alone; he will find some way — some diplomatic stratagem almost inscrutable to the eyes of common men — by which to take back every syllable he has said.

You need not fear that you will have any war with America while slavery lasts, and while you as a people maintain your opposition to the accursed system. When you cease to feel any hostility to slavery, the slaveholders will then have no fear that the slaves will desert them for you, or will hate and fight against them in favour of you. So that, if only as a means of preserving peace, it were wise policy to advocate in England the cause of the emancipation of the American slaves. But, sir, England not only has power to do great good in this matter, but it is her duty to do so to the utmost of her ability.

But I fear I am speaking too long. Oh, my friends, you are very kind, but you are not very wise in saying so, allow me to tell you, with all due deference. I must conclude, and that right early; for I have to speak again tomorrow night almost 200 miles from this place; and it becomes necessary, therefore, that I should bring my address to a close, if only from motives of self-preservation, which the Americans say is the first law of slavery.

But before I sit down, let me say a few words at parting to my London friends, as well as those from the country, for I have reason to believe that there are friends present from all parts of the United Kingdom. I look around this audience, and I see those who greeted me when I first landed on your soil. I look before me here, and I see representatives from Scotland, where I have been warmly received and kindly treated. Manchester is represented on this occasion, as well as a number of other towns. Let me say one word to all these dear friends at parting; for this is probably the last time I shall ever have an opportunity of speaking to a British audience, at all events in London.

I have now been in this country nineteen months, and I have travelled through the length and breadth of it. I came here a slave. I landed upon your shores a degraded being, lying under the load of odium heaped upon my race by the American press, pulpit, and people. I have gone through the wide extent of this country, and have steadily increased — you will pardon me for saying so, for I am loath to speak of myself — steadily increased the attention of the British public to this question. Wherever I have gone, I have been treated with the utmost kindness, with the greatest deference, the most assiduous attention; and I have every reason to love England.

Sir, liberty in England is better than slavery in America. Liberty under a monarchy is better than despotism under a democracy. Freedom under a monarchical government is better than slavery in support of the American capitol. Sir, I have known what it was for the first time in my life to enjoy freedom in this country. I say that I have here, within the last nineteen months, for the first time in my life, known what it was to enjoy liberty.

I remember, just before leaving Boston for this country, that I was even refused permission to ride in an omnibus. Yes, on account of the colour of my skin, I was kicked from a public conveyance just a few days before I left that "cradle of liberty." Only three months before leaving that "home of freedom," I was driven from the lower floor of a church, because I tried to enter as other men, forgetting my complexion, remembering only that I was a man, thinking, moreover, that I had an interest in the Gospel there proclaimed; for these reasons I went into the church, but was driven out on account of my colour. Not long before I left the shores of America I went on board several steamboats, but in every instance I was driven out of the cabin, and all the respectable parts of the ship, on to the forward deck, among horses and cattle, not being allowed to take my place with human beings as a man and a brother. Sir, I was not permitted even to go into a menagerie or to a theatre, if I wished to have gone there. The doors of every museum, lyceum and athenaeum were closed against me if I wanted to go into them. There was the gallery, if I desired to go. I was not granted any of these common and ordinary privileges of free men. All were shut against me. I was mobbed in Boston, driven forth like a malefactor, dragged about, insulted, and outraged in all directions. Every white man — no matter how black his heart — could insult me with impunity.

I came to this land — how greatly changed! Sir, the moment I stepped on the soil of England — the instant I landed on the quay at Liverpool — I beheld people as white as any I ever saw in the United States; as noble in their exterior, and surrounded by as much to commend them to admiration, as any to be found in the wide extent of America. But, instead of meeting the curled lip of scorn, and seeing the fire of hatred kindled in the eyes of Englishmen, all was blandness and kindness. I looked around in vain for expressions of insult. Yes, I looked around with wonder! for I hardly believed my own eyes. I searched scrutinizingly to find if I could perceive in the countenance of an Englishman any disapprobation of me on account of my complexion. No; there was not one look of scorn or enmity. I have travelled in all parts of the country: in England, Ireland, Scotland, and Wales. I have journeyed upon highways, byways, railways, and steamboats. I have myself gone, I might say, with almost electric speed; but at all events my trunk has been overtaken by electric speed. In none of these various conveyances, or in any class of society, have I found any curled lip of scorn, or an expression that I could torture into a word of disrespect of me on account of my complexion; not one.

Sir, I came to this city accustomed to be excluded from athenaeums, literary institutions, scientific institutions, popular meetings, from the colosseum — if there were any such in the United States — and every place of public amusement or instruction. Being in London, I of course felt desirous of seizing upon every opportunity of testing the custom at all such places here, by going and presenting myself for admission as a man. From none of them was I ever ejected. I passed through them all; your colosseums, museums, galleries of painting, even into your House of Commons; and, still more, a nobleman — I do not know what to call his office, for I am not acquainted with anything of the kind in America, but I believe his name was the Marquis of Lansdowne — permitted me to go into the House of Lords, and hear what I never heard before, but what I had long wished to hear, but which I could never have heard anywhere else, the eloquence of Lord Brougham. In none of these places did I receive one word of opposition against my entrance.

Sir, as my friend Buffum, who used to travel with me, would say, "I mean to tell these facts, when I go back to America." I will even let them know, that wherever else I may be a stranger, that in England I am at home. That whatever estimate they may form

of my character as a human being, England has no
doubt with reference to my humanity and equality.
That, however much the Americans despise and
affect to scorn the negroes, that Englishmen — the
most intelligent, the noblest and best of Englishmen —
do not hesitate to give the right hand of fellowship, of
manly fellowship, to a Negro such as I am. I will tell
them this, and endeavour to impress upon their
minds these facts, and shame them into a sense of
decency on this subject.

Why, sir, the Americans do not know that I am a
man. They talk of me as a box of goods; they speak
of me in connexion with sheep, horses, and cattle.
But here, how different! Why, sir, the very dogs of
old England know that I am a man! I was in
Beckenham for a few days, and while at a meeting
there, a dog actually came up to the platform, put his
paws on the front of it, and gave me a smile of
recognition as a man. The Americans would do well
to learn wisdom upon this subject from the very dogs
of Old England; for these animals, by instinct, know
that I am a man; but the Americans somehow or
other do not seem to have attained to the same
degree of knowledge.

But I go back to the United States not as I landed
here — I came a slave; I go back a free man. I came
here a thing — I go back a human being. I came here
despised and maligned — I go back with reputation

and celebrity; for I am sure that if the Americans were to believe one tithe of all that has been said in this country respecting me, they would certainly admit me to be a little better than they had hitherto supposed I was. I return, but as a human being in better circumstances than when I came. Still I go back to toil. I do not go to America to sit still, remain quiet, and enjoy ease and comfort.

Since I have been in this land I have had every inducement to stop here. The kindness of my friends in the north has been unbounded. They have offered me house, land, and every inducement to bring my family over to this country. They have even gone so far as to pay money, and give freely and liberally, that my wife and children might be brought to this land. I should have settled down here in a different position to what I should have been placed in the United States.

But, sir, I prefer living a life of activity in the service of my brethren. I choose rather to go home; to return to America. I glory in the conflict, that I may hereafter exult in the victory. I know that victory is certain. I go, turning my back upon the ease, comfort, and respectability which I might maintain even here, ignorant as I am. Still, I will go back, for the sake of my brethren. I go to suffer with them; to toil with them; to endure insult with them; to undergo outrage with them; to lift up my voice in their behalf; to speak and write in their vindication; and struggle in their ranks for that emancipation which shall yet be achieved by the power of truth and of principle for that oppressed people. But, though I go back thus to encounter scorn and contumely, I return gladly. I go joyfully and speedily.

I leave this country for the United States on the 4th of April, which is near at hand. I feel not only satisfied, but highly gratified, with my visit to this country. I will tell my coloured brethren how Englishmen feel for their miseries. It will be grateful to their hearts to know that while they are toiling on in chains and degradation, there are in England hearts leaping with indignation at the wrongs inflicted upon them. I will endeavour to have daguerreotyped on my heart this sea of upturned faces, and portray the scene to my brethren when I reach America; I will describe to them the kind looks, the sympathetic desires, the determined hostility to everything like slavery sitting heavily or beautifully on the brow of every auditory I have addressed since I came to England. Yes, I will tell these facts to the Negroes, to encourage their hearts and strengthen them in their sufferings and toils, and I am sure that in this I shall have your sympathy as well as their blessing.

Pardon me, my friends, for the disconnected manner in which I have addressed you; but I have spoken out of the fulness of my heart; the words that came up went out, and though not uttered altogether so delicately, refinedly, and systematically as they ought have been, still, take them as they are — the free upgushings of a heart overborne with grateful emotions at the remembrance of the kindness I have received in this country from the day I landed until the present moment. With these remarks I beg to bid all my dear friends, present and at a distance — those who are here and those who have departed — farewell![86]

---

[86] Farewell Lecture to the British People delivered at London Tavern in London, England, March 30, 1847 and published as *Farewell Speech of Mr. Frederick Douglass Previously to Embarking on Board the Cambria Upon His Return to America, Delivered at the Valedictory Soiree Given to Him at the London Tavern on March 30th, 1847*, London, 1847.

Undoing the Burdens of My Brethren – I am very glad to be here. I am very glad to be present at this Anniversary, glad again to mingle my voice with those with whom I have stood identified, with those with whom I have laboured, for the last seven years, for the purpose of undoing the burdens of my brethren, and hastening the day of their emancipation.

I do not doubt but that a large portion of this audience will be disappointed, both by the *manner* and the *matter* of what I shall this day set forth. The extraordinary and unmerited eulogies, which have been showered upon me, here and elsewhere, have done much to create expectations which, I am well aware, I can never hope to gratify. I am here, a simple man, knowing what I have experienced in Slavery, knowing it to be a bad system, and desiring, by all Christian means, to seek its overthrow. I am not here to please you with an eloquent speech, with a refined and logical address, but to speak to you the sober truths of a heart overborne with gratitude to God that we have in this land, cursed as it is with Slavery, so noble a band to second my efforts and the efforts of others, in the noble work of undoing the yoke of bondage, with which the majority of the States of this Union are now unfortunately cursed.

Since the last time I had the pleasure of mingling my voice with the voices of my friends on this platform, many interesting and even trying events have occurred to me. I have experienced, within the last eighteen or twenty months, many incidents, all of which it would be interesting to communicate to you, but many of these I shall be compelled to pass over at this time, and confine my remarks to giving a general outline of the manner and spirit with which I have been hailed abroad, and welcomed at the different places which I have visited during my absence of twenty months.

You are aware, doubtless, that my object in going from this country, was to get beyond the reach of the clutch of the man who claimed to own me as his property. I had written a book, giving a history of that portion of my life spent in the gall and bitterness of Slavery, and in which, I also identified my oppressors as the perpetrators of some of the most atrocious crimes. This had deeply incensed them against me, and stirred up within them the purpose of revenge, and, my whereabouts being known, I believed it necessary for me, if I would preserve my liberty, to leave the shores of America, and take up my abode in some other land, at least until the clamor had subsided. I went to England, monarchical England, to get rid of Democratic Slavery; and I must confess that at the very threshold I was satisfied that I had gone to the right place. Say what you will of England — of the degradation — of the poverty — and there is much of it there, — say what you will of the oppression and suffering going on in England at this time, there is Liberty there, not only for the white man, but for the Black man also. The instant that I stepped upon the shore, and looked into the faces of the crowd around me, I saw in every man a recognition of my manhood, and an absence, a perfect absence, of everything like that disgusting hate with which we are pursued in this country. I looked around in vain to see in any man's face a token of the slightest aversion to men on account of my complexion. Even the cabmen demeaned themselves to me as they did to other men, and the very dogs and pigs of old England treated me as a man! I cannot, however, my friends, dwell upon this anti-prejudice, or rather the many illustrations of the absence of prejudice against colour in England, but will proceed, at once, to defend the right and duty of invoking English aid and English sympathy for the overthrow of American slavery, for the education of coloured Americans, and to forward, in every way, the interests of humanity; inasmuch as the right of appealing to England for aid in overthrowing Slavery in this country has been called in question, in public meetings and by the press, in this city.

I cannot agree with my friend Mr. Garrison, in relation to my love and attachment to this land. I have no love for America, as such; I have no patriotism. I have no country. What country have I? The institutions of this country do not know me, do not recognize me as a man. I am not thought of, spoken of, in any direction, out of the anti-slavery ranks, as a man. I am not thought of, or spoken of, except as a piece of property belonging to some *Christian* slaveholder, and all the religious and political institutions of this country, alike pronounce me a slave and a chattel. Now, in such a country as this, I cannot have patriotism. The only thing that links me to this land is my family, and the painful consciousness that here and there are three millions of my fellow-creatures, groaning beneath the iron rod of the worst despotism that could be devised, even in Pandemonium; that here are men and brethren, who are identified with me by their complexion, identified with me by their hatred of Slavery, identified with me by their love and aspirations for liberty, identified with me by the stripes upon their backs, their inhuman wrongs and cruel sufferings. This, and this only, attaches me to this land, and brings me here to plead with you, and with this country at large, for the disenthralment of my oppressed countrymen, and to overthrow this system of Slavery which is crushing them to the earth. How can I love a country that dooms three millions of my brethren, some of them my own kindred, my own brothers, my own sisters, who are now clanking the chains of Slavery upon the plans of the South, whose warm blood is now making fat the soil of Maryland and of Alabama, and over whose crushed spirits rolls the darks shadow of oppression, shutting out and extinguishing forever, the cheering rays of that bright sun of Liberty lighted in the souls of all God's children by the Omnipotent hand of Deity itself? How can I, I say, love a country thus cursed, thus bedewed with the blood of my brethren? A country, the Church of which, and the Government of which, and the Constitution of which, is in favour of supporting and perpetuation this monstrous system of injustice and blood? I have not, I cannot have, any love for this country, as such, or for its Constitution. I desire to see its overthrow as speedily as possible, and its Constitution shriveled in a thousand fragments, rather than this foul curse should continue to remain as now.

In all this, my friends, let me make myself understood. I do not hate America as against England, or against any other country, or land. I love humanity all over the globe. I am anxious to see righteousness prevail in all directions. I am anxious to see Slavery overthrown here; but, I never appealed to Englishmen in a manner calculated to awaken feelings of hatred and disgust, or to influence their prejudices towards America as a nation, or in a manner provocative of national jealousy or ill-will; but I always appealed to their conscience — to the higher and nobler feelings of the people of that country, to enlist them in this cause. I always appealed to their manhood, that which preceded their being Englishmen, (to quote an expression of my friend Phillips,) I appealed to them as men, and I had a right to do so. They are men, and the slave is a man, and we have a right to call upon all men to assist in breaking his bonds, let them be born when, and a live where they may.

But it is asked, "What good will this do?" or "What good has it done?" "Have you not irritated, have you not annoyed your American friends, and the American people rather, than done them good?" I admit that we have irritated them. They deserve to be irritated. I am anxious to irritate the American people on this question. As it is in physics, so in morals, there are cases which demand irritation, and counter irritation. The conscience of the American public needs this irritation. And I would *blister it all over, from centre to circumference,* until it gives signs of a purer and a better life than it is no manifesting to the world.

But why expose the sins of one nation in the eyes of another? Why attempt to bring one people under the odium of another people? There is much force in this question. I admit that there are sins in almost ever country which can be best removed by means confined exclusively to their immediate locality. But such evils and such sins pre-suppose the existence of a moral power in this immediate locality sufficient to accomplish the work of renovation. But where, pray, can we go to find moral power in this nation, sufficient to overthrow Slavery? To what institution, to what party shall we apply for aid? I say, we admit that there are evils which can be best removed by influences confined to their immediate locality. But in regard to American Slavery, it is not so. It is such a giant crime, so darkening to the soul, so blinding in its moral influence, so well calculated to blast and corrupt all the human principles of our nature, so well adapted to infuse its own accursed spirit into all around it, that the people among whom it exists have not the moral power to abolish it. Shall we go to the Church for this influence? We have heard its character described. Shall we go to politicians or political parties? Have they the moral power necessary to accomplish this mighty task? They have not. What are they doing at this moment? Voting supplies for Slavery — voting supplies for the extension, the stability, the perpetuation of Slavery in this land. What is the Press doing? The same. The pulpit? Almost the same. I do not flatter myself that there is moral power in the land sufficient to overthrow Slavery, and I welcome the aid of England. And that aid will come. The growing intercourse between England and this country, by means of steam-navigation, the relaxation of the protective system in various countries in Europe, gives us an opportunity to bring in the aid, the moral and Christian aid of those living on the other side of the Atlantic. We welcome it, in the language of the resolution. We entreat our British friends to continue to send in their remonstrances across the deep, against Slavery in this land. And these remonstrances will have a powerful effect here. Sir, the Americans may tell of their ability, and I have no doubt they have it, to keep back the invader's hosts, to repulse the strongest force that its enemies may send against this country. It may boast, and it may *rightly* boast, of its capacity to build its ramparts so high that no foe can hope to scale them, to render them so impregnable as to defy the assault of the world. But, Sir, there is one thing it cannot resist, come from what quarter it may. It cannot resist TRUTH. You cannot build your forts so strong, nor your ramparts so high, nor arm yourself so powerfully, as to be able to withstand the overwhelming MORAL SENTIMENT against slavery now flowing into this land. For example; prejudice against color is continually becoming weaker in this land (and more and more consider this) sentiment as unworthy a lodgment in the breast of an enlightened community. And the American abroad dare not now, even in public conveyance, to lift his voice in defence of this disgusting prejudice.

I do not mean to say that there are no practices abroad which deserve to receive an influence favourable to their extermination, from America. I am most glad to know that Democratic freedom — not the bastard democracy, which, while loud in its protestations of regard for liberty and equality, builds up Slavery, and, in the name of Freedom, fights the battles of Despotism — is making great strides in Europe. We see abroad, in England especially happy indications of progress of American principles. A little while ago England was cursed by a Corn monopoly — by that giant monopoly, which snatched from the mouths of famishing poor the bread which you sent them from this land. The community, the *people* of England, demanded its destruction, and they have triumphed! We have aided them, and they aid us, and the mission of the two nations, henceforth, is *to serve each other.*

Sir, it is said that, when abroad, I misrepresented our country on this question. I am not aware of any misrepresentation. I stated facts, and facts only. A gentlemen of your own city, Rev. Dr. Cox, has taken particular pains to stigmatize me as having introduced the subject of Slavery illegitimately into the World Temperance Convention. But what was the fact? I went to the Convention, not as a delegate. I went into it by the invitation of the Committee of the Convention. I suppose most of you know the circumstances, but I wish to say one word in relation to the spirit and the principle which animated me at the meeting. I went into it at the invitation of the Committee, and spoke not only at their urgent request, but by public announcement. I stood on the platform on the evening referred to, and heard some eight or ten Americans address the seven thousand people assembled in that vast Hall. I heard them speak of the temperance movement in this land. I heard them eulogize the temperance societies in the highest terms, calling on England to follow their example; (and England may follow them with advantage to herself;) but I heard no reference make to the 3,000,000 of people in this country who are denied the privilege, not only of temperance, but of all other societies. I heard not a word of the American slaves, who, if seven of them were found together at a temperance meeting, or any other place, would be scourged and beaten by their cruel tyrants. Yes, nine-and-thirty lashes is the penalty required to be inflicted by the law if any of the slaves get together in a number exceeding seven, for any purpose however peaceable or laudable. And while these American gentlemen were extending their hands to me, and saying, "How do you do Mr. Douglass? I am most happy to meet you here," &c. &c. I knew that, in America, they would not have touched me with a pair of tongs. I felt, therefore, that that was the place and time to call to remembrance the 3,000,000 of slaves, whom I aspired to represent on that occasion. I did so, not maliciously, but with a desire, only to subserve the best interests of my race. I besought the American delegates, who had at first responded to my speech with shouts of applause, when they should arrive at home to extend the borders of their temperance societies so as to include the 500,000 coloured people in the Northern States of the Union. I also called to mind the fact in relation to the mob that occurred in the city of Philadelphia, in the year 1842. I stated these facts to show to the British public how difficult it is for a coloured man in this country to do anything to elevate himself or his race from this state of degradation in which they are plunged; how difficult it is for him to be virtuous or temperate, or anything but a menial, an outcast. You all remember the circumstances of the mob to which I have alluded. A number of intelligent, philanthropic, manly coloured men, desirous of snatching their coloured brethren from the fangs of intemperance, formed themselves into a procession, and walked through the streets of Philadelphia with appropriate banners and badges and mottoes. I state the fact that that procession was not allowed to proceed far, in the city of Philadelphia — the American city of Brotherly Love, the city of all others loudest in its boasts of freedom and liberty — before these noble-minded men were assaulted by the citizens, their banners torn in shreds and themselves trampled in the dust, and inhumanly beaten, and all their bright and fond hopes and anticipations, in behalf of their friends and their race, blasted by the wanton cruelty of their white fellow-citizens. And all this was done for no other reason than that they had presumed to walk through the street with temperance banners and badges, like human beings.

The statement of this fact caused the whole Convention to break forth in one general expression of intense disgust at such atrocious and inhuman conduct. This disturbed the composure of some our American representatives, who, in serious alarm, caught hold of the skirts of my coat, and attempted to make me desist from my exposition of the situation of the coloured race in this country. There was one Doctor of Divinity there, the ugliest man that I ever saw in my life, who almost tore the skirts of my coat off, so vehement was he in his *friendly* attempts to induce me to yield the floor. But fortunately the audience came to my rescue, and demanded that I should go on, and I did go on, and, I trust, discharged my duty to my brethren in bonds and the cause of human liberty, in a manner not altogether unworthy the occasion.

I have been accused of *dragging* the question of Slavery into the Convention. I had a right to do so: It was the *World's* Convention — not the Convention of any sect, or number of sects — not the Convention of any particular nation — not a man's or a woman's

Convention, not a Black man's nor a white man's Convention, but the *World's* Convention, the Convention of ALL, *Black* as well as *white, bond* as well as *free.* And I stood there, as I thought, a representative of the 3,000,000 of men whom I had left in rags and wretchedness, to be devoured by the accursed institution which stands by them, as with a drawn sword, every ready to fall upon their devoted and defenceless heads. I felt, as I said to Dr. Cox, that it was demanded of me by conscience, to speak out boldly in behalf of those whom I had left behind. And, Sir, (I think I may say this, without subjecting myself to the charge of egotism,) I deem it very fortunate for the friends of the slave, that Mr. Garrison and myself were there just at that time. Sir, the churches in this country have long repined at the position of the churches in England on the subject of Slavery. They have sought many opportunities to do away the prejudices of the English churches against American Slavery. Why, Sir, at this time there were not far from seventy ministers of the Gospel from Christian America, in England, pouring their leprous proslavery distilment into the ears of the people of that country, and by their prayers, their conversation, and their public speeches, seeking to darken the British mind on the subject of Slavery, and to create in the English public the same cruel and heartless apathy that prevails in this country in relations to the slave, his wrongs and his rights. I knew them by their continuous slandering of my race; and at this time, and under this circumstances, I deemed it a happy interposition of God, in behalf of my oppressed and misrepresented and slandered people, that one of their number should burst up through the dark incrustation of malice, and hate, and degradation, which had been thrown over them, and stand before the British public to open to them the secrets of the prison-house of bondage in America. The slave sends no delegates to the Evangelical Alliance. The slave sends no delegates to the World's Temperance Convention. Why? Because chains are upon his arms and fetters fast bind his limbs. He must be driven out to be sold at auction by some *Christian* slaveholder, and the money for which his soul is battered must be appropriated to spread the Gospel among the heathen.

Sir, I feel that it is good to be here. There is always work to be done. Slavery is everywhere. Slavery goes everywhere. Slavery was in the Evangelical Alliance, looking saintly in the person of the Rev. Dr. Smythe; it was in the World's Temperance Convention, in the person of the Rev. Mr. Kirk. Dr. Marsh went about saying, in so many words, that the unfortunate slaveholders in America were so peculiarly situated, so environed by uncontrollable circumstances, that they could not liberate their slaves; that if they were to emancipate them they would be, in many instances, cast into prison. Sir, it did me good to go around on the heels of this gentleman. I was glad to follow him around for the sake of my country, for the country is not, after all, so bad as the Rev. Dr. Marsh represented it to be.

My fellow-countrymen, what think ye he said of you, on the other side of the Atlantic? He said you were not only pro-slavery, but that you actually aided the slaveholder in holding his slaves securely in his grasp; that, in fact, you compelled him to be a slaveholder. This I deny. You are not so bad as that. You do not compel the slaveholder to be a slaveholder.

And Rev. Dr. Cox, too, talked a great deal over there; and among other things he said, "that many slaveholders — dear Christian men! — were sincerely anxious to get rid of their slaves;" and to show how difficult it is for them to get rid of their human chattels, he put the following case: A man living in a State, the laws of which compel all persons emancipating their slaves to remove hem beyond its limits, wishes to liberate his slaves, but he is too poor to transport them beyond the confines of the State in which he resides; therefore he cannot emancipate them — he is fortunately, to have on hand just at that time, which completely neutralized this very affecting statement of the Doctor's. It so happens that Messrs.

Gerrit Smith and Arthur Tappan have advertised for the especial benefit of this afflicted class of slaveholders that they have set apart the sum of $10,000 to be appropriated in aiding them to remove their emancipated slaves beyond the jurisdiction of the State, and that the money would be forthcoming on application being made for it; but *no such application was ever made!* This shows that, however truthful the statements of these gentlemen may be concerning the things of the world to come, they are lamentably reckless in their statements concerning things appertaining to this world. I do not mean to say that they would designedly tell that which is false, but they did make the statements I have ascribed to them.

And Dr. Cox and other charge me with having stirred up warlike feelings while abroad. This charge, also, I deny. The whole of my arguments and the whole of my appeals, while I was abroad, were in favour of anything else than war. I embraced every opportunity to propagate the principles of peace while I was in Great Britain. I confess, honestly, that were I not a peace-man, were I a believer in fighting at all, I should have gone through England, saying to Englishmen, as Englishmen, there are 3,000,000 of men across the Atlantic who are whipped, scourged, robbed of themselves, denied every privilege, denied the right to read the Word of God who made them, trampled under foot, denied all the rights of human beings; go to their rescue; shoulder your muskets, buckle on your knapsacks, and in the invincible cause of Human Rights and Universal Liberty, go forth, and the laurels which you shall win will be as fadeless and as imperishable as the eternal aspirations of the human soul after that freedom which every being made after God's image instinctively feels is his birth-right. This would have been my course had I been a war man. That such was not my course, I appeal to my whole career while abroad to determine.[87]

Weapons of war we have cast from the battle;
TRUTH is our armour, our watch-word is LOVE;
Hushed be the sword, and the musketry's rattle,
All our equipments are drawn from above.
Praise then the God of Truth,
Hoary age and ruddy youth,
Long may our rally be
Love, Light and Liberty,
Ever our banner the banner of Peace

---

[87] Lecture delivered before the American Anti-Slavery Society, May 11th, 1847 and published in the *National Anti-Slavery Standard*, May 20th, 1847.

Our Paper and its Prospects – We are now about to assume the management of the editorial department of a newspaper, devoted to the cause of Liberty, Humanity and Progress. The position is one which, with the purest motives, we have long desired to occupy. It has long been our anxious wish to see, in this slave-holding, slave-trading, and Negro-hating land, a printing-press and paper, permanently established, under the complete control and direction of the immediate victims of slavery and oppression.

Animated by this intense desire, we have pursued our object, till on the threshold of obtaining it. Our press and printing materials are bought, and paid for. Our office secured, and is well situated, in the centre of business, in this enterprising city. Our office Agent, an industrious and amiable young man, thoroughly devoted to the interests of humanity, has already entered upon his duties. Printers well recommended have offered their services, and are ready to work as soon as we are prepared for the regular publication of our paper. Kind friends are rallying round us, with words and deeds of encouragement. Subscribers are steadily, if not rapidly coming in, and some of the best minds in the country are generously offering to lend us the powerful aid of their pens. The sincere wish of our heart, so long and so devoutly cherished seems now upon the eve of complete realization.

It is scarcely necessary for us to say that our desire to occupy our present position at the head of an Anti-slavery Journal, has resulted from no unworthy distrust or ungrateful want of appreciation of the zeal, integrity, or ability of the noble band of white laborers, in this department of our cause; but, from a sincere and settled conviction that such a Journal, if conducted with only moderate skill and ability, would do a most important and indispensable work, which it would be wholly impossible for our white friends to do for us.

It is neither a reflection on the fidelity, nor a disparagement of the ability of our friends and fellow-laborers, to assert what "common sense affirms and only folly denies," that the man who has *suffered the wrong* is the man to *demand redress,* — that the man STRUCK is the man to CRY OUT — and that he who has *endured the cruel pangs of Slavery* is the man to *advocate Liberty.* It is evident we must be our own representatives and advocates, not exclusively, but peculiarly — not distinct from, but in connection with our white friends. In the grand struggle for liberty and equality now waging, it is meet, right and essential that there should arise in our ranks authors and editors, as well as orators, for it is in these capacities that the most permanent good can be rendered to our cause.

Hitherto the immediate victims of slavery and prejudice, owing to various causes, have had little share in this department of effort: they have frequently undertaken, and almost as frequently failed. This latter fact has often been urged by our friends against our engaging in the present enterprise; but, so far from convincing us of the impolicy of our course, it serves to confirm us in the necessity, if not the wisdom of our undertaking. That others have failed, is a reason for OUR earnestly endeavoring to succeed. Our race must be vindicated from the embarrassing imputations resulting from former non-success. We believe that what *ought* to be done, *can* be done. We say this, in no self-confident or boastful spirit, but with a full sense of our weakness and unworthiness, relying upon the Most High for wisdom and strength to support us in our righteous undertaking. We are not wholly unaware of the duties, hardships and responsibilities of our position. We have easily imagined some, and friends have not hesitated to inform us of others. Many doubtless are yet to be revealed by that infallible teacher, experience. A view of them solemnize, but do not appal us. We have counted the cost. Our mind is made up, and we are resolved to go forward.

In aspiring to our present position, the aid of circumstances has been so strikingly apparent as to almost stamp our humble aspirations with the solemn sanctions of a Divine Providence. Nine years ago, as most of our readers are aware, we were held as a slave, shrouded in the midnight ignorance of that infernal system — sunken in the depths of senility and degradation — registered with four footed beasts and creeping things — regarded as property — compelled to toil without wages — with a heart swollen with bitter anguish — and a spirit crushed and broken. By a singular combination of circumstances we finally succeeded in escaping from the grasp of the man who claimed us as his property, and succeeded in safely reaching New Bedford, Mass. In this town we worked three years as a daily laborer on the wharves. Six years ago we became a Lecturer on Slavery. Under the apprehension of being re-taken into bondage, two years ago we embarked for England. During our stay in that country, kind friends, anxious for our safety, ransomed us from slavery, by the payment of a large sum. The same friends, as unexpectedly as generously, placed in our hands the necessary means of purchasing a printing press and printing materials. Finding ourself now in a favorable position for aiming an important blow at slavery and prejudice, we feel urged on in our enterprise by a sense of duty to God and man, firmly believing that our effort will be crowned with entire success.[88]

---

[88] *The North Star*, December 3rd, 1847.

Dedicated to the Cause of the Oppressed – We solemnly dedicate the North Star to the cause of our long oppressed and plundered fellow countrymen. May God bless the offering to your good! It shall fearlessly assert your rights, faithfully proclaim your wrongs, and earnestly demand for you instant and even-handed justice. Giving no quarter to slavery at the South, it will hold no truce with oppressors at the North. While it shall boldly advocate emancipation for our enslaved brethren, it will omit no opportunity to gain for the nominally free, complete enfranchisement. Every effort to injure or degrade you or your cause — originating wheresoever, or with whomsoever — shall find in it a constant, unswerving and inflexible foe.

We shall energetically assail the ramparts of Slavery and Prejudice, be they composed of church or state, and seek the destruction of every refuge of lies, under which tyranny may aim to conceal and protect itself.

Among the multitude of plans proposed and opinions held, with reference to our cause and condition, we shall try to have a mind of our own, harmonizing with all as far as we can, and differing from any and all where we must, but always discriminating between men and measures. We shall cordially approve every measure and effort calculated to advance your sacred cause, and strenuously oppose any which in our opinion may tend to retard its progress. In regard to our position, on questions that have unhappily divided the friends of freedom in this country, we shall stand in our paper where we have ever stood on the platform. Our views written shall accord with our views spoken, earnestly seeking peace with all men, when it can be secured without injuring the integrity of our movement, and never shrinking from conflict or division when summoned to vindicate truth and justice.

While our paper shall be mainly Anti-Slavery, its columns shall be freely opened to the candid and décorous discussion of all measures and topics of a moral and humane character, which may serve to enlighten, improve, and elevate mankind. Temperance, Peace, Capital Punishment, Education, — all subjects claiming the attention of the public mind may be freely and fully discussed here.

While advocating your rights, the North Star will strive to throw light on your duties: while it will not fail to make known your virtues, it will not shun to discover your faults. To be faithful to our foes it must be faithful to ourselves, in all things.

Remember that we are one, that our cause is one, and that we must help each other, if we would succeed. We have drunk to the dregs the bitter cup of slavery; we have worn the heavy yoke; we have sighed beneath our bonds, and writhed beneath the bloody lash; — cruel mementoes of our oneness are indellibly marked in our living flesh. We are one with you under the ban of prejudice and proscription — one with you under the slander of inferiority — one with you in social and political disfranchisement. What you suffer, we suffer; what you endure, we endure. We are indissolubly united, and must fall or flourish together.

We feel deeply the solemn responsibility which we have now assumed. We have seriously considered the importance of the enterprise, and have now entered upon it with full purpose of heart. We have nothing to offer in the way of literary ability to induce you to encourage us in our laudable undertaking. You will not expect or require this at our hands. The most that you can reasonably expect, or that we can safely promise, is, a paper of which you need not be ashamed. Twenty-one years of severe bondage at the South, and nine years of active life at the North, while it has afforded us the best possible opportunity for storing our mind with much practical and important information, has left us little time for literary pursuits or attainments. We have yet to receive the advantage of the first day's schooling. In point of education, birth and rank, we are one with yourselves, and of yourselves. What we are, we are not only without help, but against trying opposition. Your knowledge of our history for the last seven years makes it unnecessary for us to say more on this point. What we have been in your cause, we shall continue to be; and not being too old to learn, we may improve in many ways. Patience and Perseverance shall be our motto.

We shall be the advocates of learning, from the very want of it, and shall most readily yield the deference due to men of education among us; but shall always bear in mind to accord most merit to those who have labored hardest, and overcome most, in the praiseworthy pursuit of knowledge, remembering "that the whole need not a physician, but they that are sick," and that "the strong ought to bear the infirmities of the weak."

Brethren, the first number of the paper is before you. It is dedicated to your cause. Through the kindness of our friends in England, we are in possession of an excellent printing press, types, and all other materials necessary for printing a paper. Shall this gift be blest to our good, or shall it result in our injury? It is for you to say. With your aid, cooperation and assistance, our enterprise will be entirely successful. We pledge ourselves that no effort on our part shall be wanting, and that no subscriber shall lose his subscription — "The North Star Shall Live." [89]

---

[89] *The North Star*, December 3, 1847.

Revolution Now Cannot Be Confined – All eyes continue fixed upon France and her infant republic, the offspring of her recent revolution. The voluminous news from that quarter do not satisfy, so much as strengthen curiosity. The more we know, the more we want to know, and the more need we have of knowing. Thanks to steam navigation and electric wires, we may almost hear the words uttered, and see the deeds done, as they transpire. A revolution now cannot be confined to the place or the people where it may commence, but flashes with lightning speed from heart to heart, from land to land, till it has traversed the globe, compelling all the members of our common brotherhood at once, to pass judgment upon its merits. The revolution of France, like a bolt of living thunder, has aroused the world from its stupor. All are up and inspecting the scene. Various are the views, and mingled are the emotions which it has created. The despots of Europe – the Tories of England, and the slaveholders of America, are astonished, confused, and terrified; while the humble poor, the toil-worn laborer, the oppressed and plundered, the world around, have heard with exultation the glorious peal, and are looking forward with ardent hopes to the glorious results of which this event is but the commencement.

Simultaneously with the fall and crash of royalty in France, a terrible noise rung out from the galling chains of fettered millions in our own land, a ray of hope penetrated the lowest confines of American slave prisons, imparting firmness of faith to the whip-scarred slave, and fear and trembling to the guilty slaveholder. The pent-up fires of freedom still live, and though bound down by strata of tyranny for ages, the sovereign element will burst all fetters. *Thank God for the event!* Slavery cannot always reign.

We occasionally see in our exchanges surprise and mortification expressed that few or no demonstrations of sympathy with France, are held in the various parts of our widely extended country. We would most respectfully ask, What sympathy have freemen with tyrants? How can the latter congratulate the former? What concord has hypocritical piety with infidel honesty? How can a nation with a manstealer in the presidential chair, and manstealers filling every other department of the government – a nation too corrupt and too mean to be fairly represented by any other than the thief and robber, sympathize with a government which has just come into existence with the glorious motto, "Liberty – Equality – Fraternity"? and has proved its sincerity by taking steps for the immediate emancipation of all its slaves, and guaranteeing the right of suffrage to all men, independent of all complexional distinction. It would be unbecoming for us to extend, and France to accept our sympathy. A nation of white men addressing "colored men" –

"*Negroes*," as "Citizens, friends, and brothers," ought not to expect much, and do not expect much sympathy from a nation which proscribes, insults, plunders and enslaves the Black man, in its very capitol. Should we venture into Washington tomorrow, a felon's doom awaits us for no earthly crime that we have committed, than that we are the child of a white man by a colored mother. While we write this, a paper has been handed us containing a detailed account of the arrest and imprisonment in Washington of seventy-seven slaves, for an attempt to escape from the land of slavery to a land of liberty; and for helping these men to escape, three white American citizens are confined in an American dungeon. In view of these facts, and the overwhelming one, that within fifteen States of this boasted republic, nearly one-half of the people are held in the most grievous and revolting bondage, and that the whole Union is solemnly sworn to keep the slave in his chains, it would be more consistent with our character for cruelty, (if not for cowardice,) to invade France with an army, with the avowed purpose of reinstating Louis Phillipe, and restoring the emancipated slaves to their tyrant masters; than to sympathize with France in her struggles for a republic.

There are only two classes in this country who are in a position to sympathize with France in her present glorious struggle in behalf of liberty, and those are the

Negroes and the Abolitionists. We have cause to rejoice and be glad; and can do so with some show of sincerity. All others stand rebuked by her noble example. The American people do not – cannot sympathize with any great movement in behalf of freedom, while fifteen States of the Union are cursed with Slavery. It is an incubus upon their spirits – a standing rebuke, a constant reproach. To be sure, when the votes of Irishmen are wanted, a slight demonstration can be made on behalf of repeal; and when the Roman Catholic influence is needed, sympathy meetings can be held for Pope Pious IX.; but all intelligent men know, that this is a mere sham – the most miserable gammon. The fact is, while Europe is becoming republican, we are becoming despotic; while France is contending for freedom, we are extending slavery; while the former are struggling to free the press, we are striving, by mobs and penal enactments, to fetter it. While France is expelling tyrants, we are glorifying them, and seeking to elevate them to the highest offices. There is no sympathy that can be called national, for France, and we ought to be ashamed to affect it. We believe Louis Phillipe would be welcomed in Washington with far more demonstrations of regard than Lamartine. We love tyrants and hate freemen.[90]

---

[90] Originally published as "France", *The North Star*, April 28th, 1848.

Force of Circumstance and the Human Condition – All people are ours, we are theirs – members of a common family, with a common destiny. In the sight of the Most High and his immutable attributes, we stand upon a common and equal footing. With Him, there is neither Jew nor Gentile, barbarian nor Scythian. He is no respecter of persons, and hath made of one blood all nations for to dwell upon all the face of the earth. ... by the force of potent circumstances, now in existence, and which for ages have existed, the colored people of this country are compelled to occupy a distinct and peculiar condition, and that it is therefore right and proper to address them especially and specifically with respect to that condition, and the rights, duties and responsibilities which of necessity attach to that condition.[91]

---

[91] Excerpted from "A Few Words to Our Own People", *The North Star*, January 19th, 1849.

What of the Night? – A crisis in the Anti-Slavery movement of this country, is evidently at hand. The moral and religious, no less than the political firmaments, North and South, at home and abroad, are studded with brilliant and most significant indications, pointing directly to a settlement of this all-commanding subject. Slavery is doomed to destruction; and of this slaveholders are rapidly becoming aware. Opposed or encouraged, the grand movement for its overthrow has, under God, attained a point of progress when its devoted advocates may press its claims in the full assurance that success will soon crown their righteous endeavors.

We have labored long and hard. The prospect has at times been gloomy, if not hopeless. At present, we feel hopeful. In our humble judgment, there is no power within reach of the slaveholder, with all their arts, cunning and depravity, which can uphold a system at once so dark, foul and bloody as that of American slavery. The power which they have derived from the unconstitutional and perfidious annexation of Texas to the United States; the vast territories which they may acquire by our atrocious war with distracted and enfeebled Mexico; the sacrilegious support which they receive from a corrupt church and degenerate priesthood; the character and position they secure by a slaveholding President, are all transient, temporary and unavailing. They are

powerful, but must give way to a mightier power. --
Like huge trees in the bed of a mighty river, they only
await the rising tide which, without effort, shall bear
them away to the vortex of destruction.

The Spirit of Liberty is sweeping in majesty over the
whole European continent, encountering and shatter-
ing dynasties, overcoming and subverting monarchies,
causing thrones to crumble, courts to dissolve, and
royalty and despotism to vanish like shadows before
the morning sun. This spirit cannot be bound by
geographical boundaries or national restrictions. It
hath neither flesh nor bones; there is no way to chain
it; swords and guns, armies and ramparts, are as
impotent to stay it as they would be if directed against
the Asiatic cholera.

We cannot but be affected. These stupendous ov-
erturnings throughout the world, proclaim in the ear
of American slaveholders, with all the terrible energy
of an earthquake, the downfall of slavery. They have
heard the royal sound -- witness their reluctance on
the floor of Congress to pass resolutions congratulating the French on the downfall of royalty and the
triumph of republicanism; witness the course of that
prince of tyrants, John C. Calhoun; witness the mean
and heartless response given by the misnamed Democrats of the country. These friends of the hell-born
system of slavery are painfully aware that the cause of
liberty and equality are one the world over; and that

its triumph in any portion of the globe foreshadows and hastens the downfall of tyranny throughout the world.

Not among the least important and significant signs of the times, are the recent debates and occurrences in Washington. A combination of events has within a few days transpired there, which may well be regarded as Providential interference in behalf of the enslaved and plundered of our land. The bold attempt of more than seventy slaves to escape their chains – their unfortunate and mortifying recapture – the wild clamor for the blood of men who are willing to aid them in their escape – the mobocratic demonstrations against the Era office – the violent and assassin speeches made in both branches of Congress – their utter failure to intimidate the noble-hearted Giddings, Palfrey, and Hale – the sovereign and increasing contempt with which these gentlemen treat the bullying speeches of these bowie-knife legislators, are not only signs, but facts, fixing attention on slavery, and demonstrating a progress in public opinion, directly pointing to the speedy overthrow of slavery, or a dissolution of our unhallowed Union. Should the latter come, the former must come; slavery is doomed in either case. God speed the day!

Never could there have been a better place, or more fitting opportunity for such facts, than at the place and time when they transpired. Slaves escaping from the Capital of the "model Republic"! What an idea! – running *from* the Temple of Liberty to be free! Then, too, our slaveholding Belshazzars were in the midst of feasting and rejoicing over the downfall of Louis Phillippe, and the establishment of a republic in France! They were all pleasure and joyous delight; "but pleasures are like poppies spread." Their joy was soon turned into moaning, their laughter into fury.

The hand-writing on the wall to these joyous congratulationists, was the fact, that more than seventy thousand dollars' worth of their human cattle had made a peaceful attempt to gain their liberty by flight. At once these thoughts of glorious liberty abroad gave way to the more urgent demands of slavery at home. These "worthless" Negroes are valuable. *These miserable creatures*, which we would gladly get rid of, must be brought back. And lo and behold! these very men who had been rejoicing over French liberty, are now armed kidnappers, and even on the Sabbath day have gone forth on the delectable business of man-hunting. Well, they have succeeded in overtaking and throttling their victims; they have brought them back before the musket's mouth, and doubtless most of them have been scourged for their temerity, and sold into Louisiana and Texas, where they will be worked to death in seven years; but as sure as there is a God, this will not be the last of it. Slavery in the District of

Columbia will receive a shock from this simple event, which no earthly power can prevent or cure. The broad eye of the nation will be opened upon slavery in the District as it has never before; the North and West feel keenly the damning disgrace of their Capital being a slave mart, and a deeper hatred of slavery will be engendered in the popular mind throughout the Union.[92]

---

[92] *The North Star*, May 5th, 1848.

The Rights of Women – One of the most interesting events of the past week, was the holding of what is technically styled a Woman's Rights Convention at Seneca Falls. The speaking, addresses, and resolutions of this extraordinary meeting was almost wholly conducted by women; and although they evidently felt themselves in a novel position, it is but simple justice to say that their whole proceedings were characterized by marked ability and dignity. No one present, we think, however much he might be disposed to differ from the views advanced by the leading speakers on that occasion, will fail to give them credit for brilliant talents and excellent dispositions. In this meeting, as in other deliberative assemblies, there were frequent differences of opinion and animated discussion; but in no case was there the slightest absence of good feeling and decorum. Several interesting documents setting forth the rights as well as the grievances of women were read. Among these was a Declaration of Sentiments, to be regarded as the basis of a grand movement for attaining the civil, social, political, and religious rights of women. We should not do justice to our own convictions, or to the excellent persons connected with this infant movement, if we did not in this connection offer a few remarks on the general subject which the Convention met to consider and the objects they seek to attain.

In doing so, we are not insensible that the bare mention of this truly important subject in any other than terms of contemptuous ridicule and scornful disfavor, is likely to excite against us the fury of bigotry and the folly of prejudice. A discussion of the rights of animals would be regarded with far more complacency by many of what are called the *wise* and *good* of our land, than would a discussion of the rights of women. It is, in their estimation, to be guilty of evil thoughts, to think that woman is entitled to equal rights with man. Many who have at last made the discovery that the Negroes have some rights as well as other members of the human family, have yet to be convinced that women are entitled to any. Eight years ago a number of persons of this description actually abandoned the anti-slavery cause, lest by giving their influence in that direction they might possibly be giving countenance to the dangerous heresy that woman, in respect to rights, stands on equal footing with man. In the judgment of such persons the American slave system, with all its concomitant horrors, is less to be deplored than this *wicked* idea. It is perhaps needless to say, that we cherish little sympathy for such sentiments or respect for such prejudices. Standing as we do upon the watchtower of human freedom, we cannot be deterred from an expression of our approbation of any movement, however humble, to improve and elevate the character of any members of the human family. While it is impossible for us to go into this subject at length, and dispose of the various objections which are often urged against such a doctrine as that of female equality, we are free to say that in respect to political rights, we hold woman to be justly entitled to all we claim for man. We go farther, and express our conviction that all political rights which it is expedient for man to exercise, it is equally so for woman. All that distinguishes man as an intelligent and account-table being, is equally true of woman, and if that government only is just which governs by the free consent of the governed, there can be no reason in the world for denying to woman the exercise of the elective franchise, or a hand in making and adminis-tering the laws of the land. Our doctrine is that "right is of no sex." We therefore bid the women engaged in this movement our humble God-speed.[93]

---

[93] *The North Star*, July 28th, 1848.

Emancipatory Universality and Revolution – I rejoice to see before me white as well as colored persons; for though this is our day peculiarly, it is not so exclusively. The great fact we this day recognize — the great truth to which we have met to do honor, belongs to the whole human family. From this meeting, therefore, no member of the human family is excluded. We have this day a free platform, to which, without respect to class, color, or condition, all are invited. Let no man here feel that he is a mere spectator — that he has no share in the proceedings of this day, because his face is of a paler hue than mine. The occasion is not one of color, but of universal man — from the purest Black to the clearest white, welcome, welcome! In the name of liberty and justice, I extend to each and to all, of every complexion, form and *feature,* a heartfelt welcome to a full participation in the joys of this anniversary.

The great act which distinguishes this day, and which you have this day heard read, is so recent, and its history perhaps so fresh in the memory of all, as to make a lengthy and minute detail of the nature and character of either superfluous. In the address which I had the honor to deliver twelve months since, on an occasion similar to this, at our neighboring town, Canandaigua, I entered quite largely into that investigation; and presuming that I now stand before thousands of the same great audience who warmly greeted me there, I shall be allowed to call your attention to a more extended view of the cause of human freedom than seemed possible at that time. The subject of human freedom, in all its grades, forms and aspects, is within the record of this day. Tyranny, in all its varied guises, may on this day be exposed — oppression and injustice denounced, and liberty held up to the admiration of all. ...

We live in stirring times, and amid thrilling events. There is no telling what a day may bring forth. The human mind is everywhere filled with expectation. The moral sky is studded with signs and wonder. High upon the whirlwind, Liberty rides as on a chariot of fire. Our brave old earth rocks with mighty agitation. Whether we look at home or abroad, Liberty greets us with the same majestic air.

We live in times which have no parallel in the history of the world. The grand commotion is universal and all-pervading. Kingdoms, realms, empires, and republics, roll to and fro like ships upon a stormy sea. The long pent up energies of human rights and sympathies, are at last let loose upon the world. The grand conflict of the angel Liberty with the monster Slavery, has at last come. The globe shakes with the contest. — I thank God that I am permitted, with you, to live in these days, and to participate humbly in this struggle. We are, Mr. President, parties to what is going on around us. We are more than spectators of the scenes that pass before us. Our interests, sympathies and destiny compel us to be parties to what is passing around us. Whether the immediate struggle be baptized by the Eastern or Western wave of the waters between us, the water is one, and the cause one, and we are parties to it. Steam, skill, and lightning, have brought the ends of the earth together. Old prejudices are vanishing. The magic power of human sympathy is rapidly healing national divisions, and bringing mankind into the harmonious bonds of a common brotherhood. In some sense, we realize the sublime declaration of the Prophet of Patmos, "And there shall be no more sea." The oceans that divided us, have become bridges to connect us, and the wide "world has become a whispering gallery." The morning star of freedom is seen from every quarter of the globe.

From spirit to spirit—from nation to nation,
From city to hamlet, thy dawning is cast;
And tyrants and slaves are like shadows of night,'

Standing in the far West, we may now hear the earnest debate of the Western world. — The means of intelligence is so perfect, as well as rapid, that we seem to be mingling with the thrilling scenes of the Eastern hemisphere.

In the month of February of the present year, we may date the commencement of the great movements now progressing throughout Europe. In France, at that time, we saw a king to all appearance firmly seated on his costly throne, guarded by two hundred thousand bayonets. In the pride of his heart, he armed himself for the destruction of liberty. A few short hours ended the struggle. A shout went up to heaven from countless thousands, echoing back to earth, "Liberty — Equality — Fraternity." The troops heard the glorious sound, and fraternized with the people in the court yard of the Tuilleries. — Instantly the King was but a man. All that was kingly fled. The throne whereon he sat was demolished; his splendid palace sacked; his royal carriage was burnt with fire; and he who had arrayed himself against freedom, found himself, like the great Egyptian tyrant, completely overwhelmed. Out of the ruins of this grand rupture, there came up a Republican Provisional Government, and snatching the revolutionary motto of "Liberty — Equality — Fraternity," from the fiery thousands who had just rolled back the tide of tyranny, they commenced to construct a State in accordance with that noble motto. Among the first of its acts, while hard pressed from without and perplexed within, beset on every hand — to the everlasting honor of that Government, it decreed the complete, unconditional emancipation of every slave throughout the French colonies. This act of justice and consistency went into effect on the 23d of last June. Thus were three hundred thousand souls admitted to the joys of freedom. — That provisional government is now no more. The brave and brilliant men who formed it, have ceased to play a conspicuous part in the political affairs of the nation. For the present, some of the brightest lights are obscured. Over the glory of the great-hearted Lamartine, the dark shadow of suspicion is cast. — The most of the members of that government are now distrusted, suspected, and slighted. — But while there remains on the earth one man of sable hue, there will be one witness who will ever remember with unceasing gratitude this noble act of that provisional government.

Sir, this act of justice to our race, on the part of the French people, has had a widespread effect upon the question of human freedom in our own land. Seldom, indeed, has the slave power of the nation received what they regarded such bad news. It placed our slaveholding Republic in a dilemma which all the world could see. We desired to rejoice with her in her republicanism, but it was impossible to do so without seeming to rejoice over abolitionism. Here inconsistency, hypocrisy, covered even the brass face of our slaveholding Republic with confusion. Even that staunch Democrat and Christian, John C. Calhoun, found himself embarrassed as to how to vote on a resolution congratulating the French people on the triumph of Republicanism over Royalty.

But to return to Europe. France is not alone the scene of commotion. Her excitable and inflammable disposition makes her an appropriate medium for lighting more substantial fires. Austria has dispensed with Metternich, while all the German States are demanding freedom; and even iron-hearted Russia is alarmed and perplexed by what is going on around her. The French metropolis is in direct communication with all the great cities of Europe, and the influence of her example is everywhere powerful. The Revolution of the 24th February has stirred the dormant energies of the oppressed classes all over the continent. Revolutions, outbreaks, and provisional governments, followed that event in almost fearful succession. A general insecurity broods over the crowned heads of Europe. Ireland, too, the land of O'Connell, among the most powerful that ever advocated the cause of human freedom — Ireland, ever chafing under oppressive rule, famine-stricken, ragged and wretched, but warm-hearted, generous and unconquerable Ireland, caught up the inspiring peal as it swept across the bosom of St. George's Channel, and again renewed her oath, to be free or die. Her cause is already sanctified by the martyrdom of Mitchell, and millions stand ready to be sacrificed in the same manner. England, too — calm, dignified, brave old England — is not unmoved by what is going on through the sisterhood of European nations. Her toiling sons, from the buzz and din of the factory and workshop, to her endless coal mines deep down below the surface of the earth, have heard the joyful sound of "Liberty — Equality — Fraternity" and are lifting their heads and hearts in hope of better days.

These facts though unfortunately associated with great and crying evils — evils which you and I, and all of us must deeply deplore, are nevertheless interesting to the lovers of freedom and progress. They show that all sense of manhood and moral life, has not departed from the oppressed and plundered masses. They prove, that there yet remains an energy, when supported with the will that can roll back the combined and encroaching powers of tyranny and injustice. To teach this lesson, the movements abroad are important. Even in the recent fierce strife in Paris, which has subjected the infant republic to a horrid baptism of blood, may be scanned a ray of goodness. The great mass of the *Blouses* behind the barricade of the Faubourgs, evidently felt themselves fighting in the righteous cause of equal rights. Wrong in head, but right in heart; brave men in a bad cause, possessing a noble zeal but not according to knowledge. Let us deplore their folly, but honor their courage; respect their aims, but eschew their means. Tyrants of the old world, and slaveholders of our own, will point in proud complacency to this awful outbreak, and say "Aha! aha! aha! *we told you so* — we told you so: this is but the result of undertaking to counteract the purposes of the Most High, who has ordained and anointed Kings and Slaveholders to rule over the people. So much for attempting to make that equal, which God made unequal!" These sentiments in other words, have already been expressed by at least one of the classes to which I have referred. To such, I say rejoice while you may, for your time is short. The day of freedom and order, is at hand. The beautiful infant may stagger and fall, but it will rise, walk and become a man. There may, and doubtless will be, many failures, mistakes and blunders attending the transition from slavery to liberty. But what then? shall the transition never be made? Who is so base, as to harbor the thought? In demolishing the old framework of the Bastille of civil tyranny, and erecting on its ruins the beautiful temple of freedom, some lives may indeed be lost; but who so craven, when beholding the noble structure — its grand proportions, its magnificent domes, its splendid towers and its elegant turrets, all pointing upward to heaven, as to say, That glorious temple ought never to have been built.[94]

---

[94] Excerpted from Lecture delivered at the West India Emancipation Day Celebration in Rochester, New York on August 1, 1848 and published as "The Revolution of 1848", *The North Star*, August 4th, 1848.

Prejudice Against Color – Let no one imagine that we are about to give undue prominence to this subject. Regarding, as we do, the feeling named above to be the greatest of all obstacles in the way of the anti-slavery cause, we think there is little danger of making the subject of it too prominent. The heartless apathy which prevails in this community on the subject of slavery — the cold-blooded indifference with which the wrongs of the perishing and heart-broken slave are regarded — the contemptuous, slanderous, and malicious manner in which the names and characters of Abolitionists are handled by the American pulpit and press generally, may be traced mainly to the malign feeling which passes under the name of prejudice against color. Every step in our experience in this country since we commenced our anti-slavery labors, has been marked by facts demonstrative of what we have just said. The day that we started on our first anti-slavery journey to Nantucket, now nine years ago, the steamer was detained at the wharf in New Bedford two hours later than the usual time of starting, in an attempt on the part of the captain to compel the colored passengers to separate from the white passengers, and to go on the forward deck of that steamer; and during this time, the most savage feelings were evinced towards every colored man who asserted his right to enjoy equal privileges with other passengers. Aside from the twenty months which we spent in England (where color is no crime, and where a man's fitness for respectable society is measured by his moral and intellectual worth), we do not remember to have made a single anti-slavery tour in any direction in this country, when we have not been assailed by this mean spirit of caste. A feeling so universal and so powerful for evil, cannot well be too much commented upon. We have used the term prejudice against color to designate the feeling to which we allude, not because it expresses correctly what that feeling is, but simply because that innocent term is usually employed for that purpose.

Properly speaking, *prejudice against color* does not exist in this country. The feeling (or whatever it is) which we call prejudice, is no less than a *murderous, hell-born hatred* of every virtue which may adorn the character of a *Black man*. It is not the Black man's color which makes him the object of brutal treatment. When he is drunken, idle, ignorant and vicious, *"Black Bill"* is a source of amusement: he is called a good-natured fellow: he is the first to touch his hat to the stranger approaching the hotel, and offer his service in holding his horse, or blacking his boots. The white gentleman tells the landlord to give "Bill" *"something to drink,"* and actually drinks with "Bill" himself! — while poor Black "Bill" will minister to the pride, vanity and laziness of white American gentlemen. While he consents to play the buffoon for their sport, he will share their regard. But let him cease to be what we have described him to be — let him shake off the filthy rags that cover him — let him abandon drunkenness for sobriety, industry for indolence, ignorance for intelligence, and give up his menial occupation for respectable employment — let him quit the hotel and go to the church, and assume there the rights and privileges of one for whom the Son of God died, and he will be pursued with the fiercest hatred. His name will be cast out as evil; and his life will be embittered with all the venom which hate and malice can generate. Thousands of colored men can bear witness to the truth of this representation. While we are servants, we are never offensive to the whites, or marks of popular displeasure. We have been often dragged or driven from the tables of hotels where colored men were officiating acceptably as waiters; and from steamboat cabins where twenty or thirty colored men in light jackets and white aprons were frisking about as servants among the whites in every direction. On the very day we were brutally assaulted in New York for riding down Broadway in company with ladies, we saw several white ladies riding with Black servants. These servants were well-dressed, proud looking men, evidently living on the fat of the land — yet they were servants. They rode not for their own, but for the pleasure and convenience of white persons. They were not in those carriages as friends or equals. They were there as appendages; they constituted a part of the magnificent equipages. They were there as the fine black horses which they drove were there — to minister to the pride and splendor of their employers. As they passed down Broadway, they were observed with admiration by the multitude; and even the poor wretches who assaulted us might have said in their hearts, as they looked upon such splendor, "We would do so too if we could." We repeat, then, that color is not the cause of our persecution; that is, it is not our color which makes our proximity to white men disagreeable. The evil lies deeper than prejudice against color. It is, as we have said, an intense hatred of the colored man when he is distinguished for any ennobling qualities of head or heart. If the feeling which persecutes us were prejudice against color, the colored servant would be as obnoxious as the colored gentleman, for the color is the same in both cases; and being the same in both cases, it would produce the same result in both cases.

We are then a persecuted people; not because we are colored, but simply because that color has for a series of years been coupled in the public mind with the degradation of slavery and servitude. In these conditions, we are thought to be in our place; and to aspire to anything above them, is to contradict the established views of the community — to get out of our sphere, and commit the provoking sin of impudence. Just here is our sin: we have been a slave; we have passed through all the grades of servitude, and have, under God, secured our freedom; and if we have become the special object of attack, it is because we speak and act among our fellow-men without the slightest regard to their or our own complexion; and further, because we claim and exercise the right to associate with just such persons as are willing to associate with us, and who are agreeable to our tastes, and suited to our moral and intellectual tendencies, without reference to the color of their skin, and without giving ourselves the slightest trouble to inquire whether the world are pleased or displeased by our conduct. We believe in human equality; that character, not color, should be the criterion by which to choose associates; and we pity the pride of the poor pale dust and ashes which would erect any other standard of social fellowship.

This doctrine of human equality is the bitterest yet taught by the abolitionists. It is swallowed with more difficulty than all the other points of the anti-slavery creed put together. "What makes a Negro equal to a white man?" "No, we will never consent to that! No, that won't do!" But stop a moment; don't [be in] a passion, keep cool. What is a white man that you do so revolt at the idea of making a Negro equal with him? Who made him? Is he an angel or a man? "A man." Very well, he is a man, and nothing but a man

— possessing the same weaknesses, liable to the same diseases, and under the same necessities to which a Black man is subject. Wherein does the white man differ from the Black? Why, one is white and the other is Black. Well, what of that? Does the sun shine more brilliantly upon the one than it does upon the other? Is nature more lavish with her gifts toward the one than toward the other? Do earth, sea and air yield their united treasures to the one more readily than to the other? In a word, "have we not all one Father?" Why then do you revolt at that equality which God and nature instituted?

The very apprehension which the American people betray on this point, is proof of the fitness of treating all men equally. The fact that they fear an acknowledgment of our equality, shows that they see a fitness in such an acknowledgment. Why are they not apprehensive lest the horse should be placed on an equality with man? Simply because the horse is not a man; and no amount of reasoning can convince the world, against its common sense, that the horse is anything else than a horse. So here all can repose without fear. But not so with the Negro. He stands erect. Upon his brow he bears the seal of manhood, from the hand of the living God. Adopt any mode of reasoning you please with respect to him, he is a man, possessing an immortal soul, illuminated by intellect, capable of heavenly aspirations, and in all things pertaining to manhood, he is at once self-evidently a man, and therefore entitled to all the rights and privileges which belong to human nature.[95]

---

[95] *The North Star*, June 13th, 1850.

First Lecture Against Human Slavery – I come before you this evening to deliver the first lecture of a course which I purpose to give in this city, during the present winter, on the subject of American Slavery.

I make this announcement with no feelings of self-sufficiency. If I do not mistake my own emotions, they are such as result from a profound sense of my incompetency to do justice to the task which I have just announced, and have now entered upon.

If any, then, demand of me why I speak, I plead as my apology, the fact that abler and more eloquent men have failed to speak, or what, perhaps, is more true, and therefore more strong, such men have spoken only on the wrong side of the question, and have thus thrown their influence against the cause of liberty, humanity and benevolence.

There are times in the experience of almost every community, when even the humblest member thereof may properly presume to teach – when the wise and great ones, the appointed leaders of the people, exert their powers of mind to complicate, mystify, entangle and obscure the simple truth – when they exert the noblest gifts which heaven has vouchsafed to man to mislead the popular mind, and to corrupt the public heart, – *then* the humblest may stand forth and be excused for opposing even his weakness to the torrent of evil.

That such a state of things exists in this community, I have abundant evidence. I learn it from the Rochester press, from the Rochester pulpit, and in my intercourse with the people of Rochester. Not a day passes over me that I do not meet with apparently good men, who utter sentiments in respect to this subject which would do discredit to savages. They speak of the enslavement of their fellow-men with an indifference and coldness which might be looked for only in men hardened by the most atrocious and villainous crimes.

The fact is, we are in the midst of a great struggle. The public mind is widely and deeply agitated; and bubbling up from its perturbed waters are many and great impurities, whose poisonous miasma demands a constant antidote.

Whether the contemplated lectures will in any degree contribute towards answering this demand, time will determine. Of one thing, however, I can assure my hearers — that I come up to this work at the call of duty, and with an honest desire to promote the happiness and well-being of every member of this community, as well as to advance the emancipation of every slave.

The audience will pardon me if I say one word more by way of introduction. It is my purpose to give this subject a calm, candid and faithful discussion. I shall not aim to shock nor to startle my hearers; but to convince their judgment and to secure their sympathies for the enslaved. I shall aim to be as stringent as truth, and as severe as justice; and if at any time I shall fail of this, and do injustice in any respect, I shall be most happy to be set right by any gentleman who shall hear me, subject, of course, to order and decorum. I shall deal, during these lectures, alike with individuals and institutions — men shall no more escape me than things. I shall have occasion, at times, to be even personal, and to rebuke sin in high places. I shall not hesitate to arraign either priests or politicians, church or state, and to measure all by the standard of justice, and in the light of truth. I shall not forget to deal with the unrighteous spirit of *caste* which prevails in this community; and I shall give particular attention to the recently enacted fugitive slave bill. I shall keep my eye upon the Congress which is to commence tomorrow, and fully inform myself as to its proceedings. In a word, the whole subject of slavery, in all its bearings, shall have a full and impartial discussion.

A very slight acquaintance with the history of American slavery is sufficient to show that it is an evil of which it will be difficult to rid this country. It is not the creature of a moment, which today is, and tomorrow is not; it is not a pigmy, which a slight blow may demolish; it is no youthful upstart, whose impertinent pratings may be silenced by a dignified contempt.

No: it is an evil of gigantic proportions, and of long standing.

Its origin in this country dates back to the landing of the pilgrims on Plymouth rock. — It was here more than two centuries ago. The first spot poisoned by its leprous presence, was a small plantation in Virginia. The slaves, at that time, numbered only twenty. They have now increased to the frightful number of three millions; and from that narrow plantation, they are now spread over by far the largest half of the American Union. Indeed, slavery forms an important part of the entire history of the American people. Its presence may be seen in all American affairs. It has become interwoven with all American institutions, and has anchored itself in the very soil of the American Constitution. It has thrown its paralyzing arm over freedom of speech, and the liberty of the press; and has created for itself morals and manners favorable to its own continuance. It has seduced the church, corrupted the pulpit, and brought the powers of both into degrading bondage; and now, in the pride of its power, it even threatens to bring down that grand political edifice, the American Union, unless every member of this republic shall so far disregard his conscience and his God to yield to its infernal behests.

That must be a powerful influence which can truly be said to govern a nation; and that slavery governs the American people, is indisputably true. If there were any doubt on this point, a few plain questions (it seems to me) could not fail to remove it. *What* power has given this nation its Presidents for more than fifty years? *Slavery.* *What* power is that to which the present aspirants to presidential honors are bowing? *Slavery.* We may call it "Union," "Constitution," "Harmony," or "American institutions," that to which such men as Cass, Dickinson, Webster, Clay and other distinguished men of this country, are devoting their energies, is nothing more or less than American slavery. It is for this that they are writing letters, making speeches, and promoting the holding of great mass meetings, professedly in favor of "*the Union.*" These men know the service most pleasing to their master, and that which is most likely to be richly rewarded. Men may "server God for nought," as did Job; but he who serves the devil has an eye to his reward. "Patriotism," "obedience to the law," "prosperity to the country," have come to mean, in the mouths of these distinguished statesmen, a mean and servile acquiescence in the most flagitious and profligate legislation in favor of slavery. I might enlarge here on this picture of the slave power, and tell of its influence upon the press in the free States, and upon the condition and rights of the free colored people of the North; but I forbear for the present. – Enough has been said, I trust, to convince all that the abolition of this evil will require time, energy, zeal, perseverance and patience; that it will require fidelity, a martyr-like spirit of self-sacrifice, and a firm reliance on Him who has declared Himself to be "*the God of the Oppressed.*" Having said thus much upon the power and prevalence of slavery, allow me to speak of the nature of slavery itself; and here I can speak, in part, from experience – I can speak with the authority of positive knowledge.

More than twenty years of my life were consumed in a state of slavery. My childhood was environed by the baneful peculiarities of the slave system. I grew up to manhood in the presence of this hydra-headed monster — not as a master — not as an idle spectator — not as the guest of the slaveholder — but as A Slave, eating the bread and drinking the cup of slavery with the most degraded of my brother-bondmen, and sharing with them all the painful conditions of their wretched lot. In consideration of these facts, I feel that I have a right to speak, and to speak *strongly*. Yet, my friends, I feel bound to speak truly.

Goading as have been the cruelties to which I have been subjected — bitter as have been the trials through which I have passed — exasperating as have been, (*and still are*), the indignities offered to my manhood — I find in them no excuse for the slightest departure from truth in dealing with any branch of this subject.

First of all, I will state, as well as I can, the legal and social relation of master and slave. A master is one — to speak in the vocabulary of the southern states — who claims and exercises a right of property in the person of a fellow-man. This he does with the force of the law and the sanction of southern religion. The law gives the master absolute power over the slave. He may work him, flog him, hire him out, sell him, and, in certain contingencies, *kill* him, with perfect impunity. The slave is a human being, divested of all rights — reduced to the level of a brute — a mere "chattel" in the eye of the law — placed beyond the circle of human brotherhood — cut off from his kind — his name, which the "recording angel" may have enrolled in heaven, among the blest, is impiously inserted in a *master's ledger*, with horses, sheep, and swine. In law, the slave has no wife, no children, no country, and no home. He can own nothing, possess nothing, acquire nothing, but what must belong to another. To eat the fruit of his own toil, to clothe his person with the work of his own hands, is considered stealing. He toils that another may reap the fruit; he is industrious that another may live in idleness; he eats unbolted meal that another may eat the bread of fine flour; he labors in chains at home, under a burning sun and biting lash, that another may ride in ease and splendor abroad; he lives in ignorance that another may be educated; he is abused that another may be exalted; he rests his toilworn limbs on the cold, damp ground that another may repose on the softest pillow; he is clad in coarse and tattered raiment that another may be arrayed in purple and fine linen; he is sheltered only by the wretched hovel that a master may dwell in a magnificent mansion; and to this condition he is bound down as by an arm of iron.

From this monstrous relation there springs an unceasing stream of most revolting cruelties. The very accompaniments of the slave system stamp it as the offspring of hell itself. To ensure good behavior, the slaveholder relies on *the whip*; to induce proper humility, he relies on *the whip*; to rebuke what he is pleased to term insolence, he relies on *the whip*; to supply the place of wages as an incentive to toil, he relies on *the whip*; to bind down the spirit of the slave, to imbrute and destroy his manhood, he relies on *the whip*, the chain, the gag, the thumb-screw, the pillory, the bowie-knife, the pistol, and the bloodhound. These are the necessary and unvarying accompaniments of the system. Wherever slavery is found, these horrid instruments are also found. Whether on the coast of Africa, among the savage tribes, or in South Carolina, among the refined and civilized, slavery is the same, and its accompaniments one and the same. It makes no difference whether the slaveholder worships the God of the Christians, or is a follower of Mahomet, he is the minister of the same cruelty, and the author of the same misery. *Slavery* is always *slavery*; always the same foul, haggard, and damning scourge, whether found in the eastern or in the western hemisphere.

There is a still deeper shade to be given to this picture. The physical cruelties are indeed sufficiently harassing and revolting; but they are as a few grains of sand on the sea shore, or a few drops of water in the great ocean, compared with the stupendous wrongs which it inflicts upon the mental, moral, and religious nature of its hapless victims. It is only when we contemplate the slave as a moral and intellectual being, that we can adequately comprehend the unparalleled enormity of slavery, and the intense criminality of the slaveholder. I have said that the slave was a man. "What a piece of work is man! How noble in reason! How infinite in faculties! In form and moving how express and admirable! In action how like an angel! In apprehension how like a God! the beauty of the world! the paragon of animals!"

The slave is a man, "the image of God," but "a little lower than the angels;" possessing a soul, eternal and indestructible; capable of endless happiness, or immeasurable woe; a creature of hopes and fears, of affections and passions, of joys and sorrows, and he is endowed with those mysterious powers by which man soars above the things of time and sense, and grasps, with undying tenacity, the elevating and sublimely glorious idea of a God. It is *such* a being that is smitten and blasted. The first work of slavery is to mar and deface those characteristics of its victims which distinguish *men* from *things*, and *persons* from *property*. Its first aim is to destroy all sense of high moral and religious responsibility. It reduces man to a mere machine. It cuts him off from his Maker, it hides from him the laws of God, and leaves him to grope his way from time to eternity in the dark, under the arbitrary and despotic control of a frail, depraved, and sinful fellowman.

As the serpent-charmer of India is compelled to extract the deadly teeth of his venomous prey before he is able to handle him with impunity, so the slave-holder must strike down the conscience of the slave before he can obtain the entire mastery over his victim.

It is, then, the first business of the enslaver of men to blunt, deaden, and destroy the central principle of human responsibility. Conscience is, to the individual soul, and to society, what the law of gravitation is to the universe. It holds society together; it is the basis of all trust and confidence; it is the pillar of all moral rectitude. Without it, suspicion would take the place of trust; vice would be more than a match for virtue; men would prey upon each other, like the wild beasts of the desert; and earth would become a *hell*.

Nor is slavery more adverse to the conscience than it is to the mind.

This is shown by the fact, that in every state of the American Union, where slavery exists, except the state of Kentucky, there are laws *absolutely* prohibitory of education among the slaves. The crime of teaching a slave to read is punishable with severe fines and imprisonment, and, in some instances, with *death itself.*

Nor are the laws respecting this matter a dead letter. Cases may occur in which they are disregarded, and a few instances may be found where slaves may have learned to read; but such are isolated cases, and only prove the rule. The great mass of slaveholders, look upon education among the slaves as utterly subversive of the slave system. I *well* remember when my mistress first announced to my master that she had discovered that I could read. His face colored at once with surprise and chagrin. He said that "I was ruined, and my value as a slave destroyed; that a slave should know nothing but to obey his master; that to give a Negro an inch would lead him to take an ell; that having learned how to read, I would soon want to know how to write; and that by-and-by I would be running away." I think my audience will bear witness to the correctness of this philosophy, and to the literal fulfillment of this prophecy.

It is perfectly well understood at the south, that to educate a slave is to make him discontented with slavery, and to invest him with a power which shall open to him the treasures of freedom; and since the object of the slaveholder is to maintain complete authority over his slave, his constant vigilance is exercised to prevent everything which militates against, or endangers, the stability of his authority. Education being among the menacing influences, and, perhaps, the most dangerous, is, therefore, the most cautiously guarded against.

It is true that we do not often hear of the enforcement of the law, punishing as a crime the teaching of slaves to read, but this is not because of a want of disposition to enforce it. The true reason or explanation of the matter is this: there is the greatest unanimity of opinion among the white population in the south in favor of the policy of keeping the slave in ignorance. There is, perhaps, another reason why the law against education is so seldom violated. The slave is *too* poor to be able to offer a temptation sufficiently strong to induce a white man to violate it; and it is not to be supposed that in a community where the moral and religious sentiment is in favor of slavery, many martyrs will be found sacrificing their liberty and lives by violating those prohibitory enactments.

As a general rule, then, darkness reigns over the abodes of the enslaved, and "how great is that darkness!"

We are sometimes told of the contentment of the slaves, and are entertained with vivid pictures of their happiness. We are told that they often dance and sing; that their masters frequently give them wherewith to make merry; in fine, that they have little of which to complain. I admit that the slave *does* sometimes sing, dance, and appear to be merry. But what does this prove? It only proves to my mind, that though slavery is armed with a thousand stings, it is not able entirely to kill the elastic spirit of the bondman. That spirit will rise and walk abroad, despite of whips and chains, and extract from the cup of nature occasional drops of joy and gladness. No thanks to the slaveholder, nor to slavery, that the vivacious captive may sometimes dance in his chains; his very mirth in such circumstances stands before God as an accusing angel against his enslaver.

But *who* tells us of the extraordinary contentment and happiness of the slave? What traveller has explored the balmy regions of our Southern country and brought back "these glad tidings of joy?" Bring him on the platform, and bid him answer a few plain questions. We shall then be able to determine the weight and importance that attach to his testimony. Is he a minister? Yes. Were you ever in a slave State, sir? Yes. May I inquire the object of your mission South? To preach the gospel, sir. Of what denomination are you? A Presbyterian, sir. To whom were you introduced? To the Rev. Dr. Plummer. Is he a slaveholder, sir? Yes, sir. Has slaves about his house? Yes, sir. Were you then the guest of Dr. Plummer? Yes, sir. Waited on by slaves while there? Yes, Did you preach for Dr. Plunner? Yes, sir. Did you spend your nights at the great house, or at the quarter among the slaves? At the great house. You had, then, no social intercourse with the slaves? No, sir. You fraternized, then, wholly with the white portion of the population while there? Yes, sir. This is sufficient, sir; you can leave the platform.

Nothing is more natural than that those who go into slave States, and enjoy the hospitality of slaveholders, should bring back favorable reports of the condition of the slave. If that ultra republican, the Hon. Lewis Cass, could not return from the Court of France, without paying a compliment to royalty simply, because King Louis Phillippe patted him on the shoulder, called him "friend," and invited him to dinner, it is not to be expected that those hungry shadows of men in the shape of ministers, that go South, can escape a contamination even more be guiling and insidious. Alas! for the weakness of poor "Pleased with a rattle, tickled with a straw!"

Why is it that all the reports of contentment and happiness among the slaves at the South come to us upon the authority of slave-holders, or (what is equally significant) of slave-holders' friends? *Why* is it that we do not hear from the slave direct? The answer to this question furnishes the darkest features of the American slave system.

It is often said, by the opponents of the anti-slavery cause, that the condition of the people of Ireland is more deplorable than that of the American slaves. *Far* be it from me to underrate the sufferings of the Irish people. They have been long oppressed; and the same heart that prompts me to plead the cause of the American bondman, makes it impossible for me *not* to sympathize with the oppressed of all lands. Yet I must say that there is no analogy between the two cases. The Irishman is poor, but he is *not* a slave. He *may* be in rags, but he is *not* a slave. He is still the master of his own body, and can say with the poet, "The hand of Douglass is his own." "The world is all before him, where to choose;" and poor as may be my opinion of the British parliament, I cannot believe that it will ever sink to such a depth of infamy as to pass a law for the recapture of fugitive Irishmen! The shame and scandal of kidnapping will long remain wholly monopolized by the American congress. The Irishman has not only the liberty to emigrate from his country, but he has liberty at home. He can write, and speak, and co-operate for the attainment of his rights and the redress of his wrongs.

The multitude can assemble upon all the green hills and fertile plains of the Emerald Isle; they can pour out their grievances, and proclaim their wants without molestation; and the press, that "swiftwinged messenger," can bear the tidings of their doings to the extreme bounds of the civilized world. They have their "Conciliation Hall," on the banks of the Liffey, their reform clubs, and their newspapers; they pass resolutions, send forth addresses, and enjoy the right of petition. But how is it with the American slave? *Where* may he assemble? *Where* is his Conciliation Hall? Where are his newspapers? Where is his right of petition? Where is his freedom of speech? his liberty of the press? and his right of locomotion? He is said to be happy; happy men can speak. But ask the slave *what* is his condition — *what* his state of mind — *what* he thinks of enslavement? and you had as well address your inquiries to the *silent dead*. There comes no *voice* from the enslaved. We are left to gather his feelings by imagining what ours would be, were our souls in his soul's stead.

If there were no other fact descriptive of slavery, than that the slave is dumb, this alone would be sufficient to mark the slave system as a grand aggregation of human horrors.

Most who are present, will have observed that leading men in this country have been putting forth their skill to secure quiet to the nation. A system of measures to promote this object was adopted a few months ago in congress.

The result of those measures is known. Instead of quiet, they have produced alarm; instead of peace, they have brought us war; and so it must ever be.

While this nation is guilty of the enslavement of three millions of innocent men and women, it is as idle to think of having a sound and lasting peace, as it is to think there is no God to take cognizance of the affairs of men. There can be no peace to the wicked while slavery continues in the land. It will be condemned; and while it is condemned there will be agitation. Nature must cease to be nature; Men must become monsters; Humanity must be transformed; Christianity must be exterminated; all ideas of justice and the laws of eternal goodness must be utterly blotted out from the human soul, — ere a system so foul and infernal can escape condemnation, or this guilty Republic can have a sound, enduring Peace.[96]

---

[96] Lecture delivered on December 1st, 1850 at Corinthian Hall, Rochester, New York and published in *The North Star*, December 5th, 1850. This unabridged version is found in a pamphlet entitled *Lectures on American Slavery*, (Buffalo, NY: Geo. Reese & Co's Power Press, 1851).

Second Lecture Against Human Slavery – In my lecture of Sunday evening last, I strove to impress those who kindly gave me their attention, with a slight idea of the all-controlling power of American slavery in the affairs of the nation.

I briefly unfolded the nature of the relation between master and slave; the cruel, arbitrary and despotic authority of the slaveholder; and I portrayed the deplorable ignorance and the deep debasement of the enslaved.

This evening I shall aim to expose further the wickedness of the slave system – to show that its evils are not confined to the Southern States; but that they overshadow the whole country; and that every American citizen is responsible for its existence, and is solemnly required, by the highest convictions of duty and safety, to labor for its utter extirpation from the land.

By some who will hear me, these propositions will be, perhaps, regarded as far too tame for the basis of a lecture on slavery at this exciting period. But I would beg such persons to remember that they are the few, not the many; and that being the exception, they afford no criterion for the course I ought to pursue on the present occasion. By them, the anti-slavery alphabet was learned perhaps twenty years ago; but the great mass of the American people, I am sorry to say, have that simple lesson yet to learn. I

design, therefore, to speak to opponents, rather than
to friends, and although I may not be able to entertain
the latter by the utterance of new truths, I may afford
them the satisfaction of hearing those truths enforced
which they have so long cherished.

Indeed, I ought to state, what must be obvious to all,
that, properly speaking, there is no such thing as *new*
truth, for truth, like the God whose attribute it is, is
eternal. In this sense, there is, indeed, nothing new
under the sun. Error may be properly designated as
old or *new*, since it is but a misconception, or an
incorrect view of the truth. Misapprehensions of what
truth is, have their beginnings and their endings.
They pass away as the race moves onward. But truth
is "from everlasting to everlasting" and can never pass
away.

Such is the truth of man's right to liberty. It existed
in the very idea of man's creation. It was *his* before
he comprehended it. He was created in it, endowed
with it, and it can never be taken from him. No laws,
no statutes, no compacts, no compromises, no constitutions, can abrogate or destroy it. It is beyond the
reach of the strongest earthly arm, and smiles at the
ravings of tyrants from its hiding place in the bosom
of God. Men may hinder its exercise, they may act in
disregard of it, they are even permitted to war against
it; but they fight against heaven and their career must

be short, for the Eternal Providence will speedily vindicate the right.

The existence of this right is self-evident. It is written upon all the powers and faculties of man. The desire for it is the deepest and strongest of all the powers of the human soul. Earth, sea, and air – great nature, with her thousand voices, proclaims it.

In the language of Addison, we may apostrophize it:

Oh, Liberty! thou Goddess, heavenly bright,
Profuse of bliss, and pregnant with delight!
Thou mak'st the glowing face of nature gay,
Giv'st beauty to the sun, and pleasure to the day.

I have said that the right to liberty is self-evident. No argument, no researches into moldy records, no learned disquisitions, are necessary to establish it. To assert it, is to call forth a sympathetic response from every human heart, and to send a thrill of joy and gladness round the world. Tyrants, oppressors and slaveholders are stunned by its utterance; while the oppressed and enslaved of all lands hail it as an angel of deliverance. Its assertion in Russia, in Austria, in Egypt, in fifteen States of the American Union, is a crime. In the harems of Turkey, and in the Southern plantations of Carolina, it is alike prohibited; for the guilty oppressors of every crime understand its *truth*, and appreciate its electric power.

Slavery is a sin, in that it comprehends a monstrous violation of the great principle of human liberty, to which I have endeavored thus to draw your attention. In this respect, it is a direct war upon the government of God. In subjecting one man to the arbitrary control of another, it contravenes the first command of the decalogue; and as upon that command rests the whole superstructure of justice, purity and brotherly kindness, slavery may be justly regarded as a warfare against all the principles of infinite goodness. It is not, however, merely with slavery as a system that I propose to deal. It has been well characterized by the faithful John Wesley as "*the sum of all villanies*," and "*the concentration of all crime.*" I prefer to speak of the villains in connection with the villainy, and of the criminals in connection with the crimes. I like the pure and stern testimony of John Wesley. It expresses the sense of a true heart in respect to the foul abomination. Adam Clarke is no less emphatic. To the traffickers in the souls and bodies of men, this great commentator says, "Oh! ye most flagitious of knaves, and worst of hypocrites! Cast off at once the mask of religion, and deepen not your endless perdition by professing the faith of our Lord Jesus Christ, while you continue in this traffic."

In contemplating the sin of slavery, and the guilt of the slaveholders, I have marveled at the coolness and self-complacency with which persons at the North often speak of having friends and relatives who are slaveholders at the South. They speak of the fact without a blush of shame, and even as though honor were conferred upon them by their slaveholding friends and relatives. What a commentary is this on the state of morals among us! Why, if the moral sentiment of the North were what it ought to be, a lady would soon tell of an abandoned sister or a pirate brother, as boast of having slaveholding relatives, for there is nothing in piracy, nothing in lewdness, that is not to be found in the slave system – indeed, slavery is a system of lewdness and piracy. Every slaveholder is the legalized keeper of ill-fame; no matter how high he may stand in Church or in State. He may be a Bishop Meade or a Henry Clay – a reputed saint or an open sinner – he is still the legalized head of a den of infamy.

As a nation we profess profound respect for chastity and the marriage institution. A violation of either is looked upon (and very properly so) with feelings of absolute horror. A maddened husband, or an outraged father, is almost justified by public opinion in taking the law into his own hand, and executing summary vengeance upon the guilty creature who, by studied arts, covers his family with shame. The laws of this commonwealth, like those of other Northern States, have thrown around innocence the most stringent protection. Our pulpits are keenly alive to the importance of the marriage institution, and the press is not a whit behind the pulpit. These things indicate, I say, a profound respect for moral purity. I will not controvert the genuineness of this seeming virtue of the community. But if it be genuine, the State of New York, must be an emancipation State, and that speedily. I hold myself ready to prove that more than a million of women, in the Southern States of this Union are, by the laws of the land, and through no fault of their own, consigned to a life of revolting prostitution; that by those laws, in many of the States, if a woman, in defense of her own innocence, shall lift her hand against the brutal aggressor, she may be lawfully put to death. I hold myself ready to prove, by the laws of the Slave States, that three millions of people of those States, are utterly incapacitated to form marriage contracts. I am also prepared to prove that slave-breeding is relied upon by Virginia as one of her chief sources of wealth. It has long been known that the best blood of old Virginia may now be found in the slave markets of New Orleans. It is also known that slave women who are nearly white, are sold in those markets, at prices which proclaim, trumpet-tongued, the accursed purposes to which they are to be devoted. Youth and elegance, beauty and inno-cence, are exposed for sale upon the auction block; while villainous monsters stand around, with pockets lined with gold, gazing with lustful eyes upon their prospective victims. But I will not go behind the scene further. I leave you to picture to yourselves what must be the state of society where marriage is not allowed by the law, and where *woman* is reduced to mere *chattel.* To the thoughtful I need say no more. You have already conceived a state of things equaling in honor and abomination, your worst conceptions of Sodom itself.

Every slaveholder is a party, a guilty party, to this awful wickedness. He owns the house, and is master of the victims. He is therefore responsible. I say again, no matter how high the slaveholder may stand in popular estimation – he may be a minister of religion, or an Honorable Member of Congress; but so long as he is a slaveholder, he deserves to be held up before the world as the patron of lewdness, and the foe of virtue. He may not be personally implicated in the wickedness; he may scrupulously maintain and respect the marriage institution for himself and for his family, for all this can be done selfishly; but while he robs any portion of the human family of the right of marriage, and takes from innocent woman the protection of the law, no matter what his individual responsibility may be, he is to be classed with the vilest of the vile, and with the basest of the base. To boast of relationship or friendly association with these infamous men – to fellowship with such men as good Christians, is a sad commentary on the morals and the religion of those who do it. It implies that their professions of purity are conventional and artificial; that there is no real soundness in them; that their virtue is seeming rather than real; that their reverence for the marriage institution is the merest affectation, and has no higher nor stronger support than that afforded by public opinion; and that their horror at its violation depends wholly upon the complexion of the parties involved, and not upon the sin committed.

I have now spoken plainly, but not more so than the nature of the case requires. If any have been shocked at the plainness of speech, I beg them to remember that *true* delicacy does not consist in a squeamish ear. In the language of the eloquent Fox, I would remind them "that true humanity does not consist in shrinking and starting at such recitals, but in a disposition of the heart to remedy the evils they all unfold. True virtue belongs rather to the mind than to the nerves, and should prompt men to charitable exertion in correcting abuses. To shudder at enormities, and do nothing to remove them, is little better than to stamp ourselves with the most pitiful and contemptible hypocrisy." To quote another author, I would say,

True modesty is a distinguished grace,
And only blushes in the proper place.
But counterfeit is base, and skulks through fear

Where 'tis a shame to be ashamed t'appear.

I pass now to the consideration of another feature of slavery. I allude to its cruelty. Much is said among us, both by the press and the pulpit, of the kindness of the slaveholders to their slaves, and of their natural attachment. The relation of master and slave has been called patriarchal, and only second in benignity and tenderness to that of the parent and child. This representation is doubtless believed by many northern people; and this may account, in part, for the lack of interest which we find among persons whom we are bound to believe to be honest and humane. *What,* then, are the facts? Here I will not quote my own experience in slavery; for this you might call one-sided testimony. I will not cite the declarations of abolitionists; for these you might pronounce exaggerations. I will not rely upon advertisements cut from newspapers; for these you might call isolated cases. But I will refer you to the laws adopted by the legislatures of the slave states. I give you such evidence, because it cannot be invalidated nor denied. I hold in my hand sundry extracts from the slave codes of our country, from which I will quote. ...

Now, if the foregoing be an indication of kindness, *what is cruelty?* If this be parental affection, *what is bitter malignity?* A more atrocious and bloodthirsty string of laws could not well be conceived of. And yet

I am bound to say that they fall short of indicating the horrible cruelties constantly practiced in the slave states.

I admit that there are individual slaveholders less cruel and barbarous than is allowed by law; but these form the exception. The majority of slaveholders find it necessary, to insure obedience, at times, to avail themselves of the utmost extent of the law, and many go beyond it. If kindness were the rule, we should not see advertisements filling the columns of almost every southern newspaper, offering large rewards for fugitive slaves, and describing them as being branded with irons, loaded with chains, and scarred by the whip. One of the most telling testimonies against the pretended kindness of slaveholders, is the fact that uncounted numbers of fugitives are now inhabiting the Dismal Swamp, preferring the untamed wilderness to their cultivated homes — choosing rather to encounter hunger and thirst, and to roam with the wild beasts of the forest, running the hazard of being hunted and shot down, than to submit to the authority of *kind* masters.

I tell you, my friends, humanity is never driven to such an unnatural course of life, without great wrong. The slave finds more of the milk of human kindness in the bosom of the savage Indian, than in the heart of his Christian master. He leaves the man of the *Bible*, and takes refuge with the man of the *toma-*

hawk. He rushes from the praying slaveholder into the paws of the bear. He quits the homes of men for the haunts of wolves. – He prefers to encounter a life of trial, however bitter, or death, however terrible, to dragging out his existence under the dominion of these *kind* masters.

The apologists for slavery often speak of the abuses of slavery; and they tell us that they are as much opposed to those abuses as we are; and that they would go as far to correct those abuses and to ameliorate the condition of the slave as anybody. The answer to that view is, that slavery is *itself* an abuse; that it lives by abuse; and dies by the absence of abuse. Grant that slavery is right; grant that the relation of master and slave may innocently exist; and there is not a single outrage which was ever committed against the slave but what finds an apology in the very necessity of the case. As was said by a slaveholder, (the Rev. A. G. Few,) to the Methodist conference, "If the relation be right, the means to maintain it are also right;" for without those means slavery could not exist. Remove the dreadful scourge — the plaited thong — the galling fetter — the accursed chain — and let the slaveholder rely solely upon moral and religious power, by which to secure obedience to his orders, and *how* long do you suppose a slave would remain on his plantation? The case only needs to be stated; it carries its own refutation with it.

Absolute and arbitrary power can never be maintained by one man over the body and soul of another man, without brutal chastisement and enormous cruelty.

To talk of *kindness* entering into a relation in which one party is robbed of wife, of children, of his hard earnings, of home, of friends, of society, of knowledge, and of all that makes this life desirable, is most absurd, wicked, and preposterous.

I have shown that slavery is *wicked* — *wicked*, in that it violates the great law of liberty, written on every human heart — *wicked*, in that it violates the first command of the decalogue — wicked, in that it fosters the most disgusting licentiousness —*wicked*, in that it mars and defaces the image of God by cruel and barbarous inflictions — *wicked*, in that it contravenes the laws of eternal justice, and tramples in the dust all the humane and heavenly precepts of the New Testament.

The evils resulting from this huge system of iniquity are not confined to the states south of Mason and Dixon's line. Its noxious influence can easily be traced throughout our northern borders. It comes even as far north as the state of New York. Traces of it may be seen even in Rochester; and travelers have told me it casts its gloomy shadows across the lake, approaching the very shores of Queen Victoria's dominions.

The presence of slavery may be explained by — as it is the explanation of — the mobocratic violence which lately disgraced New York, and which still more recently disgraced the city of Boston. These violent demonstrations, these outrageous invasions of human rights, faintly indicate the presence and power of slavery here. It is a significant fact, that while meetings for almost any purpose under heaven may be held unmolested in the city of Boston, that in the same city, a meeting cannot be peaceably held for the purpose of preaching the doctrine of the American Declaration of Independence, "that all men are created equal." The pestiferous breath of slavery taints the whole moral atmosphere of the north, and enervates the moral energies of the whole people.

The moment a foreigner ventures upon our soil, and utters a natural repugnance to oppression, that moment he is made to feel that there is little sympathy in this land for him. If he were greeted with smiles before, he meets with frowns now; and it shall go well with him if he be not subjected to that peculiarly fitting method of showing fealty to slavery, the assaults of a mob.

Now, will any man tell me that such a state of things is natural, and that such conduct on the part of the people of the north, springs from a consciousness of rectitude? No! every fibre of the human heart unites in detestation of tyranny, and it is only when the human mind has become familiarized with slavery, is accustomed to its injustice, and corrupted by its selfishness, that it fails to record its abhorrence of slavery, and does not exult in the triumphs of liberty.

The northern people have been long connected with slavery; they have been linked to a decaying corpse, which has destroyed the moral health. The union of the government; the union of the north and south, in the political parties; the union in the religious organizations of the land, have all served to deaden the moral sense of the northern people, and to impregnate them with sentiments and ideas forever in conflict with what as a nation we call *genius of American institutions*. Rightly viewed, this is an alarming fact, and ought to rally all that is pure, just, and holy in one determined effort to crush the monster of corruption, and to scatter "its guilty profits" to the winds. In a high moral sense, as well as in a national sense, the whole American people are responsible for slavery, and must share, in its guilt and shame, with the most obdurate men-stealers of the south.

While slavery exists, and the union of these states endures, every American citizen must bear the chagrin of hearing his country branded before the world as a nation of liars and hypocrites; and behold his cherished national flag pointed at with the utmost scorn and derision. Even now an American *abroad* is pointed out in the crowd, as coming from a land where men gain their fortunes by "the blood of souls," from a land of slave markets, of bloodhounds, and slave-hunters; and, in some circles, such a man is shunned altogether, as a moral pest. Is it not time, then, for every American to awake, and inquire into his duty with respect to this subject?

Wendell Phillips — the eloquent New England orator — on his return from Europe, in 1842, said, "As I stood upon the shores of Genoa, and saw floating on the placid waters of the Mediterranean, the beautiful American war ship Ohio, with her masts tapering proportionately aloft, and an eastern sun reflecting her noble form upon the sparkling waters, attracting the gaze of the multitude, my first impulse was of pride, to think myself an American; but when I thought that the first time that gallant ship would gird on her gorgeous apparel, and wake from beneath her sides her dormant thunders, it would be in defense of the African slave trade, I blushed *in utter shame* for my country."

Let me say again, *slavery is alike the sin and the shame of the American people*; it is a blot upon the American name, and the only national reproach which need make an American hang his head in shame, in the presence of monarchical governments.

With this gigantic evil in the land, we are constantly told to look *at home*; if we say ought against crowned heads, we are pointed to our enslaved millions; if we talk of sending missionaries and bibles abroad, we are pointed to three millions now lying in worse than heathen darkness; if we express a word of sympathy for Kossuth and his Hungarian fugitive brethren, we are pointed to that horrible and hell-black enactment, "THE FUGITIVE SLAVE BILL."

Slavery blunts the edge of all our rebukes of tyranny abroad — the criticisms that we make upon other nations, only call forth ridicule, contempt, and scorn. In a word, we are made a reproach and a byword to a mocking earth, and we must continue to be so made, so long as slavery continues to pollute our soil.

We have heard much of late of the virtue of patriotism, the love of country, &c., and this sentiment, so natural and so strong, has been impiously appealed to, by all the powers of human selfishness, to cherish the viper which is stinging our national life away. In its name, we have been called upon to deepen our infamy before the world, to rivet the fetter more firmly on the limbs of the enslaved, and to become utterly insensible to the voice of human woe that is wafted to us on every southern gale. We have been called upon, in its name, to desecrate our whole land by the footprints of slave-hunters, and even to engage ourselves in the horrible business of kidnapping.

I, too, would invoke the spirit of patriotism; *not* in a narrow and restricted sense, but, I trust, with a broad and manly signification; *not* to cover up our national sins, but to inspire us with sincere repentance; *not* to hide our shame from the world's gaze, but utterly to abolish the cause of that shame; *not* to explain away our gross inconsistencies as a nation, but to remove the hateful, jarring, and incongruous elements from the land; *not* to sustain an egregious wrong, but to unite all our energies in the grand effort to remedy that wrong.

I would invoke the spirit of patriotism, in the name of the law of the living God, natural and revealed, and in the full belief that "righteousness exalteth a nation, while sin is a reproach to any people." "He that walketh righteously, and speaketh uprightly; he that despiseth the gain of oppressions, that shaketh his hands from the holding of bribes, he shall dwell on high, his place of defense shall be the munitions of rocks, bread shall be given him, his water shall be sure."

We have not only heard much lately of patriotism, and of its aid being invoked on the side of slavery and injustice, but the very prosperity of this people has been called in to deafen them to the voice of duty, and to lead them onward in the pathway of sin. Thus has the blessing of God been converted into a curse. In the spirit of genuine patriotism, I warn the American people, by all that is just and honorable, to *beware*!

I warn them that, strong, proud, and prosperous though we be, there is a power above us that can "bring down high looks; at the breath of whose mouth our wealth may take wings; and before whom every knee shall bow;" and who can tell how soon the avenging angel may pass over our land, and the sable bondmen now in chains, may become the instruments of our nation's chastisement! Without appealing to any higher feeling, I would warn the American people, and the American government, to *be wise* in their day and generation. I exhort them to remember the history of other nations; and I remind them that America cannot always sit "as a queen," in peace and repose; that prouder and stronger governments than this have been shattered by the bolts of a just God; that the time *may* come when those they now despise and hate, may be needed; when those whom they now compel by oppression to be enemies, may be wanted as friends. What *has* been, *may* be again. There is a point beyond which human endurance cannot go. The crushed worm may yet turn under the heel of the oppressor. I warn them, then, with all solemnity, and in the name of retributive justice, to *look to their ways*; for in an evil hour, those sable arms that have, for the last two centuries, been engaged in cultivating and adorning the fair fields of our country, may yet become the instruments of terror, desolation, and death, throughout our borders.

We are told, by the President of the United States, in his recent message to Congress, that the American people are at peace with all the world; and this may be true in the sense in which it is used; but *what* if this may not always be the case? *What* if, by some strange vicissitude, amicable relations with Europe should be interrupted. What if *war* should take the place of diplomacy? and some principle of international law between this and some strong European power should be defeated on the battlefield? *Where* then, would be our safety? We are told, (by a Southern Statesman,) that a million of slaves are ready to "strike for freedom," at the first roll of a foreign drum; and I would ask, in his language, "How are you to sustain an assault from England or France, with this cancer in your vitals?" The slaves in, our land have reached a number *not* to be despised. They are *three* millions — a fearful multitude to be in chains. The American people numbered *three* millions when they asserted their independence; and although they contended with the strongest power on the globe, they were successful. It was the sage of the Old Dominion that said — while speaking of the possibility of a conflict between the slaves and the slaveholders— "God has no attribute that could take sides with the oppressor in such a contest. I tremble for my country when I reflect that *God* is *just,* and that his justice cannot sleep forever." Such is the warning voice of Thomas Jefferson; and every day's experience since its utterance until now, confirms its wisdom, and commends its truth.[97]

---

[97] Lecture delivered at Corinthian Hall in Rochester, New York on

No Neutral Ground Concerning Freedom and Slavery - He who comes to this country, hoping to escape *"entanglements"* on the slavery question, (as it is called by those who shrink from it,) must not only keep his mouth shut and his ears closed, but must actually put his eyes out, or cover them with bandages too thick to allow him to catch the lineaments of our national face; and in choosing one to lead him, must be sure to select an individual as blind as himself; for so sure as these conditions are not complied with, he will find his fond hopes blasted. - The line between Freedom and Slavery, in this country, is tightly drawn; and the combatants on either side are in earnest and fight hand to hand. He who chances to be on one side or on the other, if it be but in the estimation of a single hair, must fight, or die. There is no neutral ground here for any man. Father Mathew looked for such ground, but he looked with his eyes open; and this is the secret of his bad luck. Had he been deaf, dumb, and blind, he might have, peradventure, stumbled on the weak side; but he saw the strongest, and consulting his fears, he threw himself in the arms of the oppressor, because on his side was power.

December 8th, 1850. This unabridged version is found in a pamphlet entitled *Lectures on American Slavery*, (Buffalo, NY: Geo. Reese & Co's Power Press, 1851).

Kossuth[98] has tried it, and although, backed by his non-intervention doctrine; and being, perhaps, the greatest tactician of modern times, the result has been the same, and worse than the same. A tourist may visit Austria, Russia, France, Spain and the Barbary States, and perhaps escape committal or controversy; but so he may not do in the United States. Entanglement is certain. We allow no man to enter here without conflict. He must show his hand, try his strength, prove his mettle; and there's no escape.

Who are to blame for these bad manners which so annoy and perplex the stranger? – Some say the abolitionists; and they are abused on all sides soundly for the same. – Their impertinent intermeddling with foreigners, is a source of the utmost pain and mortification to the decent, well-behaved, conservative class of our citizens, many of whom would be glad to banish them to Africa with "the n****rs" if they could; for you know in this case the innocent have to suffer with the guilty. Our reputation, as a nation, is the thing that is injured; and patriotism cherishes nothing more dearly than national reputation. According to high authority, men will seek this bauble in the cannon's mouth. It is not strange, then, that our "potent, grave and reverend seniors," of Hunker stan-

---

[98] Lajos Kossuth (1802-1894) was a Hungarian statesman, freedom fighter and outstanding orator known as the Father of Hungarian Democracy.

ding, frown upon the abolitionist as an ill-mannered and mischievous set, who must be put down at all hazards. – "What," say they, "has it come to this, that a minister cannot come here from another country to preach the gospel, without being insulted by a request from these impertinent mad-caps to remember the American slave in his prayers! – that Father Mathew, the apostle of temperance, cannot come here without being bothered by an invitation to attend an anti-slavery meeting! – that noble Kossuth cannot come here to address our citizens on the great doctrines of independence, the rights of man and universal liberty, without being pestered with deputations and addresses, exhorting him to be true to himself, to his position, to his history at home and abroad, to the great doctrine of universal freedom which he preaches! Why! the bad manners of this set are intolerable!"

Such are the sentiments of our pro-slavery noodles. It is they, not we, who are at fault in this manner. They have got a foul, unnatural, loathsome abomination, to uphold against all the noble instincts of human nature; and bowing themselves before this huge and bloody idol, they call upon all men, of every land and nation, who venture withing its precincts, to "do likewise;" or at any rate, to padlock their lips, and be dumb, in regard to the monstrosity. They, not we, are the aggressors. They throw themselves athwart the current of nature, of conscience, of truth, of justice, and of the spirit of the living God. They make war on man, as well as on manners, and when we cry out against it, and call upon others to do so, we, forsooth, are meddlesome and indecorous!

We have been induced to make the foregoing remarks, in anticipation of the reception which awaits the pamphlet containing the letter to Kossuth, the title of which is given at the head of this article. The subject is a fruitful one, and we would gladly say more, but our space will not permit to do so. The letter to Kossuth, is a most searching production; and if he be not insensible to the claims of that justice he so eloquently advocates, he must be convinced by it, that he has bestowed eulogies on this nation, not deserved; that he has been playing into the hands of tyrants, worse than Austria ever knew; and that he has inflicted a wound on the cause of freedom, which he cannot too speedily do his utmost to heal.[99]

---

[99] Originally published as "Letter to Kossuth", *Frederick Douglass' Paper*, February 26th, 1852.

What to the Slave Is Your Fourth of July? – Mr. President, Friends and Fellow Citizens: He who could address this audience without a quailing sensation, has stronger nerves than I have. I do not remember ever to have appeared as a speaker before any assembly more shrinkingly, nor with greater distrust of my ability, than I do this day. A feeling has crept over me, quite unfavorable to the exercise of my limited powers of speech. The task before me is one which requires much previous thought and study for its proper performance. I know that apologies of this sort are generally considered flat and unmeaning. I trust, however, that mine will not be so considered. Should I seem at ease, my appearance would much misrepresent me. The little experience I have had in addressing public meetings, in country schoolhouses, avails me nothing on the present occasion.

The papers and placards say, that I am to deliver a 4th [of] July oration. This certainly sounds large, and out of the common way, for it is true that I have often had the privilege to speak in this beautiful Hall, and to address many who now honor me with their presence. But neither their familiar faces, nor the perfect gage I think I have of Corinthian Hall, seems to free me from embarrassment.

The fact is, ladies and gentlemen, the distance between this platform and the slave plantation, from which I escaped, is considerable – and the difficulties to be overcome in getting from the latter to the former, are by no means slight. That I am here today is, to me, a matter of astonishment as well as of gratitude. You will not, therefore, be surprised, if in what I have to say I evince no elaborate preparation, nor grace my speech with any high sounding exordium. With little experience and with less learning, I have been able to throw my thoughts hastily and imperfectly together; and trusting to your patient and generous indulgence, I will proceed to lay them before you.

This, for the purpose of this celebration, is the 4th of July. It is the birthday of your National Independence, and of your political freedom. This, to you, is what the Passover was to the emancipated people of God. It carries your minds back to the day, and to the act of your great deliverance; and to the signs, and to the wonders, associated with that act, and that day. This celebration also marks the beginning of another year of your national life; and reminds you that the Republic of America is now 76 years old. I am glad, fellow-citizens, that your nation is so young. Seventy-six years, though a good old age for a man, is but a mere speck in the life of a nation. Three score years and ten is the allotted time for individual men; but nations number their years by 2 thousands. According to this fact, you are, even now, only in the beginning of your national career, still lingering in the period of childhood. I repeat, I am glad this is so.

There is hope in the thought, and hope is much needed, under the dark clouds which lower above the horizon. The eye of the reformer is met with angry flashes, portending disastrous times; but his heart may well beat lighter at the thought that America is young, and that she is still in the impressible stage of her existence. May he not hope that high lessons of wisdom, of justice and of truth, will yet give direction to her destiny? Were the nation older, the patriot's heart might be sadder, and the reformer's brow heavier. Its future might be shrouded in gloom, and the hope of its prophets go out in sorrow. There is consolation in the thought that America is young. Great streams are not easily turned from channels, worn deep in the course of ages. They may sometimes rise in quiet and stately majesty, and inundate the land, refreshing and fertilizing the earth with their mysterious properties. They may also rise in wrath and fury, and bear away, on their angry waves, the accumulated wealth of years of toil and hardship. They, however, gradually flow back to the same old channel, and flow on as serenely as ever. But, while the river may not be turned aside, it may dry up, and leave nothing behind but the withered branch, and the unsightly rock, to howl in the abyss-sweeping wind, the sad tale of departed glory. As with rivers so with nations.

Fellow-citizens, I shall not presume to dwell at length on the associations that cluster about this day. The simple story of it is that, 76 years ago, the people of this country were British subjects. The style and title of your "sovereign people" (in which you now glory) was not then born. You were under the British Crown. Your fathers esteemed the English Government as the home government; and England as the fatherland. This home government, you know, although a considerable distance from your home, did, in the exercise of its parental prerogatives, impose upon its colonial children, such restraints, burdens and limitations, as, in its mature judgment, it deemed wise, right and proper.

But, your fathers, who had not adopted the fashionable idea of this day, of the infallibility of government, and the absolute character of its acts, presumed to differ from the home government in respect to the wisdom and the justice of some of those burdens and restraints. They went so far in their excitement as to pronounce the measures of government unjust, unreasonable, and oppressive, and altogether such as ought not to be quietly submitted to. I scarcely need say, fellowcitizens, that my opinion of those measures fully accords with that of your fathers. Such a declaration of agreement on my part would not be worth much to anybody. It would, certainly, prove nothing, as to what part I might have taken, had I lived during the great controversy of 1776. To say now that America was right, and England wrong, is exceedingly easy. Everybody can say it; the dastard, not less than the noble brave, can flippantly discant on the tyranny of England towards the American Colonies. It is fashionable to do so; but there was a time when to pronounce against England, and in favor of the cause of the colonies, tried men's souls. They who did so were accounted in their day, plotters of mischief, agitators and rebels, dangerous men. To side with the right, against the wrong, with the weak against the strong, and with the oppressed against the oppressor! here lies the merit, and the one which, of all others, seems unfashionable in our day. The cause of liberty may be stabbed by the men who glory in the deeds of your fathers. But, to proceed.

Feeling themselves harshly and unjustly treated by the home government, your fathers, like men of honesty, and men of spirit, earnestly sought redress. They petitioned and remonstrated; they did so in a decorous, respectful, and loyal manner. Their conduct was wholly unexceptionable. This, however, did not answer the purpose. They saw themselves treated with sovereign indifference, coldness and scorn. Yet they persevered. They were not the men to look back.

As the sheet anchor takes a firmer hold, when the ship is tossed by the storm, so did the cause of your fathers grow stronger, as it breasted the chilling blasts of kingly displeasure. The greatest and best of British statesmen admitted its justice, and the loftiest eloquence of the British Senate came to its support. But, with that blindness which seems to be the unvarying characteristic of tyrants, since Pharaoh and his hosts were drowned in the Red Sea, the British Government persisted in the exactions complained of.

The madness of this course, we believe, is admitted now, even by England; but we fear the lesson is wholly lost on our present rulers.

Oppression makes a wise man mad. Your fathers were wise men, and if they did not go mad, they became restive under this treatment. They felt themselves the victims of grievous wrongs, wholly incurable in their colonial capacity. With brave men there is always a remedy for oppression. Just here, the idea of a total separation of the colonies from the crown was born! It was a startling idea, much more so, than we, at this distance of time, regard it. The timid and the prudent (as has been intimated) of that day, were, of course, shocked and alarmed by it.

Such people lived then, had lived before, and will, probably, ever have a place on this planet; and their course, in respect to any great change, (no matter how great the good to be attained, or the wrong to be redressed by it), may be calculated with as much precision as can be the course of the stars. They hate all changes, but silver, gold and copper change! Of this sort of change they are always strongly in favor.

These people were called Tories in the days of your fathers; and the appellation, probably, conveyed the same idea that is meant by a more modern, though a somewhat less euphonious term, which we often find in our papers, applied to some of our old politicians.

Their opposition to the then dangerous thought was earnest and powerful; but, amid all their terror and affrighted vociferations against it, the alarming and revolutionary idea moved on, and the country with it.

On the 2d of July, 1776, the old Continental Congress, to the dismay of the lovers of ease, and the worshipers of property, clothed that dreadful idea with all the authority of national sanction. They did so in the form of a resolution; and as we seldom hit upon resolutions, drawn up in our day whose transparency is at all equal to this, it may refresh your minds and help my story if I read it.

"Resolved, That these united colonies are, and of right, ought to be free and Independent States; that they are absolved from all allegiance to the British Crown; and that all political connection between them and the State of Great Britain is, and ought to be, dissolved."

Citizens, your fathers made good that resolution. They succeeded; and today you reap the fruits of their success. The freedom gained is yours; and you, therefore, may properly celebrate this anniversary. The 4th of July is the first great fact in your nation's history — the very ring-bolt in the chain of your yet undeveloped destiny.

Pride and patriotism, not less than gratitude, prompt you to celebrate and to hold it in perpetual remembrance. I have said that the Declaration of Independence is the ring-bolt to the chain of your nation's destiny; so, indeed, I regard it. The principles contained in that instrument are saving principles. Stand by those principles, be true to them on all occasions, in all places, against all foes, and at whatever cost.

From the round top of your ship of state, dark and threatening clouds may be seen. Heavy billows, like mountains in the distance, disclose to the leeward huge forms of flinty rocks! That bolt drawn, that chain broken, and all is lost. Cling to this day — cling to it, and to its principles, with the grasp of a storm-tossed mariner to a spar at midnight.

The coming into being of a nation, in any circumstances, is an interesting event. But, besides general considerations, there were peculiar circumstances which make the advent of this republic an event of special attractiveness.

The whole scene, as I look back to it, was simple, dignified and sublime.

The population of the country, at the time, stood at the insignificant number of three millions. The country was poor in the munitions of war. The population was weak and scattered, and the country a wilderness unsubdued. There were then no means of concert and combination, such as exist now. Neither steam nor lightning had then been reduced to order and discipline. From the Potomac to the Delaware was a journey of many days. Under these, and innumerable other disadvantages, your fathers declared for liberty and independence and triumphed.

Fellow Citizens, I am not wanting in respect for the fathers of this republic. The signers of the Declaration of Independence were brave men. They were great men too — great enough to give fame to a great age. It does not often happen to a nation to raise, at one time, such a number of truly great men. The point from which I am compelled to view them is not, certainly, the most favorable; and yet I cannot contemplate their great deeds with less than admiration. They were statesmen, patriots and heroes, and for the good they did, and the principles they contended for, I will unite with you to honor their memory.

They loved their country better than their own private interests; and, though this is not the highest form of human excellence, all will concede that it is a rare virtue, and that when it is exhibited, it ought to command respect. He who will, intelligently, lay down his life for his country, is a man whom it is not in human nature to despise. Your fathers staked their lives, their fortunes, and their sacred honor, on the cause of their country. In their admiration of liberty, they lost sight of all other interests.

They were peace men; but they preferred revolution to peaceful submission to bondage. They were quiet men; but they did not shrink from agitating against oppression. They showed forbearance; but that they knew its limits. They believed in order; but not in the order of tyranny. With them, nothing was "settled" that was not right. With them, justice, liberty and humanity were "final;" not slavery and oppression. You may well cherish the memory of such men. They were great in their day and generation. Their solid manhood stands out the more as we contrast it with these degenerate times.

How circumspect, exact and proportionate were all their movements! How unlike the politicians of an hour! Their statesmanship looked beyond the passing moment, and stretched away in strength into the distant future. They seized upon eternal principles, and set a glorious example in their defense. Mark them!

Fully appreciating the hardship to be encountered, firmly believing in the right of their cause, honorably inviting the scrutiny of an on-looking world, reverently appealing to heaven to attest their sincerity, soundly comprehending the solemn responsibility they were about to assume, wisely measuring the terrible odds against them, your fathers, the fathers of this republic, did, most deliberately, under the inspiration of a glorious patriotism, and with a sublime faith in the great principles of justice and freedom, lay deep the cornerstone of the national superstructure, which has risen and still rises in grandeur around you.

Of this fundamental work, this day is the anniversary. Our eyes are met with demonstrations of joyous enthusiasm. Banners and pennants wave exultingly on the breeze. The din of business, too, is hushed. Even Mammon seems to have quitted his grasp on this day. The ear-piercing fife and the stirring drum unite their accents with the ascending peal of a thousand church bells. Prayers are made, hymns are sung, and sermons are preached in honor of this day; while the quick martial tramp of a great and multitudinous nation, echoed back by all the hills, valleys and mountains of a vast continent, bespeak the occasion one of thrilling and universal interest — a nation's jubilee.

Friends and citizens, I need not enter further into the causes which led to this anniversary. Many of you understand them better than I do. You could instruct me in regard to them. That is a branch of knowledge in which you feel, perhaps, a much deeper interest than your speaker. The causes which led to the separation of the colonies from the British crown have never lacked for a tongue. They have all been taught in your common schools, narrated at your firesides, unfolded from your pulpits, and thundered from your legislative halls, and are as familiar to you as household words. They form the staple of your national poetry and eloquence.

I remember, also, that, as a people, Americans are remarkably familiar with all facts which make in their own favor. This is esteemed by some as a national trait — perhaps a national weakness. It is a fact, that whatever makes for the wealth or for the reputation of Americans, and can be had cheap! will be found by Americans. I shall not be charged with slandering Americans, if I say I think the American side of any question may be safely left in American hands.

I leave, therefore, the great deeds of your fathers to other gentlemen whose claim to have been regularly descended will be less likely to be disputed than mine!

My business, if I have any here today, is with the present. The accepted time with God and His cause is the ever-living now.

Trust no future, however pleasant,
Let the dead past bury its dead;
Act, act in the living present,
Heart within, and God overhead.

We have to do with the past only as we can make it useful to the present and to the future. To all inspiring motives, to noble deeds which can be gained from the past, we are welcome. But now is the time, the important time. Your fathers have lived, died, and have done their work, and have done much of it well. You live and must die, and you must do your work. You have no right to enjoy a child's share in the labor of your fathers, unless your children are to be blest by your labors. You have no right to wear out and waste the hard-earned fame of your fathers to cover your indolence. Sydney Smith tells us that men seldom eulogize the wisdom and virtues of their fathers, but to excuse some folly or wickedness of their own. This truth is not a doubtful one. There are illustrations of it near and remote, ancient and modern. It was fashionnable, hundreds of years ago, for the children of Jacob to boast, we have "Abraham to our father," when they had long lost Abraham's faith and spirit. That people contented themselves under the shadow of Abraham's great name, while they repudiated the deeds which made his name great. Need I remind you that a similar thing is being done all over this country today? Need I tell you that the Jews are not the only people who built the tombs of the prophets, and garnished the sepulchres of the righteous? Washington could not die till he had broken the chains of his slaves. Yet his monument is built up by the price of human blood, and the traders in the bodies and souls of men shout — "We have Washington to *our father.*" — Alas! that it should be so; yet so it is.

The evil that men do, lives after them,
The good is oft-interred with their bones.

Fellow-citizens, pardon me, allow me to ask, why am I called upon to speak here today? What have I, or those I represent, to do with your national independence? Are the great principles of political freedom and of natural justice, embodied in that Declaration of Independence, extended to us? and am I, therefore, called upon to bring our humble offering to the national altar, and to confess the benefits and express devout gratitude for the blessings resulting from your independence to us?

Would to God, both for your sakes and ours, that an affirmative answer could be truthfully returned to these questions! Then would my task be light, and my burden easy and delightful. For who is there so cold, that a nation's sympathy could not warm him? Who so obdurate and dead to the claims of gratitude, that would not thankfully acknowledge such priceless benefits? Who so stolid and selfish, that would not give his voice to swell the hallelujahs of a nation's jubilee, when the chains of servitude had been torn from his limbs? I am not that man. In a case like that, the dumb might eloquently speak, and the "lame man leap as an hart."

But, such is not the state of the case. I say it with a sad sense of the disparity between us. I am not included within the pale of this glorious anniversary! Your high independence only reveals the immeasurable distance between us. The blessings in which you, this day, rejoice, are not enjoyed in common. — The rich inheritance of justice, liberty, prosperity and independence, bequeathed by your fathers, is shared by you, not by me. The sunlight that brought life and healing to you, has brought stripes and death to me. This Fourth [of] July is yours, not mine. You may rejoice, I must mourn. To drag a man in fetters into the grand illuminated temple of liberty, and call upon him to join you in joyous anthems, were inhuman mockery and sacrilegious irony. Do you mean, citizens, to mock me, by asking me to speak today? If so, there is a parallel to your conduct. And let me warn you that it is dangerous to copy the example of a nation whose crimes, lowering up to heaven, were thrown down by the breath of the Almighty, burying that nation in irrecoverable ruin! I can today take up the plaintive lament of a peeled and woe-smitten people!

"By the rivers of Babylon, there we sat down. Yea! we wept when we remembered Zion. We hanged our harps upon the willows in the midst thereof. For there, they that carried us away captive, required of us a song; and they who wasted us required of us mirth, saying, Sing us one of the songs of Zion. How can we sing the Lord's song in a strange land? If I forget thee, O Jerusalem, let my right hand forget her cunning. If I do not remember thee, let my tongue cleave to the roof of my mouth."[100]

Fellow-citizens; above your national, tumultuous joy, I hear the mournful wail of millions! whose chains, heavy and grievous yesterday, are, today, rendered more intolerable by the jubilee shouts that reach them. If I do forget, if I do not faithfully remember those bleeding children of sorrow this day, "may my right hand forget her cunning, and may my tongue cleave to the roof of my mouth!" To forget them, to pass lightly over their wrongs, and to chime in with the popular theme, would be treason most scandalous and shocking, and would make me a reproach before God and the world. My subject, then fellow-citizens, is AMERICAN SLAVERY. I shall see, this day, and its popular characteristics, from the slave's point of view. Standing, there, identified with the American bondman, making his wrongs mine, I do not hesitate to declare, with all my soul, that the character and conduct of this nation never looked blacker to me than on this 4th of July! Whether we turn to the declarations of the past, or to the professions of the present, the conduct of the nation seems equally hideous and revolting. America is false to the past, false to the present, and solemnly binds herself to be false to the future. Standing with God and the crushed and bleeding slave on this occasion, I will, in the name of

---

[100] King James Bible, *Psalms*, 137:1-6.

humanity which is outraged, in the name of liberty which is fettered, in the name of the constitution and the Bible, which are disregarded and trampled upon, dare to call in question and to denounce, with all the emphasis I can command, everything that serves to perpetuate slavery — the great sin and shame of America! "I will not equivocate; I will not excuse;" I will use the severest language I can command; and yet not one word shall escape me that any man, whose judgment is not blinded by prejudice, or who is not at heart a slaveholder, shall not confess to be right and just.

But I fancy I hear some one of my audience say, it is just in this circumstance that you and your brother abolitionists fail to make a favorable impression on the public mind. Would you argue more, and denounce less, would you persuade more, and rebuke less, your cause would be much more likely to succeed. But, I submit, where all is plain there is nothing to be argued. What point in the anti-slavery creed would you have me argue? On what branch of the subject do the people of this country need light? Must I undertake to prove that the slave is a man? That point is conceded already. Nobody doubts it. The slaveholders themselves acknowledge it in the enactment of laws for their government. They acknowledge it when they punish disobedience on the part of the slave. There are seventy-two crimes in the State of

Virginia, which, if committed by a Black man, (no matter how ignorant he be), subject him to the punishment of death; while only two of the same crimes will subject a white man to the like punishment. What is this but the acknowledgement that the slave is a moral, intellectual and responsible being? The manhood of the slave is conceded. It is admitted in the fact that Southern statute books are covered with enactments forbidding, under severe fines and penalties, the teaching of the slave to read or to write. When you can point to any such laws, in reference to the beasts of the field, then I may consent to argue the manhood of the slave. When the dogs in your streets, when the fowls of the air, when the cattle on your hills, when the fish of the sea, and the reptiles that crawl, shall be unable to distinguish the slave from a brute, *then* will I argue with you that the slave is a man!

For the present, it is enough to affirm the equal manhood of the Negro race. Is it not astonishing that, while we are ploughing, planting and reaping, using all kinds of mechanical tools, erecting houses, constructing bridges, building ships, working in metals of brass, iron, copper, silver and gold; that, while we are reading, writing and cyphering, acting as clerks, merchants and secretaries, having among us lawyers, doctors, ministers, poets, authors, editors, orators and teachers; that, while we are engaged in all manner of enterprises common to other men, digging gold in California, capturing the whale in the Pacific, feeding sheep and cattle on the hill-side, living, moving, acting, thinking, planning, living in families as husbands, wives and children, and, above all, confessing and worshipping the Christian's God, and looking hopefully for life and immortality beyond the grave, we are called upon to prove that we are men!

Would you have me argue that man is entitled to liberty? that he is the rightful owner of his own body? You have already declared it. Must I argue the wrongfulness of slavery? Is that a question for Republicans? Is it to be settled by the rules of logic and argumentation, as a matter beset with great difficulty, involving a doubtful application of the principle of justice, hard to be understood? How should I look today, in the presence of Americans, dividing, and subdividing a discourse, to show that men have a natural right to freedom? speaking of it relatively, and positively, negatively, and affirmatively. To do so, would be to make myself ridiculous, and to offer an insult to your understanding. — There is not a man beneath the canopy of heaven, that does not know that slavery is wrong *for him*.

What, am I to argue that it is wrong to make men brutes, to rob them of their liberty, to work them without wages, to keep them ignorant of their relations to their fellow men, to beat them with sticks, to flay their flesh with the lash, to load their limbs with irons, to hunt them with dogs, to sell them at auction, to sunder their families, to knock out their teeth, to burn their flesh, to starve them into obedience and submission to their masters? Must I argue that a system thus marked with blood, and stained with pollution, is wrong? No! I will not. I have better employments for my time and strength than such arguments would imply.

What, then, remains to be argued? Is it that slavery is not divine; that God did not establish it; that our doctors of divinity are mistaken? There is blasphemy in the thought. That which is inhuman, cannot be Divine! Who can reason on such a proposition? They that can, may; I cannot. The time for such argument is passed.

At a time like this, scorching irony, not convincing argument, is needed. O! had I the ability, and could I reach the nation's ear, I would, today, pour out a fiery stream of biting ridicule, blasting reproach, withering sarcasm, and stern rebuke. For it is not light that is needed, but fire; it is not the gentle shower, but thunder. We need the storm, the whirlwind, and the earthquake. The feeling of the nation must be quickened; the conscience of the nation must be roused; the propriety of the nation must be startled; the hypocrisy of the nation must be exposed; and its crimes against God and man must be proclaimed and denounced.

What, to the American slave, is your 4th of July? I answer: a day that reveals to him, more than all other days in the year, the gross injustice and cruelty to which he is the constant victim. To him, your celebration is a sham; your boasted liberty, an unholy license; your national greatness, swelling vanity; your sounds of rejoicing are empty and heartless; your denunciations of tyrants, brass fronted impudence; your shouts of liberty and equality, hollow mockery; your prayers and hymns, your sermons and thanks-givings, with all your religious parade, and solemnity, are, to him, mere bombast, fraud, deception, impiety, and hypocrisy — a thin veil to cover up crimes which would disgrace a nation of savages. There is not a nation on the earth guilty of practices, more shocking and bloody, than are the people of these United States, at this very hour.

Go where you may, search where you will, roam through all the monarchies and despotisms of the old world, travel through South America, search out every abuse, and when you have found the last, lay your facts by the side of the everyday practices of this nation, and you will say with me, that, for revolting barbarity and shameless hypocrisy, America reigns without a rival.

Take the American slave-trade, which, we are told by the papers, is especially prosperous just now. Ex-Senator Benton tells us that the price of men was never higher than now. He mentions the fact to show that slavery is in no danger. This trade is one of the peculiarities of American institutions. It is carried on in all the large towns and cities in one-half of this confederacy; and millions are pocketed every year, by dealers in this horrid traffic. In several states, this trade is a chief source of wealth. It is called (in contradistinction to the foreign slave-trade) "the internal slave trade." It is, probably, called so, too, in order to divert from it the horror with which the foreign slave-trade is contemplated. That trade has long since been denounced by this government, as piracy. It has been denounced with burning words, from the high places of the nation, as an execrable traffic. To arrest it, to put an end to it, this nation keeps a squadron, at immense cost, on the coast of Africa. Everywhere, in this country, it is safe to speak of this foreign slave-trade, as a most inhuman traffic, opposed alike to the laws of God and of man. The duty to extirpate and destroy it, is admitted even by our DOCTORS OF DIVINITY. In order to put an end to it, some of these last have consented that their colored brethren (nominally free) should leave this country, and establish themselves on the western coast of Africa! It is, however, a notable fact that,

while so much execration is poured out by Americans
upon those engaged in the foreign slave-trade, the
men engaged in the slave-trade between the states
pass without condemnation, and their business is deemed honorable.

Behold the practical operation of this internal slave-
trade, the American slave-trade, sustained by American politics and America religion. Here you will see
men and women reared like swine for the market.
You know what is a swine-drover? I will show you a
man-drover. They inhabit all our Southern States.
They perambulate the country, and crowd the highways of the nation, with droves of human stock. You
will see one of these human flesh-jobbers, armed with
pistol, whip and bowieknife, driving a company of a
hundred men, women, and children, from the Potomac to the slave market at New Orleans. These
wretched people are to be sold singly, or in lots, to
suit purchasers. They are food for the cotton-field,
and the deadly sugar-mill. Mark the sad procession,
as it moves wearily along, and the inhuman wretch
who drives them. Hear his savage yells and his blood-
chilling oaths, as he hurries on his affrighted captives!
There, see the old man, with locks thinned and gray.
Cast one glance, if you please, upon that young mother, whose shoulders are bare to the scorching sun, her
briny tears falling on the brow of the babe in her
arms. See, too, that girl of thirteen, weeping, *yes!*

weeping, as she thinks of the mother from whom she has been torn! The drove moves tardily. Heat and sorrow have nearly consumed their strength; suddenly you hear a quick snap, like the discharge of a rifle; the fetters clank, and the chain rattles simultaneously; your ears are saluted with a scream, that seems to have torn its way to the center of your soul! The crack you heard, was the sound of the slave-whip; the scream you heard, was from the woman you saw with the babe. Her speed had faltered under the weight of her child and her chains! that gash on her shoulder tells her to move on. Follow the drove to New Orleans. Attend the auction; see men examined like horses; see the forms of women rudely and brutally exposed to the shocking gaze of American slave-buyers. See this drove sold and separated forever; and never forget the deep, sad sobs that arose from that scattered multitude. Tell me citizens, WHERE, under the sun, you can witness a spectacle more fiendish and shocking. Yet this is but a glance at the American slave-trade, as it exists, at this moment, in the ruling part of the United States.

I was born amid such sights and scenes. To me the American slave-trade is a terrible reality. When a child, my soul was often pierced with a sense of its horrors. I lived on Philpot Street, Fell's Point, Baltimore, and have watched from the wharves, the slave ships in the Basin, anchored from the shore, with

their cargoes of human flesh, waiting for favorable
winds to waft them down the Chesapeake. There was,
at that time, a grand slave mart kept at the head of
Pratt Street, by Austin Woldfolk. His agents were sent
into every town and county in Maryland, announcing
their arrival, through the papers, and on flaming
"*hand-bills*," headed CASH FOR NEGROES. These
men were generally well dressed men, and very capti-
vating in their manners. Ever ready to drink, to treat,
and to gamble. The fate of many a slave has
depended upon the turn of a single card; and many a
child has been snatched from the arms of its mother
by bargains arranged in a state of brutal drunkenness.

The flesh-mongers gather up their victims by dozens,
and drive them, chained, to the general depot at Baltimore. When a sufficient number have been collected
here, a ship is chartered, for the purpose of conveying
the forlorn crew to Mobile, or to New Orleans. From
the slave prison to the ship, they are usually driven in
the darkness of night; for since the antislavery agitation, a certain caution is observed.

In the deep still darkness of midnight, I have been
often aroused by the dead heavy footsteps, and the
piteous cries of the chained gangs that passed our
door. The anguish of my boyish heart was intense;
and I was often consoled, when speaking to my mistress in the morning, to hear her say that the custom
was very wicked; that she hated to hear the rattle of

the chains, and the heartrending cries. I was glad to find one who sympathized with me in my horror.

Fellow-citizens, this murderous traffic is, today, in active operation in this boasted republic. In the solitude of my spirit, I see clouds of dust raised on the highways of the South; I see the bleeding foot-steps; I hear the doleful wail of fettered humanity, on the way to the slave-markets, where the victims are to be sold like horses, sheep, and swine, knocked off to the highest bidder. There I see the tenderest ties ruthlessly broken, to gratify the lust, caprice and rapa-city of the buyers and sellers of men. My soul sickens at the sight.

Is this the land your Fathers loved,
The freedom which they toiled to win?
Is this the earth whereon they moved?
Are these the graves they slumber in?

But a still more inhuman, disgraceful, and scandal-ous state of things remains to be presented. By an act of the American Congress, not yet two years old, slav-ery has been nationalized in its most horrible and revolting form. By that act, Mason and Dixon's line has been obliterated; New York has become as Virginia; and the power to hold, hunt, and sell men, women, and children as slaves remains no longer a mere state institution, but is now an institution of the whole United States. The power is co-extensive with the Star-Spangled Banner and American Christianity.

Where these go, may also go the merciless slavehunter. Where these are, man is not sacred. He is a
bird for the sportsman's gun. By that most foul and
fiendish of all human decrees, the liberty and person
of every man are put in peril. Your broad republican
domain is hunting ground for *men*. *Not* for thieves
and robbers, enemies of society, merely, but for men
guilty of no crime. Your lawmakers have commanded all good citizens to engage in this hellish sport.
Your President, your Secretary of State, your *lords,
nobles,* and ecclesiastics, enforce, as a duty you owe
to your free and glorious country, and to your God,
that you do this accursed thing. Not fewer than forty
Americans have, within the past two years, been hunted down and, without a moment's warning, hurried
away in chains, and consigned to slavery and excru-
ciating torture. Some of these have had wives and
children, dependent on them for bread; but of this,
no account was made. The right of the hunter to his
prey stands superior to the right of marriage, and to
all rights in this republic, the rights of God included!
For Black men there is neither law, justice, humanity,
nor religion. The Fugitive Slave *Law* makes mercy to
them a crime; and bribes the judge who tries them.
An American judge gets ten dollars for every victim
he consigns to slavery, and five, when he fails to do
so. The oath of any two villains is sufficient, under
this hell-black enactment, to send the most pious and

exemplary Black man into the remorseless jaws of slavery! His own testimony is nothing. He can bring no witnesses for himself. The minister of American justice is bound by the law to hear but *one* side; and *that* side, is the side of the oppressor. Let this damning fact be perpetually told. Let it be thundered around the world, that, in tyrant-killing, king-hating, people-loving, democratic, Christian America, the seats of justice are filled with judges, who hold their offices under an open and palpable *bribe*, and are bound, in deciding in the case of a man's liberty, *to hear only his accusers!*

In glaring violation of justice, in shameless disregard of the forms of administering law, in cunning arrangement to entrap the defenseless, and in diabolical intent, this Fugitive Slave Law stands alone in the annals of tyrannical legislation. I doubt if there be another nation on the globe, having the brass and the baseness to put such a law on the statute-book. If any man in this assembly thinks differently from me in this matter, and feels able to disprove my statements, I will gladly confront him at any suitable time and place he may select.

I take this law to be one of the grossest infringements of Christian Liberty, and, if the churches and ministers of our country were not stupidly blind, or most wickedly indifferent, they, too, would so regard it.

At the very moment that they are thanking God for the enjoyment of civil and religious liberty, and for the right to worship God according to the dictates of their own consciences, they are utterly silent in respect to a law which robs religion of its chief significance, and makes it utterly worthless to a world lying in wickedness. Did this law concern the "*mint, anise, and cumin*" — abridge the right to sing psalms, to partake of the sacrament, or to engage in any of the ceremonies of religion, it would be smitten by the thunder of a thousand pulpits. A general shout would go up from the church, demanding *repeal, repeal, instant repeal!* — And it would go hard with that politician who presumed to solicit the votes of the people without inscribing this motto on his banner. Further, if this demand were not complied with, another Scotland would be added to the history of religious liberty, and the stern old Covenanters would be thrown into the shade. A John Knox would be seen at every church door, and heard from every pulpit, and Fillmore would have no more quarter than was shown by Knox, to the beautiful, but treacherous queen Mary of Scotland. The fact that the church of our country, (with fractional exceptions), does not esteem "the Fugitive Slave Law" as a declaration of war against religious liberty, implies that that church regards religion simply as a form of worship, an empty ceremony, and *not* a vital principle, requiring active benevolence, justice, love and good will towards man. It esteems sacrifice above mercy; psalm-singing above right doing; solemn meetings above practical righteousness. A worship that can be conducted by persons who refuse to give shelter to the houseless, to give bread to the hungry, clothing to the naked, and who enjoin obedience to a law forbidding these acts of mercy, is a curse, not a blessing to mankind. The Bible addresses all such persons as "scribes, Pharisees, hypocrites, who pay tithe of *mint, anise, and cumin*, and have omitted the weightier matters of the law, judgment, mercy and faith."

But the church of this country is not only indifferent to the wrongs of the slave, it actually takes sides with the oppressors. It has made itself the bulwark of American slavery, and the shield of American slave-hunters. Many of its most eloquent Divines. who stand as the very lights of the church, have shamelessly given the sanction of religion and the Bible to the whole slave system. They have taught that man may, properly, be a slave; that the relation of master and slave is ordained of God; that to send back an escaped bondman to his master is clearly the duty of all the followers of the Lord Jesus Christ; and this horrible blasphemy is palmed off upon the world for Christianity.

For my part, I would say, welcome infidelity! welcome atheism! welcome anything! in preference to the gospel, *as preached by those Divines!* They convert the very name of religion into an engine of tyranny, and barbarous cruelty, and serve to confirm more infidels, in this age, than all the infidel writings of Thomas Paine, Voltaire, and Bolingbroke, put together, have done! These ministers make religion a cold and flinty-hearted thing, having neither principles of right action, nor bowels of compassion. They strip the love of God of its beauty, and leave the throng of religion a huge, horrible, repulsive form. It is a religion for oppressors, tyrants, man-stealers, and *thugs.* It is not that "*pure and undefiled religion*" which is from above, and which is "*first pure, then peaceable, easy to be entreated,* full of mercy and good fruits, *without partiality, and without hypocrisy.*" But a religion which favors the rich against the poor; which exalts the proud above the humble; which divides mankind into two classes, tyrants and slaves; which says to the man in chains, *stay there;* and to the oppressor, *oppress on;* it is a religion which may be professed and enjoyed by all the robbers and enslavers of mankind; it makes God a respecter of persons, denies His fatherhood of the race, and tramples in the dust the great truth of the brotherhood of man. All this we affirm to be true of the popular church, and the popular worship of our land and nation — a religion, a church, and a worship which, on the authority of inspired wisdom, we pronounce to be an abomination in the sight of God. In the language of Isaiah, the American church might be well addressed, "Bring no more vain ablations; incense is an abomination unto me: the new moons and Sabbaths, the calling of assemblies, I cannot away with; it is iniquity even the solemn meeting. Your new moons and your appoint-ted feasts my soul hateth. They are a trouble to me; I am weary to bear them; and when ye spread forth your hands I will hide mine eyes from you. Yea! when ye make many prayers, I will not hear. **YOUR HANDS ARE FULL OF BLOOD**; cease to do evil, learn to do well; seek judgment; relieve the oppre-ssed; judge for the fatherless; plead for the widow."[101]

The American church is guilty, when viewed in connection with what it is doing to uphold slavery; but it is superlatively guilty when viewed in connection with its ability to abolish slavery.

The sin of which it is guilty is one of omission as well as of commission. Albert Barnes but uttered what the common sense of every man at all observant of the actual state of the case will receive as truth, when he declared that "There is no power out of the church that could sustain slavery an hour, if it were not sustained in it."

Let the religious press, the pulpit, the Sunday school, the conference meeting, the great ecclesiastical, miss-ionary, Bible and tract associations of the land array

---

[101] King James Bible, *Isaiah* 1:13-17

their immense powers against slavery and slave-holding; and the whole system of crime and blood would be scattered to the winds; and that they do not do this involves them in the most awful responsibility of which the mind can conceive.

In prosecuting the anti-slavery enterprise, we have been asked to spare the church, to spare the ministry; but *how*, we ask, could such a thing be done? We are met on the threshold of our efforts for the redemption of the slave, by the church and ministry of the country, in battle arrayed against us; and we are compelled to fight or flee. From *what* quarter, I beg to know, has proceeded a fire so deadly upon our ranks, during the last two years, as from the Northern pulpit? As the champions of oppressors, the chosen men of American theology have appeared — men, honored for their so-called piety, and their real learning. The Lords of Buffalo, the Springs of New York, the Lathrops of Auburn, the Coxes and Spencers of Brooklyn, the Gannets and Sharps of Boston, the Deweys of Washington, and other great religious lights of the land have, in utter denial of the authority of Him by whom they professed to be called to the ministry, deliberately taught us, against the example of the Hebrews and against the remonstrance of the Apostles, they teach that *we ought to obey man's law before the law of God.*

My spirit wearies of such blasphemy; and how such men can be supported, as the "standing types and representatives of Jesus Christ," is a mystery which I leave others to penetrate. In speaking of the American church, however, let it be distinctly understood that I mean the great mass of the religious organizations of our land. There are exceptions, and I thank God that there are. Noble men may be found, scattered all over these Northern States, of whom Henry Ward Beecher of Brooklyn, Samuel J. May of Syracuse, and my esteemed friend (Rev. R. R. Raymond) on the platform, are shining examples; and let me say further, that upon these men lies the duty to inspire our ranks with high religious faith and zeal, and to cheer us on in the great mission of the slave's redemption from his chains.

One is struck with the difference between the attitude of the American church towards the antislavery movement, and that occupied by the churches in England towards a similar movement in that country. There, the church, true to its mission of ameliorating, elevating, and improving the condition of mankind, came forward promptly, bound up the wounds of the West Indian slave, and restored him to his liberty. There, the question of emancipation was a high religious question. It was demanded, in the name of humanity, and according to the law of the living God. The Sharps, the Clarksons, the Wilberforces, the Buxtons,

and Burchells and the Knibbs, were alike famous for
their piety, and for their philanthropy. The anti-
slavery movement *there* was not an anti-church movement, for the reason that the church took its full share
in prosecuting that movement: and the anti-slavery
movement in this country will cease to be an anti-
church movement, when the church of this country
shall assume a favorable, instead of a hostile position
towards that movement.

Americans! your republican politics, not less than
your republican religion, are flagrantly inconsistent.
You boast of your love of liberty, your superior civilization, and your pure Christianity, while the whole
political power of the nation (as embodied in the two
great political parties), is solemnly pledged to support
and perpetuate the enslavement of three millions of
your countrymen. You hurl your anathemas at the
crowned headed tyrants of Russia and Austria, and
pride yourselves on your Democratic institutions,
while you yourselves consent to be the mere *tools* and
bodyguards of the tyrants of Virginia and Carolina.
You invite to your shores fugitives of oppression from
abroad, honor them with banquets, greet them with
ovations, cheer them, toast them, salute them, protect
them, and pour out your money to them like water;
but the fugitives from your own land you advertise,
hunt, arrest, shoot and kill. You glory in your refinement and your universal education yet you maintain a

system as barbarous and dreadful as ever stained the character of a nation — a system begun in avarice, supported in pride, and perpetuated in cruelty. You shed tears over fallen Hungary, and make the sad story of her wrongs the theme of your poets, statesmen and orators, till your gallant sons are ready to fly to arms to vindicate her cause against her oppressors; but, in regard to the ten thousand wrongs of the American slave, you would enforce the strictest silence, and would hail him as an enemy of the nation who dares to make those wrongs the subject of public discourse! You are all on fire at the mention of liberty for France or for Ireland; but are as cold as an iceberg at the thought of liberty for the enslaved of America. You discourse eloquently on the dignity of labor; yet, you sustain a system which, in its very essence, casts a stigma upon labor. You can bare your bosom to the storm of British artillery to throw off a three-penny tax on tea; and yet wring the last hard earned farthing from the grasp of the Black laborers of your country. You profess to believe "that, of one blood, God made all nations of men to dwell on the face of all the earth," and hath commanded all men, everywhere to love one another; yet you notoriously hate, (and glory in your hatred), all men whose skins are not colored like your own. You declare, before the world, and are understood by the world to declare, that you "hold these truths to be self-evident, that all men are created equal; and are endowed by their Creator with certain inalienable rights; and that, among these are, life, liberty, and the pursuit of happiness;" and yet, you hold securely, in a bondage which, according to your own Thomas Jefferson, "is worse than ages of that which your fathers rose in rebellion to oppose," a seventh part of the inhabitants of your country.

Fellow-citizens! I will not enlarge further on your national inconsistencies. The existence of slavery in this country brands your republicanism as a sham, your humanity as a base pretense, and your Christianity as a lie. It destroys your moral power abroad; it corrupts your politicians at home. It saps the foundation of religion; it makes your name a hissing, and a bye-word to a mocking earth. It is the antagonistic force in your government, the only thing that seriously disturbs and endangers your Union. It fetters your progress; it is the enemy of improvement, the deadly foe of education; it fosters pride; it breeds insolence; it promotes vice; it shelters crime; it is a curse to the earth that supports it; and yet, you cling to it, as if it were the sheet anchor of all your hopes. Oh! be warned! be warned! a horrible reptile is coiled up in your nation's bosom; the venomous creature is nursing at the tender breast of your youthful republic; *for the love of God, tear away,* and fling from you the hideous monster, and *let the weight of twenty millions crush and destroy it forever!*

But it is answered in reply to all this, that precisely what I have now denounced is, in fact, guaranteed and sanctioned by the Constitution of the United States; that the right to hold and to hunt slaves is a part of that Constitution framed by the illustrious Fathers of this Republic. Then, I dare to affirm, notwithstanding all I have said before, your fathers stooped, basely stooped

To palter with us in a double sense:
And keep the word of promise to the ear,
But break it to the heart.

And instead of being the honest men I have before declared them to be, they were the veriest imposters that ever practiced on mankind. This is the inevitable conclusion, and from it there is no escape. But I differ from those who charge this baseness on the framers of the Constitution of the United States. It is a slander upon their memory, at least, so I believe. There is not time now to argue the constitutional question at length — nor have I the ability to discuss it as it ought to be discussed. The subject has been handled with masterly power by Lysander Spooner, Esq., by William Goodell, by Samuel E. Sewall, Esq., and last, though not least, by Gerritt Smith, Esq. These gentlemen have, as I think, fully and clearly vindicated the Constitution from any design to support slavery for an hour.

Fellow-citizens! there is no matter in respect to which, the people of the North have allowed themselves to be so ruinously imposed upon, as that of the pro-slavery character of the Constitution. In that instrument I hold there is neither warrant, license, nor sanction of the hateful thing; but, interpreted as it ought to be interpreted, the Constitution is a GLORIOUS LIBERTY DOCUMENT. Read its preamble, consider its purposes. Is slavery among them? Is it at the gateway? or is it in the temple? It is neither. While I do not intend to argue this question on the present occasion, let me ask, if it be not somewhat singular that, if the Constitution were intended to be, by its framers and adopters, a slave-holding instrument, why neither slavery, slaveholding, nor slave can anywhere be found in it. What would be thought of an instrument, drawn up, legally drawn up, for the purpose of entitling the city of Rochester to a track of land, in which no mention of land was made? Now, there are certain rules of interpretation, for the proper understanding of all legal instruments. These rules are well established. They are plain, common-sense rules, such as you and I, and all of us, can understand and apply, without having passed years in the study of law. I scout the idea that the question of the constitutionality or unconstitutionality of slavery is not a question for the people. I hold that every American citizen has a right to form an opinion of the constitution, and to propagate that opinion, and to use all honorable means to make his opinion the prevailing one. Without this right, the liberty of an American citizen would be as insecure as that of a Frenchman. Ex-Vice-President Dallas tells us that the Constitution is an object to which no American mind can be too attentive, and no American heart too devoted. He further says, the Constitution, in its words, is plain and intelligible, and is meant for the home-bred, unsophisticated understandings of our fellow-citizens. Senator Berrien tell us that the Constitution is the fundamental law, that which controls all others. The charter of our liberties, which every citizen has a personal interest in understanding thoroughly. The testimony of Senator Breese, Lewis Cass, and many others that might be named, who are everywhere esteemed as sound lawyers, so regard the constitution. I take it, therefore, that it is not presumption in a private citizen to form an opinion of that instrument.

Now, take the Constitution according to its plain reading, and I defy the presentation of a single pro-slavery clause in it. On the other hand it will be found to contain principles and purposes, entirely hostile to the existence of slavery.

I have detained my audience entirely too long already. At some future period I will gladly avail myself of an opportunity to give this subject a full and fair discussion.

Allow me to say, in conclusion, notwithstanding the dark picture I have this day presented of the state of the nation, I do not despair of this country. There are forces in operation, which must inevitably work the downfall of slavery. "The arm of the Lord is not shortened," and the doom of slavery is certain. I, therefore, leave off where I began, with hope. While drawing encouragement from "the Declaration of Independence," the great principles it contains, and the genius of American Institutions, my spirit is also cheered by the obvious tendencies of the age. Nations do not now stand in the same relation to each other that they did ages ago. No nation can now shut itself up from the surrounding world, and trot round in the same old path of its fathers without interference. The time was when such could be done. Long established customs of hurtful character could formerly fence themselves in, and do their evil work with social imp-unity. Knowledge was then confined and enjoyed by the privileged few, and the multitude walked on in mental darkness. But a change has now come over the affairs of mankind. Walled cities and empires have become unfashionable. The arm of commerce has borne away the gates of the strong city. Intell-igence is penetrating the darkest corners of the globe. It makes its pathway over and under the sea, as well as on the earth. Wind, steam, and lightning are its chartered agents. Oceans no longer divide, but link nations together. From Boston to London is now a holiday excursion. Space is comparatively annihilated. Thoughts expressed on one side of the Atlantic, are distinctly heard on the other.

The far off and almost fabulous Pacific rolls in grandeur at our feet. The Celestial Empire, the mystery of ages, is being solved. The fiat of the Almighty, "Let there be Light,"[102] has not yet spent its force. No abuse, no outrage whether in taste, sport or avarice, can now hide itself from the all-pervading light. The iron shoe, and crippled foot of China must be seen, in contrast with nature. Africa must rise and put on her yet unwoven garment. "Ethiopia shall stretch out her hand unto God."[103] In the fervent aspirations of William Lloyd Garrison, I say, and let every heart join in saying it:

God speed the year of jubilee
 The wide world o'er
 When from their galling chains set free,
 Th' oppress'd shall vilely bend the knee,
And wear the yoke of tyranny
 Like brutes no more.
 That year will come, and freedom's reign,
 To man his plundered fights again Restore.

---

[102] King James Bible, *Genesis* 1:3
[103] King James Bible, *Psalms* 68:31

God speed the day when human blood
    Shall cease to flow!
    In every clime be understood,
    The claims of human brotherhood,
    And each return for evil, good,
    Not blow for blow;
    That day will come all feuds to end.
    And change into a faithful friend
    Each foe.
God speed the hour, the glorious hour,
    When none on earth
    Shall exercise a lordly power,
    Nor in a tyrant's presence cower;
    But all to manhood's stature tower,
    By equal birth!
    That hour will come, to each, to all,
    And from his prison-house, the thrall Go forth.
Until that year, day, hour, arrive,
    With head, and heart, and hand I'll strive,
    To break the rod, and rend the gyve,
    The spoiler of his prey deprive —
    So witness Heaven!
    And never from my chosen post,
    Whate'er the peril or the cost,
    Be driven.[104]

---

[104] Lecture delivered at the invitation of the Ladies' Anti-Slavery Society on July 5th, 1852 at Corinthian Hall in Rochester, New York and published as *Oration delivered in Corinthian Hall, Rochester, by Frederick Douglass, July 5, 1852*, Rochester, 1852.

The Claims of the Negro Ethnologically Considered – Gentlemen of the Philozetian Society: I propose to submit to you a few thoughts on the subject of the Claims of the Negro, suggested by ethnological science, or the natural history of man. But before entering upon that subject, I trust you will allow me to make a remark or two, somewhat personal to myself. The relation between me and this occasion may justify what, in others, might seem an offence against good taste.

This occasion is to me one of no ordinary interest, for many reasons; and the honor you have done me, in selecting me as your speaker, is as grateful to my heart, as it is novel in the history of American Collegiate or Literary Institutions. Surprised as I am, the public are no less surprised, at the spirit of independence, and the moral courage displayed by the gentlemen at whose call I am here. There is felt to be a principle in the matter, placing it far above egotism or personal vanity; a principle which gives to this occasion a general, and I had almost said, a universal interest. I engage today, for the first time, in the exercises of any College Commencement. It is a new chapter in my humble experience. The usual course, at such times, I believe, is to call to the platform men of age and distinction, eminent for eloquence, mental ability, and scholarly attainments — men whose high culture, severe training, great experience, large observation, and peculiar aptitude for teaching qualify them to instruct even the already well instructed, and to impart a glow, a lustre, to the acquirements of those who are passing from the Halls of learning, to the broad theatre of active life. To no such high endeavor as this is your humble speaker fitted; and it was with much distrust and hesitation that he accepted the invitation, so kindly and perseveringly given, to occupy a portion of your attention here today.

I express the hope, then, gentlemen, that this acknowledgment of the novelty of my position, and my unaffected and honest confession of inaptitude, will awaken a sentiment of generous indulgence towards the scattered thoughts I have been able to fling together, with a view to presenting them as my humble contribution to these Commencement Exercises.

Interesting to me, personally, as this occasion is, it is still more interesting to you; especially to such of you as have completed your education, and who (not wholly unlike the gallant ship, newly launched, full rigged, and amply fitted, about to quit the placid waters of the harbor for the boisterous waves of the sea) are entering upon the active duties and measureless responsibilities incident to the great voyage of life. Before such, the ocean of mind lies outspread more solemn than the sea, studded with difficulties and perils. Thoughts, theories, ideas, and systems, so various, and so opposite, and leading to such diverse results, suggest the wisdom of the utmost precaution, and the most careful survey, at the start. A false light, a defective chart, an imperfect compass, may cause one to drift in endless bewilderment, or to be landed at last amid sharp, destructive rocks.

On the other hand, guided by wisdom, manned with truth, fidelity and industry, the haven of peace, devoutly wished for by all, may be reached in safety by all. The compensation of the preacher is full, when assured that his words have saved even one from error and from ruin. My joy shall be full, if, on this occasion, I shall be able to give a right direction to any one mind, touching the question now to be considered.

Gentlemen, in selecting the Claims of the Negro as the subject of my remarks today, I am animated by a desire to bring before you a matter of living importance — a matter upon which action, as well as thought, is required. The relation subsisting between the white and Black people of this country is the vital question of the age. In the solution of this question, the scholars of America will have to take an important and controlling part. This is the moral battlefield to which their country and their God now call them. In the eyes of both, the neutral scholar is an ignoble man. Here, a man must be hot, or be accounted cold, or, perchance, something worse than hot or cold. The lukewarm and the cowardly, will be rejected by earnest men on either side of the controversy. The cunning man who avoids it, to gain the favor of both parties, will be rewarded with scorn; and the timid man who shrinks from it, for fear of offending either party, will be despised. To the lawyer, the preacher, the politician, and to the man of letters, there is no neutral ground. He that is not for us, is against us. Gentlemen, I assume at the start, that wherever else I may be required to speak with bated breath, here, at least, I may speak with freedom the thought nearest my heart. This liberty is implied, by the call I have received to be here; and yet I hope to present the subject so that no man can reasonably say, that an outrage has been committed, or that I have abused the privilege with which you have honored me. I shall aim to discuss the claims of the Negro, general and special, in a manner, though not scientific, still sufficiently clear and definite to enable my hearers to form an intelligent judgment respecting them.

The first general claim which may here be set up, respects the manhood of the Negro. This is an elementary claim, simple enough, but not without question. It is fiercely opposed. A respectable public journal, published in Richmond, Va., bases its whole defence of the slave system upon a denial of the Negro's manhood.

"The white peasant is free, and if he is a man of will and intellect, can rise in the scale of society; or at least his offspring may. He is not deprived by law of those 'inalienable rights,' 'liberty and the pursuit of happiness,' by the use of it. But here is the essence of slavery — that we do declare the negro destitute of these powers. We bind him by law to the condition of the laboring peasant forever, without his consent, and we bind his posterity after him. Now, the true question is, have we a right to do this? If we have not, all discussions about his comfortable situation and the actual condition of free laborers elsewhere, are quite beside the point. If the negro has the same right to his liberty and the pursuit of his own happiness that the white man has, then we commit the greatest wrong and robbery to hold him a slave — an act at which the sentiment of justice must revolt in every heart — and negro slavery is an institution which that sentiment must sooner or later blot from the face of the earth." —*Richmond Examiner.*

After stating the question thus, the *Examiner* boldly asserts that the Negro has no such right — BECAUSE HE IS NOT A MAN!

There are three ways to answer this denial. One is by ridicule; a second is by denunciation; and a third is by argument. I hardly know under which of these modes my answer today will fall. I feel myself somewhat on trial; and that this is just the point where there is hesitation, if not serious doubt. I cannot, however, argue; I must assert. To know whether [a] Negro is a man, it must first be known what constitutes a man. Here, as well as elsewhere, I take it, that the "coat must be cut according to the cloth." It is not necessary, in order to establish the manhood of any one making the claim, to prove that such an one equals Clay in eloquence, or Webster and Calhoun in logical force and directness; for, tried by such standards of mental power as these, it is apprehended that very few could claim the high designation of *man*. Yet something like this folly is seen in the arguments directed against the humanity of the Negro. His faculties and powers, uneducated and unimproved, have been contrasted with those of the highest cultivation; and the world has then been called upon to behold the immense and amazing difference between the man admitted, and the man disputed. The fact that these intellects, so powerful and so controlling, are almost, if not quite, as exceptional to the general rule of humanity in one direction, as the specimen Negroes are in the other, is quite overlooked.

Man is distinguished from all other animals, by the possession of certain definite faculties and powers, as well as by physical organization and proportions. He is the only two-handed animal on the earth — the only one that laughs, and nearly the only one that weeps. Men instinctively distinguish between men and brutes. Common sense itself is scarcely needed to detect the absence of manhood in a monkey, or to recognize its presence in a Negro. His speech, his reason, his power to acquire and to retain knowledge, his heaven-erected face, his habitudes, his hopes, his fears, his aspirations, his prophecies, plant between him and the brute creation, a distinction as eternal as it is palpable. Away, therefore, with all the scientific moonshine that would connect men with monkeys; that would have the world believe that humanity, instead of resting on its own characteristic pedestal—gloriously independent — is a sort of sliding scale, making one extreme brother to the ourang-ou-tang, and the other to angels, and all the rest intermediates! Tried by all the usual, and all the unusual tests, whether mental, moral, physical, or psychological, the Negro is a man — considering him as possessing knowledge, or needing knowledge, his elevation or his degradation, his virtues, or his vices — whichever road you take, you reach the same conclusion, the Negro is a man. His good and his bad, his innocence and his guilt, his joys and his sorrows, proclaim his manhood in speech that all mankind practically and readily understand.

A very recondite author says that "man is distinguished from all other animals, in that he resists as well as adapts himself to his circumstances." He does not take things as he finds them, but goes to work to improve them. Tried by this test, too, the Negro is a man. You may see him yoke the oxen, harness the horse, and hold the plow. He can swim the river; but he prefers to fling over it a bridge. The horse bears him on his back — admits his mastery and dominion. The barnyard fowl know his step, and flock around to receive their morning meal from his sable hand. The dog dances when he comes home, and whines piteously when he is absent. All these know that the Negro is a man. Now, presuming that what is evident to beast and to bird, cannot need elaborate argument to be made plain to men, I assume, with this brief statement, that the Negro is a man.

The first claim conceded and settled, let us attend to the second, which is beset with some difficulties, giving rise to many opinions, different from my own, and which opinions I propose to combat.

There was a time when, if you established the point that a particular being is a man, it was considered that such a being, of course, had a common ancestry with the rest of mankind. But it is not so now. This is, you know, an age of science, and science is favorable to division. It must explore and analyze, until all doubt is set at rest. There is, therefore, another proposition to be stated and maintained, separately, which, in other days, (the days before the Notts, the Gliddens, the Agassizes, and Mortons, made their profound discoveries in ethnological science), might have been included in the first.

It is somewhat remarkable, that, at a time when knowledge is so generally diffused, when the geography of the world is so well understood — when time and space, in the intercourse of nations, are almost annihilated— when oceans have become bridges — the earth a magnificent ball — the hollow sky a dome — under which a common humanity can meet in friendly conclave — when nationalities are being swallowed up — and the ends of the earth brought together—I say it is remarkable — nay, it is strange that there should arise a phalanx of learned men—speaking in the name of *science* — to forbid the magnificent reunion of mankind in one brotherhood. A mortifying proof is here given, that the moral growth of a nation, or an age, does not always keep pace with the increase of knowledge, and suggests the necessity of means to increase human love with human learning.

The proposition to which I allude, and which I mean next to assert, is this: that what are technically called the Negro race, are a part of the human family, and are descended from a common ancestry, with the rest of mankind. The discussion of this point opens a comprehensive field of inquiry. It involves the question of the unity of the human race. Much has and can be said on both sides of that question.

Looking out upon the surface of the Globe, with its varieties of climate, soil, and formations, its elevations and depressions, its rivers, lakes, oceans, islands, continents, and the vast and striking differences which mark and diversify its multitudinous inhabitants, the question has been raised, and pressed with increasing ardor and pertinacity, (especially in modern times), can all these various tribes, nations, tongues, kindred, so widely separated, and so strangely dissimilar, have descended from a common ancestry? That is the question, and it has been answered variously by men of learning. Different modes of reasoning have been adopted, but the conclusions reached may be divided into two — the one YES, and the other NO. *Which* of these answers is most in accordance with facts, with reason, with the welfare of the world, and reflects most glory upon the wisdom, power, and goodness of the Author of all existence, is the question for consideration with us. On which side is the weight of the argument, rather than which side is absolutely proved?

It must be admitted at the beginning, that, viewed apart from the authority of the Bible, neither the unity, nor diversity of origin of the human family, can be demonstrated. To use the terse expression of the Rev. Dr. Anderson, who speaking on this point, says: "It is impossible to get far enough back for that." This much, however, can be done. The evidence on both sides, can be accurately weighed, and the truth arrived at with almost absolute certainty.

It would be interesting, did time permit, to give here, some of the most striking features of the various theories, which have, of late, gained attention and respect in many quarters of our country — touching the origin of mankind — but I must pass this by. The argument today, is to the unity, as against that theory, which affirms the diversity of human origin.

THE BEARINGS OF THE QUESTION

A moment's reflection must impress all, that few questions have more important and solemn bearings, than the one now under consideration. It is connected with eternal as well as with terrestrial interests. It covers the earth and reaches heaven. The unity of the human race — the brotherhood of man — the reciprocal duties of all to each, and of each to all, are too plainly taught in the Bible to admit of cavil. - The credit of the Bible is at stake — and if it be too much to say that it must stand or fall by the decision of this question, *it is* proper to say, that the value of that sacred Book — as a record of the early history of mankind — must be materially affected, by the decision of the question.

For myself I can say, my reason (not less than my feeling, and my faith) welcomes with joy, the declaration of the Inspired Apostle, "that God has made of one blood all nations of men for to dwell upon all the face of the earth." But this grand affirmation of the unity of the human race, and many others like unto it, together with the whole account of the creation, given in the early scriptures, must all get a new interpretation or be overthrown altogether, if a diversity of human origin can be maintained. - Most evidently, this aspect of the question makes it important to those who rely upon the Bible, as the sheet anchor of their hopes — and the framework of all religious truth. The young minister must look into this subject and settle it for himself, before he ascends the pulpit, to preach redemption to a fallen race.

The bearing of the question upon Revelation, is not more marked and decided than its relation to the situation of things in our country, at this moment. One *seventh* part of the population of this country is of Negro descent. The land is peopled by what may be called the most dissimilar races on the globe. The Black and the white — the Negro and the European — these constitute the American people — and, in all the likelihoods of the case, they will ever remain the principal inhabitants of the United States, in some form or other. The European population are greatly in the ascendant in numbers, wealth and power. They are the rulers of the country — the masters — the Africans are the slaves— the proscribed portion of the people— and precisely in proportion as the truth of human brotherhood gets recognition, will be the freedom and elevation, in this country, of persons of African descent. In truth, this question is at the bottom of the whole controversy, now going on between the slave-holders on the *one* hand, and the abolitionists on the other. It is the same old question which has divided the selfish from the philanthropic part of mankind in all ages. It is the question whether the rights, privileges, and immunities enjoyed by some ought not to be shared and enjoyed by all.

It is not quite two hundred years ago, when such was the simplicity (I will not now say the pride and depravity) of the Anglo-Saxon inhabitants of the British West Indies, that the learned and pious Godwin, a missionary to the West Indies, deemed it necessary to write a book, to remove what he conceived to be the injurious belief that it was sinful in the sight of God to baptize Negroes and Indians. The West Indies have made progress since that time. God's emancipating angel has broken the fetters of slavery in those islands, and the praises of the Almighty are now sung by the sable lips of eight hundred thousand freemen, before deemed only fit for slaves, and to whom even baptismal and burial rights were denied.

The unassuming work of *Godwin* may have had some agency in producing this glorious result. One other remark before entering upon the argument. It may be said that views and opinions favoring the unity of the human family, coming from one of lowly condition, are open to the suspicion that "*the wish is father to the thought*," and so, indeed, it may be. – But let it be also remembered, that this deduction from the weight of the argument on the one side, is more than counterbalanced by the pride of race and position arrayed on the other. Indeed, ninety-nine out of every hundred of the advocates of a diverse origin of the human family in this country, are among those who hold it to be the privilege of the *Anglo-Saxon* to enslave and oppress the African — and slaveholders, not a few, like the Richmond Examiner to which I have referred, have admitted, that the whole argument in defence of slavery, becomes utterly worthless the moment the African is proved to be equally a man with the Anglo-Saxon. The temptation, therefore, to read the Negro out of the human family is exceedingly strong, and may account somewhat for the repeated attempts on the part of Southern pretenders to science, to cast a doubt over the Scriptural account of the origin of mankind. If the origin and motives of most works opposing the doctrine of the unity of the human race could be ascertained, it may be doubted whether *one* such work could boast an honest parentage. Pride and selfishness, combined with mental power, never want for a theory to justify them — and when men oppress their fellow-men, the oppressor ever finds, in the character of the oppressed, a full justification for his oppression. Ignorance and depravity, and the inability to rise from degradation to civilization and respectability, are the most usual allegations against the oppressed. The evils most fostered by slavery and oppression are precisely those which slaveholders and oppressors would transfer from their system to the inherent character of their victims. Thus the very crimes of slavery become slavery's best defence. By making the enslaved a character fit only for slavery, they excuse themselves for refusing to make the slave a freeman. A wholesale method of accomplishing this result is to overthrow the instinctive consciousness of the common brotherhood of man. For, let it be once granted that the human race are of multitudinous origin, naturally different in their moral, physical, and intellectual capacities, and at once you make plausible a demand for classes, grades and conditions, for different methods of culture, different moral, political, and religious institutions, and a chance is left for slavery, as a necessary institution. The debates in Congress on the Nebraska Bill during the past winter, will show how slaveholders have availed themselves of this doctrine in support of slaveholding. There is no doubt that Messrs. Nott, Glidden, Morton, Smith and Agassiz were duly consulted by our slavery propagating statesmen.

ETHNOLOGICAL UNFAIRNESS TOWARDS THE NEGRO

The lawyers tell us that the credit of a witness is always in order. Ignorance, malice or prejudice, may disqualify a witness, and why not an author? Now, the disposition everywhere evident, among the class of writers alluded to, to separate the Negro race from every intelligent nation and tribe in Africa, may fairly be regarded as one proof, that they have staked out the ground beforehand, and that they have aimed to construct a theory in support of a foregone conclusion. The desirableness of isolating the Negro race, and especially of separating them from the various peoples of Northern Africa, is too plain to need a remark. Such isolation would remove stupendous difficulties in the way of getting the Negro in a favorable attitude for the blows of scientific Christendom.

Dr. Samuel George Morton may be referred to as a fair sample of American Ethnologists. His very able work *Crania Americana*, published in Philadelphia in 1839, is widely read in this country. - In this great work his contempt for Negroes is ever conspicuous. I take him as an illustration of what had been alleged as true of his class.

The fact that Egypt was one of the earliest abodes of learning and civilization, is as firmly established as are the everlasting hills, defying, with a calm front the boasted mechanical and architectural skill of the nineteenth century — smiling serenely on the assaults and the mutations of time, there she stands in overshadowing grandeur, riveting the eye and the mind of the modern world — upon her, in silent and dreamy wonder. Greece and Rome — and through them Europe and America — have received their civilization from the ancient Egyptians. This fact is not denied by anybody. But Egypt is in Africa. Pity that it had not been in Europe, or in Asia, or better still, in America! Another unhappy circumstance is, that the ancient

Egyptians were not white people; but were, undoubtedly, just about as dark in complexion as many in this country who are considered genuine Negroes; and that is not all, their hair was far from being of that graceful lankness which adorns the fair Anglo-Saxon head. But the next best thing, after these defects, is a positive unlikeness to the Negro. Accordingly, our learned author enters into an elaborate argument to prove that the ancient Egyptians were totally distinct from the Negroes, and to deny all relationship between. Speaking of the "Copts and Fellahs," whom everybody knows are descendants of the Egyptians, he says, "*The Copts, though now remarkably distinct from the people that surround them, derive from their remote ancestors some mixture of Greek, Arabian, and perhaps even Negro blood.*" Now, mark the description given of the Egyptians in this same work: "*Complexion brown, The nose is straight, excepting the end, where it is rounded and wide; the lips are rather thick, and the hair black and curly.*" This description would certainly seem to make it safe to suppose the presence of "*even* Negro blood." A man, in our day, with brown complexion, "nose rounded and wide, lips thick, hair black and curly," would, I think, have no difficulty in getting himself recognized as a Negro!!

The same authority tells us that the "Copts are supposed by *Neibhur, Denon* and others, to be the descendants of the ancient Egyptians"; and Dr. Morton adds, that it has often been observed that a strong resemblance may be traced between the Coptic visage and that presented in the ancient mummies and statues. Again, he says, the "*Copts can be, at most, but the degenerate remains, both physically and intellectually, of that mighty people who have claimed the admiration of all ages.*" Speaking of the Nubians, Dr. Morton says, (page 26) —

"The hair of the Nubian is thick and black — often curled, either by nature or art, and sometimes *partially frizzled*, but *never woolly.*"

Again: —

"Although the Nubians occasionally present their national characters unmixed, they generally show traces of their social intercourse with the Arabs, and even with the Negroes."

*   *   *

The repetition of the adverb here "*even,*" is important, as showing the spirit in which our great American Ethnologist pursues his work, and what deductions may be justly made from the value of his researches on that account. In everything touching the Negro, Dr. Morton, in his *Crania Americana*, betrays the same spirit. He thinks that the *Sphinx* was not the representative of an Egyptian Deity, but was a shrine, worshiped at by the degraded *Negroes* of Egypt; and this fact he alleges as the secret of the mistake made by Volney, in supposing that the Egyptians were real Negroes. The absurdity of this assertion will be very apparent, in view of the fact that the great Sphinx in question was the chief of a series, full two miles in length. Our author again repels the supposition that the Egyptians were related to Negroes, by saying there is no mention made of *color* by the historian, in relating the marriage of Solomon with Pharaoh's daughter; and, with genuine American feeling, he says, such a circumstance as the marrying of an European monarch with the daughter of a Negro would not have been passed over in silence in our day. This is a sample of the reasoning of men who reason from *prejudice* rather than from *facts*. It assumes that a *Black skin* in the East excites the same prejudice which we see here in the West. Having denied all relationship of the Negro to the ancient Egyptians, with characteristic American assumption, he says, "It is easy to prove, that whatever may have been the hue of their skin, they belong to the same race with ourselves."

Of course, I do not find fault with Dr. Morton, or any other American, for claiming affinity with Egyptians. All that goes in that direction belongs to my side of the question, and is really right.

The leaning here indicated is natural enough, and may be explained by the fact that an educated man in Ireland ceases to be an Irishman; and an intelligent Black man is always supposed to have derived his intelligence from his connection with the white race.

To be intelligent is to have one's Negro blood ignored.

There is, however, a very important physiological fact, contradicting this last assumption; and that fact is, that intellect is uniformly derived from the maternal side. Mulattoes, in this country, may almost wholly boast of Anglo-Saxon male ancestry.

It is the province of prejudice to blind; and scientific writers, not less than others, write to please, as well as to instruct, and even unconsciously to themselves, (sometimes), sacrifice what is true to what is popular. Fashion is not confined to dress; but extends to philosophy as well — and it is fashionable now, in our land, to exaggerate the differences between the Negro and the European. If, for instance, a phrenologist or naturalist undertakes to represent in portraits, the differences between the two races — the Negro and the European — he will invariably present the *highest* type of the European, and the *lowest* type of the Negro.

The European face is drawn in harmony with the highest ideas of beauty, dignity and intellect. Features regular and brow after the Websterian mold. The Negro, on the other hand, appears with features distorted, lips exaggerated, forehead depressed — and the whole expression of the countenance made to harmonize with the popular idea of Negro imbecility and degradation. I have seen many pictures of Negroes and Europeans, in phrenological and ethnological works; and all, or nearly all, excepting the work of Dr. Prichard, and that other great work, Combs' *Constitution of Man*, have been more or less open to this objection. I think I have never seen a single picture in an American work, designed to give an idea of the mental endowments of the Negro, which did anything like justice to the subject; nay, that was not infamously distorted. The heads of *A. Crummel, Henry H. Garnet, Sam'l R. Ward, Chas. Lenox Remond, W. J. Wilson, J. W. Pennington, J. I. Gaines, M. R. Delany, J. W. Loguin, J. M. Whitfield, J. C. Holly*, and hundreds of others I could mention, are all better formed, and indicate the presence of intellect more than any pictures I have seen in such works; and while it must be admitted that there are Negroes answering the description given by the American ethnologists and others, of the Negro race, I contend that there is every description of head among them, ranging from the highest Indoo Caucasian downward. If the very best type of the European is always presented, I insist that justice, in all such works, demands that the very best type of the Negro should also be taken. The importance of this criticism may not be apparent to all; — to the *Black* man it is very apparent. He sees the injustice, and writhes under its sting. But to return to Dr. Morton, or rather to the question of the affinity of the Negroes to the Egyptians.

It seems to me that a man might as well deny the affinity of the Americans to the Englishman, as to deny such affinity between the Negro and the Egyptian. He might make out as many points of difference, in the case of the one as in that of the other. Especially could this be done, if, like ethnologists, in given cases, only typical specimens were resorted to. The lean, slender American, pale and swarthy, if exposed to the sun, wears a very different appearance to the full, round Englishman, of clear, *blonde* complexion. One may trace the progress of this difference in the comm-on portraits of the American Presidents. Just study those faces, beginning with Washington; and as you come through the Jeffersons, the Adamses, and the Madisons, you will find an increasing bony and wiry appearance about those portraits, & a greater remove from that serene amplitude which characterises the countenances of the earlier Presidents. I may be mistaken, but I think this is a correct index of the change going on in the nation at large, — converting Englishmen, Germans, Irishmen, and Frenchmen into Americans, and causing them to lose, in a common American character, all traces of their former distinctive national peculiarities.

AUTHORITIES AS TO THE RESEMBLANCE OF EGYPTIANS TO NEGROES
Now, let us see what the best authorities say, as to the personal appearance of the Egyptians. I think it

will be at once admitted, that while they differ very
strongly from the Negro, debased and enslaved, that
difference is not greater than may be observed in
other quarters of the globe, among people notoriously
belonging to the same variety, the same original stock;
in a word, to the same family. If it shall be found that
the people of Africa have an African character, as
general, as well defined, and as distinct, as have the
people of Europe, or the people of Asia, the exceptional differences among them afford no ground for
supposing a difference of race; but, on the contrary, it
will be inferred that the people of Africa constitute
one great branch of the human family, whose origin
may be as properly referred to the families of Noah,
as can be any other branch of the human family from
whom they differ. Denon, in his *Travels in Egypt*,
describes the Egyptians, as of full, but "delicate and
voluptuous forms, countenances sedate and placid,
round and soft features, with eyes long and almond
shaped, half shut and languishing, and turned up at
the outer angles, as if habitually fatigued by the light
and heat of the sun; cheeks round; thick lips, full and
prominent; mouths large, but cheerful and smiling;
complexion dark, ruddy and coppery, and the whole
aspect displaying — as one of the most graphic
delineators among modern travelers has observed —
the genuine African character, of which the *Negro* is

the exaggerated and extreme representation." Again, Prichard says, (page 152) —

"Herodotus traveled in Egypt, and was, therefore, well acquainted with the people from personal observation. He does not say anything directly, as to the descriptions of their persons, which were too well known to the Greeks to need such an account, but his indirect testimony is very strongly expressed. After mentioning a tradition, that the people of Colchis were a colony from Egypt, Herodotus says, that 'there was one fact strongly in favor of this opinion — the Colchians were Black in complexion and woolly haired.'"

These are the words by which the complexion and hair of Negroes are described. In another passage, he says that

"The pigeon, said to have fled to Dodona, and to have founded the Oracle, was declared to be Black, and that the meaning of the story was this: The Oracle was, in reality, founded by a female captive from the Thebaid: she was Black, being an Egyptian." "Other Greek writers," says Prichard, "have expressed themselves in similar terms."

Those who have mentioned the Egyptians as a *swarthy* people, according to Prichard, might as well have applied the term *Black* to them, since they were doubtless of a chocolate color. The same author brings together the testimony of Eschylus and others as to the color of the ancient Egyptians, all corresponding, more or less, with the foregoing. Among the most direct testimony educed by Prichard, is, first that of Volney, who, speaking of the modern Copts, says:

"They have a puffed visage, swollen eyes, flat nose, and thick lips, and bear much resemblance to mulattoes."

Baron Larrey says, in regard to the same people:

"They have projecting cheek bones, dilating nostrils, thick lips, and hair and beard black and crisp."

Mr. Ledyard, (whose testimony, says our learned authority, is of the more value, as he had no theory to support), says:

"I suspect the *Copts* to have been the *origin* of the *Negro* race; the nose and lips correspond with those of the Negro; the hair, wherever I can see it among the people here, is curled, *not* like that of the Negroes, but like the mulattoes."

Here I leave our learned authorities, as to the resemblance of the Egyptians to Negroes.

It is not in my power, in a discourse of this sort, to adduce more than a very small part of the testimony in support of a near relationship between the present enslaved and degraded Negroes, and the ancient highly civilized and wonderfully endowed Egyptians. Sufficient has already been adduced, to show a marked similarity in regard to features, hair, color, and I doubt not that the philologist can find equal similarity in the structures of their languages. In view of the foregoing, while it may not be claimed that the ancient Egyptians were Negroes, — viz: — answering, in all respects, to the nations and tribes ranged under the general appellation, Negro; still, it may safely be affirmed, that a strong affinity and a direct relationship may be claimed by the Negro race, to *that grandest of all the nations of antiquity, the builders of the pyramids.*

But there are other evidences of this relationship, more decisive than those alleged in a general similarity of personal appearance. Language is held to be very important, by the best ethnologists, in tracing out the remotest affinities of nations, tribes, classes and families. The color of the skin has sometimes been less enduring than the speech of a people. I speak by authority, and follow in the footsteps of some of the most learned writers on the natural and ethnological history of man, when I affirm that one of the most direct and conclusive proofs of the general affinity of Northern African nations with those of West, East and South Africa, is found in the general similarity of their languages. The philologist easily discovers, and is able to point out something like the original source of the multiplied tongues now in use in that yet mysterious quarter of the globe. *Dr. R. G. Latham,* F. R. S., corresponding member of the Ethnological Society, New York — in his admirable work, entitled *Man and his Migrations* — says:

"In the languages of Abyssinia, the Gheez and Tigre, admitted, as long as they have been known at all, to be Semitic, graduate through the Amharic, the Talasha, the Harargi, the Gafat and other languages, which may be well studied in Dr. Beke's valuable comparative tables, into the Agow tongue, unequivocally indigenous to Abyssinia, and through this into the true Negro classes. But, unequivocal as may be the Semitic elements of the Berber, Coptic and Galla, their affinities with the tongues of Western and Southern Africa are more so. I weigh my words when I say, not equally, but more; changing the expression, for every foot in advance which can be made towards the Semitic tongues in one direction, the African philologist can go a yard towards the Negro ones in the other."

In a note, just below this remarkable statement, Dr. Latham says:

"A short table of the Berber and Coptic, as compared with the other African tongues, may be seen in the Classical Museum of the British Association, for 1846. In the Transactions of the Philological Society is a grammatical sketch of the Tumali language, by Dr. S. Tutsbek of Munich. The Tumali is a truly Negro language, of Kordufan; whilst, in respect to the extent to which its inflections are formed, by internal changes of vowels and accents, it is fully equal to the Semitic tongues of Palestine and Arabia."

This testimony may not serve prejudice, but to me it seems quite sufficient.

SUPERFICIAL OBJECTIONS

Let us now glance again at the opposition. A volume, on *The Natural History of the Human Species*, by Charles Hamilton Smith, quite false in many of its facts, and as mischievous as false, has been published recently in this country, and will, doubtless, be widely circulated, especially by those to whom the thought of human brotherhood is abhorrent. This writer says, after mentioning sundry facts touching the dense and spherical structure of the Negro head:

"This very structure may influence the erect gait, which occasions the practice common also to the Ethiopian, or mixed nations, of carrying burdens and light weights, even to a tumbler full of water, upon the head."

No doubt this seemed a very sage remark to Mr. Smith, and quite important in fixing a character to the Negro skull, although different to that of Europeans. But if the learned Mr. Smith had stood, previous to writing it, at our door, (a few days in succession), he might have seen hundreds of Germans and of Irish people, not bearing burdens of "*light* weight," but of *heavy* weight, upon the same vertical extremity. The carrying of burdens upon the head is as old as Oriental Society; and the man writes himself a blockhead, who attempts to find in the custom a proof of original difference. On page 227, the same writer says:

"The voice of the Negroes is feeble and hoarse in the male sex."

The explanation of this mistake in our author is found in the fact that an oppressed people, in addressing their superiors — perhaps I ought to say, their oppressors — usually assume a minor tone, as less likely to provoke the charge of intrusiveness. But it is ridiculous to pronounce the voice of the Negro feeble; and the learned ethnologist must be hard pushed, to establish differences, when he refers to this as one. Mr. Smith further declares, that

"The typical woolly haired races have never discovered an alphabet, framed a grammatical language, nor made the least step in science or art."

Now, the man is still living, (or was but a few years since), among the Mandingoes of the Western coast of Africa, who has framed an alphabet; and while Mr.

Smith may be pardoned for his ignorance of that fact, as an ethnologist, he is inexcusable for not knowing that the Mpongwe language, spoken on both sides of the Gaboon River, at Cape Lopez, Cape St. Catharine, and in the interior, to the distance of two or three hundred miles, is as truly a grammatically framed language as any extant. I am indebted, for this fact, to Rev. Dr. M. B. Anderson, President of the Rochester University; and by his leave, here is the Grammar — [holding up the Grammar]. Perhaps, of all the attempts ever made to disprove the unity of the human family, and to brand the Negro with natural inferiority, the most compendious and barefaced is the book, entitled *Types of Mankind*, by Nott and Glidden. One would be well employed in a series of Lectures directed to an exposure of the unsoundness, if not the wickedness of this work.

THE AFRICAN RACE BUT ONE PEOPLE

But I must hasten. Having shown that the people of Africa are, probably, one people; that each tribe bears an intimate relation to other tribes and nations in that quarter of the globe, and that the Egyptians may have flung off the different tribes seen there at different times, as implied by the evident relations of their language, and by other similarities; it can hardly be deemed unreasonable to suppose, that the African branch of the human species — from the once highly civilized

Egyptian to the barbarians on the banks of the Niger — may claim brotherhood with the great family of Noah, spreading over the more Northern and Eastern parts of the globe. I will now proceed to consider those physical peculiarities of form, features, hair and color, which are supposed by some men to mark the African, not only as an inferior race, but as a distinct species, naturally and originally different from the rest of mankind, and as really to place him nearer to the brute than to man.

THE EFFECT OF CIRCUMSTANCE UPON THE PHYSICAL MAN

I may remark, just here, that it is impossible, even were it desirable, in a discourse like this, to attend to the anatomical and physiological argument connected with this part of the subject. I am not equal to that, and if I were, the occasion does not require it. The form of the Negro — (I use the term *Negro*, precisely in the sense that you use the term Anglo-Saxon; and I believe, too, that the former will one day be as illustrious as the latter) — has often been the subject of remark. His flat feet, long arms, high cheek bones and retreating forehead are especially dwelt upon, to his disparagement, and just as if there were no white people with precisely the same peculiarities. I think it will ever be found, that the *well* or *ill* condition of any part of mankind, will leave its mark on the physical as well as on the intellectual part of man. A hundred instances might be cited, of whole families who have degenerated, and others who have improved in personal appearance, by a change of circumstances. A man is worked upon by what *he* works on. He may carve out his circumstances, but his circumstances will carve him out as well. I told a boot maker, in Newcastle-upon-Tyne, that I had been a plantation slave. He said I must pardon him; but he could not believe it; no plantation laborer ever had a high instep. He said he had noticed that the coal heavers and work people in low condition had, for the most part, flat feet, and that he could tell, by the shape of the feet, whether a man's parents were in high or low condition. The thing was worth a thought, and I have thought of it, and have looked around me for facts. There is some truth in it; though there are exceptions in individual cases.

The day I landed in Ireland, nine years ago, I addressed, (in company with Father Spratt and that good man who has been recently made the subject of bitter attack; I allude to the philanthropic James Haughton, of Dublin), a large meeting of the common people of Ireland, on temperance. Never did human faces tell a sadder tale. More than five thousand were assembled; and I say, with no wish to wound the feelings of any Irishman, that these people lacked only a Black skin and wooly hair, to complete their likeness to the plantation Negro. The open, uneducated

mouth — the long, gaunt arm — the badly formed foot
and ankle — the shuffling gait —the retreating forehead
and vacant expression — and, their petty quarrels and
fights — all reminded me of the plantation, and my
own cruelly abused people. Yet, that is the land of
Grattan, of Curran, of O'Connell, and of Sheridan.
Now, while what I have said is true of the common
people, the fact is, there are no more really handsome
people in the world, than the educated Irish people.
The Irishman educated, is a model gentleman; the
Irishman ignorant and degraded, compares in form
and feature with the Negro!

I am stating facts. If you go into Southern Indiana,
you will see what climate and habit can do, even in
one generation. The man may have come from New
England, but his hard features, sallow complexion,
have left little of New England on his brow. The right
arm of the blacksmith is said to be larger and stronger
than his left. The ship carpenter is at forty round-
shouldered. The shoemaker carries the marks of his
trade. One locality becomes famous for one thing,
another for another. Manchester and Lowell, in
America, Manchester and Sheffield, in England, attest
this. But what does it all prove? Why, nothing positively, as to the main point; still, it raises the inquiry —
May not the condition of men explain their various
appearances? Need we go behind the vicissitudes of
barbarism for an explanation of the gaunt, wiry, ape

like appearance of some of the genuine Negroes? Need we look higher than a vertical sun, or lower than the damp, black soil of the Niger, the Gambia, the Senegal, with their heavy and enervating miasma, rising ever from the rank growing and decaying vegetation, for an explanation of the Negro's color? If a cause, full and adequate, can be found here, *why seek further?*

The eminent Dr. Latham, already quoted, says that nine-tenths of the white population of the globe are found between 30 and 65 degrees North latitude. Only about one-fifth of all the inhabitants of the globe are white; and they are as far from the Adamic complexion as is the Negro. The remainder are — what? Ranging all the way from the brunette to jet black. There are the red, the reddish copper color, the yellowish, the dark brown, the chocolate color, and so on, to the jet black. On the mountains on the North of Africa, where water freezes in winter at times, branches of the same people who are *Black* in the valley are *white* on the mountains. The Nubian, with his beautiful curly hair, finds it becoming frizzled, crisped, and even woolly, as he approaches the great Sahara. The Portuguese, white in Europe, is brown in Asia. The Jews, who are to be found in all countries, never intermarrying, are white in Europe, brown in Asia, and Black in Africa. Again, what does it all prove? Nothing, absolutely; nothing which places the question beyond dispute; but it *does* justify the conjecture before referred to, that outward circumstances *may* have something to do with modifying the various phases of humanity; and that color itself is at the control of the world's climate and its various concomitants. It is the sun that paints the peach — and may it not be, that he paints the *man* as well? My reading, on this point, however, as well as my own observation, have convinced me that from the beginning the Almighty, within certain limits, endowed mankind with organizations capable of countless variations in form, feature and color, without having it necessary to begin a new creation for every new variety.

A powerful argument in favor of the oneness of the human family, is afforded in the fact that nations, however dissimilar, may be united in one social state, not only without detriment to each other, but, most clearly, to the advancement of human welfare, happiness and perfection. While it is clearly proved, on the other hand, that those nations freest from foreign elements present the most evident marks of deterioration. Dr. James McCune Smith, himself a colored man, a gentleman and scholar, alleges — and not without excellent reason — that this, our own great nation, so distinguished for industry and enterprise, is largely indebted to its composite character. We all know, at any rate, that now, what constitutes the very heart of the civilized world — (I allude to England) — has only risen from barbarism to its present lofty eminence, through successive invasions and alliances with her people. The Medes and Persians constituted one of the mightiest empires that ever rocked the globe. The most terrible nation which now threatens the peace of the world, to make its will the law of Europe, is a grand piece of Mosaic work, in which almost every nation has its characteristic feature, from the wild Tartar to the refined Pole.

But, gentlemen, the time fails me, and I must bring these remarks to a close. My argument has swelled beyond its appointed measure. What I intended to make special, has become, in its progress, somewhat general. I meant to speak here today, for the lonely and the despised ones, with whom I was cradled, and with whom I have suffered; and now, gentlemen, in conclusion, what if all this reasoning be unsound? What if the Negro may not be able to prove his relationship to Nubians, Abyssinians and Egyptians? What if ingenious men are able to find plausible objections to all arguments maintaining the oneness of the human race? What, after all, if they are able to show very good reasons for believing the Negro to have been created precisely as we find him on the Gold Coast — along the Senegal and the Niger — I say, what of all this? *"A man's a man for a' that."* I sincerely believe, that the weight of the argument is in favor of the unity of origin of the human race, or species — that the arguments on the other side are partial, superficial, utterly subversive of the happiness of man, and insulting to the wisdom of God. Yet, what if we grant they are not so? What, if we grant that the case, on our part, is not made out? Does it follow, that the Negro should be held in contempt? Does it follow, that to enslave and imbrute him is either *just* or *wise*? I think not. Human rights stand upon a common basis; and by all the reason that they are supported, maintained and defended, for one variety of the human family, they are supported, maintained and defended for all the human family; because all mankind have the same wants, arising out of a common nature. A diverse origin does not disprove a common nature, nor does it disprove a united destiny. The essential characteristics of humanity are everywhere the same. In the language of the eloquent Curran, "No matter what complexion, whether an Indian or an African sun has burnt upon him," his title deed to freedom, his claim to life and to liberty, to knowledge and to civilization, to society and to Christianity, are just and perfect. It is registered in the Courts of Heaven, and is enforced by the eloquence of the God of all the earth.

I have said that the Negro and white man are likely ever to remain the principal inhabitants of this country. I repeat the statement now, to submit the reasons that support it. The Blacks can disappear from the face of the country by three ways. They may be colonized, — they may be exterminated, — or, they may die out. Colonization is out of the question; for I know not what hardships the laws of the land can impose, which can induce the colored citizen to leave his native soil. He was here in its infancy; he is here in its age. Two hundred years have passed over him, his tears and blood have been mixed with the soil, and his attachment to the place of his birth is stronger than iron. It is not probable that he will be exterminated; two considerations must prevent a crime so stupendous as that — the influence of Christianity on the one hand, and the power of self interest on the other; and, in regard to their dying out, the statistics of the country afford no encouragement for such a conjecture. The history of the Negro race proves them to be wonderfully adapted to all countries, all climates, and all conditions. Their tenacity of life, their powers of endurance, their malleable toughness, would almost imply especial interposition on their behalf. The ten thousand horrors of slavery, striking hard upon the sensitive soul, have bruised, and battered, and stung, but have not killed. The poor bondman lifts a smiling face above the surface of a sea of agonies, *hoping on, hoping ever.* His tawny brother, the Indian, dies, under the flashing glance of the Anglo-Saxon. Not so the Negro; civilization cannot kill him. He accepts it — becomes a part of it. In the Church, he is an Uncle Tom; in the State, he is the most abused and least offensive. All the facts in his history mark out for him a destiny, united to America and Americans. Now, whether this population shall, by *Freedom, Industry, Virtue and Intelligence*, be made a blessing to the country and the world, or whether their multiplied wrongs shall kindle the vengeance of an offended God, will depend upon the conduct of no class of men so much as upon the Scholars of the country. The future public opinion of the land, whether antislavery or pro-slavery, whether just or unjust, whether magnanimous or mean, must redound to the honor of the Scholars of the country or cover them with shame. There is but one safe road for nations or for individuals. The fate of a wicked man and of a wicked nation is the same. The flaming sword of offended justice falls as certainly upon the nation as upon the man. God has no children whose rights may be safely trampled upon. The sparrow may not fall to the ground without the notice of his eye, and men are more than sparrows.

Now, gentlemen, I have done. The subject is before you. I shall not undertake to make the application. I speak as unto wise men. I stand in the presence of Scholars. We have met here today from vastly different points in the world's condition. I have reached here — if you will pardon the egotism — by little short of a miracle: at any rate, by dint of some application and perseverance. Born, as I was, in obscurity, a stranger to the halls of learning, environed by ignorance, degradation, and their concomitants, from birth to manhood, I do not feel at liberty to mark out, with any degree of confidence, or dogmatism, what is the precise vocation of the Scholar. Yet, this I *can* say, as a denizen of the world, and as a citizen of a country rolling in the sin and shame of Slavery, the most flagrant and scandalous that ever saw the sun, "Whatsoever things are true, whatsoever things are honest, whatsoever things are just, whatsoever things are pure, whatsoever things are lovely, whatsoever things are of good report, if there be any virtue, and if there be any praise, think on these things."[105]

---

[105] Commencement Lecture delivered to the Literary Societies at Western Reserve College in Hudson, Ohio on July 12th, 1854 and published as a *Pamphlet*, Lee, Mann & Co., Daily American Office, Rochester, New York 1854.

Comprehending the Vitality of Anti-Slavery – The growth of intelligence, the influence of commerce, steam, wind and lightning, are our allies. It would be easy to amplify this summary, and to swell the vast conglomeration of our material forces; but there is a deeper and truer method of measuring the power of our cause, and of comprehending its vitality. This is to be found in its accordance with the best elements of human nature. It is beyond the power of slavery to annihilate affinities recognized and established by the Almighty. The slave is bound to mankind, by the powerful and inextricable network of human brotherhood. His voice is the voice of man, and his cry is the cry of man in distress, and man must cease to be man before he can become insensible to that cry. It is the righteousness of the cause – the humanity of the cause – which constitutes its potency.[106]

---

[106] Excerpted from lecture delivered on March 19th, 1855 and published as *The Anti-Slavery Movement. A Lecture by Frederick Douglass, before the Rochester Ladies' Anti-Slavery Society*, Rochester, 1855.

Principled Critique of Human Slavery – In my letters and speeches, I have generally aimed to discuss the question of Slavery in the light of fundamental principles, and upon facts, notorious and open to all; making, I trust, no more of the fact of my own former enslavement, than circumstances seemed absolutely to require. I have never placed my opposition to slavery on a basis so narrow as my own enslavement, but rather upon the indestructible and unchangeable laws of human nature, every one of which is perpetually and flagrantly violated by the slave system.[107]

---

[107] Excerpted from a Letter included in the Editor's Preface to *My Bondage and My Freedom*, (New York and Auburn, New York: Miller, Orton & Mulligan, 1855).

Second Existential Meditation on Intellectual Resistance – The frequent hearing of my mistress reading the Bible—for she often read aloud when her husband was absent —soon awakened my curiosity in respect to this *mystery* of reading, and roused in me the desire to learn. Having no fear of my kind mistress before my eyes, (she had then given me no reason to fear,) I frankly asked her to teach me to read; and, without hesitation, the dear woman began the task, and very soon, by her assistance, I was master of the alphabet, and could spell words of three or four letters. My mistress seemed almost as proud of my progress, as if I had been her own child; and, supposing that her husband would be as well pleased, she made no secret of what she was doing for me. Indeed, she exultingly told him of the aptness of her pupil, of her intention to persevere in teaching me, and of the duty which she felt it to teach me, at least to read the Bible. Here arose the first cloud over my Baltimore prospects, the precursor of drenching rains and chilling blasts.

Master Hugh was amazed at the simplicity of his spouse, and, probably for the first time, he unfolded to her the true philosophy of slavery, and the peculiar rules necessary to be observed by masters and mistersses, in the management of their human chattels. Mr. Auld promptly forbade the continuance of her instruction; telling her, in the first place, that the thing itself was unlawful; that it was also unsafe, and could only lead to mischief. To use his own words, further, he said, "if you give a n****r an inch, he will take an ell;" "he should know nothing but the will of his master, and learn to obey it." "Learning would spoil the best nigger in the world;" "if you teach that n****r — speaking of myself — how to read the Bible, there will be no keeping him;" "it would forever unfit him for the duties of a slave;" and "as to himself, learning would do him no good, but probably, a great deal of harm — making him disconsolate and unhappy." "If you learn him now to read, he'll want to know how to write; and, this accomplished, he'll be running away with himself." Such was the tenor of Master Hugh's oracular exposition of the true philosophy of training a human chattel; and it must be confessed that he very clearly comprehended the nature and the requirements of the relation of master and slave. His discourse was the first decidedly antislavery lecture to which it had been my lot to listen. Mrs. Auld evidently felt the force of his remarks; and, like an obedient wife, began to shape her course in the direction indicated by her husband. The effect of his words, *on me*, was neither slight nor transitory. His iron sentences — cold and harsh — sunk deep into my heart, and stirred up not only my feelings into a sort of rebellion, but awakened within me a slumbering train of vital thought. It was a new and special revelation, dispelling a painful mystery, against which my youthful understanding had struggled, and struggled in vain, to wit: the *white* man's power to perpetuate the enslavement of the *Black* man. "Very well," thought I; "knowledge unfits a child to be a slave." I instinctively assented to the proposition; and from that moment I understood the direct pathway from slavery to freedom. This was just what I needed; and I got it at a time, and from a source, whence I least expected it. I was saddened at the thought of losing the assistance of my kind mistress; but the information, so instantly derived, to some extent compensated me for the loss I had sustained in this direction. Wise as Mr. Auld was, he evidently underrated my comprehension, and had little idea of the use to which I was capable of putting the impressive lesson he was giving to his wife. *He* wanted me to be a *slave*; I had already voted against that on the home plantation of Col. Lloyd. That which he most loved I most hated; and the very determination which he expressed to keep me in ignorance, only rendered me the more resolute in seeking intelligence. In learning to read, therefore, I am not sure that I do not owe quite as much to the opposition of my master, as to the kindly assistance of my amiable mistress. I acknowledge the benefit rendered me by the one, and by the other; believing, that but for my mistress, I might have grown up in ignorance.

. . . I lived in the family of Master Hugh, at Baltimore, seven years, during which time — as the almanac makers say of the weather—my condition was variable. The most interesting feature of my history here, was my learning to read and write, under somewhat marked disadvantages. In attaining this knowledge, I was compelled to resort to indirections by no means congenial to my nature, and which were really humiliating to me. My mistress — who, as the reader has already seen, had begun to teach me — was suddenly checked in her benevolent design, by the strong advice of her husband. In faithful compliance with this advice, the good lady had not only ceased to instruct me, herself, but had set her face as a flint against my learning to read by any means. It is due, however, to my mistress to say, that she did not adopt this course in all its stringency at the first. She either thought it unnecessary, or she lacked the depravity indispensable to shutting me up in mental darkness. It was, at least, necessary for her to have some training, and some hardening, in the exercise of the slaveholder's prerogative, to make her equal to forgetting my human nature and character, and to treating me as a thing destitute of a moral or an intellectual nature. Mrs. Auld — my mistress — was, as I have said, a most kind and tender-hearted woman; and, in the humanity of her heart, and the simplicity of her mind, she set out, when I first went to live with her, to treat me as she supposed one human being ought to treat another.

It is easy to see, that, in entering upon the duties of a slaveholder, some little experience is needed. Nature has done almost nothing to prepare men and women to be either slaves or slaveholders. Nothing but rigid training, long persisted in, can perfect the character of the one or the other. One cannot easily forget to love freedom; and it is as hard to cease to respect that natural love in our fellow creatures. On entering upon the career of a slaveholding mistress, Mrs. Auld was singularly deficient; nature, which fits nobody for such an office, had done less for her than any lady I had known. It was no easy matter to induce her to think and to feel that the curly-headed boy, who stood by her side, and even leaned on her lap; who was loved by little Tommy, and who loved little Tommy in turn; sustained to her only the relation of a chattel. I was more than that, and she felt me to be more than that. I could talk and sing; I could laugh and weep; I could reason and remember; I could love and hate. I was human, and she, dear lady, knew and felt me to be so. How could she, then, treat me as a brute, without a mighty struggle with all the noble powers of her own soul. That struggle came, and the will and power of the husband was victorious. Her noble soul was overthrown; but, he that overthrew it did not, himself, escape the consequences. He, not less than the other parties, was injured in his domestic peace by the fall.

When I went into their family, it was the abode of happiness and contentment. The mistress of the house was a model of affection and tenderness. Her fervent piety and watchful uprightness made it impossible to see her without thinking and feeling — "*that woman is a Christian.*" There was no sorrow nor suffering for which she had not a tear, and there was no innocent joy for which she had not a smile. She had bread for the hungry, clothes for the naked, and comfort for every mourner that came within her reach. Slavery soon proved its ability to divest her of these excellent qualities, and her home of its early happiness. Conscience cannot stand much violence. Once thoroughly broken down, *who* is he that can repair the damage? It may be broken toward the slave, on Sunday, and toward the master on Monday. It cannot endure such shocks. It must stand entire, or it does not stand at all. If my condition waxed bad, that of the family waxed not better. The first step, in the wrong direction, was the violence done to nature and to conscience, in arresting the benevolence that would have enlightened my young mind. In ceasing to instruct me, she must begin to justify herself to herself; and, once consenting to take sides in such a debate, she was riveted to her position. One needs very little knowledge of moral philosophy, to see *where* my mistress now landed. She finally became even more violent in her opposition to my learning to read, than was her husband himself. She was not satisfied with simply doing as *well* as her husband had commanded her, but seemed resolved to better his instruction. Nothing appeared to make my poor mistress — after her turning toward the downward path — more angry, than seeing me, seated in some nook or corner, quietly reading a book or a newspaper. I have had her rush at me, with the utmost fury, and snatch from my hand such newspaper or book, with something of the wrath and consternation which a traitor might be supposed to feel on being discovered in a plot by some dangerous spy.

Mrs. Auld was an apt woman, and the advice of her husband, and her own experience, soon demonstrated, to her entire satisfaction, that education and slavery are incompatible with each other. When this conviction was thoroughly established, I was most narrowly watched in all my movements. If I remained in a separate room from the family for any considerable length of time, I was sure to be suspected of having a book, and was at once called upon to give an account of myself. All this, however, was entirely *too late.* The first, and never to be retraced, step had been taken. In teaching me the alphabet, in the days of her simplicity and kindness, my mistress had given me the "*inch*," and now, no ordinary precaution could prevent me from taking the "*ell*."

Seized with a determination to learn to read, at any cost, I hit upon many expedients to accomplish the desired end. The plea which I mainly adopted, and the one by which I was most successful, was that of using my young white playmates, with whom I met in the street, as teachers. I used to carry, almost constantly, a copy of Webster's spelling book in my pocket; and, when sent of errands, or when play time was allowed me, I would step, with my young friends, aside, and take a lesson in spelling. I generally paid my tuition fee to the boys, with bread, which I also carried in my pocket. For a single biscuit, any of my hungry little comrades would give me a lesson more valuable to me than bread. Not everyone, however, demanded this consideration, for there were those who took pleasure in teaching me, whenever I had a chance to be taught by them. I am strongly tempted to give the names of two or three of those little boys, as a slight testimonial of the gratitude and affection I bear them, but prudence forbids; not that it would injure me, but it might, possibly, embarrass them; for it is almost an unpardonable offense to do anything, directly or indirectly, to promote a slave's freedom, in a slave state. It is enough to say, of my warm-hearted little play fellows, that they lived on Philpot street, very near Durgin & Bailey's shipyard.

Although slavery was a delicate subject, and very cautiously talked about among grown up people in Maryland, I frequently talked about it — and that very freely — with the white boys. I would, sometimes, say to them, while seated on a curb stone or a cellar door, "I wish I could be free, as you will be when you get to be men." "You will be free, you know, as soon as you are twenty-one, and can go where you like, but I am a slave for life. Have I not as good a right to be free as you have?" Words like these, I observed, always troubled them; and I had no small satisfaction in wringing from the boys, occasionally, that fresh and bitter condemnation of slavery, that springs from nature, unseared and unperverted. Of all consciences, let me have those to deal with which have not been bewildered by the cares of life. I do not remember ever to have met with a *boy*, while I was in slavery, who defended the slave system; but I have often had boys to console me, with the hope that something would yet occur, by which I might be made free. Over and over again, they have told me, that "they believed I had as good a right to be free as *they* had;" and that "they did not believe God ever made any one to be a slave." The reader will easily see, that such little conversations with my play fellows, had no tendency to weaken my love of liberty, nor to render me contented with my condition as a slave.

When I was about thirteen years old, and had succeeded in learning to read, every increase of knowledge, especially respecting the FREE STATES, added something to the almost intolerable burden of the thought — "I AM A SLAVE FOR LIFE." To my bondage I saw no end. It was a terrible reality, and I shall never be able to tell how sadly that thought chafed my young spirit. Fortunately, or unfortunately, about this time in my life, I had made enough money to buy what was then a very popular school book, viz: the *Columbian Orator.* I bought this addition to my library, of Mr. Knight, on Thames street, Fell's Point, Baltimore, and paid him fifty cents for it. I was first led to buy this book, by hearing some little boys say that they were going to learn some little pieces out of it for the Exhibition. This volume was, indeed, a rich treasure, and every opportunity afforded me, for a time, was spent in diligently perusing it. Among much other interesting matter, that which I had perused and reperused with unflagging satisfaction, was a short dialogue between a master and his slave. The slave is represented as having been recaptured, in a second attempt to run away; and the master opens the dialogue with an upbraiding speech, charging the slave with ingratitude, and demanding to know what he has to say in his own defense. Thus upbraided, and thus called upon to reply, the slave rejoins, that he knows how little anything that he can say will avail, seeing that he is completely in the hands of his owner; and with noble resolution, calmly says, "I submit to my fate." Touched by the slave's answer, the master insists upon his further speaking, and recapitulates the many acts of kindness which he has performed toward the slave, and tells him he is permitted to speak for himself. Thus invited to the debate, the quondam slave made a spirited defense of himself, and thereafter the whole argument, for and against slavery, was brought out. The master was vanquished at every turn in the argument; and seeing himself to be thus vanquished, he generously and meekly emancipates the slave, with his best wishes for his prosperity. It is scarcely necessary to say, that a dialogue, with such an origin, and such an ending — read when the fact of my being a slave was a constant burden of grief — powerfully affected me; and I could not help feeling that the day might come, when the well-directed answers made by the slave to the master, in this instance, would find their counterpart in myself.

This, however, was not all the fanaticism which I found in this *Columbian Orator*. I met there one of Sheridan's mighty speeches, on the subject of Catholic Emancipation, Lord Chatham's speech on the American war, and speeches by the great William Pitt and by Fox. These were all choice documents to me, and I read them, over and over again, with an interest that was ever increasing, because it was ever gaining in intelligence; for the more I read them, the better I understood them. The reading of these speeches added much to my limited stock of language, and enabled me to give tongue to many interesting thoughts, which had frequently flashed through my soul, and died away for want of utterance. The mighty power and heartsearching directness of truth, penetrating even the heart of a slaveholder, compelling him to yield up his earthly interests to the claims of eternal justice, were finely illustrated in the dialogue, just referred to; and from the speeches of Sheridan, I got a bold and powerful denunciation of oppression, and a most brilliant vindication of the rights of man. Here was, indeed, a noble acquisition. If I ever wavered under the consideration, that the Almighty, in some way, ordained slavery, and willed my enslavement for his own glory, I wavered no longer. I had now penetrated the secret of all slavery and oppression, and had ascertained their true foundation to be in the pride, the power and the avarice of man. The dialogue and the speeches were all redolent of the principles of liberty, and poured floods of light on the nature and character of slavery. With a book of this kind in my hand, my own human nature, and the facts of my experience, to help me, I was equal to a contest with the religious advocates of slavery, whether among the whites or among the colored people, for blindness, in this matter, is not confined to the former. I have met many religious colored people, at the south, who are under the delusion that God requires them to submit to slavery, and to wear their chains with meekness and humility. I could entertain no such nonsense as this; and I almost lost my patience when I found any colored man weak enough to believe such stuff. Nevertheless, the increase of knowledge was attended with bitter, as well as sweet results. The more I read, the more I was led to abhor and detest slavery, and my enslavers. "Slaveholders," thought I, "are only a band of successful robbers, who left their homes and went into Africa for the purpose of stealing and reducing my people to slavery." I loathed them as the meanest and the most wicked of men. As I read, behold! the very discontent so graphically predicted by Master Hugh, had already come upon me. I was no longer the light-hearted, gleesome boy, full of mirth and play, as when I landed first at Baltimore. Knowledge had come; light had penetrated the moral dungeon where I dwelt; and, behold! there lay the bloody whip, for my back, and here was the iron chain; and my good, *kind master*, he was the author of my situation. The revelation haunted me, stung me, and made me gloomy and miserable. As I writhed under the sting and torment of this knowledge, I almost envied my fellow slaves their stupid contentment. This knowledge opened my eyes to the horrible pit, and revealed the teeth of the frightful dragon that was ready to pounce upon me, but it opened no way for my escape. I have often wished myself a beast, or a bird — anything, rather than a slave. I was wretched and gloomy, beyond my ability to describe. I was too thoughtful to be happy. It was this everlasting thinking which distressed and tormented me; and yet there was no getting rid of the subject of my thoughts. All nature was redolent of it. Once awakened by the silver trump of knowledge, my spirit was roused to eternal wakefulness. Liberty! the inestimable birthright of every man, had, for me, converted every object into an asserter of this great right. It was heard in every sound, and beheld in every object. It was ever present, to torment me with a sense of my wretched condition. The more beautiful and charming were the smiles of nature, the more horrible and desolate was my condition. I saw nothing without seeing it, and I heard nothing without hearing it. I do not exaggerate, when I say, that it looked from every star, smiled in every calm, breathed in every wind, and moved in every storm.

I have no doubt that my state of mind had something to do with the change in the treatment adopted, by my once kind mistress toward me. I can easily believe, that my leaden, downcast, and discontented look, was very offensive to her. Poor lady! She did not know my trouble, and I dared not tell her. Could I have freely made her acquainted with the real state of my mind, and given her the reasons therefor, it might have been well for both of us. Her abuse of me fell upon me like the blows of the false prophet upon his ass; she did not know that an *angel* stood in the way; and — such is the relation of master and slave — I could not tell her. Nature had made us *friends*; slavery made us *enemies*. My interests were in a direction opposite to hers, and we both had our private thoughts and plans. She aimed to keep me ignorant; and I resolved to know, although knowledge only increased my discontent. My feelings were not the result of any marked cruelty in the treatment I received; they sprung from the consideration of my being a slave at all. It was slavery — not its mere incidents — that I hated. I had been cheated. I saw through the attempt to keep me in ignorance; I saw that slaveholders would have gladly made me believe that they were merely acting under the authority of God, in making a slave of me, and in making slaves of others; and I treated them as robbers and deceivers. The feeding and clothing me well, could not atone for taking my liberty from me. The smiles of my mistress could not remove the deep sorrow that dwelt in my young bosom. Indeed, these, in time, came only to deepen my sorrow. She had changed; and the reader will see that I had changed, too. We were both victims to the same overshadowing evil — she, as mistress, I, as slave. I will not censure her harshly; she cannot censure me, for she knows I speak but the truth, and have acted in my opposition to slavery, just as she herself would have acted, in a reverse of circumstances.

Whilst in the painful state of mind described in the foregoing chapter, almost regretting my very existence, because doomed to a life of bondage, so goaded and so wretched, at times, that I was even tempted to destroy my own life, I was yet keenly sensitive and eager to know any, and everything that transpired, having any relation to the subject of slavery. I was all ears, all eyes, whenever the words *slave*, *slavery*, dropped from the lips of any white person, and the occasions were not unfrequent when these words became leading ones, in high, social debate, at our house. Every little while, I could overhear Master Hugh, or some of his company, speaking with much warmth and excitement about "*abolitionists.*" Of *who* or *what* these were, I was totally ignorant. I found, however, that whatever they might be, they were most cordially hated and soundly abused by slaveholders, of every grade. I very soon discovered, too, that slavery was, in some sort, under consideration, whenever the abolitionists were alluded to. This made the term a very interesting one to me. If a slave, for instance, had made good his escape from slavery, it was generally alleged, that he had been persuaded and assisted by the abolitionists. If, also, a slave killed his master

— as was sometimes the case — or struck down his overseer, or set fire to his master's dwelling, or committed any violence or crime, out of the common way, it was certain to be said, that such a crime was the legitimate fruits of the abolition movement. Hearing such charges often repeated, I, naturally enough, received the impression that abolition — whatever else it might be — could not be unfriendly to the slave, nor very friendly to the slaveholder. I therefore set about finding out, if possible, *who* and *what* the abolitionists were, and why they were so obnoxious to the slaveholders. The dictionary afforded me very little help. It taught me that abolition was the "act of abolishing;" but it left me in ignorance at the very point where I most wanted information — and that was, as to the *thing* to be abolished. A city newspaper, the *Baltimore American*, gave me the incendiary information denied me by the dictionary. In its columns I found, that, on a certain day, a vast number of petitions and memorials had been presented to congress, praying for the abolition of slavery in the District of Columbia, and for the abolition of the slave trade between the states of the Union. This was enough. The vindictive bitterness, the marked caution, the studied reserve, and the cumbrous ambiguity, practiced by our white folks, when alluding to this subject, was now fully explained. Ever, after that, when I heard the words "abolition," or "abolition movement," mentioned, I felt the matter one of a personal concern; and I drew near to listen, when I could do so, without seeming too solicitous and prying. There was HOPE in those words. Ever and anon, too, I could see some terrible denunciation of slavery, in our papers — copied from abolition papers at the north, — and the injustice of such denunciation commented on. These I read with avidity. I had a deep satisfaction in the thought, that the rascality of slaveholders was not concealed from the eyes of the world, and that I was not alone in abhorring the cruelty and brutality of slavery. A still deeper train of thought was stirred. I saw that there was *fear*, as well as *rage*, in the manner of speaking of the abolitionists. The latter, therefore, I was compelled to regard as having some power in the country; and I felt that they might, possibly, succeed in their designs. When I met with a slave to whom I deemed it safe to talk on the subject, I would impart to him so much of the mystery as I had been able to penetrate. Thus, the light of this grand movement broke in upon my mind, by degrees; and I must say, that, ignorant as I then was of the philosophy of that movement, I believed in it from the first — and I believed in it, partly, because I saw that it alarmed the consciences of slaveholders. The insurrection of Nathaniel Turner had been quelled, but the alarm and terror had not subsided. The cholera was on its way, and the thought was present, that God was angry with the white people because of their slaveholding wickedness, and, therefore, his judgments were abroad in the land. It was impossible for me not to hope much from the abolition movement, when I saw it supported by the Almighty, and armed with DEATH!

Previous to my contemplation of the anti-slavery movement, and its probable results, my mind had been seriously awakened to the subject of religion. I was not more than thirteen years old, when I felt the need of God, as a father and protector. My religious nature was awakened by the preaching of a white Methodist minister, named Hanson. He thought that all men, great and small, bond and free, were sinners in the sight of God; that they were, by nature, rebels against His government; and that they must repent of their sins, and be reconciled to God, through Christ. I cannot say that I had a very distinct notion of what was required of me; but one thing I knew very well — I was wretched, and had no means of making myself otherwise. Moreover, I knew that I could pray for light. I consulted a good colored man, named Charles Johnson; and, in tones of holy affection, he told me to pray, and what to pray for. I was, for weeks, a poor, broken-hearted mourner, traveling through the darkness and misery of doubts and fears. I finally found that change of heart which comes by "casting all one's care" upon God, and by having faith in Jesus Christ, as the Redeemer, Friend, and Savior of those who diligently seek Him.

After this, I saw the world in a new light. I seemed to live in a new world, surrounded by new objects, and to be animated by new hopes and desires. I loved all mankind — slaveholders not excepted; though I abhorred slavery more than ever. My great concern was, now, to have the world converted. The desire for knowledge increased, and especially did I want a thorough acquaintance with the contents of the Bible. I have gathered scattered pages from this holy book, from the filthy street gutters of Baltimore, and washed and dried them, that in the moments of my leisure, I might get a word or two of wisdom from them. While thus religiously seeking knowledge, I became acquainted with a good old colored man, named Lawson. A more devout man than he, I never saw. He drove a dray [*low heavy sideless cart*] for Mr. James Ramsey, the owner of a rope-walk on Fell's Point, Baltimore. This man not only prayed three times a day, but he prayed as he walked through the streets, at his work — on his dray — everywhere. His life was a life of prayer, and his words, (when he spoke to his friends,) were about a better world. Uncle Lawson lived near Master Hugh's house; and, becoming deeply attached to the old man, I went often with him to prayer-meeting, and spent much of my leisure time with him on Sunday. The old man could read a little, and I was a

great help to him, in making out the hard words, for I
was a better reader than he. I could teach him "*the
letter*," but he could teach me "*the spirit*," and high,
refreshing times we had together, in singing, praying
and glorifying God. These meetings with Uncle Lawson went on for a long time, without the knowledge of
Master Hugh or my mistress. Both knew, however,
that I had become religious, and they seemed to
respect my conscientious piety. My mistress was still
a professor of religion, and belonged to class. Her
leader was no less a person than the Rev. Beverly
Waugh, the presiding elder, and now one of the bishops of the Methodist Episcopal church. Mr. Waugh
was then stationed over Wilk street church. I am
careful to state these facts, that the reader may be able
to form an idea of the precise influences which had to
do with shaping and directing my mind.

In view of the cares and anxieties incident to the life
she was then leading, and, especially, in view of the
separation from religious associations to which she
was subjected, my mistress had, as I have before
stated, become lukewarm, and needed to be looked
up by her leader. This brought Mr. Waugh to our
house, and gave me an opportunity to hear him exhort and pray. But my chief instructor, in matters of
religion, was Uncle Lawson. He was my spiritual
father; and I loved him intensely, and was at his house
every chance I got. This pleasure was not long allow-

ed me. Master Hugh became averse to my going to Father Lawson's, and threatened to whip me if I ever went there again. I now felt myself persecuted by a wicked man; and I *would* go to Father Lawson's, notwithstanding the threat. The good old man had told me, that the "Lord had a great work for me to do;" and I must prepare to do it; and that he had been shown that I must preach the gospel. His words made a deep impression on my mind, and I verily felt that some such work was before me, though I could not see *how* I should ever engage in its performance. "The good Lord," he said, "would bring it to pass in his own good time," and that I must go on reading and studying the scriptures. The advice and the suggestions of Uncle Lawson, were not without their influence upon my character and destiny. He threw my thoughts into a channel from which they have never entirely diverged. He fanned my already intense love of knowledge into a flame, by assuring me that I was to be a useful man in the world. When I would say to him, "How can these things be — and what can *I* do?" his simple reply was, "*Trust in the Lord.*" When I told him that "I was a slave, and a slave FOR LIFE," he said, "the Lord can make you free, my dear. All things are possible with him, only *have faith in God.*" "Ask, and it shall be given."[108] "If you want liberty,"

---

[108] King James Bible, *Matthew* 7:7

said the good old man, "ask the Lord for it, *in faith*, AND HE WILL GIVE IT TO YOU."

Thus assured, and cheered on, under the inspiration of hope, I worked and prayed with a light heart, believing that my life was under the guidance of a wisdom higher than my own. With all other blessings sought at the mercy seat, I always prayed that God would, of His great mercy, and in His own good time, deliver me from my bondage.

I went, one day, on the wharf of Mr. Waters; and seeing two Irishmen unloading a large scow of stone, or ballast, I went on board, unasked, and helped them. When we had finished the work, one of the men came to me, aside, and asked me a number of questions, and among them, if I were a slave. I told him "I was a slave, and a slave for life." The good Irishman gave his shoulders a shrug, and seemed deeply affected by the statement. He said, "it was a pity so fine a little fellow as myself should be a slave for life." They both had much to say about the matter, and expressed the deepest sympathy with me, and the most decided hatred of slavery. They went so far as to tell me that I ought to run away, and go to the north; that I should find friends there, and that I would be as free as anybody. I, however, pretended not to be interested in what they said, for I feared they might be treacherous. White men have been known to encourage slaves to escape, and then — to get the reward — they have kidnapped them, and returned them to their masters. And while I mainly inclined to the notion that these men were honest and meant me no ill, I feared it might be otherwise. I nevertheless remembered their words and their advice, and looked forward to an escape to the north, as a possible means of gaining the liberty for which my heart panted. It was not my enslavement, at the then present time, that most affected me; the being a slave *for life*, was the saddest thought. I was too young to think of running away immediately; besides, I wished to learn how to write, before going, as I might have occasion to write my own pass. I now not only had the hope of freedom, but a foreshadowing of the means by which I might, someday, gain that inestimable boon. Meanwhile, I resolved to add to my educational attainments the art of writing.

After this manner I began to learn to write: I was much in the ship yard — Master Hugh's, and that of Durgan & Bailey —and I observed that the carpenters, after hewing and getting a piece of timber ready for use, wrote on it the initials of the name of that part of the ship for which it was intended. When, for instance, a piece of timber was ready for the starboard side, it was marked with a capital "S." A piece for the larboard side was marked "L;" larboard forward, "L. F.;" larboard aft, was marked "L. A.;" starboard aft, "S. A.;" and starboard forward "S. F." I soon learned these letters, and for what they were placed on the timbers.

My work was now, to keep fire under the steam box, and to watch the ship yard while the carpenters had gone to dinner. This interval gave me a fine opportunity for copying the letters named. I soon astonished myself with the ease with which I made the letters; and the thought was soon present, "if I can make four, I can make more." But having made these easily, when I met boys about Bethel church, or any of our playgrounds, I entered the lists with them in the art of writing, and would make the letters which I had been so fortunate as to learn, and ask them to "beat that if they could." With playmates for my teachers, fences and pavements for my copy books, and chalk for my pen and ink, I learned the art of writing. I, however, afterward adopted various methods of improving my hand. The most successful, was copying the italics in Webster's spelling book, until I could make them all without looking on the book. By this time, my little "Master Tommy" had grown to be a big boy, and had written over a number of copy books, and brought them home. They had been shown to the neighbors, had elicited due praise, and were now laid carefully away. Spending my time between the ship yard and house, I was as often the lone keeper of the latter as of the former. When my mistress left me in charge of the house, I had a grand time; I got Master Tommy's copy books and a pen and ink, and, in the ample spaces between the lines, I wrote other lines, as nearly like his as possible. The process was a tedious one, and I ran the risk of getting a flogging for marring the highly prized copy books of the oldest son. In addition to these opportunities, sleeping, as I did, in the kitchen loft — a room seldom visited by any of the family, — I got a flour barrel up there, and a chair; and upon the head of that barrel I have written, (or endeavored to write,) copying from the Bible and the Methodist hymn book, and other books which had accumulated on my hands, till late at night, and when all the family were in bed and asleep. I was supported in my endeavors by renewed advice, and by holy promises from the good Father Lawson, with whom I continued to meet, and pray, and read the scriptures. Although Master Hugh was aware of my going there, I must say, for his credit, that he never executed his threat to whip me, for having thus, innocently, employed my leisure time.[109]

---

[109] Excerpted from *My Bondage and My Freedom*, (New York and Auburn, New York: Miller, Orton & Mulligan, 1855).

Thoughtlessness and the Contented Slave – To make a contented slave, you must make a thoughtless one. It is necessary to darken his moral and mental vision, and, as far as possible, to annihilate his power of reason. He must be able to detect no inconsistencies in slavery. The man that takes his earnings, must be able to convince him that he has a perfect right to do so. It must not depend upon mere force; the slave must know no Higher Law than his master's will. The whole relationship must not only demonstrate, to his mind, its necessity, but also its absolute rightfulness. If there be one crevice through which a single drop can fall, it will certainly rust away the slave's chain.[110]

---

[110] Excerpted from *My Bondage and My Freedom*, (New York and Auburn, New York: Miller, Orton & Mulligan, 1855).

Community as Resistance – For much of the happiness – or absence of misery – with which I passed this year with Mr. Freeland, I am indebted to the genial temper and ardent friendship of my brother slaves. They were, every one of them, manly, generous and brave, yes; I say they were brave, and I will add, fine looking. It is seldom the lot of mortals to have truer and better friends than were the slaves on this farm. It is not uncommon to charge slaves with great treachery toward each other, and to believe them incapable of confiding in each other; but I must say, that I never loved, esteemed, or confided in men, more than I did in these. They were as true as steel, and no band of brothers could have been more loving. There were no mean advantages taken of each other, as is sometimes the case where slaves are situated as we were; no tattling; no giving each other bad names to Mr. Freeland; and no elevating one at the expense of the other. We never undertook to do anything, of any importance, which was likely to affect each other, without mutual consultation. We were generally a unit, and moved together. Thoughts and sentiments were exchanged between us, which might well be called very incendiary, by oppressors and tyrants; and perhaps the time has not even now come, when it is safe to unfold all the flying suggestions which arise in the minds of intelligent slaves.[111]

---

[111] Excerpted from *My Bondage and My Freedom*, (New York

Keeping Down the Spirit of Insurrection pt. II – Judging from my own observation and experience, I believe these holidays to be among the most effective means, in the hands of slaveholders, of keeping down the spirit of insurrection among slaves.

To enslave men, successfully and safely, it is necessary to have their minds occupied with thoughts and aspirations short of the liberty of which they are deprived. A certain degree of attainable good must be kept before them. The young man can go wooing; the married man can visit his wife; the father and mother can see their children; the industrious and money loving can make a few dollars; the great wrestler can win laurels; the young people can meet, and enjoy each other's society; the drunken man can get plenty of whisky; and the religious man can hold prayer meetings, preach, pray and exhort during the holidays. Before the holidays, these are pleasures in prospect; after the holidays, they become pleasures of memory, and they serve to keep out thoughts and wishes of a more dangerous character. Were slaveholders at once to abandon the practice of allowing their slaves these liberties, periodically, and to keep them, the year round, closely confined to the narrow circle of their homes, I doubt not that the south would blaze with insurrections. These holidays are conductors or safety valves to carry off the explosive

and Auburn, New York: Miller, Orton & Mulligan, 1855).

elements inseparable from the human mind, when reduced to the condition of slavery. But for these, the rigors of bondage would become too severe for endurance, and the slave would be forced up to dangerous desperation. Woe to the slaveholder when he undertakes to hinder or to prevent the operation of these electric conductors. A succession of earthquakes would be less destructive, than the insurrectionary fires which would be sure to burst forth in different parts of the south, from such interference.

Thus, the holidays, become part and parcel of the gross fraud, wrongs and inhumanity of slavery. Ostensibly, they are institutions of benevolence, designed to mitigate the rigors of slave life, but, practically, they are a fraud, instituted by human selfishness, the better to secure the ends of injustice and oppression. The slave's happiness is not the end sought, but, rather, the master's safety. It is not from a generous unconcern for the slave's labor that this cessation from labor is allowed, but from a prudent regard to the safety of the slave system. I am strengthened in this opinion, by the fact, that most slaveholders like to have their slaves spend the holidays in such a manner as to be of no real benefit to the slaves. It is plain, that everything like rational enjoyment among the slaves, is frowned upon; and only those wild and low sports, peculiar to semi-civilized people, are encouraged. All the license allowed, appears to have no other object than to disgust the slaves with their temporary freedom, and to make them as glad to return to their work, as they were to leave it. By plunging them into exhausting depths of drunkenness and dissipation, this effect is almost certain to follow. I have known slaveholders resort to cunning tricks, with a view of getting their slaves deplorably drunk. A usual plan is, to make bets on a slave, that he can drink more whisky than any other; and so to induce a rivalry among them, for the mastery in this degradation. The scenes, brought about in this way, were often scandalous and loathsome in the extreme. Whole multitudes might be found stretched out in brutal drunkenness, at once helpless and disgusting. Thus, when the slave asks for a few hours of virtuous freedom, his cunning master takes advantage of his ignorance, and cheers him with a dose of vicious and revolting dissipation, artfully labeled with the name of LIBERTY. We were induced to drink, I among the rest, and when the holidays were over, we all staggered up from our filth and wallowing, took a long breath, and went away to our various fields of work; feeling, upon the whole, rather glad to go from that which our masters artfully deceived us into the belief was freedom, back again to the arms of slavery. It was not what we had taken it to be, nor what it might have been, had it not been abused by us. It was about as well to be a slave to *master*, as to be a slave to *rum* and *whisky*.

I am the more induced to take this view of the holiday system, adopted by slaveholders, from what I know of their treatment of slaves, in regard to other things. It is the commonest thing for them to try to disgust their slaves with what they do not want them to have, or to enjoy. A slave, for instance, likes molasses; he steals some; to cure him of the taste for it, his master, in many cases, will go away to town, and buy a large quantity of the *poorest* quality, and set it before his slave, and, with whip in hand, compel him to eat it, until the poor fellow is made to sicken at the very thought of molasses. The same course is often adopted to cure slaves of the disagreeable and inconvenient practice of asking for more food, when their allowance has failed them. The same disgusting process works well, too, in other things, but I need not cite them.[112]

---

[112] Excerpted from *My Bondage and My Freedom*, (New York and Auburn, New York: Miller, Orton & Mulligan, 1855).

Sober Mind a Threat to Slavery pt. II – When a slave is drunk, the slaveholder has no fear that he will plan an insurrection; no fear that he will escape to the north. It is the sober, thinking slave who is dangerous, and needs the vigilance of his master, to keep him a slave.[113]

---

[113] Excerpted from *My Bondage and My Freedom*, (New York and Auburn, New York: Miller, Orton & Mulligan, 1855).

Who Will Take Tare of the Philosophy? – In the summer of 1841, a grand anti-slavery convention was held in Nantucket, under the auspices of Mr. Garrison and his friends. Until now, I had taken no holiday since my escape from slavery. Having worked very hard that spring and summer, in Richmond's brass foundery — sometimes working all night as well as all day — and needing a day or two of rest, I attended this convention, never supposing that I should take part in the proceedings. Indeed, I was not aware that anyone connected with the convention even so much as knew my name. I was, however, quite mistaken. Mr. William C. Coffin, a prominent abolitionist in those days of trial, had heard me speaking to my colored friends, in the little schoolhouse on Second street, New Bedford, where we worshiped. He sought me out in the crowd, and invited me to say a few words to the convention. Thus sought out, and thus invited, I was induced to speak out the feelings inspired by the occasion, and the fresh recollection of the scenes through which I had passed as a slave. My speech on this occasion is about the only one I ever made, of which I do not remember a single connected sentence. It was with the utmost difficulty that I could stand erect, or that I could command and articulate two words without hesitation and stammering. I trembled in every limb. I am not sure that my embarrassment was not the most effective part of my speech, if speech it could be called. At any rate, this is about the only part of my performance that I now distinctly remember. But excited and convulsed as I was, the audience, though remarkably quiet before, became as much excited as myself. Mr. Garrison followed me, taking me as his text; and now, whether I had made an eloquent speech in behalf of freedom or not, his was one never to be forgotten by those who heard it. Those who had heard Mr. Garrison oftenest, and had known him longest, were astonished. It was an effort of unequaled power, sweeping down, like a very tornado, every opposing barrier, whether of sentiment or opinion. For a moment, he possessed that almost fabulous inspiration, often referred to but seldom attained, in which a public meeting is transformed, as it were, into a single individuality — the orator wielding a thousand heads and hearts at once, and by the simple majesty of his all controlling thought, converting his hearers into the express image of his own soul. That night there were at least one thousand Garrisonians in Nantucket! At the close of this great meeting, I was duly waited on by Mr. John A. Collins — then the general agent of the Massachusetts anti-slavery society — and urgently solicited by him to become an agent of that society, and to publicly advocate its anti-slavery principles. I was reluctant to take the proffered position. I had not been quite three years from slavery — was honestly distrustful of my ability — wished to be excused; publicity exposed me to discovery and arrest by my master; and other objections came up, but Mr. Collins was not to be put off, and I finally consented to go out for three months, for I supposed that I should have got to the end of my story and my usefulness, in that length of time.

Here opened upon me a new life —a life for which I had had no preparation. I was a "graduate from the peculiar institution," Mr. Collins used to say, when introducing me, "*with my diploma written on my back!*" The three years of my freedom had been spent in the hard school of adversity. My hands had been furnished by nature with something like a solid leather coating, and I had bravely marked out for myself a life of rough labor, suited to the hardness of my hands, as a means of supporting myself and rearing my children. Now what shall I say of this fourteen years' experience as a public advocate of the cause of my enslaved brothers and sisters? The time is but as a speck, yet large enough to justify a pause for retrospection — and a pause it must only be.

Young, ardent, and hopeful, I entered upon this new life in the full gush of unsuspecting enthusiasm. The cause was good; the men engaged in it were good; the means to attain its triumph, good; Heaven's blessing must attend all, and freedom must soon be given to the pining millions under a ruthless bondage. My whole heart went with the holy cause, and my most fervent prayer to the Almighty Disposer of the hearts of men, were continually offered for its early triumph. "Who or what," thought I, "can withstand a cause so good, so holy, so indescribably glorious. The God of Israel is with us. The might of the Eternal is on our side. Now let but the truth be spoken, and a nation will start forth at the sound!" In this enthusiastic spirit, I dropped into the ranks of freedom's friends, and went forth to the battle. For a time I was made to forget that my skin was dark and my hair crisped. For a time I regretted that I could not have shared the hardships and dangers endured by the earlier workers for the slave's release. I soon, however, found that my enthusiasm had been extravagant; that hardships and dangers were not yet passed; and that the life now before me, had shadows as well as sunbeams.

Among the first duties assigned me, on entering the ranks, was to travel, in company with Mr. George Foster, to secure subscribers to the *Anti-slavery Standard* and the *Liberator*. With him I traveled and lectured through the eastern counties of Massachusetts. Much interest was awakened — large meetings assembled. Many came, no doubt, from curiosity to hear what a Negro could say in his own cause. I was generally introduced as a "*chattel*" — a "*thing*" — a piece of southern "*property*" — the chairman assuring the audience that it could speak. Fugitive slaves, at that time, were not so plentiful as now; and as a fugitive slave lecturer, I had the advantage of being a "*brand new fact*" — the first one out. Up to that time, a colored man was deemed a fool who confessed himself a runaway slave, not only because of the danger to which he exposed himself of being retaken, but because it was a confession of a very low origin! Some of my colored friends in New Bedford thought very badly of my wisdom for thus exposing and degrading myself. The only precaution I took, at the beginning, to prevent Master Thomas from knowing where I was, and what I was about, was the withholding my former name, my master's name, and the name of the state and county from which I came. During the first three or four months, my speeches were almost exclusively made up of narrations of my own personal experience as a slave. "Let us have the facts," said the people. So also said Friend George Foster, who always wished to pin me down to my simple narrative. "Give us the facts," said Collins, "we will take care of the philosophy." Just here arose some embarrassment. It was impossible for me to repeat the same old story month after month, and to keep up my interest in it. It was new to the people, it is true, but it was an old story to me; and to go through with it night after night, was a task altogether too mechanical for my nature. "Tell your story, Frederick," would whisper my then revered friend, William Lloyd Garrison, as I stepped upon the platform. I could not always obey, for I was now reading and thinking. New views of the subject were presented to my mind. It did not entirely satisfy me to *narrate* wrongs; I felt like *denouncing* them. I could not always curb my moral indignation for the perpetrators of slaveholding villainy, long enough for a circumstantial statement of the facts which I felt almost everybody must know. Besides, I was growing, and needed room. "People won't believe you ever was a slave, Frederick, if you keep on this way," said Friend Foster. "Be yourself," said Collins, "and tell your story." It was said to me, "Better have a *little* of the plantation manner of speech than not; 'tis not best that you seem too learned." These excellent friends were actuated by the best of motives, and were not altogether wrong in their advice; and still I must speak just the word that seemed to *me* the word to be spoken *by* me.

At last the apprehended trouble came. People doubted if I had ever been a slave. They said I did not talk like a slave, look like a slave, nor act like a slave, and that they believed I had never been south of Mason and Dixon's line. "He don't tell us where he came from — what his master's name was — how he got away — nor the story of his experience. Besides, he is educated, and is, in this, a contradiction of all the facts we have concerning the ignorance of the slaves." Thus, I was in a pretty fair way to be denounced as an impostor. The committee of the Massachusetts anti-slavery society knew all the facts in my case, and agreed with me in the prudence of keeping them private. They, therefore, never doubted my being a genuine fugitive; but going down the aisles of the churches in which I spoke, and hearing the free spoken Yankees saying, repeatedly, "*He's never been a slave, I'll warrant ye*," I resolved to dispel all doubt, at no distant day, by such a revelation of facts as could not be made by any other than a genuine fugitive. In a little less than four years, therefore, after becoming a public lecturer, I was induced to write out the leading facts connected with my experience in slavery, giving names of persons, places, and dates — thus putting it in the power of any who doubted, to ascertain the truth or falsehood of my story of being a fugitive slave. This statement soon became known in Maryland, and I had reason to believe that an effort would be made to recapture me.

It is not probable that any open attempt to secure me as a slave could have succeeded, further than the obtainment, by my master, of the money value of my bones and sinews. Fortunately for me, in the four years of my labors in the abolition cause, I had gained many friends, who would have suffered themselves to be taxed to almost any extent to save me from slavery. It was felt that I had committed the double offense of running away, and exposing the secrets and crimes of slavery and slaveholders. There was a double motive for seeking my reënslavement — avarice and vengeance; and while, as I have said, there was little probability of successful recapture, if attempted openly, I was constantly in danger of being spirited away, at a moment when my friends could render me no assistance. In traveling about from place to place — often alone — I was much exposed to this sort of attack. Any one cherishing the design to betray me, could easily do so, by simply tracing my whereabouts through the antislavery journals, for my meetings and movements were promptly made known in advance. My true friends, Mr. Garrison and Mr. Phillips, had no faith in the power of Massachusetts to protect me in my right to liberty. Public sentiment and the law, in their opinion, would hand me over to the tormentors. Mr. Phillips, especially, considered me in danger, and said, when I showed him the manuscript of my story, if in my place, he would throw it into the fire. Thus, the reader will observe, the settling of one difficulty only opened the way for another; and that though I had reached a free state, and had attained a position for public usefulness, I was still tormented with the liability of losing my liberty.[114]

---

[114] Excerpted from *My Bondage and My Freedom*, (New York and Auburn, New York: Miller, Orton & Mulligan, 1855).

The Dred Scott Decision - Mr. CHAIRMAN, FRIENDS, and FELLOW CITIZENS: While four millions of our fellow countrymen are in chains — while men, women, and children are bought and sold on the auction-block with horses, sheep, and swine — while the remorseless slave-whip draws the warm blood of our common humanity — it is meet that we assemble as we have done today, and lift up our hearts and voices in earnest denunciation of the vile and shocking abomination. It is not for us to be governed by our hopes or our fears in this great work; yet it is natural on occasions like this, to survey the position of the great struggle which is going on between slavery and freedom, and to dwell upon such signs of encouragement as may have been lately developed, and the state of feeling these signs or events have occasioned in us and among the people generally. It is a fitting time to take an observation to ascertain where we are, and what our prospects are.

To many, the prospects of the struggle against slavery seem far from cheering. Eminent men, North and South, in Church and State, tell us that the omens are all against us. Emancipation, they tell us, is a wild, delusive idea; the price of human flesh was never higher than now; slavery was never more closely entwined about the hearts and affections of the southern people than now; that whatever of conscientious scruple, religious conviction, or public policy, which opposed the system of slavery forty or fifty years ago, has subsided; and that slavery never reposed upon a firmer basis than now. Completing this picture of the happy and prosperous condition of this system of wickedness, they tell us that this state of things is to be set to our account. Abolition agitation has done it all. How deep is the misfortune of my poor, bleeding people, if this be so! How lost their condition, if even the efforts of their friends but sink them deeper in ruin!

Without assenting to this strong representation of the increasing strength and stability of slavery, without denouncing what of untruth pervades it, I own myself not insensible to the many difficulties and discouragements that beset us on every hand. They fling their broad and gloomy shadows across the pathway of every thoughtful colored man in this country. For one, I see them clearly, and feel them sadly. With an earnest, aching heart I have long looked for the realization of the hope of my people. Standing, as it were, barefoot, and treading upon the sharp and flinty rocks of the present, and looking out upon the boundless sea of the future, I have sought, in my humble way, to penetrate the intervening mists and clouds, and, perchance, to descry, in the dim and shadowy distance, the white flag of freedom, the precise speck of time at which the cruel bondage of my people should end, and the long entombed millions rise from the foul grave of slavery and death. But of that time I can know nothing, and you can know nothing. All is uncertain at that point. One thing, however, is certain; slaveholders are in earnest, and mean to cling to their slaves as long as they can, and to the bitter end. They show no sign of a wish to quit their iron grasp upon the sable throats of their victims. Their motto is, "a firmer hold and a tighter grip" for every new effort that is made to break their cruel power. The case is one of life or death with them, and they will give up only when they must do that or do worse.

In one view slaveholders have a decided advantage over all opposition. It is well to notice this advantage — the advantage of complete organization. They are organized; and yet were not at the pains of creating their organizations. The State governments, where the system of slavery exists, are complete slavery organizations. The church organizations in those States are equally at the service of slavery; while the Federal Government, with its army and navy, from the chief magistracy in Washington, to the Supreme Court, and thence to the chief marshalship at New York, is pledged to support, defend, and propagate the crying curse of human bondage. The pen, the purse, and the sword, are united against the simple truth, preached by humble men in obscure places.

This is one view. It is, thank God, only one view; there is another, and a brighter view. David, you know, looked small and insignificant when going to meet Goliath, but looked larger when he had slain his foe. The Malakoff was, to the eye of the world, impregnable, till the hour it fell before the shot and shell of the allied army. Thus hath it ever been. Oppression, organized as ours is, will appear invincible up to the very hour of its fall. Sir, let us look at the other side, and see if there are not some things to cheer our heart and nerve us up anew in the good work of emancipation.

Take this fact — for it is a fact — the anti-slavery movement has, from first to last, suffered no abatement. It has gone forth in all directions, and is now felt in the remotest extremities of the Republic.

It started small, and was without capital either in men or money. The odds were all against it. It literally had nothing to lose, and everything to gain. There was ignorance to be enlightened, error to be combatted, conscience to be awakened, prejudice to be overcome, apathy to be aroused, the right of speech to be secured, mob violence to be subdued, and a deep, radical change to be inwrought in the mind and heart of the whole nation. This great work, under God, has gone on, and gone on gloriously.

Amid all changes, fluctuations, assaults, and adverses of every kind, it has remained firm in its purpose, steady in its aim, onward and upward, defying all opposition, and never losing a single battle. Our strength is in the growth of antislavery conviction, and this has never halted.

There is a significant vitality about this abolition movement. It has taken a deeper, broader, and more lasting hold upon the national heart than ordinary reform movements. Other subjects of much interest come and go, expand and contract, blaze and vanish, but the huge question of American Slavery, comprehending, as it does, not merely the weal or the woe of four millions, and their countless posterity, but the weal or the woe of this entire nation, must increase in magnitude and in majesty with every hour of its history. From a cloud not bigger than a man's hand, it has overspread the heavens. It has risen from a grain not bigger than a mustard seed. Yet see the fowls of the air, how they crowd its branches.

Politicians who cursed it, now defend it; ministers, once dumb, now speak in its praise; and presses, which once flamed with hot denunciations against it, now surround the sacred cause as by a wall of living fire. Politicians go with it as a pillar of cloud by day, and the press as a pillar of fire by night. With these ancient tokens of success, I, for one, will not despair of our cause.

Those who have undertaken to suppress and crush out this agitation for Liberty and humanity, have been most woefully disappointed. Many who have engaged to put it down, have found themselves put down. The agitation has pursued them in all their meanderings, broken in upon their seclusion, and, at the very moment of fancied security, it has settled down upon them like a mantle of unquenchable fire. Clay, Calhoun, and Webster each tried his hand at suppressing the agitation; and they went to their graves disappointed and defeated.

Loud and exultingly have we been told that the slavery question is settled, and settled forever. You remember it was settled thirty-seven years ago, when Missouri was admitted into the Union with a slaveholding constitution, and slavery prohibited in all territory north of thirty-six degrees of north latitude. Just fifteen years afterwards, it was settled again by voting down the right of petition, and gagging down free discussion in Congress. Ten years after this it was settled again by the annexation of Texas, and with it the war with Mexico. In 1850 it was again settled. This was called a final settlement. By it slavery was virtually declared to be the equal of Liberty, and should come into the Union on the same terms. By it the right and the power to hunt down men, women, and children, in every part of this country, was conceded to our southern brethren, in order to keep them in the Union. Four years after this settlement, the whole question was once more settled, and settled by a settlement which unsettled all the former settlements.

The fact is, the more the question has been settled, the more it has needed settling. The space between the different settlements has been strikingly on the decrease. The first stood longer than any of its successors.

There is a lesson in these decreasing spaces. The first stood fifteen years — the second, ten years — the third, five years — the fourth stood four years — and the fifth has stood the brief space of two years.

This last settlement must be called the Taney settlement. We are now told, in tones of lofty exultation, that the day is lost — all lost — and that we might as well give up the struggle. The highest authority has spoken. The voice of the Supreme Court has gone out over the troubled waves of the National Conscience, saying peace, be still.

This infamous decision of the Slaveholding wing of the Supreme Court maintains that slaves are, within the contemplation of the Constitution of the United States, property; that slaves are property in the same sense that horses, sheep, and swine are property; that the old doctrine that slavery is a creature of local law is false; that the right of the slaveholder to his slave does not depend upon the local law, but is secured wherever the Constitution of the United States extends; that Congress has no right to prohibit slavery anywhere; that slavery may go in safety anywhere under the star-spangled banner; that colored persons of African descent have no rights that white men are bound to respect; that colored men of African descent are not and cannot be citizens of the United States.

You will readily ask me how I am affected by this devilish decision — this judicial incarnation of wolfishness! My answer is, and no thanks to the slaveholding wing of the Supreme Court, my hopes were never brighter than now.

I have no fear that the National Conscience will be put to sleep by such an open, glaring, and scandalous tissue of lies as that decision is, and has been, over and over, shown to be.

The Supreme Court of the United States is not the only power in this world. It is very great, but the Supreme Court of the Almighty is greater. Judge Taney can do many things, but he cannot perform impossibilities. He cannot bale out the ocean, annihilate this firm old earth, or pluck the silvery star of liberty from our Northern sky. He may decide, and decide again; but he cannot reverse the decision of the Most High. He cannot change the essential nature of things — making evil good, and good, evil.

Happily for the whole human family, their rights have been defined, declared, and decided in a court higher than the Supreme Court. "There is a law," says Brougham, "above all the enactments of human codes, and by that law, unchangeable and eternal, man cannot hold property in man."

Your fathers have said that man's right to liberty is self-evident. There is no need of argument to make it clear. The voices of nature, of conscience, of reason, and of revelation, proclaim it as the right of all rights, the foundation of all trust, and of all responsibility. Man was born with it. It was his before he comprehended it. The *deed* conveying it to him is written in the centre of his soul, and is recorded in Heaven. The sun in the sky is not more palpable to the sight than man's right to liberty is to the moral vision. To decide against this right in the person of Dred Scott, or the humblest and most whip-scarred bondman in the land, is to decide against God. It is an open rebellion against God's government. It is an attempt to undo what God |has| done, to blot out the broad distinction instituted by the *All-Wise* between men and things, and to change the image and superscription of the everliving God into a speechless piece of merchandise.

Such a decision cannot stand. God will be true though every man be a liar. We can appeal from this hell-black judgment of the Supreme Court, to the court of common sense and common humanity. We can appeal from man to God. If there is no justice on earth, there is yet justice in heaven. You may close your Supreme Court against the Black man's cry for justice, but you cannot, thank God, close against him the ear of a sympathising world, nor shut up the Court of Heaven. All that is merciful and just, on earth and in Heaven, will execrate and despise this edict of Taney.

If it were at all likely that the people of these free States would tamely submit to this demonical judgment, I might feel gloomy and sad over it, and possibly it might be necessary for my people to look for a home in some other country. But as the case stands, we have nothing to fear.

In one point of view, we, the abolitionists and colored people, should meet this decision, unlooked for and monstrous as it appears, in a cheerful spirit. This very attempt to blot out forever the hopes of an enslaved people may be one necessary link in the chain of events preparatory to the downfall and complete overthrow of the whole slave system.

The whole history of the anti-slavery movement is studded with proof that all measures devised and executed with a view to allay and diminish the antislavery agitation, have only served to increase, intensify, and embolden that agitation. This wisdom of the crafty has been confounded, and the counsels of the ungodly brought to nought. It was so with the Fugitive Slave Bill. It was so with the Kansas-Nebraska Bill; and it will be so with this last and most shocking of all proslavery devices, this Taney decision.

When great transactions are involved, where the fate of millions is concerned, where a long enslaved and suffering people are to be delivered, I am superstitious enough to believe that the finger of the Almighty may be seen bringing good out of evil, and making the wrath of man redound to his honor, hastening the triumph of righteousness.

The American people have been called upon, in a most striking manner, to abolish and put away forever the system of slavery. The subject has been pressed upon their attention in all earnestness and sincerity. The cries of the slave have gone forth to the world, and up to the throne of God. This decision, in my view, is a means of keeping the nation awake on the subject. It is another proof that God does not mean that we shall go to sleep, and forget that we are a slaveholding nation.

Step by step we have seen the slave power advancing; poisoning, corrupting, and perverting the institutions of the country; growing more and more haughty, imperious, and exacting. The white man's liberty has been marked out for the same grave with the Black man's.

The ballot box is desecrated, God's law set at nought, armed legislators stalk the halls of Congress, freedom of speech is beaten down in the Senate. The rivers and highways are infested by border ruffians, and white men are made to feel the iron heel of slavery.

This ought to arouse us to kill off the hateful thing. They are solemn warnings to which the white people, as well as the Black people, should take heed.

If these shall fail, judgment, more fierce or terrible, may come. The lightning, whirlwind, and earthquake may come. Jefferson said that he trembled for his country when he reflected that God is just, and his justice cannot sleep forever. The time may come when even the crushed worm may turn under the tyrant's feet. Goaded by cruelty, stung by a burning sense of wrong, in an awful moment of depression and desperation, the bondman and bondwoman at the south may rush to one wild and deadly struggle for freedom. Already slaveholders go to bed with bowie knives, and apprehend death at their dinners. Those who enslave, rob, and torment their cooks, may well expect to find death in their dinner-pots.

The world is full of violence and fraud, and it would be strange if the slave, the constant victim of both fraud and violence, should escape the contagion. He, too, may learn to fight the devil with fire, and for one, I am in no frame of mind to pray that this may be long deferred.

Two remarkable occurrences have followed the presidential election, one was the unaccountable sickness traced to the National Hotel at Washington, and the other was the discovery of a plan among the slaves, in different localities, to slay their oppressors.

Twenty or thirty of the suspected were put to death. Some were shot, some hanged, some burned, and some died under the lash. One brave man owned himself well acquainted with the conspiracy, but said he would rather die than disclose the facts. He received seven hundred and fifty lashes, and his noble spirit went away to the God who gave it. The name of this hero has been by the meanness of tyrants suppressed. Such a man redeems his race. He is worthy to be mentioned with the Hoffers and Tells, the noblest heroes of history. These insurrectionary movements have been put down, but they may break out at any time, under the guidance of higher intelligence, and with a more invincible spirit.

> The fire thus kindled, may be revived again;
> The flames are extinguished, but the embers remain;
> One terrible blast may produce an ignition,
> Which shall wrap the whole South in wild conflagration.
>
> The pathway of tyrants lies over volcanoes;
> The very air they breathe is heavy with sorrows;
> Agonizing heart-throbs convulse them while sleeping,
> And the wind whispers Death as over them sweeping.

By all the laws of nature, civilization, and of progress, slavery is a doomed system. Not all the skill of politicians, North and South, not all the sophistries of Judges, not all the fulminations of a corrupt press, not all the hypocritical prayers, or the hypocritical refusals to pray of a hollow-hearted priesthood, not all the devices of sin and Satan, can save the vile thing from extermination.

Already a gleam of hope breaks upon us from the southwest. One Southern city has grieved and astonished the whole South by a preference for freedom. The wedge has entered. Dred Scott, of Missouri, goes into slavery, but St. Louis declares for freedom. The judgment of Taney is not the judgment of St. Louis.

It may be said that this demonstration in St. Louis is not to be taken as an evidence of sympathy with the slave; that it is purely a white man's victory. I admit it. Yet I am glad that white men, bad as they generally are, should gain a victory over slavery. I am willing to accept a judgment against slavery, whether supported by white or Black reasons — though I would much rather have it supported by both. He that is not against us, is on our part.

Come what will, I hold it to be morally certain that, sooner or later, by fair means or foul means, in quiet or in tumult, in peace or in blood, in judgment or in mercy, slavery is doomed to cease out of this otherwise goodly land, and liberty is destined to become the settled law of this Republic.

I base my sense of the certain overthrow of slavery, in part, upon the nature of the American Government, the Constitution, the tendencies of the age, and the character of the American people; and this, notwithstanding the important decision of Judge Taney.

I know of no soil better adapted to the growth of reform than American soil. I know of no country where the conditions for affecting great changes in the settled order of things, for the development of right ideas of liberty and humanity, are more favorable than here in these United States.

The very groundwork of this government is a good repository of Christian civilization. The Constitution, as well as the Declaration of Independence, and the sentiments of the founders of the Republic, give us a platform broad enough, and strong enough, to support the most comprehensive plans for the freedom and elevation of all the people of this country, without regard to color, class, or clime.

There is nothing in the present aspect of the anti-slavery question which should drive us into the extravagance and nonsense of advocating a dissolution of the American Union as a means of overthrowing slavery, or freeing the North from the malign influence of slavery upon the morals of the Northern people. While the press is at liberty, and speech is free, and the ballot-box is open to the people of the sixteen free States; while the slaveholders are but four hundred thousand in number, and we are fourteen millions; while the mental and moral power of the nation is with us; while we are really the strong and they are the weak, it would look worse than cowardly to retreat from the Union.

If the people of the North have not the power to cope with these four hundred thousand slaveholders inside the Union, I see not how they could do so outside the Union; indeed, I see not how they could get out of the Union. The strength necessary to move the Union must ever be less than is required to break it up. If we have got to conquer the slave power to get out of the Union, I for one would much rather conquer, and stay in the Union. The latter, it strikes me, is the far more rational mode of action.

I make these remarks in no servile spirit, nor in any superstitious reverence for a mere human arrangement. If I felt the Union to be a curse, I should not be far behind the very chiefest of the disunion Abolitionists in denouncing it. But the evil to be met and abolished is not in the Union. The power arrayed against us is not a parchment.

It is not in changing the dead form of the Union, that slavery is to be abolished in this country. We have to do not with the dead, but the living; not with the past, but the living present.

Those who seek slavery in the Union, and who are everlastingly dealing blows upon the Union, in the belief that they are killing slavery, are most woefully mistaken. They are fighting a dead form instead of a living and powerful reality. It is clearly not because of the peculiar character of our Constitution that we have slavery, but the wicked pride, love of power, and selfish perverseness of the American people. Slavery lives in this country not because of any paper Constitution, but in the moral blindness of the American people, who persuade themselves that they are safe, though the rights of others may be struck down.

Besides, I think it would be difficult to hit upon any plan less likely to abolish slavery than the dissolution of the Union. The most devoted advocates of slavery, those who make the interests of slavery their constant study, seek a dissolution of the Union as their final plan for preserving slavery from Abolition, and their ground is well taken. Slavery lives and flourishes best in the absence of civilization; a dissolution of the Union would shut up the system in its own congenial barbarism.

The dissolution of the Union would not give the North one single additional advantage over slavery to the people of the North, but would manifestly take from them many which they now certainly possess.

Within the Union we have a firm basis of anti-slavery operation. National welfare, national prosperity, national reputation and honor, and national scrutiny; common rights, common duties, and common country, are so many bridges over which we can march to the destruction of slavery. To fling away these advantages because James Buchanan is President, or Judge

Taney gives a lying decision in favor of slavery, does not enter into my notion of common sense.

Mr. Garrison and his friends have been telling us that, while in the Union, we are responsible for slavery; and in so telling us, he and they have told us the truth. But in telling us that we shall cease to be responsible for slavery by dissolving the Union, he and they have not told us the truth.

There now, clearly, is no freedom from responsibility for slavery, but in the Abolition of slavery. We have gone too far in this business now to sum up our whole duty in the cant phrase of "no Union with slaveholders."

To desert the family hearth may place the recreant husband out of the sight of his hungry children, but it cannot free him from responsibility. Though he should roll the waters of three oceans, between him and them, he could not roll from his soul the burden of his responsibility to them; and, as with the private family, so in this instance with the national family. To leave the slave in his chains, in the hands of cruel masters, who are too strong for him, is not to free ourselves from responsibility. Again: If I were on board of a pirate ship, with a company of men and women whose lives and liberties I had put in jeopardy, I would not clear my soul of their blood by jumping in the long boat, and singing out no union with pirates. My business would be to remain on board, and while I never would perform a single act of piracy again, I should exhaust every means given me by my position, to save the lives and liberties of those against whom I had committed piracy. In like manner, I hold it is our duty to remain inside this Union, and use all the power to restore [to the] enslaved millions their precious and God-given rights. The more we have done by our voice and our votes, in times past, to rivet their galling fetters, the more clearly and solemnly comes the sense of duty to remain, to undo what we have done. Where, I ask, could the slave look for release from slavery if the Union were dissolved? I have an abiding conviction founded upon long and careful study of the certain effects of slavery upon the moral sense of slave-holding communities, that if the slaves are ever delivered from bondage, the power will emanate from the free States. All hope that the slaveholders will be self-moved to this great act of justice, is groundless and delusive. Now, as of old, the Redeemer must come from above, not from beneath. To dissolve the Union would be to withdraw the emancipating power from the field.

But I am told this is the argument of expediency. I admit it, and am prepared to show that what is expedient in this instance is right. "Do justice, though the heavens fall." [*Fiat justitia ruat caelum*]

Yes, that is a good motto, but I deny that it would be doing justice to the slave to dissolve the Union and leave the slave in his chains to get out by the clemency of his master, or the strength of his arms. Justice to the slave is to break his chains, and going out of the union is to leave him in his chains, and without any probable chance of getting out of them.

But I come now to the great question as to the constitutionality of slavery. The recent slaveholding decision, as well as the teachings of anti-slavery men, make this a fit time to discuss the constitutional pretensions of slavery.

The people of the North are a law abiding people. They love order and respect the means to that end. This sentiment has sometimes led them to the folly and wickedness of trampling upon the very life of law, to uphold its dead form. This was so in the execution of that thrice accursed Fugitive Slave Bill. Burns and Simms, were sent back to the hell of slavery after they had looked upon Bunker Hill, and heard liberty thunder in Faneuil Hall. The people permitted this outrage in obedience to the popular sentiment of reverence for law. While men thus respect law, it becomes a serious matter so to interpret the law as to make it operate against liberty. I have a quarrel with those who fling the Supreme Law of this land between the slave and freedom. It is a serious matter to fling the weight of the Constitution against the cause of human liberty, and those who do it, take upon them a heavy responsibility. Nothing but absolute necessity, shall, or ought to drive me to such a concession to slavery.

When I admit that slavery is constitutional, I must see slavery recognized in the Constitution. I must see that it is there plainly stated that one man of a certain description has a right of property in the body and soul of another man of a certain description. There must be no room for a doubt. In a matter so important as the loss of liberty, everything must be proved beyond all reasonable doubt.

The well known rules of legal interpretation bear me out in this stubborn refusal to see slavery where slavery is not, and only to see slavery where it is.

The Supreme Court has, in its day, done something better than make slaveholding decisions. It has laid down rules of interpretation which are in harmony with the true idea and object of law and liberty.

It has told us that the intention of legal instruments must prevail; and that this must be collected from its words. It has told us that language must be construed strictly in favor of liberty and justice.

It has told us where rights are infringed, where fundamental principles are overthrown, [and] where the general system of the law is departed from, the Legislative intention must be expressed with irresistible clearness, to induce a court of justice to suppose a design to effect such objects.

These rules are as old as law. They rise out of the very elements of law. It is to protect human rights, and promote human welfare. Law is in its nature opposed to wrong, and must everywhere be presumed to be in favor of the right. The pound of flesh, but not one drop of blood, is a sound rule of legal interpretation.

Besides there is another rule of law as well [as] of common sense, which requires us to look to the ends for which a law is made, and to construe its details in harmony with the ends sought.

Now let us approach the Constitution from the stand-point thus indicated, and instead of finding in it a warrant for the stupendous system of robbery, comprehended in the term slavery, we shall find it strongly against that system.

"We, the people of the United States, in order to form a more perfect Union, establish justice, insure domestic tranquility, provide for the common defence, promote the general welfare, and secure the blessings of liberty to ourselves and our posterity, do ordain and establish this constitution for the United States of America."

Such are the objects announced by the instrument itself, and they are in harmony with the Declaration of

Independence, and the principles of human well-being.

Six objects are here declared, "Union," "defence," "welfare," "tranquility," and "justice," and "liberty."

Neither in the preamble nor in the body of the Constitution is there a single mention of the term *slave* or *slave holder*, *slave master* or *slave state*, neither is there any reference to the color, or the physical peculiarities of any part of the people of the United States. Neither is there anything in the Constitution standing alone, which would imply the existence of slavery in this country.

"We, the people" — not we, the white people — not we, the citizens, or the legal voters — not we, the privileged class, and excluding all other classes but we, the people; not we, the horses and cattle, but we the people — the men and women, the human inhabitants of the United States, do ordain and establish this Constitution, &c.

I ask, then, any man to read the Constitution, and tell me where if he can, in what particular that instrument affords the slightest sanction of slavery?

Where will he find a guarantee for slavery? Will he find it in the declaration that no person shall be deprived of life, liberty, or property, without due process of law? Will he find it in the declaration that the Constitution was established to secure the blessings of liberty? Will he find it in the right of the people to be secure in their persons and papers, and houses, and effects? Will he find it in the clause prohibiting the enactment by any State of a bill of attainder? These all strike at the root of slavery, and any one of them, but faithfully carried out, would put an end to slavery in every State in the American Union.

Take, for example, the prohibition of a bill of attainder. That is a law entailing on the child the misfortunes of the parent. This principle would destroy slavery in every State of the Union.

The law of slavery is a law of attainder. The child is property because its parent was property, and suffers as a slave because its parent suffered as a slave.

Thus the very essence of the whole slave code is in open violation of a fundamental provision of the Constitution, and is in open and flagrant violation of all the objects set forth in the Constitution.

While this and much more can be said, and has been said, and much better said, by Lysander Spooner, William Goodell, Beriah Green, and Gerrit Smith, in favor of the entire unconstitutionality of slavery, what have we on the other side?

How is the constitutionality of slavery made out, or attempted to be made out?

First, by discrediting and casting away as worthless the most beneficent rules of legal interpretation; by disregarding the plain and common sense reading of the instrument itself; by showing that the Constitution does not mean what it says, and says what it does not mean, by assuming that the WRITTEN Constitution is to be interpreted in the light of a SECRET and UNWRITTEN understanding of its framers, which understanding is declared to be in favor of slavery.

It is in this mean, contemptible, underhand method that the Constitution is pressed into the service of slavery. They do not point us to the Constitution itself, for the reason that there is nothing sufficiently explicit for their purpose; but they delight in supposed intentions — intentions nowhere expressed in the Constitution, and everywhere contradicted in the Constitution.

Judge Taney lays down this system of interpreting in this wise: "The general words above quoted would seem to embrace the whole human family, and, if they were used in a similar instrument at this day, would be so understood. But it is too clear for dispute that the enslaved African race were not intended to be included, and formed no part of the people who framed and adopted this declaration; for if the language, as understood in that day, would embrace them, the conduct of the distinguished men who framed the Declaration of Independence would have been utterly and flagrantly inconsistent with the principles they asserted; and instead of the sympathy of mankind, to which they appealed, they would have deserved and received universal rebuke and reprobation."

"It is difficult, at this day, to realize the state of public opinion respecting that unfortunate class with the civilized and enlightened portion of the world at the time of the Declaration of Independence and the adoption of the Constitution; but history shows they had, for more than a century, been regarded as beings of an inferior order, and unfit associates for the white race, either socially or politically, and had no rights which white men are bound to respect; and the Black man might be reduced to slavery, bought and sold, and treated as an ordinary article of merchandise. This opinion, at that time, was fixed and universal with the civilized portion of the white race. It was regarded as an axiom of morals, which no one thought of disputing, and every one habitually acted upon it, without doubting, for a moment, the correctness of the opinion. And in no nation was this opinion more fixed, and generally acted upon, than in England; the subjects of which government not only seized them on the coast of Africa, but took them, as ordinary merchandise, to where they could make a profit on them. The opinion, thus entertained, was universally maintained on the colonies this side of the Atlantic; accordingly, Negroes of the African race were regarded by them as property, and held and bought and sold as such in every one of the thirteen colonies which united in the Declaration of Independence, and afterwards formed the Constitution."

The argument here is, that the Constitution comes down to us from a slaveholding period and a slaveholding people; and that, therefore, we are bound to suppose that the Constitution recognizes colored persons of African descent, the victims of slavery at that time, as debarred forever from all participation in the benefit of the Constitution and the Declaration of Independence, although the plain reading of both includes them in their beneficent range.

As a man, an American, a citizen, a colored man of both Anglo-Saxon and African descent, I denounce this representation as a most scandalous and devilish perversion of the Constitution, and a brazen misstatement of the facts of history.

But I will not content myself with mere denunciation; I invite attention to the facts.

It is a fact, a great historic fact, that at the time of the adoption of the Constitution, the leading religious denominations in this land were anti-slavery, and were laboring for the emancipation of the colored people of African descent.

The church of a country is often a better index of the state of opinion and feeling than is even the government itself.

The Methodists, Baptists, Presbyterians, and the denomination of Friends, were actively opposing slavery, denouncing the system of bondage, with language as burning and sweeping as we employ at this day.

Take the Methodists. In 1780, that denomination said: "The Conference acknowledges that slavery is contrary to the laws of God, man, and nature, and hurtful to society — contrary to the dictates of conscience and true religion, and doing to others that we would not do unto us." In 1784, the same church declared, "that those who buy, sell, or give slaves away, except for the purpose to free them, shall be expelled immediately." In 1785, it spoke even more stringently on the subject. It then said: "We hold in the deepest abhorrence the practice of slavery, and shall not cease to seek its destruction by all wise and proper means."

So much for the position of the Methodist Church in the early history of the Republic, in those days of darkness to which Judge Taney refers.

Let us now see how slavery was regarded by the Presbyterian Church at that early date.

In 1794, the General Assembly of that body pronounced the following judgment in respect to slavery, slaveholders, and slaveholding.

"1st Timothy, 1st chapter, 10th verse: 'The law was made for man-stealers.' 'This crime among the Jews exposed the perpetrators of it to capital punishment.' Exodus, xxi, 15. —And the apostle here classes them with sinners of the first rank. The word he uses in its original import, comprehends all who are concerned in bringing any of the human race into slavery, or in retaining them in it. Stealers of men are all those who bring off slaves or freemen, and keep, sell, or buy them. 'To steal a freeman,' says Grotius, 'is the highest kind of theft.' In other instances, we only steal human property, but when we steal or retain men in slavery, we seize those who, in common with ourselves, are constituted, by the original grant, lords of the earth."

I might quote, at length, from the sayings of the Baptist Church and the sayings of eminent divines at this early period, showing that Judge Taney has grossly falsified history, but will not detain you with these quotations.

The testimony of the church, and the testimony of the founders of this Republic, from the declaration downward, prove Judge Taney false: as false to history as he is to law.

Washington and Jefferson, and Adams, and Jay, and Franklin, and Rush, and Hamilton, and a host of others, held no such degrading views on the subject as are imputed by Judge Taney to the Fathers of the Republic.

All, at that time, looked for the gradual but certain abolition of slavery, and shaped the constitution with a view to this grand result.

George Washington can never be claimed as a fanatic, or as the representative of fanatics. The slaveholders impudently use his name for the base purpose of giving respectability to slavery. Yet, in a letter to Robert Morris, Washington uses this language — language which, at this day, would make him a terror of the slaveholders, and the natural representative of the Republican party.

"There is not a man living, who wishes more sincerely than I do, to see some plan adopted for the abolition of slavery; but there is only one proper and effectual mode by which it can be accomplished, and that is by Legislative authority; and this, as far as my suffrage will go, shall not be wanting."

Washington only spoke the sentiment of his times. There were, at that time, Abolition societies in the slave States — Abolition societies in Virginia, in North Carolina, in Maryland, in Pennsylvania, and in Georgia — all slaveholding States. Slavery was so weak, and liberty so strong, that free speech could attack the monster to its teeth. Men were not mobbed and driven out of the presence of slavery, merely because they condemned the slave system. The system was then on its knees imploring to be spared, until it could get itself decently out of the world.

In the light of these facts, the Constitution was framed, and framed in conformity to it.

It may, however, be asked, if the Constitution were so framed that the rights of all the people were naturally protected by it, how happens it that a large part of the people have been held in slavery ever since its adoption? Have the people mistaken the requirements of their own Constitution?

The answer is ready. The Constitution is one thing, its administration is another, and, in this instance, a very different and opposite thing. I am here to vindicate the law, not the administration of the law. It is the written Constitution, not the unwritten Constitution, that is now before us. If, in the whole range of the Constitution, you can find no warrant for slavery, then we may properly claim it for liberty.

Good and wholesome laws are often found dead on the statute book. We may condemn the practice under them and against them, but never the law itself. To condemn the good law with the wicked practice, is to weaken, not to strengthen our testimony.

It is no evidence that the Bible is a bad book, because those who profess to believe the Bible are bad. The slaveholders of the South, and many of their wicked allies at the North, claim the Bible for slavery; shall we, therefore, fling the Bible away as a pro-slavery book? It would be as reasonable to do so as it would be to fling away the Constitution.

We are not the only people who have illustrated the truth, that a people may have excellent law, and detestable practices. Our Savior denounces the Jews, because they made void the law by their traditions. We have been guilty of the same sin.

The American people have made void our Constitution by just such traditions as Judge Taney and Mr. Garrison have been giving to the world of late, as the true light in which to view the Constitution of the United States. I shall follow neither. It is not what Moses allowed for the hardness of heart, but what God requires, [which] ought to be the rule.

It may be said that it is quite true that the Constitution was designed to secure the blessings of liberty and justice to the people who made it, and to the posterity of the people who made it, but was never designed to do any such thing for the colored people of African descent.

This is Judge Taney's argument, and it is Mr. Garrison's argument, but it is not the argument of the Constitution. The Constitution imposes no such mean and satanic limitations upon its own beneficent operation. And, if the Constitution makes none, I beg to know what right has any body, outside of the Constitution, for the special accommodation of slave-holding villainy, to impose such a construction upon the Constitution?

The Constitution knows all the human inhabitants of this country as "the people." It makes, as I have said before, no discrimination in favor of, or against, any class of the people, but is fitted to protect and preserve the rights of all, without reference to color, size, or any physical peculiarities. Besides, it has been shown by William Goodell and others, that in eleven out of the old thirteen States, colored men were legal voters at the time of the adoption of the Constitution.

In conclusion, let me say, all I ask of the American people is, that they live up to the Constitution, adopt its principles, imbibe its spirit and enforce its provisions.

When this is done, the wounds of my bleeding people will be healed, the chain will no longer rust on their ankles, their backs will no longer be torn by the bloody lash, and liberty, the glorious birthright of our common humanity, will become the inheritance of all the inhabitants of this highly favored country.[115]

---

[115] *Two Speeches by Frederick Douglass; One on West India Emancipation . . . and the Other on the Dred Scott Decision, Delivered in New York, on the Occasion of the Anniversary of the American Abolition Society*, May, 1857 (Rochester: C. P. Dewey, 1857).

The Ballot and the Bullet – "He has preached both the ballot and the bullet as means by which slavery is to be destroyed and men have refused to employ either the one or the other, and the preacher has become discouraged. Let him discard both the ballot and the bullet, and as the best agent for the enfranchisement of man wield the sword of the spirit which divides Truth from Error, which separates between the Right and the Wrong. Then, when the weapon falls from his hand in death, he will be able to say with a cheerful tone and exulting heart, 'By this have I conquered.'"

The advice given above is addressed to our friend Gerrit Smith, by the *Anti-Slavery Bugle*, an organ of the non-voting theory. It sounds to us very much like nonsense, but may strike others differently. If the anti-slavery cause has failed, the ballot and the bullet are as little to blame for it as is the so-called *"sword of the spirit*," which simply means, in the columns of the *Bugle*, telling men to do that which Garrisonians will not do themselves. They tell the Government to pass laws for the abolition of slavery, but will not themselves vote for such a law. They tell their State legislatures to pass Personal Liberty Bills, but will not themselves vote for such men as will pass such bills. They denounce pro-slavery voting, but will not themselves cast an anti-slavery vote. Their cry is "no union with slaveholders," and yet they equally, with others, help to support the Government and consume the produce of the slave. Their money goes equally with others into the national treasury, and into the pockets of slave-drivers. While they "discard" both the ballot and the bullet, they seem to give no better proof of vitality and power than those who discard neither. Far be it from us to undervalue the power of truth when honestly addressed to the hearts and consciences of men; but truth to be efficient must be uttered in action as well as in speech.

If speech alone could have abolished slavery, the work would have been done long ago. What we want is an anti-slavery Government, in harmony with anti-slavery speech, one which will give effect to our words, and translate them into acts. For this, the ballot is needed, and if this will not be heard and heeded, then the bullet. We have had cant enough, and are sick of it. When anti-slavery laws are wanted, anti-slavery men should vote for them, and when a slave is to be snatched from the hand of a kidnapper, physical force is needed, and he who gives it proves himself a more useful anti-slavery man than he who refuses to give it, and contents himself by talking of a "sword of the spirit."[116]

---

[116] *Douglass' Monthly*, October, 1859.

Captain John Brown Not Insane – One of the most painful incidents connected with the name of this old hero, is the attempt to prove him insane. Many journals have contributed to this effort from a friendly desire to shield the prisoner from Virginia's cowardly vengeance. This is a mistaken friendship, which seeks to rob him of his true character and dim the glory of his deeds, in order to save his life. Was there the faintest hope of securing his release by this means, we would choke down our indignation and be silent. But a Virginia court would hang a crazy man without a moment's hesitation, if his insanity took the form of hatred of oppression; and this plea only blasts the reputation of this glorious martyr of liberty, without the faintest hope of improving his chance of escape.

It is an appalling fact in the history of the American people, that they have so far forgotten their own heroic age, as readily to accept the charge of insanity against a man who has imitated the heroes of Lexington, Concord, and Bunker Hill.

It is an effeminate and cowardly age, which calls a man a lunatic because he rises to such self-forgetful heroism, as to count his own life as worth nothing in comparison with the freedom of millions of his fellows. Such an age would have sent Gideon to a madhouse, and put Leonidas in a strait-jacket. Such a people would have treated the defenders of Thermopylae as demented, and shut up Caius Marcus in bedlam. Such a marrowless population as ours has become under the debaucheries of Slavery, would have struck the patriot's crown from the brow of Wallace, and recommended blisters and bleeding to the heroic Tell. Wallace was often and again as desperately forgetful of his own life in defense of Scotland's freedom, as was Brown in striking for the American slave; and Tell's defiance of the Austrian tyrant, was as far above the appreciation of cowardly selfishness as was Brown's defiance of the Virginia pirates. Was Arnold Winkelried insane when he rushed to his death upon an army of spears, crying "make way for Liberty!" Are heroism and insanity synonyms in our American dictionary? Heaven help us! when our loftiest types of patriotism, our sublimest historic ideals of philanthropy, come to be treated as evidence of moon-struck madness. Posterity will owe everlasting thanks to John Brown for lifting up once more to the gaze of a nation grown fat and flabby on the garbage of lust and oppression, a true standard of heroic philanthropy, and each coming generation will pay its installment of the debt. No wonder that the aiders and abettors of the huge, overshadowing and many-armed tyranny, which he grappled with in its own infernal den, should call him a madman; but for those who profess a regard for him, and for human freedom, to join in the cruel slander, "is the unkindest cut of all."

Nor is it necessary to attribute Brown's deeds to the spirit of vengeance, invoked by the murder of his brave boys. That the barbarous cruelty from which he has suffered had its effect in intensifying his hatred of slavery, is doubtless true. But his own statement, that he had been contemplating a bold strike for the freedom of the slaves for ten years, proves that he had resolved upon his present course long before he, or his sons, ever set foot in Kansas. His entire procedure in this matter disproves the charge that he was prompted by an impulse of mad revenge, and shows that he was moved by the highest principles of philanthropy. His carefulness of the lives of unarmed persons — his humane and courteous treatment of his prisoners — his cool self-possession all through his trial — and especially his calm, dignified speech on receiving his sentence, all conspire to show that he was neither insane or actuated by vengeful passion; and we hope that the country has heard the last of John Brown's madness. The explanation of his conduct is perfectly natural and simple on its face. He believes the Declaration of Independence to be true, and the Bible to be a guide to human conduct, and acting upon the doctrines of both, he threw himself against the serried ranks of American oppression, and translated into heroic deeds the love of liberty and hatred of tyrants, with which he was inspired from both these forces acting upon his philanthropic and heroic soul.

This age is too gross and sensual to appreciate his deeds, and so calls him mad; but the future will write his epitaph upon the hearts of a people freed from slavery, because he struck the first effectual blow.

Not only is it true that Brown's whole movement proves him perfectly sane and free from merely revengeful passion, but he has struck the bottom line of the philosophy which underlies the abolition movement. He has attacked slavery with the weapons precisely adapted to bring it to the death. Moral considerations have long since been exhausted upon slaveholders. It is in vain to reason with them. One might as well hunt bears with ethics and political economy for weapons, as to seek to "pluck the spoiled out of the hand of the oppressor" by the mere force of moral law. Slavery is a system of brute force. It shields itself behind might, rather than right. It must be met with its own weapons. Capt. Brown has initiated a new mode of carrying on the crusade of freedom, and his blow has sent dread and terror throughout the entire ranks of the piratical army of slavery. His daring deeds may cost him his life, but priceless as is the value of that life, the blow he has struck, will, in the end, prove to be worth its mighty cost. Like Samson, he has laid his hands upon the pillars of this great national temple of cruelty and blood, and when he falls, that temple will speedily crumble to its final doom, burying its denizens in its ruins.[117]

---

[117] *Douglass' Monthly*, November 1859.

The Real Peril of the Republic - Denied, as we are, by a feeling in the country which we will not now stop to characterize, the humble privilege of active exertion with others in upholding the national flag and suppressing the present raging slaveholding rebellion, the next best thing, perhaps, is to watch the course of the conflict, observe the weak points of the enemy, mark the mistakes of friends, declare the sources of danger, and to point out the true method of avoiding them. Speaking as we do, only once in each month, our communication ought to possess something of the quality of history. Indeed, a paper published monthly can be, in these fast times, a newspaper to but very few. The mission of our journal is, therefore, to be a faithful recorder, not of all events touching the great conflict going on between liberty and slavery in this country, whether in the field or in the councils of the nation, but of the most important of them, and enough of them, to enable all, whether nearby or afar off, who may read our journal, to form an intelligent judgment in respect to the character of the whole controversy. In this capacity of recorder, it is our duty, as already stated, to observe and criticise what is passing before us.

Let it, then, be borne in mind, that if this great American Government of ours — the pride of its people, and the admiration of the friends of freedom throughout the world —shall now, in this the first great trial of its strength, go down into the gloomy depths of social confusion, and into the midnight darkness of wild anarchy and chaos, the fact will not be explained by the tremendous power or extraordinary ability arrayed against it — for the rebels are notoriously a miserable, ill clad, ill fed, ill armed and poverty-stricken set. — This is a well ascertained fact. Our Government will not perish by these miserable foes, nor by want of a good cause to defend, or the necessary physical material to defend that cause. On this point there is no doubt anywhere at the North, or at the South, at home or abroad. Our Government is opulent in all the materials and munitions of war. Men and money flow to its standard in defeat as well as in victory, like the rushing waters of Erie to those of Ontario. All that great wealth, physical bravery, and military skill can do to save the country, will doubtless be done. If we fail, we shall fail by moral causes, not by outward strength, but by internal weakness. Physical power is important — bread is indispensable — but nations, no more than individuals, can live by bread alone. The thing which we wish here and now to urge upon public attention, and which is the central ideal of all our lectures through the country, is, that no amount of physical courage or strength can possibly supply the place of *wisdom and justice.*

In the prosecution of the war, thus far, our Government has shown its poverty and destitution nowhere more than in respect to these virtues. It has not been wise, because it has blindly refused to cultivate the friendship and welcome the co-operation of the four million slaves, the main dependence of the rebels for the money and means for overthrowing the Government. It has not been just in that it has doggedly refused to give liberty to these bondmen, when it has clearly the right and the power to do so, and when it was plainly its duty to do so.

Herein is the weakness of the Government, and if it fails, the failure will be terribly aggravated by this reflection. If the Government could fall in a manly struggle to advance the cause of freedom and justice towards a long enslaved people, it would be glorious even in its fall. But we are fighting no such battle, and hence are trammeled and weakened both from within and from without. — We are still fighting the enemy with only one hand, leaving the other not free, but fettered. We not only refuse to strike the slaveholders with both hands, but so completely disable ourselves by slavery as to give them decided advantages in striking us with both theirs.—The old folly is still upon us, and doing us the utmost damage—the delusive and neither-hot-nor-cold spirit of compromise. Our Government is still in bondage to fear, not that which the battle field inspires, but of the political power of slavery. It is regarded the rock which breaks in pieces all who fall upon it, and grinds into powder all upon whom it falls. Hence we are endeavoring to whip the slaveholders without seriously hurting them. In other words, we are allowing our contempt for the rights of man, and our old scrupulous regard for the interests of slaveholders to control all our movements towards the rebels, hoping to gain by conciliation instead of conquering by arms. Does a poor slave escape from his bondage and seek refuge within our lines on the Potomac—Gen. Banks promptly permits his recapture and rendition to bondage. Does a man of color offer his services to the Government to aid in suppressing the slaveholding rebellion — his application is contemptuously rejected. Does a Massachusetts regiment allow a few colored servants of the officers to appear in uniform — the Secretary of War, Mr. Cameron, at once orders them to be disrobed. Does Major-General Freemont proclaim that the slaves of traitors and rebels shall be hereafter treated as free men — the President of the United States comes promptly forward to shield the rebels from such extreme punishment.

The future historian will look at the facts of this war for the suppression of rebellion with astonishment. He will marvel at the conduct of the Government, and if he writes truly, he will write that while the people had heroism in the field, they had cowardice in the Cabinet, and that the latter counteracted the good effected by the former; that while the brave

Northern troops thought they were pouring out their warm hearts' blood for universal liberty, the Cabinet was plotting that no harm should come to slavery; that while a faithful General was levelling his heaviest bolt at the head of rebellion in Missouri, the President was interposing a statute book to soften the blow.

But we are told that this is but the anti-slavery view of the action of the Government towards the war. We admit it, and plead that it is exceedingly difficult for us, or for anybody else, to contemplate the action of the Federal Government in reference to the present slaveholding rebellion, without making slavery our base line of observation. Every doctrine, principle and measure of the rebels has reference to that system. All that they say of the right of self-government, the defence of their institutions, their homes and their firesides, has no other meaning than the security, safety, prosperity and ascendency of slavery. The war on their part is a war for slavery, and only for slavery. This is at once the motive, the object, and the means of prosecuting the war. For slavery they brave all danger, endure all hardships, and perpetrate all crimes. This is the unconcealed and everywhere apparent purpose of the rebels. We repeat this, not because it is unknown, but because the fact is sought to be ignored, or is but imperfectly recognized by the Government at Washington.

Up to the present moment it deals only with the fact of rebellion. It sees two or three hundred thousand armed rebels marshaled for the overthrow of the Government, for the dissolution of the Union, and for the erection of a new Government and a new Union on the ruins of the old Government and the old Union; but it does not trouble itself with any other fact.

Herein is the secret of the disapproval of General Fremont's Proclamation. That document strikes the rebellion at its source. It looks beyond the effect to the cause, and dares to grapple with that cause. It has in it not only the vigor of the warrior, but the wisdom of the statesman. Until the Government shall take similar ground to that proclaimed at St. Louis, it will have failed to have returned the only true and logical answer to the rebels and traitors, and to secure for itself the respect and sympathy of the friends of freedom the world over, and what is better still, the consciousness of having conformed to the highest dictates of justice and wisdom.[118]

---

[118] *Douglass' Monthly*, October 1861.

What Shall Be Done with the Slaves If Emancipated?
– It is curious to observe, at this juncture, when the existence of slavery is threatened by an aroused nation, when national necessity is combining with an enlightened sense of justice to put away the huge abomination forever, that the enemies of human liberty are resorting to all the old and ten thousand times refuted objections to emancipation with which they confronted the abolition movement twenty-five years ago. Like the one stated above, these pro-slavery objections have their power mainly in the slavery-engendered prejudice, which everywhere pervades the country. Like all other great transgressions of the law of eternal rectitude, slavery thus produces an element in the popular and depraved moral senti-ment favorable to its own existence. These objections are often urged with a show of sincere solicitude for the welfare of the slaves themselves. It is said, what will you do with them? they can't take care of themselves; they would all come to the North; they would not work; they would become a burden upon the State, and a blot upon society; they'd cut their masters' throats; they would cheapen labor, and crowd out the poor white laborer from employment; their former masters would not employ them, and they would necessarily become vagrants, paupers and criminals, overrunning all our alms houses, jails and prisons. The laboring classes among the whites would

come in bitter conflict with them in all the avenues of labor, and regarding them as occupying places and filling positions which should be occupied and filled by white men; a fierce war of races would be the inevitable consequence, and the Black race would, of course, (being the weaker,) be exterminated. In view of this frightful, though happily somewhat contradictory picture, the question is asked, and pressed with a great show of earnestness at this momentous crisis of our nation's history, What shall be done with the four million slaves if they are emancipated?

This question has been answered, and can be answered in many ways. Primarily, it is a question less for man than for God — less for human intellect than for the laws of nature to solve. It assumes that nature has erred; that the law of liberty is a mistake; that freedom, though a natural want of the human soul, can only be enjoyed at the expense of human welfare, and that men are better off in slavery than they would or could be in freedom; that slavery is the natural order of human relations, and that liberty is an experiment. What shall be done with them?

Our answer is, do nothing with them; mind your business, and let them mind theirs. Your *doing* with them is their greatest misfortune. They have been undone by your doings, and all they now ask, and really have need of at your hands, is just to let them alone. They suffer by every interference, and succeed best by being let alone. The Negro should have been let alone in Africa — let alone when the pirates and robbers offered him for sale in our Christian slave markets — (more cruel and inhuman than the Mohammedan slave markets) — let alone by courts, judges, politicians, legislators and slave-drivers — let alone altogether, and assured that they were thus to be let alone forever, and that they must now make their own way in the world, just the same as any and every other variety of the human family. As colored men, we only ask to be allowed to do with ourselves, subject only to the same great laws for the welfare of human society which apply to other men, Jews, Gentiles, Barbarian, Sythian. Let us stand upon our own legs, work with our own hands, and eat bread in the sweat of our own brows. When you, our white fellow-countrymen, have attempted to do anything for us, it has generally been to deprive us of some right, power or privilege which you yourselves would die before you would submit to have taken from you. When the planters of the West Indies used to attempt to puzzle the pure minded Wilberforce with the question, How shall we get rid of slavery? his simple answer was, "quit stealing." In like manner, we answer those who are perpetually puzzling their brains with questions as to what shall be done with the Negro, "let him alone and mind your own business." If you see him plowing in the open field, leveling the forest, at work with a spade, a rake, a hoe, a pick-axe, or a bill — let him alone; he has a right to work. If you see him on his way to school, with spelling book, geography and arithmetic in his hands — let him alone. Don't shut the door in his face, nor bolt your gates against him; he has a right to learn — let him alone. Don't pass laws to degrade him. If he has a ballot in his hand, and is on his way to the ballotbox to deposit his vote for the man whom he thinks will most justly and wisely administer the Government which has the power of life and death over him, as well as others — let him *alone*; his right of choice as much deserves respect and protection as your own. If you see him on his way to the church, exercising religious liberty in accordance with this or that religious persuasion — let him alone. — Don't meddle with him, nor trouble yourselves with any questions as to what shall be done with him.

The great majority of human duties are of this negative character. If men were born in need of crutches, instead of having legs, the fact would be otherwise. We should then be in need of help, and would require outside aid; but according to the wiser and better arrangement of nature, our duty is done better by not hindering than by helping our fellow-men; or, in other words, the best way to help them is just to let them help themselves.

We would not for one moment check the outgrowth of any benevolent concern for the future welfare of the colored race in America or elsewhere; but in the name of reason and religion, we earnestly plead for justice before all else. Benevolence with justice is harmonious and beautiful; but benevolence without justice is a mockery. Let the American people, who have thus far only kept the colored race staggering between partial philanthropy and cruel force, be induced to try what virtue there is in justice. First pure, then peaceable — first just, then generous. — The sum of the Black man's misfortunes and calamities are just here: He is everywhere treated as an exception to all the general rules which should operate in the relations of other men. He is literally scourged beyond the beneficent range of truth and justice. — With all the purifying and liberalizing power of the Christian religion, teaching, as it does, meekness, gentleness, brotherly kindness, those who profess it have not yet even approached the position of treating the Black man as an equal man and a brother. The few who have thus far risen to this requirement, both of reason and religion, are stigmatized as fanatics and enthusiasts.

What shall be done with the Negro if emancipated? Deal justly with him. He is a human being, capable of judging between good and evil, right and wrong, liberty and slavery, and is as much a subject of law as any other man; therefore, deal justly with him. He is, like other men, sensible of the motives of reward and punishment. Give him wages for his work, and let hunger pinch him if he don't work. He knows the difference between fullness and famine, plenty and scarcity. "But will he work?" Why should he not? He is used to it, and is not afraid of it. His hands are already hardened by toil, and he has no dreams of ever getting a living by any other means than by hard work. But would you turn them all loose? Certainly! We are no better than our Creator. He has turned them loose, and why should not we?

But would you let them all stay here? — Why not? What better is *here* than *there*? Will they occupy more room as freemen than as slaves? Is the presence of a Black freeman less agreeable than that of a Black slave? Is an object of your injustice and cruelty a more ungrateful sight than one of your justice and benevolence? You have borne the one more than two hundred years — can't you bear the other long enough to try the experiment? "But would it be safe?" No good reason can be given why it would not be. There is much more reason for apprehension from slavery than from freedom. Slavery provokes and justifies incendiarism, murder, robbery, assassination, and all manner of violence. — But why not let them go off by themselves? That is a matter we would leave exclusively to themselves. Besides, when you, the American people, shall once do justice to the enslaved colored people, you will not want to get rid of them.

Take away the motive which slavery supplies for getting rid of the free Black people of the South, and there is not a single State, from Maryland to Texas, which would desire to be rid of its Black people. Even with the obvious disadvantage to slavery, which such contact is, there is scarcely a slave State which could be carried for the unqualified expulsion of the free colored people. Efforts at such expulsion have been made in Maryland, Virginia and South Carolina, and all have failed, just because the Black man as a freeman is a useful member of society. To drive him away, and thus deprive the South of his labor, would be as absurd and monstrous as for a man to cut off his right arm, the better to enable himself to work.

There is one cheering aspect of this revival of the old and thread-bare objections to emancipation — it implies at least the presence of danger to the slave system. When slavery was assailed twenty-five years ago, the whole land took the alarm, and every species of argument and subterfuge was resorted to by the defenders of slavery. The mental activity was amazing; all sorts of excuses, political, economical, social, ethical, theological and ethnological, were coined into barricades against the advancing march of anti-slavery sentiment. The same activity now shows itself, but has added nothing new to the argument for slavery or against emancipation. — When the accursed slave system shall once be abolished, and the Negro, long cast out from the human family, and governed like a beast of burden, shall be gathered under the divine government of justice, liberty and humanity, men will be ashamed to remember that they were ever deluded by the flimsy nonsense which they have allowed themselves to urge against the freedom of the long enslaved millions of our land. That day is not far off.

O hasten it in mercy, gracious Heaven![119]

---

[119] *Douglass' Monthly*, January 1862.

Emancipation Proclaimed – Common sense, the necessities of the war, to say nothing of the dictation of justice and humanity have at last prevailed. We shout for joy that we live to record this righteous decree. Abraham Lincoln, President of the United States, Commander-in-Chief of the army and navy, in his own peculiar cautious, forbearing and hesitating way, slow, but we hope sure, has, while the loyal heart was near breaking with despair, proclaimed and declared: "*That on the first of January, in the year of our lord one thousand, eight hundred and sixty-three, all persons held as slaves within any State or any designated part of a State, the people whereof shall then be in rebellion against the United States, shall be thenceforward and forever free.*" "Free forever" oh! long enslaved millions, whose cries have so vexed the air and sky, suffer on a few more days in sorrow, the hour of your great deliverance draws nigh! oh! ye millions of free and loyal men who have earnestly sought to free your bleeding country from the dreadful ravages of revolution and anarchy, lift up now your voices with joy and thanksgiving for with freedom to the slave will come peace and safety to your country. President Lincoln has embraced in this proclamation the law of Congress passed more than six months ago, prohibiting the employment of any part of the army and naval forces of the United States, to return fugitive slaves to their masters commanded all officers of the army and navy to respect and obey its provisions. He has still further declared his intention to urge upon the Legislature of all the slave States not in rebellion the immediate or gradual abolishment of slavery. But read the proclamation for it is the most important of any to which the President of the United States has ever signed his name.

Opinions will widely differ as to the practical effect of this measure upon the war. All that class at the North who have not lost their affection for slavery will regard the measure as the very worst that could be devised, and as likely lead to endless mischief. All their plans for the future have been projected with a view to a reconstruction of the American Government upon the basis of compromise between slaveholding and non-slaveholding States. The thought of a country unified in sentiments, objects and ideas, has not entered into their political calculations, and hence this newly declared policy of the Government, which contemplates one glorious homogeneous people, doing away at a blow with the whole class of compromisers and corrupters will meet their stern opposition. Will that opposition prevail? Will it lead the President to reconsider and retract? Not a word of it. Abraham Lincoln may be slow, Abraham Lincoln may desire peace even at the price of leaving our terrible national sore untouched, to fester on for generations, but Abraham Lincoln is not the man to reconsider, retract and contradict words and purposes solemnly proclaimed over his official signature.

The careful, and we think, the slothful deliberation which he has observed in reaching this obvious policy, is a guarantee against retraction. But even if the temper and spirit of the President himself were other than what they are, events greater than the President, events which have slowly wrung this proclamation from him may be relied on to carry him forward in the same direction. To look back now would only load him with heavier evils, while diminishing his ability, for overcoming those with which he now has to contend. To recall his proclamation would only increase rebel pride, rebel sense of power and would be hailed as a direct admission of weakness on the part of the Federal Government, while it would cause heaviness of heart and depression of national enthusiasm all over the loyal North and West. No, Abraham Lincoln, will take no step backward. His word has gone out over the country and the world, giving joy and gladness to the friends of freedom and progress wherever those words are read, and he will stand by them, and carry them out to the letter. If he has taught us to confide in nothing else, he has taught us to confide in his word. The want of Constitutional power, the want of military power, the tendency of the measure to intensify Southern hate, and to exasperate the rebels, the tendency to drive from him all that class of Democrats at the North, whose loyalty has been conditioned on his restoring the union as it was, slavery and all, have all been considered, and he has taken his ground notwithstanding. The President, doubtless saw, as we see, that it is not more absurd to talk about restoring the union, without hurting slavery, than restoring the union without hurting the rebels. As to exasperating the South, there can be no more in the cup than the cup will hold, and that was full already. The whole situation having been carefully scanned, before Mr. Lincoln could be made to budge an inch, he will now stand his ground. Border State influence, and the influence of half loyal men have been exerted and have done their worst. The end of these two influences is implied in this proclamation. Hereafter, the inspiration as well as the men and the money for carrying on the war will come from the North, and not from half loyal border States.

The effect of this paper upon the disposition of Europe will be great and increasing. It changes the character of the war in European eyes and gives it an important principle as an object, instead of national pride and interest. It recognizes, and declares the real nature of the contest, and places the North on the side of justice and civilization, and the rebels on the side of robbery and barbarism. It will disarm all purpose on the part of European Government to intervene in favor of the rebels and thus cast off at a blow one source of rebel power. All through the war thus far, the rebel ambassadors in foreign countries have been able to silence all expression of sympathy with the North as to slavery. With much more than a show of truth, they said that the Federal Government, no more than the Confederate Government, contemplated the abolition of slavery.

But will not this measure be frowned upon by our officers and men in the field? We have heard of many thousands, who have resolved that they will throw up their commissions and lay down their arms, just so soon as they are required to carry on a war against slavery. Making all allowances for exaggeration there are doubtless far too many of this sort in the loyal army. Putting this kind of loyalty and patriotism to the test, will be one of the best collateral effects of the measure. Any man who leaves the field on such a ground will be an argument in favor of the proclamation, and will prove that his heart has been more with slavery than with his country. Let the army be cleansed from all such pro-slavery vermin, and its health and strength will be greatly improved. But there can be no reason to fear the loss of many officers or men by resignation or desertion. We have no doubt that the measure was brought to the attention of most of our leading Generals, and blind as some of them have seemed to be in the earlier part of the war, most of them have seen enough to convince them that there can be no end to this war that does not end slavery. At any rate, we may hope that for every proslavery man that shall start from the ranks of our loyal army, there will be two anti-slavery men to fill up the vacancy, and in this war one truly devoted to the cause of Emancipation is worth two of the opposite sort.

Whether slavery will be abolished in the manner now proposed by President Lincoln, depends of course upon two conditions, the first specified and the second implied. The first is that the slave States shall be in rebellion on after the first day of January 1863 and the second is we must have the ability to put down that rebellion. About the first there can be very little doubt. The South is thoroughly in earnest and confident. It has staked everything upon the rebellion. Its experience thus far in the field has rather increased its hopes of final success than diminished them. Its armies now hold us at bay at all points, and the war is confined to the border States slave and free. If Richmond were in our hands and Virginia at our mercy, the vast regions beyond would still remain to be subdued. But the rebels confront us on the Potomac, the Ohio, and the Mississippi. Kentucky, Maryland, Missouri, and Virginia are in debate on the battle fields and their people are divided by the line which separates treason from loyalty. In short we are yet, after eighteen months of war, confined to the outer margin of the rebellion. We have scarcely more than touched the surface of the terrible evil. It has been raising large quantities of food during the past summer. While the masters have been fighting abroad, the slaves have been busy working at home to supply them with the means of continuing the struggle. They will not down at the bidding of this Proclamation, but may be safely relied upon till January and long after January. A month or two will put an end to general fighting for the winter. When the leaves fall we shall hear again of bad roads, winter quarters and spring campaigns. The South which has thus far withstood our arms will not fall at once before our pens. All fears for the abolition of slavery arising from this apprehension may be dismissed. Whoever therefore, lives to see the first day of next January, should Abraham Lincoln be then alive and President of the United States may confidently look in the morning papers for the final proclamation, granting freedom, and freedom forever, to all slaves within the rebel States. On the next point nothing need be said. We have full power to put down the rebellion. Unless one man is more than a match for four, unless the South breeds braver and better men than the North, unless, slavery is more precious than liberty, unless a just cause kindles a feebler enthusiasm than a wicked and villinous one, the men of the loyal States will put down this rebellion and slavery, and all the sooner will they put down that rebellion by coupling slavery with that object. Tenderness towards slavery has been the loyal weakness during the war. Fighting the slave-holders with one hand and holding the slaves with the other, has been fairly tried and has failed. We have now inaugurated a wiser and better policy, a policy which is better for the loyal cause than an hundred thousand armed men. The Star Spangled banner is now the harbinger of Liberty and the millions in bondage, inured to hardships, accustomed to toil, ready to suffer, ready to fight, to dare and to die, will rally under that banner wherever they see it gloriously unfolded to the breeze. Now let the Government go forward in its mission of Liberty as the only condition of peace and union, by weeding out the army and navy of all such officers as the late Col. Miles, whose sympathies are now known to have been with the rebels. Let only the men who assent heartily to the wisdom and the justice of the anti-slavery policy of the Government be lifted into command; let the Black man have an arm as well as a heart in this war, and the tide of battle which has thus far only waved backward and forward, will steadily set in our favor. The rebellion suppressed, slavery abolished, and America will, higher than ever, sit as a queen among the nations of the earth.

Now for the work. During the interval between now and next January, let every friend of the long enslaved bondman do his utmost in swelling the tide of anti-slavery sentiment, by writing, speaking, money and example. Let our aim be to make the North a unit in favor of the President's policy, and see to it that our voices and votes, shall forever extinguish that latent and malignant sentiment at the North, which has from the first cheered on the rebels in their atrocious crimes against the union, and has systematically sought to paralyze the national arm in striking down the slaveholding rebellion. We are ready for this service or any other, in this, we trust the last struggle with the monster slavery.[120]

---

[120] *Douglass' Monthly*, October 1862.

The Work of the Future – Already it seems well to look forward to the future to which we are hastening. No nation was ever called to the contemplation of a destiny more important and solemn than ours. Great duties and responsibilities are devolved upon us. Liberty, order, and civilization are staked against a slaveholding despotism, and social anarchy. Today we have to put down a stupendous rebellion. To-morrow we shall have to reconstruct the whole fabric of Southern society, and bring order out of anarchy. It is a tremendous undertaking. When the armies of the rebellion are entirely demoralized, broken and scattered beyond the possibility of organized opposition to the National Government, when the flag of the Union shall wave from the battlements of every fortress in the South: When slavery the grim and guilty motive for this horrid war shall have been abolished, when the poor whites of the South shall have been delivered from the rule and sway of the slaveholding class, when sullen, silent, and gloomy but subdued hate shall settle upon the Southern mind, then will come the time for the exercise of the highest of all human faculties. A profounder wisdom, a holier zeal, than belongs to the prosecution of war, will be required. Courage and patriotism are chiefly needed now, a holy philanthropy and a deep insight into human nature will be needed then. The sea of thought and feeling lashed into rage and fury by the war will remain to be calmed into the steady motions of peace and safety. The war will leave Southern Society like a ship driven by the storm, without rudder or compass. State and National constitutions, holding but feeble sway and exciting but feeble reverence. The people left to themselves, will each be disposed to do after his own mind, and the discomfited rebels, may among themselves, fulfill the prediction of Mr. Stephens of Georgia, who said he expected yet to see the rebels cutting each others throats. The structure of the American Constitution and Government imply the existence among the whole people a fraternal good will, an earnest spirit of co-operation for the common good, a mutual dependence of all upon each and of each upon all. The Government is not enthroned above the people but is of, by and through the people. A despotic form of Government with its standing armies, holds its existence in large measure independently of the people and in some sort against the people, looking at them very much as a slaveholder regards his slaves, to be worked and fed when obedient, and to be flogged and otherwise punished when they disobey. When such people raise an insurrection and are put down, the path before them is plain and simple: *It is submission.* To obey is the fulfillment of the whole Law of despotism. — But our form of Government contemplates in such a case something more than mere cold obedience. It not only requires this, but a cordial co-operation. Its whole machinery is deranged when one of its parts fail to perform its functions. The rebellion has paralyzed the Federal Government in all the rebel States, but putting down the rebels in arms does not necessarily cure this paralysis. The benumbed or dead state must be called into life, and for this the highest wisdom must be imployed. The State Senate, the State Legislature, the State Courts, the State Governors, and officers generally have to be gathered in under the fold of the Constitution and Union, and brought to co-operate in good faith with the National Government. How all this shall be done, is one of the great questions of the future. Foreseeing this State of things, Mr. Sumner of the Senate, with the comprehensive grasp of a true statesmanship proposed that the States in rebellion shall be Governed as Territories. Though denounced and repudiated at the time, this theory of conducting the rebel States back to their former position will in the end be adopted.

It would be absurd and ridiculous to expect that the conquered traitors will at once cordially cooperate with the Federal Government. They must be set aside for a new class of men, men who have hitherto exercised but little influence in the State. For this, we shall have to Educate the people. The arduous task of the future will be to make the Southern people see and appreciate Republican Government, as a blessing of inestimable value, and to be maintained at any and every cost. They have got to be taught that slavery which they have valued as a blessing has ever been their direct calamity and curse. — The work before us is nothing less than a radical revolution in all the modes of thought which have flourished under the blighting slave system. The idea that labor is an evil, that work is degrading and that idleness is respectable, must be dispelled and the idea that work is honorable made to take its place. — Above all they must be taught that the liberty of a part is never to be secured by the enslavement or oppression of any. Neither the slave or the slaveholder can instantly throw off the sentiments inspired and ground into them by long years of tyranny on the one hand and of abject and cringing submission on the other. The master will carry into the new relation of liberty much of the insolence, caprice and pretention exercised by him while the admitted lord of the lash. The slave in his turn will be bound in the invisible chains of slavery long after his iron chains are broken and forever buried out of sight. There is no such thing as immediate Emancipation either for the master or for the slave. Time experience and culture must gradually bring society back to the normal condition from which long years of slavery have carried all under its iron sway.

Then for the freed men: What shall be their status in the new condition of things? Shall they exchange the relation of slavery to individuals, only to become the slaves of the community at large, having no rights which anybody is required to respect, subject to a code of Black laws, denying them school privileges, denying them the right of suffrage, denying them the right to sit as jurors, denying them the right to testify in courts of Law, denying them the right to keep and bear arms, denying them the right of speech, and the right of petition? Or shall they have secured to them equal rights before the law. Oh! that the heart of this unbelieving nation could be at once brought to a faith in the Eternal Laws of justice, justice for all men, justice now and always, justice without reservation or qualification except those suggested by mercy and love. It is not likely however, that at the outset, the Southern people, will consent to an absolutely just and humane policy towards the newly Emancipated Black people so long enslaved and degraded. One, therefore, of the labors and duties which will require the exertions of those who have heretofore remembered those in bonds as bound with them, will be to ameliorate the condition of the partially Emancipated. The whole South, as it never was before the abolition of slavery will become missionary ground. The family relation which has had no real existence under the reign of slavery, will remain to be established, schools for the education of dusky millions will be required, and all the elevating and civilizing institutions of the country must be extended to these people. Men full of faith in the race, and of the sacred fire of love, must walk among these slavery smitten columns of humanity and lift their forms towards Heaven. Verily, the work does not end with the abolition of slavery but only begins. Slavery has been the great hinderance. It has stood athwart the pathway of knowledge and progress, dreading nothing so much as the enlightenment of its slaves. This old and grim obstacle removed, and jets of heavenly light will speedily illumine the land long covered with darkness cruelty and crime.[121]

---

[121] *Douglass' Monthly*, November 1862.

To Be the Slave of Society at Large? – This is scarcely a day for prose. It is a day for poetry and song, a new song. These cloudless skies, this balmy air, this brilliant sunshine, (making December as pleasant as May,) are in harmony with the glorious morning of liberty about to dawn upon us. Out of a full heart and with sacred emotion, I congratulate you my friends, and fellow citizens, on the high and hopeful condition, of the cause of human freedom and the cause of our common country, for these two causes are now one and inseparable and must stand or fall together. We stand today in the presence of a glorious prospect. This sacred Sunday in all the likelihoods of the case, is the last which will witness the existence of legal slavery in all the Rebel slave-holding States of America. Henceforth and forever, slavery in those States is to be recognized, by all the departments [of] the American Government, under its appropriate character as an unmitigated robber and pirate, branded as the sum of all villainy, an outlaw having no rights which any man white or colored is bound to respect. It is difficult for us who have toiled so long and hard, to believe that this event, so stupendous, so far reaching and glorious is even now at the door. It surpasses our most enthusiastic hopes that we live at such a time and are likely to witness the downfall, at least the legal downfall of slavery in America. It is a moment for joy, thanksgiving and Praise.

Among the first questions that tried the strength of my childhood mind — was first why are colored people slaves, and the next was will their slavery last forever? From that day onward, the cry that has reached the most silent chambers of my soul, by day and by night has been How long! How long oh! Eternal Power of the Universe, how long shall these things be?

This inquiry is to be answered on the first of January 1863.

That this war is to abolish slavery I have no manner of doubt. The process may be long and tedious but that that result must at last be reached is among the undoubted certainties of the future! Slavery once abolished in the Rebel States, will give the death wound to slavery in the border States. When Arkansas is a free State, Missouri cannot be a slave State.

Nevertheless. This is no time for the friends of freedom to fold their hands and consider their work at an end. The price of Liberty is eternal vigilance. Even after slavery has been legally abolished, and the rebellion substantially suppressed, even when there shall come representatives to Congress from the States now in rebellion, and they shall have repudiated the miserable and disastrous error of disunion, or secession, and the country shall have reached a condition of comparative peace, there will still remain an urgent necessity for the benevolent activity of the men and the women who have from the first opposed slavery from high moral conviction.

Slavery has existed in this country too long and has stamped its character too deeply and indelibly, to be blotted out in a day or a year, or even in a generation. The slave will yet remain in some sense a slave, long after the chains are taken from his limbs, and the master will retain much of the pride, the arrogance, imperiousness and conscious superiority, and love of power, acquired by his former relation of master. Time, necessity, education, will be required to bring all classes into harmonious and natural relations.

But the South will not be the only part of the country demanding vigilance and exertion on the part of the true friends of the colored people. Our chief difficulty will [be] hereafter, as it has been heretofore with proslavery doughfaces, at the North. A dog will continue to scratch his neck even after the collar is removed. The sailor a night or two after reaching land feels his bed swimming from side to side, as if tossed by the sea. Daniel Webster received a large vote in Massachusetts after he was dead. It will not be strange if many Northern men whose politics, habits of thought, and accustomed submission to the slave power, leads them to continue to go through the forms of their ancient servility long after their old master slavery is in his grave.

Law and the sword can and will, in the end abolish slavery. But law and the sword cannot abolish the malignant slaveholding sentiment which has kept the slave system alive in this country during two centuries. Pride of race, prejudice against color, will raise their hateful clamor for oppression of the Negro as heretofore. The slave having ceased to be the abject slave of a single master, his enemies will endeavor to make him the slave of society at large.

For a time at least, we may expect that this malign purpose and principle of wrong will get itself more or less expressed in party presses and platforms. Pro-Slavery political writers and speakers, will not fail to inflame the ancient prejudice against the Negro, by exaggerating his faults and concealing or disparaging his virtues. A crime committed by one of the hated race, while any excellence found in one Black man will grudgingly be set to his individual credit. Hence we say that the friends of freedom, the men and women of the land who regard slavery as a crime and the slave as a man will still be needed even after slavery is abolished.[122]

---

[122] Remarks given at Zion Church in Rochester, New York on December 28, 1862 and published in *Douglass' Monthly*, January 1863.

Valedictory – My Respected Readers: —I beg to state that my relation to you as the Editor and publisher of a Journal devoted to the cause of Emancipation is, for the present, ended. That journal which has continued, under one form and designation or another, during nearly sixteen years, covering a period remarkable for the intensity and fierceness of the moral struggle between slavery and freedom, will be discontinued from the date of this publication.

In making this simple announcement emotions are excited for which I shall not attempt to find words to give suitable expression. — Although the result has been reached naturally, logically and necessarily, it is nevertheless accepted reluctantly and sadly. My relation to my readers has been in a high degree friendly, and in taking this formal leave of those readers, at home and abroad, I feel that I am taking leave of my true and tried friends. Great principles of justice and the most enduring sympathies known to the heart of man have united us in the cause of the American slave and swept us along the tide of these eventful sixteen years together. I know well enough, and knew from the first that my hold upon you, was not the result of shining talents or high mental attainments. I came to you fresh from the house of American bondage, with only such learning as I had stolen or picked up in the darkness of twenty-two years of slavery, and in a few years of liberty and toil. Yet you were pleased to receive me, and were not ashamed to cheer me on in my mission of deliverance to my enslaved people. Out of a full heart, my dear respected friends, I thank you at this parting, for your long continued and ever faithful cooperation. I shall never cease to regard these years of Editorial toil on my part and of sympathy and support on your part, as among the most cheerful and happy of my life.

But you will ask me, Why do you cease the publication of your paper? "Why not continue to speak and write as formerly — Slavery is not yet abolished." The inquiry is pertinent and I will give it my answer: and to answer it more perfectly I will first answer it negatively. First then, I wish it distinctly understood, that I do not discontinue the publication of my paper because it can no longer be supported. In this respect my paper has been highly favored from the first. The kind friends, who in England, seventeen years ago gave me the means of purchasing a printing press, have stood by me through all the years of my journal and generously helped me in every time of need. The same friends would doubtless help me hereafter as heretofore, if the journal were continued, and needed their help for its continuance.

Again, I cannot allow that my course is dictated by a love of change or adventure. My stability is quite equal to that of most men. My paper, ends its existence in the same room on the same street where it began. It has been during these sixteen years, immovable in its principles as it has been permanent in its local habitation. Often called elsewhere as more desirable localities for being heard and felt over the country, I have still remained in Rochester, and shown no taste for experimenting anywhere. Many times I could have sold my establishment, and formed alliances with other papers, but remembering that those who put me in possession of the press desired me to conduct it, I have refused all proposals for either sale or alliance. Neither do I discontinue the paper because I think that speaking and writing against slavery and its twin monster prejudice against the colored race are no longer needful. Such writing and speaking will be necessary so long as slavery and proscription shall remain in this country and in the world. Happily, however, I can write now through channels which were not opened fully to these subjects, when my journal was established. It will be grateful to my friends, especially to those over the sea, to know that, the *New York Independent* and the *New York Tribune*, both powerful periodicals, counting their readers, by the hundred thousand, welcome to their ample columns the best utterances in behalf of my race of which I am capable. These journals with many others, in my own town and elsewhere, are now quite ready to listen to what the colored man has to say for himself and for his much questioned and doubted people. Besides these, there is now, as there was not, at the beginning, a paper published in the city of New York by colored men entitled *The Anglo-African,* to whose columns all colored writers may gain access. I, at least have never been refused a place in its columns. — Indeed, I may say with gratitude and without boasting, that humble as I am in origin and despised as is the race to which I belong, I have lived to see the leading presses of the country, willing and ready to publish any argument or appeal in behalf of my race, I am able to make. So that while speaking and writing are still needful, the necessity for a special organ for my views and opinions on slavery no longer exists. To this extent at least, my paper has accomplished the object of its existence. It has done something towards battering down that dark and frowning wall of partition between the working minds of two races, hitherto thought impregnable. It found me an illiterate fugitive from slavery, and by the mental exercise, in reflection and reading its publication imposed, and made indispensable, it has educated myself, and other colored men up to the average power of thought and expression of our times.

Let it also be understood that I do not abandon my paper, because I shall cease to think and write upon vital social questions concerning colored men and women. I shall think, write and speak as I have opportunity, while the slave needs a pen to plead his cause, or a voice to expose his wrongs before the people.

So much dear readers, negatively, and to prevent misapprehension. I will now tell affirmatively and directly why I lay down my pen and paper. The United States are now in the bitterest pangs of civil war. Slavery is the cause of this terrible war, and its abolition is decreed by one of the parties to the war. I am with the abolition party in war as in peace. I discontinue my paper, because I can better serve my poor bleeding country-men whose great opportunity has now come, by going South and summoning them to assert their just liberty, than I can do by staying here. I am going South to assist Adjutant General Thomas, in the organization of colored troops, who shall win for the millions in bondage the inestimable blessings of liberty and country.

Slavery has chosen to submit her claims to the decision of the God of battles. She has deliberately taken the sword and it is meet that she should perish by the sword. Let the oppressor fall by the hand of the oppressed, and the guilty slaveholder, whom the voice of truth and reason could not reach, let him fall by the hand of his slave. It is in accordance with the All-Wise orderings of Providence that it should be so. Eternal justice can thunder forth no higher vindication of her majesty nor proclaim a warning more salutary to a world steeped in cruelty and wickedness, than in such a termination of our system of slavery. Reason, argument, appeal, —all moral influences have been applied in vain. The oppressor has hardened his heart, blinded his mind and deliberately rushed upon merited destruction. Let his blood be upon his own head. That I should take some humble part in the physical as well as the moral struggle against slavery and urge my long enslaved people to vindicate their manhood by bravely striking for their liberty and country is natural and consistent. I have indicated my course. You may not approve it, but I am sure you will appreciate the convictions of duty which impel me to it. With a heart full and warm with gratitude to you for all that you have done in furtherance of the cause of those to whom I have devoted my life, I bid you an affectionate farewell.[123]

---

[123] *Douglass' Monthly*, August 1863. Dated Aug 16, 1863.

What the Black Man Wants - Mr. President. —I have not heard the resolutions read, but I have listened to the speeches of Mr. Phillips and Mr. Thompson, and I do not feel, at this time, like entering into the discussion of the questions which I suppose, from these speeches, to be involved in the resolutions. I came here, as I come always to the meetings in New England, as a listener, and not as a speaker; and one of the reasons why I have not been more frequently to the meetings of this Society has been because of the disposition on the part of some of my friends to call me out upon the platform, even when they knew that there was some difference of opinion and of feeling between those who rightfully belong to this platform and myself; and for fear of being misconstrued, as desiring to interrupt or disturb the proceedings of these meetings, I have usually kept away, and have thus been deprived of that educating influence, which I am always free to confess is of the highest order, descending from this platform. I have felt, since I have lived out West, that in going there, I parted from a great deal that was valuable; and I feel, every time I come to these meetings that I have lost a great deal by making my home west of Boston, west of Massachusetts; for, if anywhere in the country there is to be found the highest sense of justice, or the truest demands for my race, I look for it in the East, I look for it here. The ablest discussions of the whole question of our rights occur here, and to be deprived of the privilege of listening to those discussions is a great deprivation.

I do not know, from what has been said, that there is any difference of opinion as to the duty of abolitionists at the present moment. I went with every word uttered by Mr. Phillips, and with almost every word uttered by Mr. Thompson. How can we get up any difference at this point, or at any point, where we are so united, so agreed? I went especially, however, with that word of Mr. Phillips to which, if to any exception was taken by Mr. Thompson, and that is, the criticism of Gen. Banks and Gen. Banks's policy. I hold that that policy is our chief danger at the present moment; that it practically enslaves the Negro, and makes the Proclamation of 1863 a mockery and delusion. What is freedom? It is the right to choose one's own employment. Certainly, it means that, if it means anything; and when any individual or combination of individuals undertakes to decide for any man when he shall work, where he shall work, at what he shall work, and for what he shall work, he or they practically reduce him to slavery. He is a slave. That I understand Gen. Banks to do — to determine for the so-called freedman when, and where, and at what, and for how much he shall work, when he shall be punished, and by whom punished. It is absolute slavery. It defeats the beneficent intentions of the government, if it has beneficent intentions, in regard to the freedom of our people.

I have had but one idea for the last three years to present to the American people, and the phraseology in which I clothe it is the old abolition phraseology. I am for the "immediate, unconditional and universal" enfranchisement of the Black man, in every State of the Union. Without this, his liberty is a mockery; without this, you might as well almost retain the old name of slavery for his condition; for, in fact, if he is not the slave of the individual master, he is the slave of society, and holds his liberty as a privilege, not as a right. He is at the mercy of the mob, and has no means of protecting himself.

It may be objected, however, that this pressing of the Negroes' right to suffrage is premature. Let us have slavery abolished, it may be said, let us have labor organized, and then, in the natural course of events, the right of suffrage will be extended to the Negro. I do not agree with this. The constitution of the human mind is such, that if it once disregards the conviction forced upon it by a revelation of truth, it requires the exercise of a higher power to produce the same conviction afterwards. The American people are now in tears. The Shenandoah has run blood — the best blood of the North. All around Richmond the blood of New England and of the North has been shed — of your sons, your brothers, and your fathers. We all feel, in the existence of this rebellion, that judgments terrible, widespread, far-reaching, overwhelming, are abroad in the land; and we feel, in view of these judgments, just now, a disposition to learn righteousness. This is the hour. Our streets are in mourning, tears are falling at every fireside, and under the chastisement of this rebellion, we have almost come up to the point of conceding this great, this all-important right of suffrage. I fear that if we fail to do it now, if Abolitionists fail to press it now, we may not see, for centuries to come, the same disposition that exists at this moment. Hence, I say, now is the time to press this right.

It may be asked, "Why do you want it? Some men have got along very well without it. Women have not this right." Shall we justify one wrong by another? That is a sufficient answer. Shall we at this moment justify the deprivation of the Negro of the right to vote because someone else is deprived of that privilege? I hold that women as well as men have the right to vote, and my heart and my voice go with the movement to extend suffrage to woman. But that question rests upon another basis than that on which our right rests. We may be asked, I say, why we want it. I will tell you why we want it. We want it because it is our right, first of all. No class of men can, without insulting their own nature, be content with any deprivation of their rights. We want it, again, as a means for educating our race. Men are so constituted that they derive their conviction of their own possibilities largely from the estimate formed of them by others. If nothing is expected of a people, that people will find it difficult to contradict that expectation. By depriving us of suffrage, you affirm our incapacity to form an intelligent judgment respecting public men and public measures; you declare before the world that we are unfit to exercise the elective franchise, and by this means lead us to undervalue ourselves, to put a low estimate upon ourselves, and to feel that we have no possibilities like other men. Again, I want the elective franchise, for one, as a colored man, because ours is a peculiar government, based upon a peculiar idea, and that idea is universal suffrage. If I were in a monarchical government, or an autocratic or aristocratic Government, where the few bore rule and the many were subject, there would be no special stigma resting upon me because I did not exercise the elective franchise. It would do me no great violence. Mingling with the mass, I should partake of the strength of the mass; I should be supported by the mass, and I should have the same incentives to endeavor with the mass of my fellow-men; it would be no particular burden, no particular deprivation. But here, where universal suffrage is the rule, where that is the fundamental idea of the government, to rule us out is to make us an exception, to brand us with the stigma of inferiority, and to invite to our heads the missiles of those about us. Therefore I want the franchise for the Black man.

There are, however, other reasons, not derived from any consideration merely of our rights, but arising out of the condition of the South and of the country — considerations which have already been referred to by Mr. Phillips — considerations which must arrest the attention of statesmen. I believe that when the tall heads of this rebellion shall have been swept down, as they will be swept down, when the Davises and Toombses and Stephenses and others who are leading in this rebellion shall have been blotted out, there will be this rank undergrowth of treason, to which reference has been made, growing up there, and interfering with and thwarting the quiet operation of the Federal Government in those States. You will see those traitors handing down from sire to son the same malignant spirit which they have manifested and which they are now exhibiting, with malicious hearts, broad blades and bloody hands in the field, against our sons and brothers. That spirit will still remain; and whoever sees the Federal Government extended over those Southern States will see that government in a strange land and not only in a strange land but in an enemy's land. A postmaster of the United States in the South will find himself surrounded by a hostile spirit; a collector in a Southern port will find himself surrounded by a hostile spirit; a United States marshal or United States judge will be surrounded there by a hostile element. That enmity will not die out in a year, will not die out in an age. The Federal Government will be looked upon in those States precisely as the governments of Austria and France are looked upon in Italy at the present moment. They will endeavor to circumvent, they will endeavor to destroy the peaceful operation of this government. Now, where will you find the strength to counterbalance this spirit, if you do not find it in the Negroes of the South! They are your friends, and have always been your friends. They were your friends even when the Government did not regard them as such. They comprehended the genius of this war before you did. It is a significant fact, it is a marvellous fact, it seems almost to imply a direct interposition of Providence, that this war, which began in the interest of slavery on both sides, bids fair to end in the interests of liberty on both sides. It was begun, I say, in the interest of slavery, on both sides. The South was fighting to take slavery out of the Union and the North fighting to keep it in the Union; the South fighting to get it beyond the limits of the United States Constitution, and the North fighting to retain it within those limits, the South fighting for new guarantees and the North fighting for the old guarantees; — both despising the Negro, both insulting the Negro. Yet the Negro, apparently endowed with wisdom from on high, saw more clearly the end from the beginning than we did. When Seward said the status of no man in the country would be changed by the war, the Negro did not believe him. When our generals sent their underlings in shoulder straps to hunt the flying Negro back from our lines into the jaws of slavery from which he had escaped, the Negroes thought that a mistake had been made, and that the intentions of the Government had not been rightly understood by our officers in shoulder straps, and they continued to come into our lines, threading their way through bogs and fens, over briars and thorns, fording streams, swimming rivers, bringing us tidings as to the safe path to march, and pointing out the dangers that threatened us. They are our only friends in the South, and we should be true to them in this their trial hour, and see to it that they have the elective franchise.

I know that we are inferior to you in some things — virtually inferior. We walk about among you like dwarfs among giants. Our heads are scarcely seen above the great sea of humanity. The Germans are superior to us; the Irish are superior to us; the Yankees are superior to us; they can do what we cannot, that is, what we have not hitherto been allowed to do. But, while I make this admission, I utterly deny that we are originally, or naturally, or practically, or in any way, or in any important sense, inferior to anybody on this globe. This charge of inferiority is an old dodge.

It has been made available for oppression on many occasions. It is only about six centuries since the blue-eyed and fair-haired Anglo-Saxons were considered inferior by the haughty Normans, who once trampled upon them. If you read the history of the Norman Conquest, you will find that this proud Anglo-Saxon was once looked upon as of coarser clay than his Norman master, and might be found in the highways and byways of old England laboring with a brass collar on his neck, and the name of his master marked upon it. You were down then! You are up now. I am glad you are up, and I want you to be glad to help us up also.

The story of our inferiority is an old dodge, as I have said; for wherever men oppress their fellows, wherever they enslave them, they will endeavor to find the needed apology for such enslavement and oppression in the character of the people oppressed and enslaved. When we wanted, a few years ago, a slice of Mexico, it was hinted that the Mexicans were an inferior race, that the old Castilian blood had become so weak that it would scarcely run down hill, and that Mexico needed the long, strong and beneficent arm of the Anglo-Saxon care extended over it. We said that it was necessary to its salvation, and a part of the "manifest destiny" of this Republic, to extend our arm over that dilapidated government. So, too, when Russia wanted to take possession of a part of the Ottoman Empire, the Turks were "an inferior race." So, too, when England wants to set the heel of her power more firmly in the quivering heart of old Ireland, the Celts are "an inferior race." So, too, the Negro, when he is to be robbed of any right which is justly his, is "an inferior man." It is said that we are ignorant; I admit it. But if we know enough to be hung, we know enough to vote. If the Negro knows enough to pay taxes to support the Government, he knows enough to vote—taxation and representation should go together. If he knows enough to shoulder a musket and fight for the flag, fight for the Government, he knows enough to vote. If he knows as much when he is sober as an Irishman knows when drunk, he knows enough to vote, on good American principles.

But I was saying that you needed a counterpoise in the persons of the slaves to the enmity that would exist at the South after the rebellion is put down. I hold that the American people are bound, not only in self-defence, to extend this right to the freedmen of the South, but they are bound by their love of country and by all their regard for the future safety of those Southern States to do this — to do it as a measure essential to the preservation of peace there. But I will not dwell upon this. I put it to the American sense of honor. The honor of a nation is an important thing. It is said in the Scriptures, "What doth it profit a man if he gain the whole world, and lose his own soul!"[124] It may be said also, what doth it profit a nation if it gain the whole world, but lose its honor? I hold that the American Government has taken upon itself a solemn obligation of honor to see that this war, let it be long or let it be short, let it cost much, or let it cost little, — that this war shall not cease until every freedman at the South has the right to vote. It has bound itself to do it. What have you asked the Black men of the South, the Black men of the whole country to do? Why, you have asked them to incur the deadly enmity of their masters, in order to befriend you and to befriend this government. You have asked us to call down, not only upon ourselves, but upon our children's children, the deadly hate of the entire Southern people. You have called upon us to turn our backs upon our masters, to abandon their cause and espouse yours; to turn against the South and in favor of the North; to shoot down the Confederacy and uphold the flag — the American flag. You have called upon us to expose ourselves to all the subtle machinations of their malignity for all time. And now, what do you propose to do when you come to make peace? To reward your enemies, and trample in the dust your friends? Do you intend to sacrifice the very men who have come to the rescue of your banner in the South and incurred the lasting displeasure of their

---

[124] King James Bible, *Matthew* 16:26, *Mark* 8:36

masters thereby? Do you intend to sacrifice them, and reward your enemies? Do you mean to give your enemies the right to vote, and take it away from your friends? Is that wise policy? Is that honorable? Could American honor withstand such a blow? I do not believe you will do it. I think you will see to it that we have the right to vote. There is something too mean in looking upon the Negro when you are in trouble as a citizen, and when you are free from trouble as an alien. When this nation was in trouble, in its early struggles, it looked upon the Negro as a citizen. In 1776, he was a citizen. At the time of the formation of the Constitution, the Negro had the right to vote in eleven States out of the old thirteen. In your trouble you have made us citizens. In 1812, Gen. Jackson addressed us as citizens, "fellow citizens." He wanted us to fight. We were citizens then! And now, when you come to frame a conscription bill, the Negro is a citizen again. He has been a citizen just three times in the history of this government, and it has always been in time of trouble. In time of trouble we are citizens. Shall we be citizens in war, and aliens in peace? Would that be just?

I ask my friends who are apologizing for not insisting upon this right, where can the Black man look in this country for the assertion of this right if he may not look to the Massachusetts Anti-Slavery Society? Where under the whole heavens can he look for sympathy in asserting this right if he may not look to this platform? Have you lifted us up to a certain height to see that we are men, and then are any disposed to leave us there, without seeing that we are put in possession of all our rights? We look naturally to this platform for the assertion of all our rights, and for this one especially. I understand the anti-slavery societies of this country to be based on two principles—first, the freedom of the blacks of this country; and, second, the elevation of them. Let me not be misunderstood here. I am not asking for sympathy at the hands of Abolitionists, sympathy at the hands of any. I think the American people are disposed often to be generous rather than just. I look over this country at the present time, and I see Educational Societies, Sanitary Commissions, Freedmen's Association, and the like, — all very good; but in regard to the colored people, there is always more that is benevolent, I perceive, than just, manifested towards us. What I ask for the Negro is not benevolence, not pity, not sympathy, but simply justice. The American people have always been anxious to know what they shall do with us. Gen. Banks was distressed with solicitude as to what he should do with the Negro. Everybody has asked the question, and they learned to ask it early of the abolitionists: "What shall we do with the Negro?" I have had but one answer from the beginning. Do nothing with us! Your doing with us has already played the mischief with us. Do nothing with us! If the apples will not remain on the tree of their own strength, if they are worm-eaten at the core, if they are early ripe and disposed to fall, let them fall! I am not for tying or fastening them on the tree in any way, except by nature's plan, and if they will not stay there let them fall. And if the Negro cannot stand on his own legs, let him fall also. All I ask is, give him a chance to stand on his own legs! Let him alone! If you see him on his way to school, let him alone, — don't disturb him! If you see him going to the dinner table at a hotel, let him go! If you see him going to the ballot box, let him alone! — don't disturb him! If you see him going into a workshop, just let him alone, — your interference is doing him positive injury. Gen. Banks's "preparation" is of a piece with this attempt to prop up the Negro. Let him fall if he cannot stand alone! If the Negro cannot live by the line of eternal justice, so beautifully pictured to you in the illustration used by Mr. Phillips, the fault will not be yours, it will be His who made the Negro, and established that line for his government. Let him live or die by that. If you will only untie his hands, and give him a chance, I think he will live. He will work as readily for himself as the white man. A great many delusions have been swept away by this war. One was, that the Negro would not work; he has proved his ability to work. Another was, that the Negro would not fight;

that he possessed only the most sheepish attributes of humanity; was a perfect lamb, or an "Uncle Tom"; disposed to take off his coat whenever required, fold his hands, and be whipped by anybody who wanted to whip him;—but the war has proved that there is a great deal of human nature in the Negro, and that he will fight, as Mr. Quincy, our President, said, in earlier days than these, "when there is a reasonable probability of his whipping anybody." But here I am talking away, and taking up the time which belongs to others.[125]

---

[125] Lecture delivered at the Annual Meeting of the Massachusetts Anti-Slavery Society in Boston, Massachusetts on January 26, 1865 and published in *The Equality of all Men before the Law Claimed and Defended in speeches by Hon. William D. Kelley, Wendell Phillips, and Frederick Douglass*, (Boston, 1865) pp.36-39.

The Struggle to Be as The Question Forced Upon Us - ... first indications, whether observed in the silent, mysterious phenomena of physical nature, or in the moral or intellectual developments of human society, are always interesting to thoughtful men. Every age has its prophet or its Messiah. We are ever waiting and watching like good Simeon for our babe of Bethlehem. John Brown used to say he had looked over our people as over a dark sea, in the hope of seeing a head rise up with a mind to plan and a hand to deliver. Any movement of the water arrested his attention. In all directions, we desire to catch the first sign. The first sign of clear weather on the ocean after a season of darkness and storm; the first sign of returning health after long and weary months of wasting fever; the first sign of rain after a famine, threatening drouth; the first indication of spring, silently releasing the knotty and congealed earth from the frosty fetters of winter; the first sign of peace after the ten thousand calamities, horrors, desolations and alarms of war, evermore bring joy and gladness to the human heart.

The mind of man has a special attraction towards first objects. It delights in the dim and shadowy outlines of the coming fact. There is a calm and quiet satisfaction in the contemplation of present attainments; but the great future, and the yet unattained, awaken in the soul the deepest springs of poetry and enthusiasm.

... the present is a critical moment for the colored people of this country; our fate for weal or for woe, it may be yet for many generations, trembles now in the balance. No man can tell which way the scale will turn. ...

It is the misfortune of our class that it fails to derive due advantages from the achievements of its individual members, but never fails to suffer from the ignorance or crimes of a single individual with whom the class is identified. ... The public, with the mass of ignorance – notwithstanding that ignorance has been enforced and compelled among our people, hitherto – has sternly denied the representative character of our distinguished men. They are treated as exceptions, individual cases, and the like. They contend that the race, as such, is destitute of the subjective original elemental condition of a high self-originating and self-sustaining civilization.

Such is the sweeping and damaging judgment pronounced in various high quarters against our race; and such is the current opinion against which colored people have to advance, if they advance at all. A few years ago, we met this unfavorable theory as best we could in three ways. We pointed to our assailants and traducers to the ancient civilization of Northern Africa. We traced the entangled threads of history and of civilization back to their sources in Africa. We called attention to the somewhat disagreeable fact – agreeable to us, but not so to our Teutonic brethren – that the arts, appliances and blessings of civilization flourished in the very heart of Ethiopia, at a time when all Europe floundered in the depths of ignorance and barbarism. We dwelt on the grandeur, magnificence and stupendous dimensions of Egyptian architecture, and held up the fact, now generally admitted, that that race was master of mechanical forces of which the present generations of men are ignorant.

We pointed to the nautical skill commercial enterprise and military prowess of Carthage, and justly claimed relationship with those great nations of antiquity. We are a dark people – so were they. They stood between us and the Europeans in point of complexion, as well as in point of geography. We have contended – and not illogically – that if the fact of color was no barrier to civilization in their case, it cannot be in ours.

... Where under the whole heavens was there ever a race so blasted and withered, so shorn and bereft of all opportunities for development as ourselves? It would seem that the whole Christian world had combined for the destruction of our race, and had summoned heaven and hell, philosophy and revelation, to assist in the work. Our history has been but a track of blood. Gaunt and hungry sharks have followed us on slave ships by the sea, and the hungrier and greedier slave-drivers have followed us during all these years with the bloody slave-whip on land. The question forced upon us at every moment of our generation has not been, as with other races of men, how shall we adorn, beautify, exalt and ennoble life, but how shall we retain life itself. The struggle with us was not to do, but to be. Mankind lost sight of our human nature in the idea of our being property, and the whole machinery of society was planned, directed and operated to the making us a stupid, spiritless, ignorant, besotted, brutified, and utterly degraded race of men.

Thus far we have derived little advantage from any apologies we have made or from any explanations we have patiently given. Our relationship to the ancient Egyptians has been denied; the progress made by the enlightened people of the West Indies is not believed, and men still insist that the fault of our ignorance is not in slavery, but in ourselves. ... Now, what are those elemental and original powers of civilization about which men speak and write so earnestly, and which white men claim for themselves and deny the Negro? I answer that they are simply consciousness of wants and ability to gratify them. Here the whole machinery of civilization, whether moral, intellectual or physical, is set in motion.

Man is distinguished from all other animals, but in nothing is he distinguished more than in this, namely, resistance, active and constant resistance, to the forces of physical nature. All other animals submit to the same conditions and limitations from generation to generation. The bear is today as he was a thousand years ago. Nature provides him with food, clothing and shelter, and he is neither wiser nor better because of the experience of his bearish ancestors. Not so with man. He learns from the past, improves upon the past, looks back upon the past, and hands down his knowledge of the past to after-coming generations of men, that they may carry their achievements to a still higher point. To lack this element of progress is to resemble the lower animals, and to possess it is to be men.[126]

---

[126] Excerpted from Lecture delivered at the Inauguration of The Douglass Institute in Baltimore, Maryland on September 29th, 1865 and published in *The Liberator*, October 13th, 1865.

Reconstruction – The assembling of the Second Session of the Thirty-ninth Congress may very properly be made the occasion of a few earnest words on the already much-worn topic of reconstruction.

Seldom has any legislative body been the subject of a solicitude more intense, or of aspirations more sincere and ardent. There are the best of reasons for this profound interest. Questions of vast moment, left undecided by the last session of Congress, must be manfully grappled with by this. No political skirmishing will avail.

The occasion demands statesmanship. Whether the tremendous war so heroically fought and so victoriously ended shall pass into history a miserable failure, barren of permanent results, — a scandalous and shocking waste of blood and treasure, — a strife for empire, as Earl Russell characterized it, of no value to liberty or civilization, — an attempt to re-establish a Union by force, which must be the merest mockery of a Union, — an effort to bring under Federal authority States into which no loyal man from the North may safely enter, and to bring men into the national councils who deliberate with daggers and vote with revolvers, and who do not even conceal their deadly hate of the country that conquered them; or whether, on the other hand, we shall, as the rightful reward of victory over treason, have a solid nation, entirely delivered from all contradictions and social antagonisms, based upon loyalty, liberty, and equality, must be determined one way or the other by the present session of Congress. The last session really did nothing which can be considered final as to these questions. The Civil Rights Bill and the Freedmen's Bureau Bill and the proposed constitutional amendments, with the amendment already adopted and recognized as the law of the land, do not reach the difficulty, and cannot, unless the whole structure of the government is changed from a government by States to something like a despotic central government, with power to control even the municipal regulations of States, and to make them conform to its own despotic will. While there remains such an idea as the right of each State to control its own local affairs, — an idea, by the way, more deeply rooted in the minds of men of all sections of the country than perhaps any one other political idea, — no general assertion of human rights can be of any practical value. To change the character of the government at this point is neither possible nor desirable. All that is necessary to be done is to make the government consistent with itself, and render the rights of the States compatible with the sacred rights of human nature.

The arm of the Federal government is long, but it is far too short to protect the rights of individuals in the interior of distant States. They must have the power to protect themselves, or they will go unprotected, spite of all the laws the Federal government can put upon the national statute-book.

Slavery, like all other great systems of wrong, founded in the depths of human selfishness, and existing for ages, has not neglected its own conservation. It has steadily exerted an influence upon all around it favorable to its own continuance. And today it is so strong that it could exist, not only without law, but even against law. Custom, manners, morals, religion, are all on its side everywhere in the South; and when you add the ignorance and servility of the ex-slave to the intelligence and accustomed authority of the master, you have the conditions, not out of which slavery will again grow, but under which it is impossible for the Federal government to wholly destroy it, unless the Federal government be armed with despotic power, to blot out State authority, and to station a Federal officer at every crossroad. This, of course, cannot be done, and ought not even if it could. The true way and the easiest way is to make our government entirely consistent with itself, and give to every loyal citizen the elective franchise, — a right and power which will be ever present, and will form a wall of fire for his protection.

One of the invaluable compensations of the late Rebellion is the highly instructive disclosure it made of the true source of danger to republican government. Whatever may be tolerated in monarchical and despotic governments, no republic is safe that tolerates a privileged class, or denies to any of its citizens equal rights and equal means to maintain them. What was theory before the war has been made fact by the war.

There is cause to be thankful even for rebellion. It is an impressive teacher, though a stern and terrible one. In both characters it has come to us, and it was perhaps needed in both. It is an instructor never a day before its time, for it comes only when all other means of progress and enlightenment have failed. Whether the oppressed and despairing bondman, no longer able to repress his deep yearnings for manhood, or the tyrant, in his pride and impatience, takes the initiative, and strikes the blow for a firmer hold and a longer lease of oppression, the result is the same, — society is instructed, or may be.

Such are the limitations of the common mind, and so thoroughly engrossing are the cares of common life, that only the few among men can discern through the glitter and dazzle of present prosperity the dark outlines of approaching disasters, even though they may have come up to our very gates, and are already within striking distance. The yawning seam and corroded bolt conceal their defects from the mariner until the storm calls all hands to the pumps. Prophets, indeed, were abundant before the war; but who cares for prophets while their predictions remain unfulfilled, and the calamities of which they tell are masked behind a blinding blaze of national prosperity?

It is asked, said Henry Clay, on a memorable occasion, Will slavery never come to an end? That question, said he, was asked fifty years ago, and it has been answered by fifty years of unprecedented prosperity. Spite of the eloquence of the earnest Abolitionists, — poured out against slavery during thirty years, — even they must confess, that, in all the probabilities of the case, that system of barbarism would have continued its horrors far beyond the limits of the nineteenth century but for the Rebellion, and perhaps only have disappeared at last in a fiery conflict, even more fierce and bloody than that which has now been suppressed.

It is no disparagement to truth, that it can only prevail where reason prevails. War begins where reason ends. The thing worse than rebellion is the thing that causes rebellion. What that thing is, we have been taught to our cost. It remains now to be seen whether we have the needed courage to have that cause entirely removed from the Republic. At any rate, to this grand work of national regeneration and entire purification Congress must now address itself, with full purpose that the work shall this time be thoroughly done. The deadly upas, root and branch, leaf and fibre, body and sap, must be utterly destroyed. The country is evidently not in a condition to listen patiently to pleas for postponement, however plausible, nor will it permit the responsibility to be shifted to other shoulders. Authority and power are here commensurate with the duty imposed. There are no cloudflung shadows to obscure the way. Truth shines with brighter light and intenser heat at every moment, and a country torn and rent and bleeding implores relief from its distress and agony.

If time was at first needed, Congress has now had time. All the requisite materials from which to form an intelligent judgment are now before it. Whether its members look at the origin, the progress, the termination of the war, or at the mockery of a peace now existing, they will find only one unbroken chain of argument in favor of a radical policy of reconstruction. For the omissions of the last session, some excuses may be allowed. A treacherous President stood in the way; and it can be easily seen how reluctant good men might be to admit an apostasy which involved so much of baseness and ingratitude. It was natural that they should seek to save him by bending to him even when he leaned to the side of error. But all is changed now. Congress knows now that it must go on without his aid, and even against his machinations. The advantage of the present session over the last is immense. Where that investigated, this has the facts. Where that walked by faith, this may walk by sight. Where that halted, this must go forward, and where that failed, this must succeed, giving the country whole measures where that gave us half-measures, merely as a means of saving the elections in a few doubtful districts. That Congress saw what was right, but distrusted the enlightenment of the loyal masses; but what was forborne in distrust of the people must now be done with a full knowledge that the people expect and require it. The members go to Washington fresh from the inspiring presence of the people. In every considerable public meeting, and in almost every conceivable way, whether at courthouse, schoolhouse, or crossroads, indoors and out, the subject has been discussed, and the people have emphatically pronounced in favor of a radical policy. Listening to the doctrines of expediency and compromise with pity, impatience, and disgust, they have everywhere broken into demonstrations of the wildest enthusiasm when a brave word has been spoken in favor of equal rights and impartial suffrage. Radicalism, so far from being odious, is now the popular passport to power. The men most bitterly charged with it go to Congress with the largest majorities, while the timid and doubtful are sent by lean majorities, or else left at home. The strange controversy between the President and Congress, at one time so threatening, is disposed of by the people. The high reconstructive powers which he so confidently, ostentatiously, and haughtily claimed, have been disallowed, denounced, and utterly repudiated; while those claimed by Congress have been confirmed.

Of the spirit and magnitude of the canvass nothing need be said. The appeal was to the people, and the verdict was worthy of the tribunal. Upon an occasion of his own selection, with the advice and approval of his astute Secretary, soon after the members of Congress had returned to their constituents, the President quitted the executive mansion, sandwiched himself between two recognized heroes, — men whom the whole country delighted to honor, — and, with all the advantage which such company could give him, stumped the country from the Atlantic to the Mississippi, advocating everywhere his policy as against that of Congress. It was a strange sight, and perhaps the most disgraceful exhibition ever made by any President; but, as no evil is entirely unmixed, good has come of this, as from many others. Ambitious, unscrupulous, energetic, indefatigable, voluble, and plausible, — a political gladiator, ready for a "set-to" in any crowd, — he is beaten in his own chosen field, and stands today before the country as a convicted usurper, a political criminal, guilty of a bold and persistent attempt to possess himself of the legislative powers solemnly secured to Congress by the Constitution. No vindication could be more complete, no condemnation could be more absolute and humiliating. Unless reopened by the sword, as recklessly threatened in some circles, this question is now closed for all time.

Without attempting to settle here the metaphysical and somewhat theological question (about which so much has already been said and written), whether once in the Union means always in the Union, — agreeably to the formula, Once in grace always in grace, — it is obvious to common sense that the rebellious States stand today, in point of law, precisely where they stood when, exhausted, beaten, conquered, they fell powerless at the feet of Federal authority. Their State governments were overthrown, and the lives and property of the leaders of the Rebellion were forfeited. In reconstructing the institutions of these shattered and overthrown States, Congress should begin with a clean slate, and make clean work of it. Let there be no hesitation. It would be a cowardly deference to a defeated and treacherous President, if any account were made of the illegitimate, one-sided, sham governments hurried into existence for a malign purpose in the absence of Congress. These pretended governments, which were never submitted to the people, and from participation in which four millions of the loyal people were excluded by Presidential order, should now be treated according to their true character, as shams and impositions, and supplanted by true and legitimate governments, in the formation of which loyal men, Black and white, shall participate.

It is not, however, within the scope of this paper to point out the precise steps to be taken, and the means to be employed. The people are less concerned about these than the grand end to be attained. They demand such a reconstruction as shall put an end to the present anarchical state of things in the late rebellious States, — where frightful murders and wholesale massacres are perpetrated in the very presence of Federal soldiers. This horrible business they require shall cease. They want a reconstruction such as will protect loyal men, Black and white, in their persons and property; such a one as will cause Northern industry, Northern capital, and Northern civilization to flow into the South, and make a man from New England as much at home in Carolina as elsewhere in the Republic. No Chinese wall can now be tolerated. The South must be opened to the light of law and liberty, and this session of Congress is relied upon to accomplish this important work.

The plain, common-sense way of doing this work, as intimated at the beginning, is simply to establish in the South one law, one government, one administration of justice, one condition to the exercise of the elective franchise, for men of all races and colors alike. This great measure is sought as earnestly by loyal white men as by loyal Blacks, and is needed alike by both. Let sound political prescience but take the place of an unreasoning prejudice, and this will be done.

Men denounce the Negro for his prominence in this discussion; but it is no fault of his that in peace as in war, that in conquering Rebel armies as in reconstructing the rebellious States, the right of the Negro is the true solution of our national troubles. The stern logic of events, which goes directly to the point, disdaining all concern for the color or features of men, has determined the interests of the country as identical with and inseparable from those of the Negro.

The policy that emancipated and armed the Negro — now seen to have been wise and proper by the dullest — was not certainly more sternly demanded than is now the policy of enfranchisement. If with the Negro was success in war, and without him failure, so in peace it will be found that the nation must fall or flourish with the Negro.

Fortunately, the Constitution of the United States knows no distinction between citizens on account of color. Neither does it know any difference between a citizen of a State and a citizen of the United States. Citizenship evidently includes all the rights of citizens, whether State or national. If the Constitution knows none, it is clearly no part of the duty of a Republican Congress now to institute one. The mistake of the last session was the attempt to do this very thing, by a renunciation of its power to secure political rights to any class of citizens, with the obvious purpose to allow the rebellious States to disfranchise, if they should see fit, their colored citizens. This unfortunate blunder must now be retrieved, and the emasculated citizenship given to the Negro supplanted by that contemplated in the Constitution of the United States, which declares that the citizens of each State shall enjoy all the rights and immunities of citizens of the several States, — so that a legal voter in any State shall be a legal voter in all the States.[127]

---

[127] *Atlantic Monthly*, December 1866.

About the Editor

A. Shahid Stover is a writer, existential philosopher, and Black radical intellectual who serves as the editor-in-chief of *The Brotherwise Dispatch.*

Stover is the author of several philosophical works –
Existential Liberation Critique (2026),
Epistemic Ruptures, Insurgent Philosophy (2022),
Being and Insurrection (2019) and
Hip Hop Intellectual Resistance (2009).

Stover writes and lives in New York City.